Like some Anne Rice vampire, it was always late at night when he called, always dark out there whenever you ran into him. You got the feeling he hardly ever saw daylight, didn't approve of it. On a completely different schedule to everyone else, always sleeping until four or five in the afternoon, these late-night rendezvous had the incongruous effect of making you feel as though he was always a little bit more awake than you, or indeed anyone else around him. Not that it made him smarter or more fun to be with—just that it ensured things tended to be done on his terms, whether they be long, complicated meetings or simple phone conversations. Even an accidental collision on the street didn't seem to catch him off guard. It was as though he just expected strange things to happen to him—all the time.

—from *W.A.R.*

W.A.R.

Also by Mick Wall

W.A.R.

The Unauthorized Biography
of William Axl Rose

MICK WALL

St. Martin's Press
New York

www.stmartins.com

Wall, Mick.
    W.A.R. : the unauthorized biography of William Axl Rose / Mick Wall.—1st U.S. ed.
        p. cm.
    First published in Great Britain by Sidgwick & Jackson.
    Includes bibliographical references.
    ISBN-13: 978-0-312-37767-0
    ISBN-10: 0-312-37767-3
    1. Rose, Axl, 1962– 2. Rock musicians—United States—Biography. I. Title. II. Title: William Axl Rose.

ML420.R87575 W35 2008
782.42166092—dc22
[B]

                                                                    2007047208

First published in Great Britain by Sidgwick & Jackson, an imprint of Pan Macmillan Ltd

First U.S. Edition: February 2008

10 9 8 7 6 5 4 3 2 1

FOR LINDA, EVIE, MOLLIE AND MICHAEL

This book could not have been written without the generous help and support of the following people:

Linda Wall, Robert Kirby, Ingrid Connell, Ross Halfin, Jon Hotten, Damian McGee, and Matthew Corner.

Thanks also to Slash, Duff, Izzy and Steven, for always being themselves.

And of course to Axl, who could never have been anyone else.

Contents

PART FOUR

CHINESE CURSE

W.A.R.

Introduction

GUNS OR KNIVES, MOTHERFUCKER

Like some Anne Rice vampire, it was always late at night when he called, always dark out there whenever you ran into him. You got the feeling he hardly ever saw daylight, didn't approve of it. On a completely different schedule to everyone else, always sleeping until four or five in the afternoon, these late night rendezvous had the incongruous effect of making you feel as though he was always a little bit more awake than you, or indeed anyone else around him. Not that it made him smarter or more fun to be with – just that it ensured things tended to be done on his terms, whether they be long, complicated meetings or simple phone conversations. Even an accidental collision on the street didn't seem to catch him off-guard. It was as though he just expected strange things to happen to him – all the time.

Of course, back then, this was exactly the sort of thing I most craved from my rock stars, but since it was the boring 1980s, hardly ever got – that lurking sense of . . . not danger exactly, nor even real excitement, just something *additional*. That creeping feeling that this was one rock star that might just bust out at any moment and say or do something no one else dared. Even though rock had officially been declared dead by the British music press almost ten years before, to the point where I felt I had actually seen the corpse rotting by the roadside many times during my own decade-long career working for that same press, I couldn't help but be seduced by the strange promise this driven individual with the long red hair and pinched little face seemed to hold out: that not only was rock not dead, but that, in the time-honoured phrase, we hadn't seen nuthin' yet. In fact, he would make sure of it. That seemed to be the deal he was offering us anyway.

For a while he seemed to be able to deliver on it too. Even though we couldn't really be sure at the time, looking back now, twenty years later, it seems obvious: Guns N' Roses were the last of the all-time great rock bands. That is, the last of the all-time great rock bands that didn't consider what they did was in any way ironic or – perish the thought – embarrassing. Not even on some subconscious level. That's what the twentysomethings who now walk around in their 'post-modern' GN'R T-shirts never seem to have considered. That once upon a time, this stuff wasn't funny; it was real. Okay, maybe it *was* funny by the time Guns N' Roses first became famous, but for those of us who were the twentysomethings back then the most pleasing aspect of this phenomenon was just how quickly they wiped the smiles off everybody's faces.

Watching the band perform in London at the Hammersmith Odeon, as it was still known in October 1987, there was no room for doubt: this was rock with a capital 'R'. This was rock that did – not – give – a – fuck. Like Axl screamed in one of his most famous songs, you were in the jungle, baby. And you were gonna die . . .

Even those *NME*-reading so-called pop sophisticates, who will still tell you The Smiths were the last great rock band, couldn't entirely deny the frightening reality of Guns N' Roses. Deep down inside, they knew The Smiths were simply too self-conscious to be a truly transcendent rock band; that Morrissey's hand-wringing, über-fan angst would always prevail over good-looking Johnny Marr's low-slung rock sensibility. Certainly, there appeared to be no such problems regarding W. Axl Rose – the one that only came out at night – or his leather-clad buddy Slash. Not then anyway. All that stuff would only become apparent later, when it was already over and none of us were supposed to care any more.

Needless to say, as time went by and the empty, unproductive years seemed to have cluttered up his mind like cigarette butts in an ashtray, it became clear just how ridiculous the whole last-great-rock-band premise was, both for Axl and for those of us that had once, just for a minute, actually believed in it – or rather were seen to believe. Viewed from a distance, until his recent return to the stage – his second comeback in the last five years, the previous one in 2002 having ended with the almost immediate collapse of his first US tour for ten years – it seemed that things hadn't just fallen apart, they had dwindled to the point of near total obscurity.

Yet it must have been great being a teenage Guns N' Roses fan in the late-1980s, finding a real-deal rock band to call your own that didn't belong to the generations before. Until then the arbiters of rock taste were a collection of older brothers and young dads who scoffed at the MTV-friendly, niche-driven likes of Def Leppard, Bon Jovi and their poodle-headed pals, throwing their Zeppelin, Sabbath and Purple albums on the table like a royal flush at a poker game for greenhorns. Now they had to admit it: that Guns N' Roses song, 'Sweet Child O' Mine', that their kid brother/son told them about, it was good – fucking good. As was that other one they'd seen the video for, 'Paradise City'. In fact, they might even invest in a copy of the album those tunes came from, *Appetite for Destruction*. Why not? Over thirty million other people would do exactly the same during that period – that's more people than ever bought the Beatles' *Sgt. Pepper*, more copies sold than any solitary album by U2 or the Rolling Stones; more albums sold, in fact, than Bob Dylan has managed in his entire career.

Even when the *NME*-reading, brother-dad axis appeared to get their own back with the grand-scale arrival in 1991 of Nirvana, the band that history now tells us made groups like Guns N' Roses obsolete overnight, it didn't actually change a thing. The groups that looked and tried to sound like Guns N' Roses – the second-raters like Mötley Crüe and Poison – their flames were certainly extinguished by the wave of new 'grunge' stars Nirvana's unforeseen success ushered in. Not Guns N' Roses, though. They didn't become obsolete, though their career did grind to an ignominious halt a couple of years later.

But if things were somehow different now and that original five-man line-up actually got back together, or even if just four out of five of them could make it back into the studio, the odds are the album they produced would easily sell another twenty million copies. The fact that it's been more than fifteen years since he last released an album of original material, yet W. Axl Rose can still headline arenas and festivals all over the world with a band that has absolutely nothing in common with Guns N' Roses except its legal right to the name, proves just how strong the demand is for the original line-up. In fact, it's such a no-brainer it's amazing that even Axl has not yet succumbed to its lure.

Of course, some will say that it's only as things should be. That in our minds' eye the original band has become even more cartoonish in their extended twilight than they were in their heyday, right down to their rent-a-rocker clothes and profoundly silly names – Axl, Slash, Duff, Izzy, and whoever the drummer was that week. That they belong not here and now but in our cloudy collective memories, briefly illuminated every so often when MTV throws the 'Sweet Child O' Mine' video into semi-rotation again, or some radio station blows the dust off the edited-down CD single. No, they never did quite fulfill their musical promise, despite the simultaneous release in 1991 of two surprisingly enterprising double-albums – Axl's typically overambitious scheme to seal the band's immortality at a time when a simple straightforward album release would have done the job much better.

We have to bear in mind all those things. It should not be forgotten, however, that for all their fashion-mishaps and cultural clangers, for those of us who were actually there at the shows first time around, there was never any doubt in our hearts and minds that what we were witnessing was something very special. Guns N' Roses might have been the last of the dinosaurs, or the last gunslingers in Dodge, or as *Kerrang!* memorably dubbed them in the first major article written about them outside America, 'the most dangerous band in the world'. Whatever they had, it was always – always – worth taking the trouble to seek out and savour. Now that they're gone – really gone, whatever the Axl apologists have to say about it on their sad little chat-rooms and hollow footsteps fan-sites – it's worth remembering what all the fuss was about. And what killed them off, finally, in the end.

Two decades on since he was the most famous and sought-after rock star on the planet, one wonders what it is that W. Axl

Rose thinks he is doing with his rock star life. Why the tedious on-off-on-off-etc-etc-etc saga still, as I write, surrounding the puzzlingly titled *Chinese Democracy* album, which he has now spent more than a decade and, according to *Rolling Stone*, $13 million trying and failing to make his next release? It is fifteen years since his last album! Compared to, say, the Beatles, who released their entire oeuvre in approximately half that time, this is a monumental gap to fill. No ostensibly functioning major rock artist has ever left such a yawning chasm between record releases. Put another way, you could fit the entire twelve-year, nine-album career of Led Zeppelin – another phenomenally successful band regarded as recklessly uncommercial in their lifetime, refusing to release obvious hit singles or even appear on TV – into this period and still end up with three years to spare. Whole genres have come and gone since Axl last sanctioned the release of an original Guns N' Roses album: grunge, Britpop, electronica, Americana, nu-metal, Emo . . . the list is farcically long and still growing. Indeed, it's been so long since Guns N' Roses last released a new album that, strictly speaking, the band itself no longer exists. So frustrated by the unbelievable amount of time it has taken their erstwhile frontman to try to get to grips with the challenge of recording a new album that, one by one, they have either quit or been fired. But then, it seems like almost everyone who knows Axl Rose falls out of his company sooner or later: band members, managers, PRs, record company associates, wives, girlfriends, friends of friends – and, of course, plenty of writers too, including this one. For many, our crimes were essentially variations on the same theme: foolishly telling the king he has no clothes. Our punishment: at best, banishment from the court of King Axl; at worst, public and private humiliation and legal battles. In my own case, it led to him actually putting my name in a song: 'Get In The Ring', from the *Use Your Illusion II* album, one of the most sulphurous tracks Guns N' Roses would ever record, in which Axl proclaimed loudly that I and three others – Bob Guccione Jr. of *Spin*, Andy Secher of *Hit Parader* and some unnamed hack at *Circus* magazine – were guilty of ripping off the kids as well as printing lies. Dirty deeds for which we were roundly invited to suck his dick.

Did I print lies? Of course not. I never set out to do anything other than tell the story of Guns N' Roses as it unfolded around me. The band fights, the drug problems, the model girlfriends and estranged wives, the cancelled shows and bloody riots, the two fans trampled to death in the mud at Castle Donington in 1988 . . . What was there left to make up? Back then, in the air-guitar 1980s, you had to work fast just to write it all down. For me the truth, as ever, is much more prosaic. I believe I had simply shown myself to be beyond his complete control. A condition Axl appears to have found intolerable even amongst his own band-mates. As far as Axl was concerned, you were either for him or against him. There was no middle-ground allowed. And therein lies a great deal of the problem with being Axl Rose. Here was a young guy from nowhere, arriving with a talent so effusive the impact he would make on the world was almost immediate. A young guy who appeared to be on his way to becoming the most significant, certainly the most successful, rock artist of his gener-ation. And yet he often seemed willing to throw it all away for . . . what? An argument over who had the final word? Or who was the boss of you? What?

I first met Guns N' Roses backstage at the Manchester Apollo in October 1987, on one of five dates on the band's first UK tour. I was there on assignment for *Kerrang!* – the first magazine of any prominence to cover the band in depth – and was warmly welcomed backstage. Unlike drummer Steven Adler ('You can't get Quaaludes in England? That sucks, dude!'), or guitarist Slash, (rarely seen anywhere back then without an open bottle of Jack Daniels in his hand), Axl struck me on first acquaintance as the only sensible one among them, an opinion I was to revise drastically over the years. At the time, though, he seemed intelli-gent, approachable, a little over-serious perhaps, but then maybe that's what happened when you were the leader of a gang of party animals like Guns N' Roses – for despite the presence of various managers and bigwigs, Axl was clearly the one in charge, even then. Which made his later attempts at securing yet more control inexplicable: there was never any doubt who was the boss of Guns N' Roses. It was always Axl. Even when they tried to kick him out, as they did just a few months later, it was clear the band wouldn't be able to carry on without him.

Their rise to superstardom over the next twelve months – as their debut album, *Appetite for Destruction*, began its inexorable rise towards the number one spot in both Britain and America – happened to coincide with my own gradual relocation to Los Angeles, where they were based. Our paths would cross a great deal over the next three years. Mainly, I got to know Slash, an easy-going sheep-in-wolf's clothing who had yet to learn how to say no to anything. He never bothered to hide his generally mixed feelings about Axl. 'He's a great front man,' he told me, 'and great front men are hard to find. But he's also . . .' He waved his cigarette around while he struggled to find the right word. '. . . Axl. And you have to deal with that, too.' Other mutual friends echoed those sentiments. 'Axl is a sweetheart,' said one, 'but he's also different, you know? He likes to do what he likes to do, whatever time of day or night it is.' Uh, huh. And that made him different from other rock stars in what way? 'Wait and see,' they said. 'You'll find out . . .'

Sure enough, West Hollywood being the self-contained rock village it was in the late-1980s, I ran into Axl on quite a few occasions throughout this period. Not yet the reclusive figure he would later become, donning disguises so as not to be recognized, it wasn't unusual back then to find him hanging out at well-known LA haunts like the Cat Club (run by one-time rival Faster Pussycat singer Taime Downe). Despite the already colossal fame of the band, there were no bodyguards back then. Instead he was usually accompanied by the same close-knit circle of pre-fame friends and relatives he always surrounded himself with. Friends, 'street kids' as he called them, such as West Arkeen, who would share the credits with Axl on various Guns N' Roses songs; Del James, whose access to Axl would help secure him a career as a magazine writer; Robert John, a previously unknown photographer whose proximity to the GN'R throne would also win him a string of high-profile assignments; and Axl's younger half-brother, Stuart, an amiable small-town guy along for the ride.

Axl was always friendly on such occasions. Unlike Slash or

the others, who would enter a club as though they were about to walk onstage, Axl liked to keep a low profile; lurking in the DJ-booth at the Cat; slipping to the toilets in the kitchen of the Rainbow rather than risk the rabble of the public johns. By 1989, he had sprouted a huge red beard and taken to wearing his glasses and a baseball cap whenever he went out. As disguises go, it was a pretty good one and in stark contrast to the back-combed, beautifully made-up voodoo doll of the videos then rotating on MTV. I recall him once taking a group of us outside to see the flash, giant-sized speakers he'd just bought and had fitted into his new sports car. When he hit the 'play' button Metallica's 'Eye Of The Beholder' came blaring out. It sounded louder than in the club, the car's shiny leather upholstery visibly vibrating. He stood there enjoying our awed expressions. 'Kicks ass, huh?' he grinned as he pressed 'pause'. Then he climbed behind the wheel, started the engine, hit 'play' again and roared off down the street, pounding the steering wheel with one hand in time to the monstrously loud music.

Of course, I'd heard all the stories. Walk-outs, cancelled shows, band fights, busted-up rooms . . . there had already been several long before Guns N' Roses became famous for them. But in my naiveté that was a side of the singer I never imagined I would have to endure personally. Because of the numerous favourably slanted magazine articles I'd written about the band, I flattered myself that they saw me as a friend, someone who would look the other way rather than write something that would upset or embarrass them, someone they could relax and be themselves around. Why else would they have given me a gold record with my name on it for their 1988 mini-album, *GN'R Lies*?

Then, late one night in January 1990, I got the call that would lead to the end of that cosy misconception. I happened to be staying at the Hollywood home of the band's PR. When Axl called her at around midnight, raging about something he'd just read in *Kerrang!*, she offered to let him speak to me, to see if I could help. Seizing the opportunity, Axl demanded I go straight to his apartment where he would make some sort of 'statement'. I remember being mildly put out because I was just about to go to bed. But I wasn't going to pass up the chance of catching Axl Rose 'in the mood to talk', as he growlingly put it, so I hurriedly got myself together and picked up my tape-recorder. I didn't know the address so the PR drove me there. In fact, she sat in on the whole interview, which made it doubly disconcerting when Axl later tried to claim I had made parts of it up – and the PR dutifully backed him. But then, having once been a rock PR myself, I knew that that's what good PRs do: back their clients to the hilt, right or wrong. It's not the writer who's paying their bills.

Picture the scene: Axl, then the biggest rock star in the world, answers the door to his surprisingly modest West Hollywood apartment by yanking it nearly off its hinges, then storming down the corridor. You follow him into the lounge, try and say hello but he's already in full flow. Standing there in crumpled T-shirt and jeans, his big red beard covering most of his scrunched-up, freckled face, raging about Mötley Crüe singer Vince Neil, who has been 'saying some shit' in *Kerrang!* – specifically, Neil's claim to have punched-out GN'R guitarist Izzy Stradlin for 'messing' with Vince's wife, a former mud-wrestler from the Tropicana named Sharise.

Axl, who went to school with Izzy and still sees him as his only real friend in the band, says this is 'bullshit'. Now Vince must pay. 'Guns or knives, motherfucker,' Axl snarls, 'I don't care. I just wanna smash his plastic face.' This last comment was a sarcastic reference to Vince's supposedly hush-hush cosmetic surgery. 'Turn on the tape-recorder,' he growled. My journalist's antennae twitching madly, I hurriedly did as he said. I mean, just *try* and make up an intro to a feature for *Kerrang!*, circa 1990, as good as that. It was so insanely ridiculous, so marvellously over the top I had to stop myself from laughing out loud. Yet the dust it kicked up when the interview was eventually published in April that year was even more unbelievable, and far less funny – at least to me. Not then.

Axl disowned the interview almost as soon as it appeared. I heard through intermediaries that he didn't believe he would 'talk like that'. Even though I had phoned him and read him the most inflammatory parts of the piece before sending it in to the magazine, just to make sure he still wanted me to go ahead. I remember his defiantly laughing voice on the phone: 'I stand by every fuckin' word, man!'

When I learned that he was now all but accusing me of making the story up, I felt shattered. To be accused of lying when you've told the truth is bad enough. To be branded a liar by the person whose 'truth' it is you have been uniquely trusted to convey (this was no normal interview-request I had put in with the record company) is particularly hard to bear. Worse still, I couldn't figure out why he'd do it. The only thing I could think of was that maybe someone from the Crüe office had lodged a complaint and that Axl – embarrassed by something he'd said months before and that he could no longer be bothered to defend or explain – had simply told them the journalist had made the whole thing up. How often have we heard the same excuse applied by other recalcitrant stars caught out saying or doing something they later regretted?

It wasn't until years later that I heard of another possibility. According to *The Dirt*, the official Mötley Crüe autobiography published in 2001, Vince Neil was so riled when he read my interview with Axl that he repeatedly tried to contact him to organize a proper fist-fight, including going public with an invitation to a brawl between the two to be broadcast live on MTV. However Vince claims in his book that, after agreeing through intermediaries to meet up with Axl and fight it out at least half-a-dozen times 'Axl chickened out'. It was a shame, Vince said, because 'the only thing that would have given me more pleasure than a number one record was breaking Axl Rose's nose'. He added: 'I wanted to beat the shit out of that little punk and shut him up for good. But I never heard from him: not that day, not that month, not that year, not that century. But the offer still stands.'

None of which would be very surprising to anybody who knew Vince, who was a tough Mexican kid who'd grown up fighting in the street. Vince walked the walk; he felt Axl merely liked to talk – or sing – about it. Maybe, at some point, he tried to talk his way out of the mess he was in with Vince – exacerbated by the fact that everybody else in GN'R and the Crüe hung out in almost identical circles – by claiming the rotten fuckin' limey journalist had made the whole thing up.

I first heard about 'Get In The Ring' when Guns N' Roses bassist Duff McKagan – who came up with the tune and original words – told me about it excitedly at a Christmas party as far back as 1989. Originally called 'Why Do You Look at Me When You Hate Me?' it was the Sid Vicious-worshipping, Seattle punk Duff who was to have sung it. He gave me a drunken verse or two in my ear at the party and it sounded like a bad impression of Sid doing 'My Way'. When, over a year later, Axl's bonnet was buzzing with so many bees he co-opted the song for his own purposes and re-title it 'Get In The Ring', I'm told Duff was not exactly thrilled, his big solo moment gone (though he did enjoy the spotlight elsewhere on *Use Your Illusion II* with the Johnny Thunders-esque 'So Fine'). Axl, though, was clearly on a mission. His target: me and anybody else he believed had got in his way.

Because my Guns N' Roses fan biography, *The Most Dangerous Band in the World*, was published around the same time as the *Use Your Illusion I* and *II* albums were released in 1991, it was generally assumed that the song was in direct response to the book. Not so. While Axl may have disapproved of me publishing a book without his prior consent or knowledge, it seems pretty clear now that the crux of the matter came back to that ill-starred interview he gave to me about how he was going to 'kill' Vince Neil. But then, as I and so many others were to discover, push· the right buttons and Axl appeared ready to metaphorically 'kill' anyone. Me, Vince, and eventually his own band, all of whom would be gone within the next five years, leaving Axl to soldier on with an endless parade of session men, maintaining the Guns N' Roses legend in name only.

I tell this story now, not because that's what this new book is all about, but in order to declare any perceived conflict of interest and get the whole tawdry affair out of the way as quickly as possible. This book is not about score-settling. It is about trying to uncover the complicated truth behind the *Wizard Of Oz*-like façade William Bruce Bailey erected for himself the day he became W. Axl Rose; to try and explain, for better or worse, who and what he really is – and why.

For despite his behaviour towards me and others like me, Axl Rose remains one of the most intriguing rock stars it has been my fortune to work with. Not because of his talent, which many feel he has almost wilfully squandered these past fifteen years, making one bad decision after another in a career which now bears all the nasty gashes and jagged scars of the habitual self-harmer. And certainly not because of his personality, which appears to combine love and hate in such a way as to allow moments of fury, distrust and stubborn pride to co-exist, apparently without incongruity, with the thoughtful, generous feelings he shows to those few who have remained loyal to him and his cause, no matter what. But because, for all his contracts and bodyguards, there has never been a rock star whose fundamental needs and motivations have been brought so painfully to bear on his own career as W. Axl Rose. The only others I can think of who come close are Elvis Presley and Michael Jackson, and in the case of the former you could perhaps forgive him because – unlike Axl, who became a rock star at a time when it had seemingly all been done before – there were no precedents for Elvis to adhere to, no rules to follow because none existed until he came along. In the case of the latter, he has spent so long squirming beneath the unforgiving heat of the media spotlight that we all feel we know something of what the problem is with Michael Jackson. Compared to him, the story of W. Axl Rose remains a complete mystery to most people, even his most ardent fans – one might say, *especially* to his most ardent fans.

Ultimately, this is not the story of a monster, though it would be easy to make it appear so. It is the story of what happened to a lonely badly treated boy from small-town America who grew up believing that rock music would provide not only an escape from childhood horrors but would sanctify his soul – and who was proved at least partly right. But a child, nevertheless, who never quite found the solution to his loneliness. And whose bitter and constant hitting out – verbally, emotionally, even musically – has ultimately been directed in one direction: towards himself.

Once upon a time, W. Axl Rose was quite rightly regarded as the most famous, most talented, most sought-after young rock star in the world. These days, he is regarded by some as almost a Howard Hughes figure; the bearded, sun-baked, wild-eyed survivor stalking the desert island he washed up on after his ship sank. Indeed, there is little that is funny about this story and far too much that is simply tragic.

How did it happen? And why did it happen? This book is my attempt to turn on the lights in the blacked-out room where the real Axl Rose has been hiding all these years. To throw back the dusty old curtains, open the locked windows and let some air into the chokingly unhealthy environment. Some of it will make for unsettling reading, especially to those who have stood in line for tickets or been waiting all this time for a new album. But then what did they think was really going on here?

Whatever it was, think again . . .

Part One

ONE IN A MILLION

Being unwanted, unloved, uncared for . . .
I think that is a much greater hunger,
a much greater poverty than the person
who has nothing to eat.

MOTHER TERESA

Chapter One

WHAT'S SO CIVIL ABOUT WAR ANYWAY?

Slash once told me that the rest of the band had a saying about Axl, that you couldn't really consider yourself his friend until you'd told him at least once to fuck off. Yet that was something Slash and the band would find harder and harder to do as time went by and Guns N' Roses became more and more successful. Mainly because they knew by then that there was no pushing him, and that if you did he was just as likely to jack the whole thing in and walk out, even if it meant cutting off his nose to spite his face. But also because anyone who really knew him understood that the one person he was usually fighting hardest with was himself. That he is, was and always would be his own worst enemy. But why? Who was he deep down inside, and what had happened to make him so perpetually at odds with everyone and everything? According to those who despised him, it was because Axl was 'a hick'. Even his childhood friend Izzy told me he was 'just this little guy' that had come from 'nowhere'.

But surely there was more to it than that? Back in the late-1980s, before the shutters came down and I was consigned to Axl's 'shit list', I occasionally found myself in the same company as his amiable half-brother, Stuart. Getting to know Stuart provided a unique insight into Axl's small-town origins. Once, staying at an apartment in LA where Stuart was a frequent visitor, I was boiling eggs in the kitchen one morning when I asked him to fetch some egg-cups.

He looked at me, puzzled. 'Egg *what*?' he said in his sing-song Midwestern accent.

'Egg-cups,' I repeated.

'Huh?'

'You know, for putting eggs in?'

'Say what?'

Jesus Christ. I went to fetch them myself. 'Egg-cups, see?' He looked but no light came on. 'What do you call them then?' I asked.

'Uh, we don't call 'em nuthin. I never saw nuthin like that before . . .'

I looked at him. 'Are you taking the piss, Stuart?'

'No, sir. Where I'm from, we don't put 'em in no cups, we just peel 'em and suck 'em.'

I looked again. He wasn't joking. I thought of Axl and tried to imagine him as a kid, sitting there sucking eggs, his thick, black-framed spectacles sliding down his freckled nose. It was surprisingly easy. Then I thought of that same child growing old enough to run away from home and hitch a ride to Los Angeles, walking down Sunset Boulevard for the first time with his hunched-up shoulders and permanently glowering expression, frightened yet utterly fascinated by everything he sees, from the tall palm trees that speak of an exalted kind of paradise to the strip clubs and late-night bars suggestive of another, entirely different sort of high life. Wanting to embrace it yet at the same time instinctively repelled, his upbringing counting against him as surely as the old-fashioned jeans and baseball cap he's wearing. Or as Axl once said: 'I have a lot of damage, and I'm not saying that like, "Oh, pity me" or anything. Instead of being myself, I was definitely a product of my environment, and that was something [Guns N' Roses] has thrown back in the world's face. "You don't like us? Fuck you! You helped create us! Your ways of doing things helped make sure we exist the way we are." We didn't have a choice to exist any other way.'

William Bruce Rose Junior was born on 6 February 1962, in Lafayette, Indiana, a small college town on the banks of the Wabash River.

As an Aquarian, Axl seems to conform to some of the astrological stereotype. Known as the sign of the Thinker, Aquarians tend towards ultra-independence, refusing to be tied down in any given situation for long. Idealistic yet rational, they are adept at gathering information from several different channels at once and processing it – often while the rest of the world assumes they are sleeping. On the positive side, although they can be difficult to get to know well, given the right relationship a typical Aquarian can also be extremely faithful and supportive. Even then, however, their need to preserve a significant degree of privacy and autonomy is paramount. They like to be helpful to others but strongly resent it if they feel they are deliberately being used. At their best, Aquarians are usually lively, original and inventive. Revelling in standing out from the crowd, they can be tremendously creative, with an inbuilt attraction to anything different. Indeed, they are recognized as the most eccentric sign in the zodiac and usually exhibit an abiding love of the unconventional.

Aquarians can be unpredictable. They have strong opinions about everything, and can sometimes be stubborn when pushed in a corner. They are so reliant on their own feelings and observations, they sometimes find themselves out of sync with others.

Some of these character traits will be familiar to anyone who has ever known or worked with Axl – not least his former band mates. 'We call him the Ayatollah,' Slash told me jokingly but with a certain weariness when we first met. 'With Axl, it's always been *his* way or the highway.'

It would seem the roots of whatever really drives Axl can be traced back directly to his troubled beginnings in Indiana. Today, the area known as Greater Lafayette is one of those decorously bland country towns that calls itself a city (population approximately 90,000) and has long characterized the vast, culturally limited plains of the American Midwest. The sort of place most smart kids dream of running away from. Even the public market on 5th Street where Axl hung out as a teenager has a musty middle-aged air; circled by tall, Italianate brick buildings dating from the 1850s, when the railroads first arrived and the marshy frontier settlement first became a proper wife-and-kids town. Farming, manufacturing and trade have always been the mainstays of Lafayette life. Before Axl, its most famous inhabitant was John Purdue, founder of the local university, who died in 1876.

The arrival in the 1960s of Interstate 65 opened up the nascent city. Sixty-three miles from Indianapolis and 125 miles from Chicago, by the time William Rose was born the population of Greater Lafayette was booming, the product of a generation of Second World War veterans, many of whom had taken advantage of the GI Bill to attend Purdue University, moving into the area en masse and starting families, buying up thousands of prefabricated, made-in-Lafayette 'National' homes. (At one point, in the late-1940s, admissions staff at Purdue were processing more than a hundred applications a day.) Situated on the west side of the river, Purdue University opening its doors to so many marked the beginning of the East–West split that still serves as a dividing line for the local community. Now regarded as one of the leading American colleges for agriculture, engineering and technology, with more than 37,000 students enrolled on the West Lafayette campus alone, the university is the area's biggest employer.

While downtown would remain the busy heart of Lafayette, by the 1960s there were numerous shopping centres dotted around. As Barbara Church, a former classmate of Axl's, says now, 'There's two different towns separated by the Wabash River. On the west side of town – the West Lafayette – would be the university, and on the east side of town would be mostly the factories.'

It was on the poorer Eastside, on 24th Street, that the young Axl grew up. Unlike the mostly professional home-owners that populated the City of West Lafayette – regarded locally as home to the Purdue academics and professionals – residents of the Eastside, known simply as the City of Lafayette, tended to work either at A.E. Staley's corn syrup plants, or the ALCOA aluminium plant, or at the sprawling Eli Lilly Pharmaceuticals factory, which had opened in 1954. As such, according to Church, the Lafayette she and 'Bill', as she still calls Axl, grew up in was 'a conservative, downhome kind of town. At the time we were children, it was a small town with a park and an ice-cream parlour and kids riding their bikes and playing hide and seek in the alleys.'

That said, any notions of Axl having enjoyed the idyllic white picket-fence Midwestern childhood depicted in so many Stephen

Spielberg movies are quickly dispelled by the discovery that his father, also William Rose, was a notorious local trouble-maker who would soon abandon his pretty teenage wife, Sharon, and their baby son, never to be seen again. Though his mother would do everything in her power to keep this important part of his past out of her son's reach as he was growing up, as the result of what he called his work with 'regression therapy', Axl would later claim he'd been 'aware' of the problems surrounding his parents' troubled relationship even as a baby in the womb. 'My real father was a pretty fucked-up individual,' he was quoted as telling *Rolling Stone* writer Kim Neely. 'I didn't like the way he treated me before I was born. So when I came out, I was just wishing the motherfucker was dead.' He reportedly added that he didn't care what people made of statements like that. Everything about his life had been stored in his mind, he believed, 'from very early on'. For years, he had simply 'blacked out' the worst aspects of his ghastly childhood. It was only through the regression therapy that the worst memories had come back.

Most shocking of all were the 'repressed memories' he was reported to have recovered of William Rose Senior sexually abusing him as a child. According to *Rolling Stone* he said that his father had 'fucked me in the ass when I was two'. William Rose died in the 1980s, 'killed and buried in several miles of strip mining in Illinois', as Axl told me. His mother, Sharon, died from cancer in 1996, so we only have the singer's version of events. Axl also reportedly told *Rolling Stone* about how his real father once 'kidnapped me, because someone wasn't watching me.' He was also quoted in *RIP* as saying, 'With the help of regression therapy I uncovered that my real dad, not my stepdad, sexually abused me.'

William Rose abandoned the family when baby Bill was just two years old. When Sharon remarried after her divorce came through a couple of years later, her new husband, a Pentecostal preacher by the name of the Reverend L. Stephen Bailey – or 'Beetle' as he was sometimes known to his church friends – legally adopted the toddler and gave him his own surname. Far from being the end of his familial problems, the arrival of a strict, extremely religious stepfather must surely have sent the unhappy boy even deeper into his emotional shell.

Modern Pentecostalism of the kind practised by L. Stephen Bailey began around the turn of the twentieth century, when a young woman named Agnes Ozman was reported to have 'received the gift of tongues' during a prayer meeting in 1901 at Charles Fox Parham's Bethel Bible College in Topeka, Kansas. It was Parham, formerly a Methodist minister, who later formulated the doctrine that speaking in tongues was 'Bible evidence' of the Baptism of the Holy Spirit. As a result, the Pentecostal movement within Protestant Christianity places special emphasis on what it describes as the 'gifts of the Holy Spirit', as demonstrated in the Biblical account of the Day of Pentecost. Pentecostals believe that one can only truly be 'saved' and made 'acceptable to God' by believing in Jesus as the Lord and Saviour in the most literal terms, and that all events depicted in the Bible, no matter how fantastic, are true – though 'truth' as a concept is not limited to the realm of 'reason'.

As such, most Pentecostals like Stephen Bailey believe that the baptism in the Holy Spirit is always accompanied, certainly in its earliest stages, by the experience of speaking in tongues, also known as glossolalia. Hence, perhaps, Axl's off-hand remark years later that he once heard his stepfather singing in fluent Japanese, even though he didn't know the language. Most Pentecostal churches also accept the corollary that those who don't speak in tongues have not received the blessing they call 'The Baptism of the Holy Spirit'. Even more strongly held is the Pentecostal belief in 'holding witness to unbelievers', i.e. spreading the word, in the most vigorous terms. 'The Great Commission' to spread the 'Good News of the Kingdom of God', claimed to have been spoken by Jesus directly before his Ascension, is perceived by Pentecostals as the most important command Jesus gave. (As described in Mark 16:15 and Matthew 28: 19–20.) Or as Axl later put it, 'The Bible was shoved down my throat, and it really distorted my point of view . . . We were taught "You must fear God."'

Axl had two half-siblings, Amy and Stuart. According to *Rolling Stone* Axl told how Stephen Bailey routinely beat his children for such transgressions as singing along to pop songs on the radio or watching the 'wrong' television programmes – that is, on those days when they were actually allowed to have the TV switched on. Stephen Bailey has not commented publicly on these accusations. 'I was brainwashed in a Pentecostal church,' Axl would later tell his friend Del James. He was not 'against churches or religion', he said, but his particular church which 'was filled with self-righteous hypocrites who were child abusers and child molesters. These were people who'd been damaged in their own childhoods and in their lives. These were people who were finding God but still living with their damage and inflicting it upon their children.'

Axl would be reported as saying that it was this background that poisoned his own adult attitudes to women. 'Women were evil. Everything was evil. I had a really distorted view of sexuality and women.' Forbidden even from watching actors kiss on-screen, by the time Axl was in his teens his stepfather had conditioned his children so completely that they voluntarily turned their heads away whenever anything remotely sexual appeared on the television. 'We scolded each other. My mom allowed all of this to happen because she was too insecure to be without my stepfather.'

Indeed, it wasn't only his father and stepfather who Axl felt had a disastrous influence on him as a child. Years later, he would also blame his mother for the 'hatred for women' he admitted was part of his motivation behind the lyrics of infamous Guns N' Roses songs such as 'Back Off Bitch' and 'Locomotive'. As he was reported as saying to *Rolling Stone*: 'Basically, I've been rejected by my mother since I was a baby. She's picked my stepfather over me ever since he was around.' He reportedly even partly blamed his maternal grandmother for his negative feelings towards women. 'I've gone back and done the work and found out I overheard my grandma going off on men when I was four. And I've had problems with my own masculinity because of that. I was pissed off at my grandmother for her problem with men and how it made me feel about being a man. So I wrote about my feelings in the songs.'

As a result of his deeply unhappy background, Bill grew up

a shy bespectacled boy with hunched shoulders, an almost permanent frown on his face and a reluctance to make eye contact with anyone he didn't already know intimately (a personality tic that would remain embedded long into adulthood). Even with the other kids at school, young Bill tended to keep himself to himself. Asked years later whether he had any favourite childhood memories, Axl replied, 'As in a good time? Wow! I guess it would be when the three of us kids were playing and getting along with my stepfather, wrestling around, kind of getting away from whatever was going on and all relating and having fun as little kids.'

But it didn't happen very often and even then, he said, his stepfather was able to spoil it for him somehow. According to *Metallix*, he observed, 'My stepfather had shot a video of our entire family and of his entire family, all the way back to [pictures of] great-great-grandfathers, and he compiled this video. Through doing certain work with my family, with understanding what was going on there now, it was very strange, very surreal, and very disturbing.' To somehow purge himself of his stepfather's influence he would later use a clip from the video in the promo for the 1991 'Live And Let Die' single. 'I use a shot in the beginning from when I was about three or four years old. I come in the door with a toy gun and my dad happened to film it . . . He sent it to me with some sound effects over it and a comment, kind of putting me down, letting me know he's still on top of things or whatever. But that's not the fact and I don't accept it, so it's like, "No, I'm using it my way, and that's me, and don't forget it."'

The only positive element his stepfather seemed to have instilled in him was an interest in music, an aptitude for which he demonstrated from an early age. At five, he had begun singing in the Pentecostal church choir. Later, he also sang in the Bailey Trio with Stuart and Amy, while learning to play church hymns on the piano. To his stepfather's chagrin, however, young Bill was also partial to the pop music he would hear occasionally on the tiny transistor radio his mother had surreptitiously given him.

Later in life, he would recall how he used to sing Elvis Presley songs in front of the smaller children at recess when he was in the third grade: 'I wasn't allowed to listen to music except for old

Elvis Presley and Jimmy Swaggart gospel records.' Swaggart would go on to become America's leading TV evangelist, before resigning from his ministry in February 1988 after he was photographed with a prostitute. In front of a congregation of over 7,000 in Baton Rouge, Louisiana, and a television audience of millions, he wept as he confessed to 'moral failure'. Turning to his wife, Frances, he sobbed, 'I have sinned against you and I beg your forgiveness.' Swaggart's confession was all the more acute as he himself had recently denounced rival TV evangelist Jim Bakker over his extramarital affair with his secretary Jessica Hahn. 'I was raised on Jimmy Swaggart religious tapes from when I was five,' said Axl. 'We had a reel-to-reel deck and we bought 'em all. This just went on for years and years and years.' Barbara Church, a classmate from his first school, Oakland Elementary, also recalls a lonely-looking Bill 'walking around in the playground singing a lot. And I remember him being in the choir. I remember Bill having a very low voice and not thinking that he was very remarkable, or anything outstanding as far as having a singing voice that was wonderful.'

As a boy Bill was also quite athletic, running and winning cross-country races at school. And yet there was always a terrible schism in his mind about what it all meant; winning prizes for learning Bible verses, yet feeling unable to believe wholeheartedly in the extreme values his stepfather preached endlessly to him and others. The emotional conflicts these feelings caused would betray themselves in all sorts of unpleasant ways. As Axl reportedly revealed to *Rolling Stone*, he was plagued by nightmares throughout his childhood. Sleeping on the top bunk of the bunk bed he shared with Stuart, the nightmares were sometimes so physically affecting he would toss and turn himself right out of bed and onto the floor. Once, he hit the ground so hard his front teeth went through his lower lip. This went on 'for years' he said.

The pain and frustration would seep like blood through a bandage in other ways too. Once fond of model-making, he would now routinely smash his model airplanes as soon as he had built them, enjoying the sight of their mangled bodies in bits on the floor of his bedroom, their broken wings jutting out like spikes. Inevitably, his school work suffered too. By the time he was sixteen he was playing truant so often he decided one day to stop going to school completely. Until then, the way he is reported as telling it, 'On the placement tests in school, I was always in the top three per cent.' He went back as a senior, 'then dropped out again. I couldn't make school work for me. I was having to read books, sing songs, draw pictures of things that didn't stimulate or excite me. It just didn't do anything for me. So I dropped out and started drawing and painting at home and spending a lot of my time in the library. Basically I started putting myself through Axl's school of subjects that I wanted to learn about.'

Increasingly, he turned to music as an outlet. But once again his stepfather deeply disapproved of Axl's fondness for 'the devil's music'. The only time he and the other children were allowed to listen to the radio with impunity was on Sunday afternoons, when his stepfather would switch it on for his own selfish reasons. 'That's when he and Mom had their special time together,' Axl recalled, 'and we had to take our naps. They would put on the radio so we wouldn't overhear anything. But rock'n'roll was a bad and evil thing.'

Nevertheless, his musical tastes continued to broaden in spite of his limited exposure to it at home. 'It wasn't necessarily the words in the songs but the melody and the feelings expressed in songs that somehow became a friend of mine when I was a child. I was denied feeling any way other than how my stepfather told me I should feel continually, about anything and everything. But in music, I could listen and realize you could feel other ways or new ways. It was okay, because here were manifestations of those other feelings.' More and more he knew that 'whether my dad liked them or not, they existed'.

Like most American kids his age, Bill grew up approving strongly of rockers like Aerosmith and Kiss. But because of his love of piano, his most favourite artists tended to be those whose work contained a higher level of musicality or classically influenced styles: Elton John, Queen, Todd Rundgren and the Electric Light Orchestra. 'I'm an old ELO fanatic,' he told me. 'I love old ELO – *Out Of The Blue*, that period. I went to see 'em play when I was a kid and shit like that. I mean, I respect [ELO singer-songwriter] Jeff Lynne for being Jeff Lynne, but *Out Of The Blue* is an awesome album.'

He added that later Guns N' Roses songs such as the ponderous, epically proportioned 'November Rain', with its kitchen-sink orchestral arrangement, which Axl said he'd begun writing as a child, were in effect his own attempt to emulate the ELO sound of the 1970s. He then proceeded to list all the qualities he most admired about Jeff Lynne. 'Well, one: he's got stamina. Two: he's used to working with a lot of material. Three: he's used to working with all kinds of instrumentation. Four: he's used to working with all kinds of different styles of music. Five: he wrote all his own material. Six: he produced it.' He paused and lit a cigarette, shaking his head in wonder. 'That's a lot of concentration, and a lot of energy needed.'

He said he'd even like to get Lynne to produce some tracks for the band: an ambition that remains unfulfilled. Nevertheless, it was obvious, I remarked, that Axl's tastes in music were more far-reaching than one anticipated from the average heavy metal singer. 'I sure fuckin' hope so,' he smiled. On another occasion, he said he felt his stepfather's antipathy towards the music he wished to explore as a teenager had made him a late starter. 'I seem to have pulled it together on my own [but] it took a long time and . . . even to this day, I still have to deal with, you know, coming to grips with certain things that happened during my childhood, and certain things I wasn't allowed to do and allowed to hear and everything like that. So, I'm still exploring every field of music I possibly can. And I feel I got a lot of catching up to do.'

To try and find out more, I once asked him to pick three songs from his childhood that, for whatever reason, he felt summed up or helped form his musical tastes back then. He thought about it for a moment then treated me to one of his rare wintry smiles. The first song he picked was Led Zeppelin's 'D'Yer Maker', a track from their *Houses of the Holy* album, and a US hit single in the summer of 1973. He still pronounced it *Dyer* Maker, until I explained that it was actually a play on the word 'Jamaica' – said with an English accent – based on the song's self-conscious reggae-feel.

He stared at me. 'Wow. I never knew that. When I was in grade school I used to write down the names of, like, all the novelty songs. Like "Spiders and Snakes" [by Terry Jacks] and stuff like that. Then I heard "D'Yer Maker" and I made fun of it like crazy. I was telling everybody about this weird song I'd heard on the radio. So I'm laughing at it and this and that, but by recess in the afternoon I'm sitting in the corner with my pocket radio and I just had to hear that song again. I mean, I *had* to hear it. That was, like, the first case of "*I have to hear that song.*" I had it going through my head and I had to hear it.'

It was his belated discovery of Zeppelin's music, he said, that 'got me into hard rock'. Axl was just eleven at the time and had never heard of them before. 'I heard that and then I was hooked. After that I was Led Zeppelin all the way. That song just blew my mind. I thought, how does he write like this? How does he feel like this? I mean, 'cos everything around me was, like, religious and strict. Even though we were in a city we went to a country church and stuff. I mean, the language was so much different. There was no, whoa, cool vibe and stuff, like in that Zeppelin song. It was like, how did he think like that, you know?'

The second track that influenced him most back then, he said, was 'Benny And The Jets' from the 1973 Elton John double album, *Goodbye Yellow Brick Road*. Axl said he was also a great fan of Elton John's lyricist, Bernie Taupin. So much so, he'd like to have interviewed Taupin about his lyrics. He intimated that he had even run the idea past a few magazine editors but that, so far, there had been no takers. (How many editors would bite an arm off for such an opportunity now? Interestingly, when asked for his opinion of the young Guns N' Roses singer's lyrics, Taupin graciously replied that he was 'an admirer', particularly of the lyrics to 'Sweet Child O' Mine'.)

'Elton John is just the baddest!' Axl grinned. 'There's nobody badder when it comes to attacking the piano and using it in a rock sense. I mean, you're gonna tell me that "Saturday Night's Alright For Fighting" or "Grow Some Funk Of Your Own", or like, "Ballad Of A Well-Known Gun" or "Somebody Saved My Life Tonight" and things like that, ain't heavy songs? There's no way! Those guys wrote seven number one albums in the US from, like, '72 to '75. Bernie Taupin was twenty-five years old, writing off the top of his head, writing albums in two hours! And the guy's vocabulary and education . . .' He shook his head in awe.

'It was so amazing they decided to go rock'n'roll rather than go classical or whatever. And they blended all these different styles – amazing! And "Benny And The Jets", with the ambience and the sound and the way it's recorded, made me *want* the stage. That's the song that made me want the stage, 'cos it made me think about a concert and being on a stage and the way it would sound in a room. Things miked out and this and that. Plus, it just reminded me of the glam scene that was going on then around America and the clubs that I would read about in the old *Creem* magazine and stuff like that . . . Elton John's singing is amazing and that piano solo can't be touched. It's an amazing record. Then when I got the piano book and was trying to learn the song, I discovered the guy's playing ten fingers of the weirdest chords in the world, you know? It's like, what made him think to hit this combination of five notes that makes the initial bomp-bomp-bomp? It's not just, like, a major note, it's all these weird combinations. He just pulls stuff off that nobody else does.'

Would he consider Elton John's music a major influence on his own songwriting style? 'Sure,' he nodded approvingly. 'I've played piano in a style influenced by Elton John and Billy Joel. But it's minimalistic [*sic*]. I know what I can and what I can't do, so I aim it real carefully. But it's basically influenced off Elton John's attack – and his singing. If you want to learn how to sing all different styles, try singing like Elton John – anything from the blues on. It amazes me that radio in America doesn't give Elton John the space that they give Led Zeppelin, the Beatles and the Stones. You know, you don't have the Elton John Hour, yet you can have 400,000 people going to Central Park to see Elton John, and you're gonna have sold-out tours all over the country. I don't understand it . . . I haven't met a group of people that after you've played everything all night and you put on an Elton John record, that don't go, "Cool . . ." and kickback, and like it that the album's on. Any of the first seven or eight albums, you put one of those on and everyone just relaxes . . . It makes you feel good 'cos of the vibrations in the styles of the songs, the styles of writing. And the way they take you so many different places on, like, one album.'

Axl's third and last choice of most influential track was the most surprising: 'I'm Not In Love', a number one single in 1974, in both Britain and America, for 10cc. 'For me,' he said, 'that song goes back and forth along with "Layla" by Derek and the Dominos and Metallica's "Fade To Black". As weird a cross as it may seem, those three songs are my favourite songs of all time. But we were talking about when I was young. "Layla" I didn't get into til I was a bit older.'

The fascination with 10cc began, he explained, at a drugstore he used to stop by on his way to piano lessons as a teenager. 'It was very nice and conservative but had this liquor section that you weren't allowed into unless you were twenty-one – they had magazines like *Playboy* and stuff like that. So I would go there early and I'd hang out for hours in this drugstore. Like, steal a look at these magazines. I was really into *Oui* magazine. The photography was amazing. And I'm just discovering girls and stuff like that and I'm, like, going with the girls in my school and stuff, in my class. But they're boring. But in these magazines, like, these are women and they're great, you know? All right!

'Well, "I'm Not In Love" was always on in this place. And the production is so amazing. It's this guy who is in love, but yeah, doesn't want to be in love, or whatever. Doesn't want to deal with it. He's contradicting himself all the way through the record. Plus, it's like, the coolest attitude. It's like . . .' He began to sing softly, 'I keep your picture . . . on the wall . . . It hides a nasty [sic] stain . . . that's lying there . . .' He stopped and looked down at his shoes. 'That's so, like, nonchalant, so cool. But the production and the song has always stuck. Whenever I'm having a heavy emotional situation, or meeting someone, it's like, I'll get in the car and I'll just turn on the ignition and that song will always be on the radio! I mean, that song messes with my life, man.'

He was thirteen and in the eighth grade at Jefferson High School when he first made friends with Jeffrey Isbell, who would become the catalyst that led to Bill singing in his first rock band. Born the same year as his new friend, Izzy, as he became known at school, recalls how 'we rode bikes, smoked pot, got into trouble – it was pretty Beavis and Butt-Head, actually.' Coming from 'a semi-musical background' in which his grandmother had played drums ('She even had a band, these old ladies who'd play swing and jazz at parties') Izzy was already tinkering with drums and guitar when he met Axl. What first made him think about starting his own band was watching David Cassidy in the kids' TV show *The Partridge Family*. 'I'd watch *The Partridge Family* on TV and think, that looks good. I'll do that.'

Where Axl could be all fire and righteous loathing, Izzy was the kind of guy that liked to slip in and out of a room unnoticed, unobtrusive as a shadow. Quieter than Axl, though no less intense, the two forged an unlikely yet strangely familial bond. Hanging out with Izzy, it wasn't long before Bill made up his own mind about what he wanted to do. As he later said, 'I remember when I was in junior high and they talked about finding a goal – "Yeah, I'm gonna do this, I'm gonna do that" – all just trying to impress the teacher to get a grade. If they got a good grade, they got an allowance. I was like, "No. I wanna be in a band and I wanna do great things." So I got an F for thinking grandiose thoughts.'

Izzy would later laughingly tell me how even his earliest memory of Axl at Jefferson High involved some form of conflict. 'I remember the first day at school there was this big fucking commotion. I heard all these books hit the ground, yelling, and then he went running past. A bunch of fucking teachers chasing him down the hallway . . .' The two of them later ended up sitting next to each other in driver's education class – which is where they finally met. 'He's a fucking horrible driver but that's kind of where we got to know each other.' When Izzy became the drummer in a school band, it wasn't long before he had per-suaded his flame-haired 'crazy friend' to come along and have a go at singing. 'I thought, well, here's a guy who's completely crazy, he'd be a fucking great singer. We had to coax him a bit [and] it didn't go so well in the early days. Sometimes he would just come over and stand around, like he was embarrassed. Or he'd start to sing and then he'd just leave. Walk out and I wouldn't see him again for like three days! Some things don't change, huh?' he added with a rueful smile.

Talking to Izzy a decade after his decision to leave the band he had helped Axl make famous, he had a far more prosaic take on the cause of his former band mate's overbearing personality. 'In high school, you know, Axl, he had long, red hair, he was a little guy and he got a lot of shit [because of it]. I think he never got laid, too, in school. He never got no pussy at school, Axl. So now the guy's a big fucking rock star, he's got the chicks lined up, he's got money and he's got people . . . and the power went to this guy's head.'

With such a deep and abiding interest in music, Bill Bailey might easily have gone on to become a first class student in the subject. Instead, by the age of seventeen, he was in danger of turning into a full-fledged juvenile delinquent. Already filled with rage at the dysfunctional environment he was forced to grow up in, the tipping point came with the accidental discovery of the truth about his real father, William Rose. Brought up to believe that Stephen Bailey was his biological father, when Bill came across old family insurance papers while rifling through some drawers at home one day, he was baffled to discover the name 'Rose' on the forms. Searching some more, he then discovered his mother's old high school diploma – with her surname also listed as 'Rose' – he confronted his parents demanding to know the meaning of this. That was when the truth finally came out. Even then, however, neither Sharon nor Stephen was prepared to discuss the matter properly with their son. 'They always just freaked out whenever anything was mentioned about my real father.' His mother's eyes would 'turn black' and his stepfather would begin to rant and rave.

Left to his own devices Bill was at first confused, then dismayed – then utterly outraged. For the first time in his life, he found the strength to stand up to his stepfather. No longer able to control the boy, Bailey eventually kicked him out. All of which must have only fed the seventeen-year-old's already inward look-ing personality. As he later told Del James, 'I was separated from myself at an early age, and my stepfather made sure I never put myself back together, with his confusing mixed messages.'

Unable to face the truth, Bailey had accused his stepson of 'doing drugs and drinking and all this stuff that I wasn't doing'. Looking for any excuse to be rid of the troublesome teenager, the final bust-up was, ludicrously, over the length of his hair. 'I was kicked out of my house for not cutting my hair. And it was above my ears at the time.' Not unnaturally, he decided, 'Well, if I'm gonna be accused of all these things, I might as well find out what they're all about. And, you know, maybe I got on the wrong track.'

He had always been the kid in trouble at school; the oddball with red hair who studied 'sissy' piano. Now, living away from home, staying at his maternal grandmother's small house, he had his first brushes with the law – mainly for misdemeanours such as 'public consumption [of alcohol]' and 'disturbing the peace'. Over the next two years he would serve time at various weekend correctional centres, including a short stretch in County Jail after he turned eighteen when he didn't have the money to pay a fine.

Other times, he was busted, he said, simply because 'the cops hated me. I got thrown in jail over twenty times and five of those times I was guilty.' He became so used to courtroom procedure, often he would defend himself. 'I didn't trust the public defenders for shit.' Tippecanoe County Court records state that Axl spent a total of ten days in County Jail as an adult over a period from July 1980 to September 1982, on charges of battery, contributing to the delinquency of a minor, public intoxication, criminal trespass and mischief. Before that, he had been arrested as a juvenile four times.

Gina Siler, who later became his girlfriend, recalls this period well. She met him at her seventeenth birthday party, when she was a senior in high school. Axl was twenty and had already hitched and bussed back and forth to LA a couple of times, following in the tracks of Izzy, who had moved there in 1981. Axl had plans to join him permanently but had so far not been able to manage it. 'He had on a long trench coat, dark glasses; collar pulled up, and said he was trying to stay away from the police,' Gina was reported as saying in *Spin* magazine. 'I asked: "What happened?" He said: "Nothing. They just always bother me. They always harass me, no matter where I am." But he would do some pretty wild things.' Axl and his friends, including Dana Gregory, 'would go out and drink and do some stupid things, like smash windows along Main Street'.

After she got to know him, though, Gina realized it wasn't always his fault and that there was some truth in what he said about the police constantly hassling him. He had been walking down the street once, she said, 'it was probably two o'clock in the morning. From the back, he looks very effeminate, with his long hair – not common for that area – and very thin legs, and he had a long coat on. These police were making comments, making gestures, because they thought he was a woman. Until he turned around, and they were very embarrassed to find out it was a male. So they started hassling him, because they were homophobic as hell. They questioned him, and then found out it was Bill Bailey, who'd obviously been in trouble before, and threw him in jail.' He later phoned Gina from his police cell, begging her to come down and bail him out. Dutifully, she skipped school the next day and met him down at the courthouse, where he was brought out still in handcuffs. He was released the same day on condition of bail, which Gina paid for in cash from her own savings.

Inevitably, Axl began to see himself as something of a rock'n'roll martyr. As he later told Del James, 'You're taught to believe that it's normal to get smacked in the head if you don't eat your food. By the time you're in your teens, you're like, "Gimme a beer. Life's a bitch."' As far as he saw it, what had happened to him as a disaffected teenager was a fairly common experience for those young men that became mixed up in the music business. Not only the ones that ended up singing about it but those that bought the records, too. 'There's a lot of people involved in rock'n'roll who were running from something. They got involved with drugs and alcohol to help ease their pain. A large portion – probably the majority – of rockers and metal fans are damaged people who are trying to find some way to express themselves. They can relate to the anger, the pain, the frustration of the band that's performing.'

Axl certainly could. Another friend of his from those days, Dana Gregory's wife, Monica, tells how 'he got hassled a lot, for a variety of reasons'. More than once, 'All the cops came in and basically beat the crap out of Axl.' Why? 'Just because.' As time went by, Axl – as he always did – applied his own rationale to the situation.

'Sometimes,' he said, 'it was just the vibe' he gave off. 'An authority figure can pick up that vibe and feel it as a challenge to his authority, and take it as a threat . . . they immediately sense this guy could be a threat. That he probably *is* a threat, so let's eliminate this threat.' Once, in Chicago, 'I was held down by eight police. I'm on like a brick floor, realizing this guy can take my head and just – bash! And there was nothing I could do if he were to do that.' Not surprisingly, he decided, 'I don't like being vulnerable.'

And yet it became increasingly hard for him to live any other way. Having dropped out of school, the road to college was closed to him. Instead, Axl hung out with like-minded friends such as Izzy and David Lank (who would later also go to LA to form the band Mank Rage), Monica and Dana Gregory, Mike Staggs (another who ended up in LA, in a band called Dumpster who would later open on occasion for Guns N' Roses), and other musicians including David Pyle and Anna Hoon (whose younger brother, Shannon, would achieve fame as the singer in Blind Melon). They all hung out on David Lank's front porch, smoking and drinking cheap hooch, or at Axl's grandmother's home (where he lived after his parents kicked him out), an old wooden house behind a frozen-custard shop adjacent to run-down Columbian Park.

Columbian Park was also a good place to go to after dark. 'We ruled that place at night,' says Dana. They would pick the lock on the old piano case that was built into the outdoor stage and Axl would play for them into the small hours. Not far from the stage was a large memorial stone with a list of names carved into it of all the sons of Lafayette who had 'made the supreme sacrifice in defence of our country'. Unbeknown to Axl, it included the name of William Rose, almost certainly Axl's great-great-great-grandfather, who had been killed in the same Civil War that Axl would later write about in one of his most memorable songs, called simply 'Civil War' and concluding with the line: 'What's so civil about war, anyway?'

The only other local hang-out that would allow them through its doors was a small bar called the Stabilizer. But you needed money to spend there, so mainly they hung out at David's or Axl's grandmother's place. Axl would lay mattresses down in his room and the gang would loll around while he tinkled at the small piano he had moved in there. 'You could get really artistic in whatever way you wanted to,' Monica later recalled. '[Axl] would just sit down and play the most beautiful things . . . He turned me on to Elton John, 'cos he used to do a lot of Elton John. The creative side he had was so intense.'

Dana remembers Axl mostly playing Thin Lizzy songs. 'But the only time I ever really heard him sing was in the bathroom. He'd be in there for an hour doing God knows what. Prancing around like a woman, for all I know.'

And what of Axl's life in Lafayette was reflected in his music, did he think? 'The anger, man,' he says. 'I'd say he got that here.' Others who knew him back then felt that Axl was simply a born troublemaker. Even Izzy, who saw both sides of his friend, said, 'If it wasn't for the band, I just hate to think what he'd have done.'

Dana recalls how on the night Axl finally left for LA for good, he spray-painted on a wall outside Columbian Park: 'Kiss my ass, Lafayette. I'm out of here.'

'I wish I'd taken a picture of that.'

It's since been suggested that at one stage the Lafayette authorities began proceedings to have the young reprobate locked up and branded as a habitual criminal, and that Axl eventually left town on the advice of his lawyer, who had seen the writing on the wall. Or as Axl was later reported as telling *Rolling Stone*, 'It finally reached a point where I realized I was gonna end up in jail, 'cos I kept fucking with the system . . . once you've pissed off a detective, it's a vengeance rap back there.

'They tried everything. They busted me illegally in my own

backyard for drinking. They tried to get me as a habitual criminal, which can mean a life in prison. My lawyer got the case thrown out of court. I left and came to California. They told me not to leave, but I left anyway. My lawyer took care of it. I didn't go back for a long time. Now when I go back to see my family, I avoid the police there. I try to avoid all police in general.'

When Izzy left for LA, after graduating from high school at eighteen (the only member of the original GN'R line-up to do so), Bill decided to follow him. By now he had also changed his name, putting even more distance between himself and his loathed stepfather by re-adopting his birth-name of William Rose, albeit shortened to W. Rose. He may have hated Stephen Bailey but that didn't mean he was prepared to forgive his biological father his sins either. As he would later explain, 'I am "W" Rose because "William" was an asshole.'

With or without Izzy, he had already decided he wanted to have his own band. 'I was working on it since about eighth grade, with a conscious effort, you know? Like, I had all the right clothes. Stack-heeled shoes . . . the bell-bottoms, and the wide shirts with the huge collars. I remember one girl went off at me one day, going "You look like you're a rock star!" I was like, thank you very much! I was very happy about that. I was succeeding.' Pundits have noted that 'Axl Rose' is an anagram of 'oral sex', which may have appealed to the rebellious young man. But the real reasons behind his name-change were of course much more prosaic.

At seventeen, he had looked on enviously as his friend Dana, who played rudimentary bass, started rehearsing with a band they called Axl, a name inspired by the wheel-axle of a skateboard. Soon Bill was telling girls he was in the band too. David Lank helped them design a huge banner for the band emblazoned with the letters A-X-L. Bill fancied himself as the keyboard player. 'I used to play with this guitar player named Paul [Tobias, aka Paul Huge] and I learned about blues and emotionalism through him – he was a big [Jimmy] Page fanatic.' Years later, Tobias was destined to make a dramatic reappearance in the story of Guns N' Roses but for now the fledgling 'band' was never a very solid proposition, the line-up never quite solidifying long enough to play gigs. But Bill really liked the name Axl, eventually deciding to make it his own.

It wasn't until he first made it down to Izzy's pad in LA that Bill finally got serious about wanting his own band, or even calling himself Axl. 'I had a small apartment in Huntington Beach,' Izzy recalled, 'and Bill used to come down and crash on the floor. He was always coming out to visit [and] getting lost. Then, at the end of '82, he came back out with this girl and rented an apartment. That's when he finally stayed . . .' 'This girl' was Gina Siler. In a *Spin* article in 1991 Gina jokingly called herself 'the missing link' because she said Axl no longer acknowledged her; his ability to blank out the past when he wanted to is a trait he would repeat over the coming years.

In the summer of 1982, boasting of his adventures down in LA with Izzy, he told Gina she should go with him the next time he went. But, according to Gina, she was already a student at Purdue and LA seemed a long way off. Instead, she let Axl stay with her and they spent the summer holidays hanging out, getting drunk, taking LSD together and painting the walls of her dorm in psychedelic colours. She later recalled how Axl would write page after page of poetry, including many verses dedicated to her. They also spent time enjoying more downhome pursuits such as skateboarding and playing Frisbee, staying up all night listening to albums by Axl favourites including Queen, Nazareth, AC/DC and the Sex Pistols.

When the holidays finally came to an end in September, Gina said she got ready to go back to college and Axl began to talk again of splitting for LA. He liked Gina but Lafayette was a drag. She says he asked if she was sure she didn't want to come with him?

Chapter Two

JUST A HICK ON THE STRIP

Although Los Angeles has long been the epicentre of the movie industry, its place at the heart of the American music business is a comparatively recent phenomenon. In fact, it wasn't until the early 1990s – long after Guns N' Roses had become an established hit act – that LA overtook New York as America's number one music biz metropolis. Most of the big record companies didn't even have offices on the West Coast until the late 1950s, and even then their biggest power-brokers like Mo Ostin at Warner Bros weren't considered in the same creative light as East Coast legends such as Ahmet Ertegun at Atlantic. Despite the success of established crossover Hollywood stars Frank Sinatra and Elvis Presley or East Coast pop émigrés Bobby Darin and Phil Spector, until then there had simply never been an identifiable music scene in LA the way there was in New York.

Post-war, LA was mainly known as a jazz backwater, the home of off-centre 'cool sounds' practitioners like Gerry Mulligan, Chet Baker and native Angelinos Art Pepper and later Herb Alpert, all of whom became known for a more laidback, 'cocktail' version of what was then considered the more authentically 'down beat' sound of classic New York jazzmen like Charlie Parker and, in his wake, the comet-trail of bebop stars that followed. Later on, while the rest of the world was rocking to the shocking new rhythms of Elvis Presley, Jerry Lee Lewis, Chuck Berry and Little Richard, the best LA could offer up was Ricky Nelson – the clean-cut sixteen-year-old who sprang to fame as the good-looking son in his real-life dad's TV sitcom, *The Adventures Of Ozzie and Harriet*.

Rather than inject any sense of rock's subversive power into the Hollywood mainstream, Nelson's success merely reinforced the homespun, land-of-opportunity Ozzie'n'Harriet picture most people had in their minds of LA in the 1950s. Typically, until the

Beach Boys came along in the mid-1960s with their own equally manufactured idea of the LA teen sound (Brian Wilson, the shy, overweight pop genius behind their biggest hits had never been near a surfboard in his life), Hollywood's main contribution to the new phenomenon was in films such as *Rebel Without A Cause* (1955), *The Girl Can't Help It* (1956) and *Jailhouse Rock* (1957). As the maverick LA-based record producer Kim Fowley once explained, 'The music business here was always a bastard child of the movie industry. It was only in later years that they became equal, and you had the situation where MTV was free advertising for the latest Schwarzenegger movie.' The latter was a reference to the video for the 1991 Guns N' Roses single 'You Could Be Mine', which featured scenes from Arnie's megabucks new *Terminator II* movie, that summer's big Hollywood blockbuster.

Just as it had everywhere else in the 1960s, the advent of the Beatles changed everything in the LA music business. While San Francisco would quickly assume the intellectual high ground in California, with 'flower power' groups such as the Grateful Dead and Jefferson Airplane looking down their noses at what was considered the more dissipated scene groggily evolving in LA, suddenly Hollywood had spawned a group like the Byrds (who *Newsweek* dubbed 'the Dylanized Beatles'), soon to be followed by The Doors, whose Dionysian rock-as-shamanistic-ritual made them the first successful American group to fully embrace the sense of LA noir that Guns N' Roses would also later tap into.

But by the time Hollywood had caught up with – and assimilated – the catalytic cultural shift brought about by the Beatles, enough at least to successfully imitate their likeness if not their essence, with the TV show *The Monkees* and its spin-off hits, the music scene in LA had already moved on. Now everyone who was anyone was grooving to that collision of folk, country and rock that would become known as the Laurel Canyon sound, epitomized by such minstrel singer-songwriter waifs and cosmic boys as Jackson Browne, James Taylor, Joni Mitchell, Crosby, Stills and Nash and, most famously, the Eagles.

That none of these people had been born within a hundred miles of Los Angeles hardly mattered. One way or another, they had all gravitated there, and in so doing adopted both the lifestyle and the sounds they heard when they got there – that peculiarly erotic Southern Californian mix of warm summer air, the tang of smog, the hint of sea breeze and the hazy fug of good grass – to produce something that became uniquely of its time and place.

No sooner were these artists firmly established in the public's mind as quintessentially Californian, however, than LA underwent another seismic shift, brought about yet again by the arrival of a whole new sound and look from Britain, where the glam rock of David Bowie, T. Rex, Roxy Music and – for a time, while improbably spangled clothes and giant stack-heels were still fashionable – former plain-Jane rock and rollers like Elton John, Rod Stewart and others now held sway.

Throwing down the welcome mat for glam in LA came a weedy-looking kid newly arrived from San Francisco named Rodney Bingenheimer. With his blond-bob Brian Jones haircut and seeming inability to stop talking, Rodney initially found favour hanging out with still-cool bands like the Byrds at Ben Frank's coffee shop, before latching on to the possibilities of glam rock in 1973 and opening his own club on Hollywood Boulevard, Rodney Bingenheimer's English Disco.

Eschewing live performances in favour of a non-stop rotation of music by Bowie, Bolan et al, within weeks Rodney's English Disco became the most fashionable club in LA. Soon the walls of his private office at the club were decorated in pictures of him with all the stars of the day: Rodney with Bowie, Rodney with Spector, Rodney with Jagger, Lennon, even Elvis. And then there were the girls that flocked to the club. Rodney was in luck there, too. Although the glam scene had a large gay following, Rodney was pure het-cat. 'Rodney fucked movie-star bitches you would not believe,' Kim Fowley told the writer Barney Hoskyns. 'He got so much cunt that in his early thirties he had a stroke. Allegedly, Led Zeppelin paid the hospital bill – a hundred thousand dollars – because he had no insurance.'

Ah, yes . . . Led Zeppelin. If glam never really rose above the status of a cult in LA – albeit an influential one – the music of Led Zeppelin would virtually take over the city throughout the 1970s as sales of their albums outstripped even those of the

Rolling Stones by an astonishing 2:1 ratio. Zeppelin singer Robert Plant – himself a self-proclaimed devotee of the West Coast sound – would later recall ruefully how 'the people who lived in Laurel Canyon avoided us,' considering the Zeppelin boys and their wayward entourage far too uncivilized for their weed-and-wine evenings beneath the stars, stroking their acoustic guitars and writing barely disguised songs about each other's love lives.

Zeppelin, meanwhile, cavorted openly with drugs and groupies, holding sleazy court at their favourite half-moon tables at the Rainbow Bar & Grill while residing at the Riot House – as they dubbed their favourite Sunset Strip hotel, the Hyatt House – supported by a tough road crew and wreaking havoc wherever they went. For many long-time Hollywood habitués this was the beginning of the LA music scene's bleakest period, when the twin demons of unlimited drugs and money – and the dark unforgiving worlds they opened the doors to – would begin to run rampant along its sunburned streets and boulevards. Even LA's most famous groupie, Pamela Des Barres, then involved in a lengthy on–off affair with Zeppelin guitarist and leader Jimmy Page, would decry the malign influence the band would have on her hometown, telling Barney Hoskyns: 'As much as I really loved Zeppelin, they kind of fucked things up in LA. The magic really went out of rock'n'roll.'

But even Led Zeppelin's apocalyptic reign would eventually come to an end. Their last US tour was in 1977, but by then it wasn't only the music business in LA that was shape-shifting, but across the world. Yet again, the spark came from England, this time from a group of even more snot-nosed young artists intent on bringing the entire music business to its knees, led by an iconic spiky orange-haired figurehead with the faux-naif name of Johnny Rotten, singer and controversial spokesman with London's numero uno punk rockers, the Sex Pistols.

A far less brash but still self-consciously 'new wave' of rock artists – less concerned with musical prowess and more interested in saying something new, as evinced by startling 'art-rock' performers like Patti Smith, Television and, less intellectual but perhaps even more influential, the Ramones – had been hardening like a scab on the New York club scene since 1975.

The arrival in the UK a year later of even more musically revolutionary and certainly more radically named and attired groups like the Pistols (following in their boot-steps, the Damned, the Clash, the Jam, the Stranglers, the Buzzcocks and many others), effected a ground zero approach to rock in the late-1970s. Suddenly, everything that had gone before – up to and including major arena-rock artists like Zeppelin, Pink Floyd and the Eagles – was deemed overindulgent and – most heinous of all – 'boring'.

But while this punishingly restrictive form of thinking played well in the critically elitist circles of London and New York, sunny LA was always going to be a tougher nut to crack for the po-faced, only-after-dark punk bands. With its car-dominant, palm-treed, poolside ambience, the moneyed-up mien of Hollywood proved such a hostile environment for most punk bands they didn't even try and find a niche there. Indeed, while the original UK punk triumvirate of the Sex Pistols, the Clash and the Damned would become cult figures in LA circles, none would play there on a regular basis (the Sex Pistols not at all) and none would ever achieve mainstream US hits.

Bill Bailey was fifteen the first time he heard of the Sex Pistols, and though in years to come he would pay lip service to the pride of place they came to occupy in the annals of bad-boy rock, musically they completely passed him by, as did most of the new wave releases of the late-1970s. Next to his Queen, Elton John and ELO albums, what the Pistols played sounded intolerably brutish, unsophisticated and, well, dull. Bill was in good company. That's what most small-town American rock fans back then thought of the Sex Pistols and their cruddy likes, if they thought about them at all.

Future Guns N' Roses guitarist Saul Hudson – already jokingly called 'Slash' by his father and his friends because of the boy's tendency to 'answer back at them' in sarcastic one-liners – was thirteen when he first heard the Sex Pistols. Having only just arrived in Los Angeles from London two years before, he was more accustomed to the gritty sound the first wave of British punk bands advocated than his future band mate, Axl. However, his main memories of punk now are of how 'ridiculous' it quickly became. 'There was something to be said about what [British] punk meant socially and politically. It was a great emotional outburst. Whereas in LA you had bands like the Germs, just trying to jump on the band-wagon. It wasn't the same. How punky can you be living in LA? Come on!' The only LA punk band Slash ever had any time for was Fear, who didn't come along until the early 1980s. 'They kicked all the other LA punk bands' asses. I used to sell Quaaludes outside their shows.'

In fact, LA's initial response to Brit-punk was to give the world The Runaways – five teenage girls who could barely play their instruments but succeeded briefly in the late-1970s, as (what their Svengali-producer Kim Fowley unashamedly described) 'a pure jailbait act'. Indeed, Fowley admitted he had first put the band together not so much to cash-in on punk as simply to cash in: a sort of bridge-cum-collision between the last vestiges of glam and the onset of punk. But if The Runaways were generally considered by most latter-day American punk fans to be 'bogus', they probably did more to ignite the local LA punk scene in the 1970s than any of their more revered peers. As Pat Smear, guitarist with one of the very first authentically punk Hollywood bands the Germs (and now with Dave Grohl's Foo Fighters) recalls, The Runaways 'primed kids for punk, even if people don't want to admit it now'.

Suddenly, the same West Hollywood clubs that had once been the home of James Taylor and Joni Mitchell were being taken over by hastily formed LA bands like the Germs, the Dogs, the Pop!, the Bags, X and the Weirdos. With the sole exception of the Germs (now remembered chiefly for their psychotic singer Darby Crash, who died after self-administering a deliberate heroin overdose in December 1980), none of these bands would achieve lasting fame, or even become that well known outside their own limited circle of dedicated fans. But the punk die was cast and by the time word had spread to the suburbs of LA in 1978, punk in its purist form had been forced to mutate into a style more fitting with the prevailing cultural climate.

Gone were the conceptual conceits of original punk entrepreneurs like Pistols manager Malcolm McLaren and Clash manager Bernie Rhodes. In their place came a much more dead-ahead mentality, epitomized by a breed of younger, faster, angrier and much more stridently in-your-face bands that deemed themselves not punk but 'hardcore'. Suburban would-be warrior-souls like Black Flag (from Hermosa Beach), the Screws and the Outsiders (both from Huntington Beach) and several other short-lived South Bay outfits like the Adolescents, most of whom had started out as surfers or beach-punks. As Black Flag guitarist Greg Ginn recalled, 'We had skateboards, we roller-skated up and down the Strand. It made sense to revolt eventually.'

By the end of the 1970s, Los Angeles and its environs were no longer seen simply as the home of good grass, beautiful women, cheap wine and easy, free-ride living. In the end it wasn't glam rock, Led Zeppelin or even punk that killed off the old Laurel Canyon scene in LA. It was an act of suicide. Punk may have been running riot in the clubs and the suburbs but, in truth, it hardly ever troubled the American Top 40. Instead, the whole city had become synonymous in the public mind with coke-snorting, zillion-selling rock sophisticates like members of Fleetwood Mac and the Eagles; or ex-pat rockers turned mainstream disco-divas like Rod Stewart, Elton John and David Bowie, all of them living in their own air-tight, security-cordoned wings of the Hotel Californian dream, lost in the smoke of their own fame, making music for and about each other, to be flogged wholesale to those who wandered like cattle outside their golden, electrified gates.

For the first time it became clear to the outside world that there was something rotten lying beneath the black silk sheets of their king-sized Hollywood beds. It shouldn't have come as news. For while LA had long embodied certain seemingly unshakable Californian ideals – from the Beach Boys singing sweetly about surfing and sun-kissed girls to Stevie Nicks crooning seductively about a mystical Welsh witch named 'Rhiannon' – as far back as the silent movie era there had always existed a dark underbelly at odds with the butter-wouldn't-melt image of LA purveyed by countless films, records and TV shows. The same nitty-gritty reality of life behind the cool facade of cocktails by the pool and drive-ins full of Cadillacs and continental coupés.

Long before the jazzers and folkies had purloined the clubs

along the Strip for their own shaky designs, LA had been the home of Hollywood, whose infinitely sordid movie industry made the music business of the 1970s look like a toddler's playgroup. Even the biggest movie stars had always been happy to share their after-hours playground with nefarious characters such as Frank Sinatra crony Sam Giancana, Bugsy Siegal, the mob's first full-time West Coast man, and proto-Hollywood bad boy and real-life gangster George Raft.

Then there were the less instantly recognizable but equally notorious fringe players like Kenneth Anger (the black magic-dabbling cult filmmaker whose *Hollywood Babylon* books first lifted the lid on the gruesome details of off-screen LA life) and, even lower down the scale, Charles Manson (whose inability to break into the LA music business precipitated his psychotic revenge killings), on to eccentric, if briefly successful, mavericks like Phil Spector (the nerdy, asthmatic wunderkind whose first hit, 'To Know Him Is To Love Him', was cribbed from his mother's inscription on his suicidal father's headstone) and so many others that by the 1960s every waitress in LA seemed to be an aspiring Barbra Streisand; every pretty-boy bellhop a potential Warren Beatty. That meant a lot of dreams eventually left behind like cigarette butts littering the gutter.

Drugs were hardly new either. Marijuana had been a staple of the LA music scene since the mid-1960s and heroin-use stretched back to the jazz era. And, of course, LSD played as significant a part in shaping the hazy-daze sound of LA in the late-1960s as cocaine would the following decade. Indeed, by the time Bill Bailey stepped off the Greyhound bus from Lafayette in 1982 – a scene he was to later idealize in the first Guns N' Roses video, 'Welcome To The Jungle', where he is chewing straw as he gazes warily around him at the teeming street life – his mind already caught up in the pulsing neon ooze – it could be argued that LA had seen and done so much already that its whole music scene had become irredeemably passé. Certainly, American rock music was going through its most stale period since the post-Elvis, pre-Beatles era.

Punk may have left its bloody fingerprints all over pocket-sized scenes in almost every major American city, but it had never really broken through to the mainstream – no artist had ever appeared on prime time TV and accused Barbara Walters of being a 'fucking rotter' the way the Sex Pistols did to Bill Grundy – and by 1982 even the Eagles and Fleetwood Mac were no longer chart-certainties as both groups lurched towards break-up, or breakdown. Whatever, dude. Instead, the charts were now dominated by middle-aged radio-friendly rock behemoths like Journey, REO Speedwagon and Styx. Such was the paucity of excitement, it was a time when a band like the Police – another middle-aged rock band, this time from England, but with a gimmick (rock gently laced with reggae au lait) and a good-looking frontman (the memorably named Sting) – would be regarded by mainstream American audiences as innovative and even important.

The only real promise of unabashed excitement in the LA rock scene right then lay in the realms of heavy metal, in particular the brash, ostensibly uncommercial strand of metal as purveyed by outré British line-ups like Judas Priest and Iron Maiden. As a result, most of the bands performing for the first time in the Hollywood clubs of 1982 were – if not glam-punk – then out-and-out British heavy metal imitators. Axl's first stabs at forming a band in LA were to be no exception.

Even the arrival into the American charts in the mid-1980s of arguably more exciting MTV-driven newcomers like the fresh-faced and full-figured Madonna and the new-in-town punk-gone-pop Billy Idol couldn't disguise the essential blandness of the strictly non-threatening era, as illustrated most spectacularly by the back-slapping spectacle of the 1985 'USA For Africa' single and subsequent Live Aid concert in Philadelphia.

While rock was apparently intent on repositioning itself as something intrinsically useful, or even worthy, the artists' label masters were also remoulding themselves, not into globe-straddling charities, but giant, one-size-fits-all corporations. By the end of the decade, CBS would be sold to Sony, MCA to Matsushita, both Island and A&M to PolyGram, with Warner Bros left to merge with Time. The heyday of 'boutique' independent labels such as Herb Alpert and Jerry Moss's A&M and in the UK Richard Branson's Virgin was fast coming to an end.

David Geffen, whose Asylum Records had set the template for artist-led independent labels in the early 1970s, now fronted his own eponymously named label. But that had been set up with an entirely different philosophy from his idealistic Asylum operation. As Don Henley, founding member of Asylum's most successful signing, the Eagles, would observe in 1993, 'David Geffen used to care about music and his artists. But he's not in the record business any more. He's in the David Geffen business.' While Geffen kept faith with latter-day signings like Neil Young and Joni Mitchell, he now looked to the massive sales provided by the more generic likes of Asia, Aerosmith and Whitesnake to keep his company afloat. As such, Geffen Records would become the most successful independent label of the 1980s, with projected revenues for 1989 alone tipping $175 million – precipitating their own sale to MCA in 1990 for a staggering $545 million.

Geffen himself was the first to admit that his company's success was largely down, not to his own signings, as it had been in Asylum's heyday, but to the astute acquisitions made by his two most talented A&R executives, John Kalodner and Tom Zutaut. The former made his mark by relaunching the fallen-by-the-wayside musical careers of fading stars such as Cher and Aerosmith, the latter by having his finger on the pulse of the new heavy metal scene then developing in LA, as epitomized by the huge success of local Sunset Strip boys-made-good, Van Halen, whose high-octane guitar-shredding sound transformed the hard rock landscape in the early-1980s.

In the wake of Van Halen came a raft of like-minded local outfits, all with the same back-combed hairstyles, open-tuned guitars and lurid death's head body insignia courtesy of Sunset Strip Tattoos, situated across the street from the Hyatt House. Out-for-action groups like London, W.A.S.P., Rätt, Quiet Riot, Poison and, most famously, Mötley Crüe, whose debut album, *Too Fast For Love*, was released, punk-style, on their own Leathur Records label in 1982 and proceeded to sell over 20,000 copies in LA alone. 'Within two years, the Strip had gone from lip-gloss to cock-stink,' Kim Fowley later opined. Suddenly 'everybody had to beat up policemen and shoot heroin in their feet . . . The tits got bigger, the men got dumber, and the music got uglier.'

Tom Zutaut had signed the Crüe when he was at the new Warners-Elektra-Atlantic alliance (WEA), and by 1985 they were rivalling Van Halen for album sales, propelled into the charts by their raucous top ten cover of Brownsville Station's corny classic, 'Smokin' In The Boys' Room'. When Zutaut decamped to Geffen, his first priority was to find a band that could replicate the success of Mötley Crüe. When he saw Guns N' Roses for the first time, he knew his chance had come.

Although Mötley Crüe's bad-boy reputation was based on solid fact – culminating in the conviction for manslaughter of singer Vince Neil after the death in a car he was driving of Hanoi Rocks drummer 'Razzle' Dingley (drunk at the wheel, Neil had driven head-on into an oncoming vehicle) – musically, they had little of real substance to back it up, beyond a clutch of memorable titles – 'Shout At The Devil', 'Looks That Kill' – and a knack for 'X-rated' videos like the one set in a biker's titty bar for 'Girls, Girls, Girls'. It was immediately clear to Zutaut that while Guns N' Roses clearly shared most of the Crüe's offstage proclivities, musically they had a lot more going for them. Unlike Mötley Crüe or Poison, Guns N' Roses weren't merely a facsimile of the Stones-cum-Aerosmith-cum-Sex Pistols. They wore the same clothes, played the same clubs and even shared many of the same fans as their immediate Hollywood rivals, but there was one crucial difference: they were the real deal.

According to Slash, the roots of the band's musical appeal lay in an equal disdain for both the LA punk scene and the LA metal scene. 'We were the only five guys here who could have made up this band at the time. We just didn't fit in. And we had such a hard time from not fitting in that we were very tough, very brash. People say "What's the gimmick?" you know? But there never was no fucking gimmick.' Guns N' Roses would provide their own definition of punk and metal. 'It's all centred on attitude, breaking away from the norm of what's acceptable, doing your own thing.' They would be punk in the same sense that 'The Who was a great punk band.' It wasn't about safety-pins and haircuts. 'When punk became popular, I never changed my hair or clothes or even my drugs.' Real punk rock should be about 'people expressing themselves honestly. Being an individual.'

In the end, though, it wasn't any one thing but more a lurid hybrid of all LA's most flamboyant 1970s styles that would inform the musical outlook of Guns N' Roses – the wistful acoustic confessionals of Neil Young, the self-regarding glam of Bowie, the uncompromising hard rock of Led Zeppelin, the fearsomely attitudinal punk of the Sex Pistols (and their LA counterparts Fear) and, latterly, the unabashed heavy metal of Van Halen and Judas Priest.

For Axl, the best rock music was never just about one thing anyway. 'I've always looked at things in a versatile sense because of Queen, ELO, Elton John,' he told *Rolling Stone* in 1989. 'Whenever their newest record would come out and have all these other kinds of music on it, at first I'd only like this song or that song. But after a period of time listening to it, it would open my mind up to so many different styles. I really appreciate them for that. That's something I've always wanted to be able to achieve. It's important to show people all forms of music, basically try to give people a broader point of view.'

Although Guns N' Roses would come to be seen as the quintessential LA band, like Axl none of the five members of what would become recognized as the classic line-up of the band was born there. First to arrive was Steven Adler, a Kiss and Aerosmith fanatic born in Cleveland, Ohio, on 22 January 1965. Later on, Steven would describe himself simply as 'from Hollywood, born and raised in America,' but he didn't arrive in LA until he was already at grade school. He grew up the archetypal California boy; sun-streaked blond hair, tanned and tattooed, with eyes as blue and vacant as the postcard sky above the Hollywood hills.

The first record he ever remembers playing was 'Working My Way Back To You Babe' by the Four Seasons, when he was five. He first met Slash when he was eleven, after crashing into him with his skateboard at Bancroft Junior High School, where they were both pupils. By then Steven already had dreams of becoming a guitar player like his hero, Ace Frehley of Kiss. It was Steven, in fact, who first turned his new buddy on to the idea of becoming a guitarist. The pair would sit together at Steven's grandmother's house, where he had been sent to live after his parents broke up, banging away on an old guitar plugged into a small amplifier, cranked up as loud as it would go.

Saul Hudson had been born in Stoke-on-Trent, England, on 23 July 1965, the elder of two sons of a black American mom, Ola, and a white English dad, Tony. Both were variously connected with the music business – Tony as a graphic designer, notably for the sleeve of the 1973 Joni Mitchell album, *Court and Spark*, and Ola as a clothes and costume designer, styling the Pointer Sisters and David Bowie (who she dated when she designed the clothes for his first starring role in the 1975 cult movie *The Man Who Fell To Earth*). Slash, as he became known as an adolescent, grew up in a fashionable flat in Hampstead, north London. 'I grew up in a kind of rebellious hippy household,' he told me. 'I was given a lot of freedom as a kid. I started saying the word "fuck" when I was, like, seven or eight years old, telling my parents to fuck off all the time. I guess some people found that shocking.'

When they split when he was eleven, Slash went to live initially with his dad in Laurel Canyon, where he says he was 'fortunate to have been exposed to such an overindulgent, egotistical, just basically ridiculous rock'n'roll environment. I watched all these things go down. I watched people go down. I watched a lot of heavy shit go down and I learned from it.' For a time, he found himself playing with the kids of his dad's Canyon neighbours including Neil Young, while David Bowie and Ola once took him to visit Iggy Pop, who was then a patient at a mental hospital. Bowie was 'the first guy to replace my dad when my mom and dad separated. I can remember him tucking me up in bed.'

Not long after, his parents' complex lives meant he was sent to live with his maternal grandmother in Hollywood. By the time he met Steven Adler, Slash was already growing his dark curly hair over his face, not as a concession to rock'n'roll fashion, but because he was shy and didn't want anyone to see into his eyes. Hanging out with the brash Steven helped knock down his protective wall, bringing out his unexpectedly gregarious side.

'That was also when I started drinking,' he said. 'If I don't have a drink I sink into myself. And I like it, I like being drunk! It helps me; it brings me out of my shell.' He could never 'deal with people in a social situation when I'm sober.'

Slash and Steven attended their first proper rock concert together when they were twelve, a performance by Kiss at the LA amusement park Magic Mountain. Later that night, drunk on wine and the excitement of their first show, they cemented their friendship in an 'Indian blood brother' ceremony, according to Steven, when they cut each other's wrists with a knife then placed them together so the blood would flow into each other's veins, vowing to become rock stars when they grew up.

Because of his parents' association with the music business, Slash had already amassed a huge collection of records. 'I used to listen to The Who, Joni Mitchell, Led Zeppelin, Minnie Ripperton, the Stones, Chaka Khan . . . Just everything we had in there.' Until he met Steven, however, the thought of actually picking up an instrument and learning how to play it had never crossed his mind. Steven would 'just plug in and turn it all the way up and bang on it real loud, and I was just fuckin' fascinated by it.' In order to join in, he bought himself a 'plank of wood with a few strings on it for five bucks' and took a few elementary guitar lessons, before quitting in favour of sitting at home and playing along to his Aerosmith and Led Zeppelin albums. 'Back then I didn't know the difference between bass and lead guitar, or any of that shit. I basically chose guitar 'cos it had more strings.'

It was his grandmother who bought him his first proper electric guitar: 'A Gibson Explorer copy that I flipped out on. Unfortunately, it was a piece of crap. Then I got a Memphis Les Paul copy. At rehearsal one day, I ended up sticking it through a wall neck first, because I could not keep the thing in tune!'

He practised all the time, whether he was with Steven or not. 'I was a workaholic, playing twelve hours a day. I picked it up really quickly because I was naive in a way. I wasn't star struck, and I wasn't so flipped out by other guitar players that they intimidated me. I didn't feel like I was trying to reach some goal – I was just learning.' Being single-minded, 'once I got into guitar, that's all I did. It basically replaced school.'

Of course, playing guitar wasn't all Slash and Steven got up to as teenagers running wild in Hollywood. While Slash experienced his first hangover at twelve, Steven had been smoking pot since he was eleven. By the time they were thirteen, both boys had also lost their virginities. According to Steven, by the time he and Slash were fourteen, they were both 'veteran Hollywood street kids'. Recalling for me once what he described as 'a typical day in Hollyweird', Steven said: 'When Slash and I lived with our grandmothers, we could do anything. I would cover for him and he would cover for me. We ditched school every day and walked up and down Santa Monica or Sunset, basically, looking for a good time . . . any kind of good time. We'd go out and meet chicks – old women – who would take us back to their Beverly Hills homes. They'd give us booze, coke, they'd feed us, really whatever we wanted. All we had to do was fuck them . . . In return for a blow job, I'd get a little dope . . . Slash and I would be gone for days. When I'd finally stumble back home to my grandmother's, I would use Slash as an excuse. "I told you I was spending the night at Slash's." "That's right", she'd say.'

Meanwhile, the better Slash got at guitar, the less interested Steven became in trying to keep up. Instead, for a time he fancied himself as a singer, the two of them toying with the idea of forming and fronting their own band, for which Steve had come up with a name: Road Crew. By the time they were seventeen, it became obvious that it wasn't going to work and Steven, somewhat belatedly but no less enthusiastically, took to the idea of becoming the drummer in their notional band, beating on his long-suffering grandmother's pots and pans. Finding he actually had a talent for it, he began saving up for his first proper drum-kit. 'I never took a drum lesson in my life,' he would boast. 'I learned from watching and listening very closely to other drummers, plus wanting it real bad and believing in myself.' The better Steven got at beating the drums, the more seriously both boys started to take the idea of making Road Crew into a real band playing real gigs. 'It was a great little band,' Slash would later tell me. 'Sort of like [early] Metallica but without a singer.'

No longer constrained by school, having both dropped out,

they also found various ways to 'make a buck' while waiting for the band to turn into something more concrete. At different times over the next three years Steven would 'mop bowling alleys, sweep floors at the 7–Eleven, wash dishes, wait on tables . . . I had a lot of goofy jobs.' Slash was less industrious, picking up cash by selling weed to friends and Quaaludes to other would-be musicians on the Strip.

According to Steven, 'habitation' took the form of shacking up with girls who also happened to have 'lots of cash and drugs' – mostly strippers. As far as Slash and Steven were concerned it was all par for the course. As Slash later told me, they had 'done some crazy things, but never really bad things to hurt anybody or screw anyone up. We're not into that. We're into having fun. As long as we don't hurt anybody or rip anybody off, there's nothing wrong with having a good time.'

About the same time that Steven and Slash were dropping out of school and hanging out in strip clubs, Izzy Stradlin, newly arrived from Lafayette, was just starting to take his first tentative steps towards making a life for himself in Los Angeles. Speaking to Izzy twenty years later, he recalled his early days in LA partly with a shudder and partly with wry amusement. All he really knew back then, he told me, was that he 'had to get out of Lafayette – I fuckin' hated the place back then.' It had 'always been the plan' to go down to LA. 'The weather was better and that's where everything was.' Hitching his way to Hollywood, he found himself a cheap place to rent – 'a small apartment in Huntington Beach, out in the 'burbs' – and worked on getting himself involved in a band, any band.

As such, his first gig was as the drummer in Orange County punk band Naughty Women. He lasted just one gig after discovering the band liked to perform in drag. 'What a bunch of fucking wankers they were! I had no idea . . . They didn't tell me that bit; when I met them and we were rehearsing in Orange County they were all wearing street clothes. Then at the first gig they all came out in pink spandex, fucking Afros and make-up. I was like, "Holy shit, what's this?" The crowd threw bottles at us and beat the hell out of the singer. So that was my initiation into Los Angeles rock.'

Naughty Women was followed by an equally short-lived stint in The Atoms. But when part of his drum kit was stolen, he sold the rest of it, bought a bass guitar with the proceeds and joined another local South Bay outfit called Shire. 'That didn't last either,' he said, mainly because by then he'd decided what he really wanted to do was play guitar. Being the guitarist 'seemed cooler' than being drummer and, most crucially, a guitar was simply 'easier to write songs on'.

Izzy had only been in town for a few months when he heard from his old hometown buddy, Bill, asking if he could visit, maybe stay a couple of weeks. Izzy shrugged and said 'sure,' offering to let Bill crash on his floor. Before Izzy had set off for LA, Bill had toyed for a while with the idea of trying his luck in New York City. Only 800 miles from Lafayette – as opposed to more than 2,000 miles to LA – not only was New York geographically closer to Lafayette, culturally it was a place Bill might have felt more instantly at home in, with streets you could walk on, a subway you could ride, and a proliferation of cosmopolitan street life totally unlike the tanned, car-hopping, cooler-than-thou denizens that would initially make him feel so isolated in downtown LA.

The only thing New York didn't have going for it was that Bill didn't know anyone there. At least the long journey to LA would be rewarded at the end of it with the promise of a beer and a shared roof over his head with someone who knew him from home. Even so, it was a long trip and the first time he made it, it took him almost a week to get there, hitching part of the way, riding the Greyhound bus the rest of it. Axl once laughingly recalled how he arrived in LA 'with a back-pack, a can of Mace in one hand and a piece of steel in the other'. He added that when he finally got to Fullerton, the small working-class suburb where Izzy was now living, 'I thought it was just the smallest city . . . I rode the bus around for two days, never found Izzy.'

When they did finally meet up, at first Axl wondered what he'd let himself in for. Regarded as a hick from the sticks by most of Izzy's new friends, he found it hard to fit in. Riding the bus back home from that first trip, he wasn't sure if he really liked the place enough to go back. Intolerable as family life at home in Lafayette had become, LA was something else again, full of people and events he'd never experienced before. 'I didn't experience stuff like real racism until I came to LA,' he told me. 'All these black guys at the bus station hassling me. I was scared.'

The wide-eyed country boy arriving in the big bad city, though he would never say so out loud, he wasn't sure at first if he could handle it. 'I went back and forth from Indiana eight times my first year in Hollywood,' he said. 'I'd never been in a city this big and was fortunate enough to have this black dude help me find my way. He guided me to the RTD station and showed me what bus to take, because I couldn't get a straight answer out of anybody . . . People kept coming up trying to sell me joints and stuff. In downtown LA the joints are usually bogus, or they'll sell you drugs that can kill you. It's a really ugly scene.' The only similarity with Lafayette was in the way the cops treated him. 'When I sat down after walking in circles for three hours, the cops told me to get off the streets. The cops down there have seen so much slime that they figure if you have long hair, you're probably slime also.'

Something else he'd never experienced directly before as a young adult was open homosexuality. Hitching to LA, he said, had been fraught with danger in that respect, including one incident which left its mark on him. 'I hitchhiked a lot and I got hassled an awful lot. I was very naive, and very tired, and a guy picked me up and said I could crash at his hotel, and I woke up with the man trying to rape me,' he was quoted as saying in *Interview* magazine. His response had been to go for his assailant. 'I was so frightened. I had a straight-edge razor and was freaking out: "Don't ever touch me again!" Then the guy ran out the door. I was so scared and I felt so violated.' He grabbed his stuff and left. It was the middle of the night, 'in the middle of nowhere outside of St Louis'. He walked alone along the highway for hours before he dared stick his thumb out again.

Though he didn't consciously realize it then, he said, the experience was made even worse for him, he felt, by the subconscious knowledge of 'what had gone on in my childhood and what I had pretty much buried – and didn't even remember'. In a later interview with *Rolling Stone* he was quoted as claiming this experience was also partly responsible for the fact that he was now so uncomfortable around gay men. 'I've had some very bad experiences with homosexuals, that's why I have the attitude I have.'

Having returned home to Lafayette bragging about his adventures it wasn't long before Axl found himself out on the highway hitching again. LA was freaky, for sure, but life in Lafayette was just plain dumb and miserable. He forced himself to go back down there again, if nothing else just for something to do. It wasn't until after he'd met Gina Siler that he worked up the courage to make a more permanent move to LA. With Gina by his side, he figured he wouldn't be so totally alone. Together they would make a go of it. And so after much debate Gina says she finally agreed to join Axl, as he was now usually known, finishing high school early in order to drive down with him in her car to LA on 19 December 1982, moving into 'some shit hole' Axl had rented for them at 1921 Whitley Avenue, Hollywood. Even though the sun was shining it was just a few days before Christmas when they arrived, and at first Gina wondered what she'd done. According to her it was exciting, too, and the couple spent New Year's Eve talking about how great their new life together in LA was going to be.

Axl would later be quoted as saying in an early interview that up until Guns N' Roses signed their record deal he had 'lived on the streets for five years. I never lived in one place for more than two months, always crashing at people's houses.' These early years were chaotic though initially Gina provided some stability. According to Gina Axl spent the first half of 1983 living with her on and off in their small dingy apartment on Whitley Avenue. There were times, she confirmed, when Axl did live on the streets, but usually only 'after I'd kick him out because I got tired of trying to support the both of us, and I got tired of fighting . . . I helped him out quite a bit. I don't think he likes to think about that, though.'

Clearly there were other things affecting the way Axl thought about things. Even once he was settled in LA, at first he couldn't make up his mind what it was he wanted to do: hunker down to a so-called normal life, or really try and make a go of it as a rock musician. Friends from those days recall how one moment he was debating whether to dye his hair black or blond, the next he was wondering aloud whether he should simply throw the towel in and cut off all his hair. He would spend days and weeks agonizing over the 'right thing to do'. As he later recalled, 'My parents would say, "Come back home and go to college and we'll pay for it." But I would reply, "No, I have to do this now."'

Even his name became a matter of internal debate. Some days he would prefer to be known as plain old Bill, some days he would only answer to Axl. Already known for his mood-swings, it became hard even for those close to him to know what might set him off; insecurity seemed to dog him. For a long time after he moved to LA he didn't even like to talk about growing up in the Midwest; he didn't want to be seen as a hick any more, preferring to portray himself as a Mr Mystery. Gina says he would live with her, periodically, for the next two-and-a-half years. She would later tell how between 1982 and 1985 they were engaged 'at least nine times', though a wedding date was never actually planned. 'I lived with him during that period of "Bill" to "Bill/Axl" to "Axl". It was the strangest thing,' she later told *Spin* magazine. 'Some days I didn't know who the hell he was, I didn't know what to do, because I didn't know what person he was.'

Confusion reigned. 'When I was living in Indiana,' Axl later explained, 'I was labelled a punk, a punk rocker. When I moved to LA, the punks called me a hippy and didn't want anything to do with me. The Hollywood rock scene was a war zone back then. I tried out for a punk band and didn't make it because they said I sounded like Robert Plant. I was bummed because I thought I had a gig and really liked the music.'

According to Gina, Axl 'was made to be a musician. I went to West LA Community College, and had some cheesy part-time job somewhere. We lived there for five months, and then I moved out. He stayed there, and then Izzy moved in for a while. In fact, while we were living there he got into the band Hollywood Rose. There were times when he would take my car to practice. I would help him do his make-up.'

It was during one of his periodic break-ups with Gina that Axl first rented a small rundown apartment with Izzy on Crescent Heights and Sunset. As soon as they were back together, however, he began sleeping over at her place again. Gina claims it was also she who had paid for the famous rose tattoo on his arm that says: 'W. Axl Rose'. It was a birthday present. Gina's version of Axl during this period also belies the popular image of Axl's lifestyle during those hand-to-mouth years. While it was true they often barely had enough money to eat, rather than spend what money they had on drugs Axl liked to keep himself in shape with regular workouts.

But then Axl would get in fights with all sorts of people. Once he got angry, Gina said, it was almost impossible for him to turn it off. 'I don't think he's even conscious of what he does, or how angry he gets. I always thought that there was something chemical that happened to him when he was angry. That image of him sitting in that electric chair in that video "Welcome To The Jungle", looking crazed, says it all. That's what he looks like when he's pissed off.'

Ultimately she decided Axl was 'extremely intelligent' and a 'nit-picky perfectionist' who just blew up when things didn't 'go smoothly or to his liking'. It was something she had witnessed 'on many occasions, smashing things and breaking things and yelling and screaming – holes through walls'. Behaviour that according to their legal depositions as reported by *Rolling Stone* could be said to be repeated with his first wife Erin Everly and later his fiancée Stephanie Seymour.

In the end Gina said she couldn't take it any more and left LA, relocating to Phoenix. There was talk of a possible reconciliation towards the end of 1985 but by then Axl was fronting the first line-up of Guns N' Roses and things had changed irrevocably. 'It was a huge apartment,' she recalled in *Spin*. 'And these people were just sleeping everywhere.' She was met at the airport by Axl and a new friend she didn't recognize and who he didn't bother to properly introduce: 'I was really pissed because they were doing heroin. Really pissed. God, that weekend was awful. All we ever did was fight.' The last time she says she saw him was a few months before the first GN'R album was released in 1987, and again she was bitterly disappointed. 'All he said to me was, "I can't wait until this album's done, because I want to lock myself in a room . . . and do heroin." '

With Izzy still vacillating between instruments and bands, Axl's first LA gig was as the singer in a band called Rapid Fire, who he performed a handful of badly attended shows with at the start of 1983. In May that year, however, they managed to make a rough one-take demo, recording the songs 'Ready To Rumble', 'All Night Long', 'The Prowler' and 'On The Run' – all fairly sub-Judas Priest fare. Copies of the cassette were sent out sporadically to various club owners and record company A&R departments but nobody ever called back. Quickly losing heart, Axl began to look for something else to do. With Izzy also now scratching around for a gig, forming a band together 'just seemed the obvious thing to do'.

The two would look for inspiration by catching as many gigs along the Strip as they could blag their way into without paying. Axl recalled the first time he and Izzy walked into the Roxy. Mötley Crüe's first major label album *Shout At The Devil* had just been released and 'everyone was in leather and studs'. At one point he looked up and saw Crüe members Vince Neil and Nikki Sixx 'leaning over a rail trying to figure out who the fuck we were!' But because they didn't blend in, he said, 'It took three years to start getting accepted in LA.' He remembered 'standing at the Troubadour and people wouldn't talk to me. I didn't know what to say to them, so you just watched and learned for a long, long time . . . you drifted around. You stayed in friends' garages, cars, stayed one step ahead of the sheriffs.'

By now Izzy had also introduced Axl to another guitarist named Chris Weber. When Izzy moved to LA, practically the first people he'd hooked up with were Weber and another guitar-playing friend, Tracii Guns, both of whom had been students at Hollywood's famous Fairfax High School (alma mater for such future music legends as Jerry 'Hound Dog' Lieber, Herb Alpert,

Jan and Dean and others). It was Tracii and Chris who first introduced Izzy to late-night Strip haunts like the Rainbow, the Roxy, the Whisky, the Troubadour and the Starwood. Tracii would later recall that Izzy had worn a dress in the first band he saw him in, 'and I think somebody beat his ass, so he joined this band called Shire, which was a Scorpions kind of metal band. That's when I became friends with him.'

Tracii already had plans for the type of band he wanted to play in and Izzy was still busy fooling around with Shire, so at first Axl talked to Chris in terms of resurrecting the singer's idea for a band called Axl. 'We were all outcasts who got together and pooled our talents,' Axl said. Even though they had no money, 'When we started we wanted to be the coolest, sexiest, meanest, nastiest, loudest, funnest band.'

But with little money they were forced to make ends meet any way they could. Getting a regular job was obviously out of the question. Instead, they took on a variety of weird and wonderful pastimes to bring in some cash. At one stage, Axl and Izzy became professional cigarette smokers for a research team of doctors and scientists at UCLA. Izzy told me, 'One day I'm going through the paper and there's an ad that says: "Smokers needed, $10 an hour". So I said, "Fuck, this seems like easy work. That's all we do anyway." And so we called this place and they said, "Yeah, come on down."

After Izzy started joining in with the new band, Axl changed his mind again and announced the band would be called Rose. Other members of the fledgling Rose line-up included drummer Johnny Kreiss (aka Johnny Christ), who had responded to an ad they'd placed in the local free-sheet *The Recycler*, and bassist Rick Mars (soon to be replaced by Andre Roxx). The band's first show was at a small out-of-town club called The Orphanage. Soon, however, they embellished their name to the more glamorous-sounding Hollywood Rose and were chalking up support slots and occasional headline appearances at better-known LA venues like the Troubadour, the Country Club and Madam Wong's East, sharing the bill with better-known local bands such as Mondo Cain, Bitch, The Mercenaries and Candy.

Poison singer Brett Michaels recalls seeing the band playing at Madame Wong's East. 'There were maybe fifteen people in the club and Axl was playing as if he were in front of a million people.' With Axl starting to flirt with a glam image – back-combing his long red hair into the style he would become famous for in Guns N' Roses, and experimenting for the first time with Gina's make-up bag – they certainly created a look. But their music was still generic Sunset Strip heavy metal, leaning on cover versions, barely one up from what Axl had been doing in Rapid Fire. Writing with Chris and Izzy, it was now that Axl started to come up with some of the earliest tunes that would later feature, more fully formed, in the Guns N' Roses repertoire, including one tune originally called 'My Way Your Way' which later turned up on *Appetite For Destruction* as 'Anything Goes'.

By the start of 1984 the band was ready to make a demo, a five-track cassette featuring 'My Way Your Way' and four other stand-out original songs from their live set: 'Killing Time' and 'Rocker', plus 'Wreckless' (which later evolved in Guns N' Roses into 'Reckless Life') and 'Shadow Of Your Love'. Listening to the demo now, more than two decades later, in truth there's very little to recommend it. With the exception of Axl's anguished throaty vocal and the now familiar chorus to 'My Way Your Way', there's nothing there that really ties the band to the one that would sign a major deal with Geffen Records just two years later. Instead, particularly on tracks like the self-consciously aggressive 'Killing Time' and the cringe-making 'Rocker', replete with cheesy 'crazy' laugh at the end, they sound like tennis-racquets-in-front-of-the-mirror Judas Priest wannabes crossed with an Americanized early Iron Maiden.

Even Axl's voice is still very much a work in progress, infused with the histrionics of a Zeppelin-era Robert Plant, only not nearly as technically adept. 'Shadow Of Your Love' is just more of the same riff-grinding. Only 'Wreckless', with its battering, heads-down rhythm sounds remotely like the early, pre-signed Guns N' Roses.

Nevertheless, it was just the sort of demo-tape to convince LA club owners that the band could at least play, and a string of one-off gigs throughout the spring and summer of 1984 quickly followed – including, most notoriously, an 'after hours party'

show at Shamrock Studios on Santa Monica Boulevard which
didn't begin until 2.00 a.m. and didn't end till past dawn. It was
not the sort of tape, however, that would have a top-drawer
record company A&R scout reaching for his chequebook. Not
yet anyway.

Chapter Three

DREAM HOUSE IN HELL

Although things had started promisingly for Hollywood Rose, by September 1984, following a difficult show at the Music Machine opening for the self-avowedly Christian 'white metal' band Stryper – a more inappropriate setting for a band like Hollywood Rose it would have been hard to arrange – Axl and Izzy threw in the towel and split the band up the very next day. Izzy joined London – led by lead guitarist Lizzy Grey, who originally formed the group in conjunction with a pre-Mötley Nikki Sixx – while Axl joined guitarist Tracii Guns in the prototype LA Guns with Ole Beich on bass and Rob Gardner on drums; the latter both local LA boys well known to the others. As Tracii later recalled, 'A bunch of people revolved in and out of Hollywood Rose – it's the way these bands are. Izzy got an offer to join this band called London, so he left. Axl ended up singing for LA Guns until he got in a fight with our manager. But Axl decided we should continue writing songs together.'

LA Guns also briefly featured, at one point, a corkscrew-haired, mulatto guitarist. 'We ran an ad for a heavy metal, punk, glam guitarist, blues-influenced,' Axl remembered, 'and Slash showed up.' Slash had also been on the bill at the Stryper show in a short-lived band called Black Sheep. Although his tenure in Hollywood Rose lasted only a matter of weeks, according to Mark Canter, owner of the Jewish delicatessen Canter's where Slash and Steven liked to hang out – because they knew Mark and he would always comp them coffee and a lox and bagel sandwich – it was at this juncture that Axl and Slash wrote 'Welcome To The Jungle'. 'Living the way they did just gave them more things to write about,' Mark said. ' "Welcome To The Jungle" was the first song they wrote together, and it tells you everything.'

Generally, though, things didn't go to Axl's liking, not least because of the new band's name, a fact which meant the rest of its members tended to see Tracii as its leader, rather than Axl. After just a few weeks Axl managed to lure Tracii away from his own band to join him and Izzy in the temporary resurrection of Hollywood Rose for a special New Year's Eve show at the Dancing Waters club – this time, with Gardner on drums and Steve Darrow on bass. (Slash hadn't lasted long, his dislike of playing 'second banana' to Tracii, a guitarist he considered less gifted than himself, meant he'd quickly ruled himself out of the group.)

Even though the club was packed that night because it was New Year's Eve, Axl and Tracii were both encouraged enough by the size of the turn-out to believe they were on to something and resolved to continue with this revised line-up on a more permanent basis, though not as Hollywood Rose. Tracii still saw himself as the leader of the group and so Axl proposed a compromise: that the new group should contain both their surnames in its title. Hence, Guns N' Roses.

The first gig the newly named band played was at the Troubadour on 26 March 1985. The hand-drawn flyer they produced for the show read simply: *'LA Guns and Hollywood Rose presents the band Guns N' Roses'*. The band's line-up was essentially the same as it had been in LA Guns – with Ole Beich back on bass – except with Izzy taking the spot vacated by Slash. The only let-down this time was the size of the audience on that inaugural occasion: just two paying customers showed up. Clearly the new band would have their work cut out building a regular following. As Izzy said, 'We didn't have anything else to do so we just kinda stuck at it. But it was kinda all over the place at the start.'

Within weeks, Ole Beich was out of the picture again and the band placed a notice in the free classified ads section of local music paper *Music Connection*. They got only one reply: a bass player, new to most of them, named Michael McKagan – or 'Duff', as he introduced himself. Born in Seattle, Washington, on 5 February 1965, the youngest of eight children, McKagan would later tell me how he had grown up in a family 'surrounded by music'. His father, he said, had sung in a barber-shop quartet and most of his brothers and sisters could play at least one instrument. It was his older brother, Bruce, also a bass player, who showed him his first few rudimentary guitar chords. Tall and rangy, at school he was a popular athlete. 'I played football, basketball and baseball. I was good at all three. But I hated jocks by the time I was in ninth grade.'

Beneath the bull in a china shop exterior he was also smart and an honour student before dropping out of high school to tour with various punk bands. As a teenager growing up in Jet City, as Seattle was known in the 1970s due to the presence of the giant Boeing factory, Duff had played drums or bass for 'over thirty of these New Wave-type bands', including the Fastbacks, Fartz, Silly Killers, the Veins and, most famously, Ten Minute Warning. Although punk was what he was into – hence his 'punk nickname' – all his brothers and sisters 'were hippies' and so he kept his ears open and his tastes broad. 'I couldn't figure out what I wanted to play. I got a record by Prince and was like, "Wow, this guy played everything." All my older brothers and sisters liked James Gang, Sly and the Family Stone, Hendrix, Vanilla Fudge . . . Maybe it was mainstream stuff, but they were hippies. I liked the soulful and ripping stuff and Zeppelin, too. I saw Grandmaster Flash and Melle Mel when they came to Seattle, but mainly I was into Prince and I still am.'

At one point he was on the verge of becoming the drummer in English second-wave punks, the Angelic Upstarts. 'The band came to Seattle years ago and they crashed at the house of a friend of mine, so I got to know them,' he said. 'Then out of the blue one day they called me from San Francisco, said they were looking for a new drummer and asked if I'd be interested.' Duff went as far as rehearsing with the Upstarts but backed out when it was pointed out that joining them would also entail moving to live in England. 'I was shit-scared of making such a jump back then. So I turned 'em down and stayed with the band I was with.'

But not for long. Still only twenty years old but already a veteran of and 'bored shitless' by the limited Seattle scene, Duff decided it was time to strike out on his own somewhere new and more promising – specifically, Los Angeles. And so, in January 1985, Duff and his friend, former Ten Minute Warning drummer

Greg Gilmore, moved down to LA, where they immediately began responding to ads in the music press and attending auditions.

Renting a tiny, cockroach-infested apartment together, Duff was also looking for a fresh start. As he would later say, some in his circle in Seattle had become rather too fond of heroin. The irony that he would escape Seattle only to end up in LA 'in a band with three heroin addicts in it' was not lost on him. Not that he was exactly an angel in that department either. Having regularly smoked pot from the age of ten, by the time he was fifteen he had graduated to snorting coke.

The decision to move to LA had also prompted a return to the bass. Recently, Duff had been making it as a guitarist again. But, as he recalled years later, 'I had heard all these stories about LA, you know, that there were millions of great guitar players there already. And I really didn't think I was good enough to be one of the top guys. So just to get a fuckin' foot in the door, I decided to get a bass and an amp and go down to LA that way.'

The first band he hooked up with after his arrival was a ramshackle two-man outfit called Road Crew. The band was always looking for musicians because nobody except Slash and Steven ever stayed for long. Duff had been given Slash's phone number and called him up 'thinking he'd be some old punk guy with a name like that'. Because of Slash's quiet mumble on the phone, 'I could barely understand him. But he said their influences were Aerosmith, Alice Cooper, AC/DC, Motörhead, so I thought, cool, I'll try it out.' Duff's 'audition' was at the coffee counter of Canter's. Duff was still very much the punk, and his hair was cut spiky-short and dyed various shades of red, black and blond. 'So I walk in there still expecting to find some old punk rock guy. Slash and Steven were there with their girlfriends and they were all completely wasted. And their girlfriends immediately thought I was a homo because of my hair.' Nevertheless, neither side was exactly in a position to turn the other down, and so for a short spell in the spring of 1985 Duff joined Slash and Steven in Road Crew.

According to everyone involved, Road Crew was one of those bands that barely made it out of the garage; rehearsals were infrequent, gigs practically non-existent. In fact, both Slash and

Steven would audition for other bands, sometimes together, as was the case when they both showed up for a try-out with the soon-to-be-famous Poison (Steven was rejected, Slash was offered the gig but baulked at 'putting on make-up and shit' and soon quit); sometimes separately behind each other's backs (as happened during Slash's brief tenure in Black Sheep).

But it was while Duff was in Road Crew that he and Slash came up with a riff and chorus to a song called 'Paradise City'. Duff had written a line about the city where the girls were pretty while he was still in Seattle. It was Slash who came up with the chiming guitar riff. Greg Gilmore also attended a few of their practices. Disillusioned by the haphazard nature of Slash and Steven's lives, Gilmore quickly decided he'd had enough and moved back to Seattle, where he would later join local scene-makers Mother Love Bone, which also included Jeff Ament and Stone Gossard, later founding members of Pearl Jam.

By then, however, even the good-natured Duff was beginning to lose patience with his new-found friends. As he later told me, 'I hated Steven. He was a real little asshole. I love him now to death, but he'll tell you himself, he was an asshole then.' All of which Duff could have coped with had the band been more proactive. But 'nothing was really happening and I split.' Instead, he started scanning the Musicians Wanted sections of the music press again, which was where he found Axl's phone number. 'That line-up was really pretty bad, though. I was beginning to wonder why I was bothering with a band that was just like all the other bands I'd been in, in Seattle. It was already called Guns N' Roses, but there was another guy on guitar called Tracii and a different drummer [Rob Gardener], and it was a real iffy band. Like, I would hardly show up for rehearsal, and that is not like me. I am always the first guy to show up at rehearsal, the first guy to do everything like that.'

What finally saved the day was Duff's ingenuity. Out of desperation to make something happen, Duff took it upon himself to book the band some gigs, using his old contacts in Seattle. 'I booked us this tour – just up and down the West Coast.' When, at the last minute, Tracii and Rob 'pussied out' (according to

Duff) of doing the dates, Duff was furious. 'Rob and Tracii suddenly chickened out, like, three days before the thing was due to start. Like, "Oh, we don't know if we wanna do it . . ." I was like, fuck you! So we got Slash and Steven in the band at the last minute, and it clicked. We had three days to rehearse and everybody was like, "Okay, we'll give it a shot." '

Talking to *Spin* magazine six years later, Tracii Guns had rather different memories of why he didn't make that fateful tour. 'I just wanted to get away for a week or something, and I recall Axl or Izzy calling and leaving a message – "We got rehearsal this week" – and I just ignored it. I didn't hear anything for a couple of days and then finally the whip came down – "Slash is going to play guitar because you haven't come to rehearsal." '

Slash and Steven certainly weren't up to anything else at the time. 'Me and Steven were basically back to being a two-man band,' Slash said. 'The main problem was we'd never been able to find a singer, and when Duff called at first I went along with the idea of stealing Axl for my own band.'

What Duff didn't know was that Axl, Izzy, Slash and Steven already knew each other in that roundabout Hollywood way. Axl had first met and played with Slash in Hollywood Rose, of course. But Izzy knew Slash mainly through their shared fondness for heroin. In order to keep up his own steadily worsening habit, Izzy had begun dealing occasionally on the side, and Slash – also on the verge of developing his own nasty habits – had latterly become one of his regular customers. As for Steven, Izzy wasn't sure where he knew the little blond-haired dude from, but Axl knew he'd seen him around in all sorts of weird places, some of them gigs, some of them not.

As Steven later explained to me in 1999, 'I'd like to be able to tell you the name of the girl whose apartment I was leaving when I first met Axl Rose. She was a stripper – worked a club on La Cienega – and she had a thing for rockers. She was always good for a lay and a twenty dollar bill. She lived in a second-story apartment in a building built around a pool.' He was 'halfway down the stairs' one day 'when this skinny little dude almost runs me over. He's wearing a black leather vest and a cap, maybe to affect a dangerous attitude but he's looking more like a fag whore. Then, I recognize him. He's the friend of Slash's latest smack-pusher Izzy. I have never heard him sing but Slash swears Axl can front a band. He recognizes me, too. And we agree we should jam together some time. I watch him head up the stairs – and I'll be damned, he heads for my girlfriend's apartment. Okay, she wasn't my girlfriend anymore than I was her boyfriend . . . apparently. If I could only remember her name. Someday I'll ask Axl if he remembers. She's the first thing we ever shared.'

After two days and thirty-six hours of non-stop rehearsal, Axl, Izzy, Duff, Slash and Steven loaded up a friend's van and set off on their first tour as Guns N' Roses. Quickly christened the Hell Tour, about a hundred miles outside of LA, bombing along on Interstate 5, the van broke down. Undeterred, they simply got out and levelled their thumbs at the highway. 'We were all standing by the side of the road dressed in our stage clothes,' Duff laughingly told me. 'Five guys in striped tight pants and boots out in the middle of Oregon.' Picked up by a friendly truck-driver who dropped them off by the side of the road a day later, next to help them were 'two ex-hippy girls from San Francisco – they passed us and then they remembered back in the hippy days when nobody would pick them up, so they came around and we piled in'. The band was also grateful for some 'radical pot brownies' the girls fed them. 'Then when we finally got to Seattle,' Duff said, 'we had to play on other people's equipment and we were just wasted. It was our first gig and we sucked really bad. But it was hilarious, too. The whole trip went from bad to worse. But the playing was coming together and we knew that if we could get through that, we could get through anything.'

Their first gig was on Sunday 8 June 1985, headlining the Omni Room in Seattle with Duff's former band the Fastbacks opening for them. Exactly thirteen people turned up. Afterwards, they discovered that most of the local club owners hadn't even expected them to show up and therefore hadn't bothered advertising the dates. As a result, instead of the $250-per-show Duff had agreed over the phone, they were lucky most nights if they pocketed $50 in cash. Occasionally they received a pitcher of beer and a book of McDonald's meal-tickets as payment.

Slash thought they'd never make it back to LA in one piece. But despite the adversity, said Duff, 'That is when the band really clicked. We all stuck together. We went out and played a shitty first gig; we had no transportation back, and we had to bum a lift with this chick who was a junky. It was horrible. After that though we knew, okay, this is for real.' Or as Slash put it with a shrug, 'No one died, no one fainted, we all survived. And we've been pushing ourselves that way ever since.'

For Duff and Slash at least it was obvious. Seattle was 'the turning point'; Guns N' Roses was 'the right band with the right songs at the right time'. Duff said, 'You're in a band and there's always a loose link, in the end. Always. Every band I'd ever been in before, there'd always be one person, or two, that wasn't cutting it. This band, it was finally like, Okay, this is it! You could feel it at the first rehearsal. It just felt right.' Or as Slash later put it, Guns N' Roses may have left for Seattle as 'different parts of two or three different bands' but they would return as one: 'fully-blooded'. A bond was forged that would see them through the next incredible five years.

If Seattle was, as Duff said, 'a turning point' for the new band, for Axl it was also a welcome new beginning in another way. Apart from the music, which was suddenly coming together in a way he had never experienced before, on a personal level he had never felt so unthreatened; an important consideration for the sometimes crushingly insecure fledgling frontman. As Slash says, 'Axl always had this kind of *vision* of where he wanted to be, what he wanted the band to be. He didn't like people he thought were trying to hold him back.' That included anyone who questioned that vision. With Tracii out of the group, the last real challenge to his authority had gone and Axl was ready to assume the full-time role of leader.

Duff was bubbling with enthusiasm, but in a good way. Like Axl, he wanted to rehearse regularly and get the show on the road as soon as possible, but he didn't try and write the songs for Axl, while Slash and Izzy, who were more involved in the songwriting process, were so laidback their voices were easy to tune out. And anyway, they owed him: Izzy for sticking up for him when Slash made it clear he thought he would do a better job as the sole guitarist in the band (something Axl rejected out of hand, insisting that he and Izzy came as a team); and Slash because he knew 'good singers were rarer than rocking-horse shit', and that he had already blown his chances with Axl once before. Only Steven the new drummer could be a pain sometimes, with his know-all wisecracks and loud mouth. You could tell Steven once fancied himself as a singer. Well, that was all right, as long as he didn't get in the way.

To the outside world, the new Guns N' Roses line-up was very much a band in the traditional sense: equal partners in every way. For many, including Duff, the real musical genius of the new band wasn't Axl but Slash. As Duff later told me, having known Slash 'from, like, this kid where I thought, okay, he's just another good guitar player, to, like, this total fuckin' monstrosity' that he had become by 1985, 'as a musician, I appreciated him so much, you know?' Axl would go on to become 'just amazing, but to me, like when we first got together, I wasn't sure about Axl. I was like, he's good but I don't know. But that was when we had those other two cats in the band and the band was not working. But when this band clicked, Axl all of a sudden clicked. It took something finally for him to click and it took something for Slash to click, but when it did it *really* did.'

Michelle Young, an old high school friend of both Slash and Steven who met Axl for the first time after they joined Guns N' Roses, recalls a twenty-three-year-old hick with a chip on his shoulder. 'Axl was always like, "I'm from Indiana". He would wear blue-and-white-striped Dolphin shorts, cowboy boots, and a cropped T-shirt. I'd say, "I'm not going down Melrose with you dressed like that!" He was very insecure, very naive, but he knew he had something.'

With Tracii gone, initially there was some discussion about changing the name of the band. Heads Of Amazon and even AIDS were among the alternative names briefly considered, both of which Axl thought funny, but in the end everyone agreed that nothing they had come up with sounded quite as neat as Guns N' Roses. As before, their first official show in LA was at the Troubadour on a typically under-crowded week-night; billed on their hand-made flyers as: '*A Rock N Roll Bash Where Everyones [sic] Smashed!*'

Owned by folk enthusiast Doug Weston and originally based on the old boho coffee-houses that had populated the Strip in the 1950s, the Troubadour started out on La Cienega in West Hollywood as a safe haven for folk acts old and new, though it tended to favour the more eclectic and experimental outfits that knocked on its old wooden doors. By 1961, when the Troubadour moved to 9081 Santa Monica Boulevard (where it still resides today), the club became famous locally for its Monday night 'hootenannies'. Everyone from the least known folk 'minstrel' to future stars of the genre such as Judy Collins and Phil Ochs would turn up there to either sing or just hang out.

But the Troub's real contribution to the LA music scene occurred in the latter part of the 1960s, when names such as David Crosby and Gene Clark became regulars. Then unknowns like Don Henley and Jackson Browne propped up the bar, waiting for an opportunity to get up and show what they could do. As Henry 'Tad' Diltz of the Modern Folk Quartet once recalled, 'The place would be absolutely packed with agents and managers and record company people.' So much so that by the early 1970s, the Troub had become the most legendary club on the Strip. Many artists – including Elton John, who completed a famous 1970 residency there – now credit the Troubadour for providing the launch-pad to American success.

However, by the time Izzy introduced his old hometown buddy Axl to the Troubadour in 1983, the heyday of the club had long since passed. With the era of the singer-songwriter gone, the club had closed briefly in 1976, only to re-open for business a year later as a more generic rock venue ready to attract a wider variety of artist. This once hippy stronghold had even willingly opened its doors to punk, but following an unnerving night in 1977 during which over-zealous fans of the Bags overturned tables and terrorized club staff in what police later described as a 'mini-riot', the club subsequently banned all punk bands (and their unruly fans) from the venue. (The Germs and their fans were also banned from the Whisky A Go-Go for much the same reason that same year, as were the Weirdos and their fans from the Starwood after setting fire to the American flag onstage during a 4th of July gig.)

A decade on the Troub was mainly the preserve of the heavy metal crowd. Where once regular performers included Gram Parsons, Linda Ronstadt and Neil Young, the stage now became a home-from-home for big-haired LA screamers like Quiet Riot, Mötley Crüe, Rätt and Poison, to name the best-known. As a result, it was almost inevitable that this would be the LA club where Guns N' Roses first became well known. Their fame had spread in the months since the anonymous debut of the Axl'n'Tracii line-up three months earlier, and even though their first show with the new Slash–Duff–Steven line-up was another Monday night no-hoper, the place was surprisingly crowded. The vibe was unmistakable. 'We did Mondays at the Troubadour; then we were doing Tuesdays,' Duff recalled. 'That was like God for us at the time, just opening for bands at the Troubadour. We were all like, "Wow, this is it!" '

Even so, Axl and the new band found themselves victims of the recently installed 'pay to play' system, a rule hastily drawn up by nervous club-bookers after a new City ordinance banned posters and flyers from being put up on telegraph poles and trees. As a result, bands now had to agree to pay for the cost of their own tickets, so that if they didn't sell them they would be out of pocket rather than the club. Fair or not, it certainly worked as a powerful incentive for the band to try everything they could to get people along to the shows. Playing Mondays or Tuesdays, the slowest nights of the week, their weekends were spent walking back and forth along the Strip, cruising the bars and clubs, selling as many tickets as they could of the 500 they'd been allocated, for between $5 and $10 to anyone crazy enough to stump up the cash in advance.

As well as the Troubadour, that June they also played the Stardust Ballroom for the first time, and the Roxy on Sunset (next-door to the Rainbow) in August. '*Diamonds In The Rough*' read the flyers for the latter gig, which was exactly what they were. Back at the Troub their performances were now so good that by September they had started selling out Wednesday and

Thursday nights. Soon they found themselves moved to week-ends, at which point they pretty much became the house band. This, as they saw it, was the big time. 'Welcome To The Jungle' read the flyers for their first Saturday night show at the Troub. 'It was like we were rock stars, but just in Hollywood,' says Steven.

The chemistry between the new five-piece was immediately apparent to everyone who saw them. Even when they were off musically, they exuded charisma, particularly Axl and Slash, who were fast becoming the visual and creative focus of the band. Often there would be outbursts of violence at their shows. Some-times this was a side-effect of a fully revved-up LA crowd letting off steam at the weekend. Sometimes, according to Steven's inter-view with Classic Rock, it seemed sparked by the singer's behav-iour. 'He would leave the stage in the middle of every single show we played. Or he wouldn't get there on time. I'd say, "What are you doing?" He would kick me in the balls, which he'd done numerous times. The first week I knew Axl, he kicked me in the balls!'

Almost from their first shows in LA, the band's reputation was built on stories of hard drugs, sex and wilfully nihilistic behaviour, rumours and accusations the band did nothing to dispel and everything to fuel. Regular flyers for their gigs now proclaimed the group 'Fresh from detox!' Which wasn't true, of course, in fact quite the reverse: the intoxication was only just beginning. At first, this meant the usual on-the-road 'remedies' of weed, speed and – if someone else was buying – the occasional gram of coke. Slash and Izzy, however, had already descended to heroin long before they had the money to afford it. As Izzy cheerfully informed me a decade later, apart from playing in the band, 'selling drugs' was his chief preoccupation during this period, mainly to other rock musicians including, he said, Aerosmith guitarist Joe Perry.

Another rock star Izzy didn't mind scoring for was Nikki Sixx of Mötley Crüe. By then the Crüe were on to their third platinum album and Nikki had bought himself a house on Valley Vista Boulevard in Sherman Oaks, where, as he later wrote in his autobiography, The Dirt, he 'shot up to five hundred and one thousand dollars worth of drugs a day. We went through bags of heroin, rocks of cocaine, cases of Cristal, and whatever pills we could get our hands on. At first it was a big party, Izzy Stradlin would be rolled up in a ball in front of the fireplace.' One night, two girls Nikki didn't know knocked on the door and said they were with a guy named Axl from a group called Guns N' Roses, 'I think I've heard of him,' he told them. 'I know his guitar player or something.' Not that this was any guarantee of hospitality. When Nikki invited the girls in and they asked if they could bring Axl with them, he told them no. The girls took him up on his kind offer and Axl was left alone outside, too shy to knock on the door himself.

Slash certainly made no bones when we first met about his fondness for 'the bad boy', as he called heroin. The first time I formally interviewed him, in LA in June 1988, he had just finished, as he put it, 'smoking a foil' when I turned up at his hotel. 'I don't see nothin' wrong with it,' he smiled woozily. 'I got it under control.' He certainly wasn't 'as bad as I used to be on it, back before we were signed'. Or as he put it in a Q interview in 1991: 'I just liked it. I liked the way it felt. And fuck, I didn't know if I did it four or five days in a row I'd get fucking hooked on it! And that's a different subject altogether. That drug takes you over mentally and physically, so much that to come back is hard.'

Axl was more discreet than his new band mates but no less curious. He was never a regular drug user and inevitably tended to rationalize his interest much more than the others, who in his eyes were merely thrill-seekers. He was later quoted by Del James for an interview in RIP, saying 'It's not like we're the most intelligent bunch, but as far as street sense – hanging out, doing drugs, partying, girls and shit like that – we know and understand a lot. It's like we purposely put ourselves through street school. I didn't know how to pick up chicks, so I used to stand outside the Rainbow and watch how this goes down. I didn't know shit about doing drugs, so I learned what's safe and what's not, how to get it, how to do it properly and everything else that's involved.' As far as Axl was concerned it was all part of learning 'how to survive' in the music business.

Although the band was still mostly reliant on cover versions to keep their growing audiences happy – including scalding hot versions of Aerosmith's 'Mama Kin', Elvis's 'Heartbreak Hotel', the Stones' 'Jumping Jack Flash' and Rose Tattoo's 'Nice Boys Don't Play Rock'n'Roll' – they were also busy writing a clutch of original tunes, drawing on each of their respective pasts but also on the new energy they discovered playing together. Thus, Slash and Duff's chiming chorus and refrain about the city where the girls were pretty was fleshed out by Axl's extra verses and near-hysterical delivery, turning it into an anthem for the city none of them had been born in yet all now saw as home. Older Hollywood Rose-era material like Slash and Axl's ferociously full-on 'Welcome To The Jungle' now began to feature regularly in the live set, as did the re-titled 'Anything Goes' and one of the first tunes Axl and Izzy wrote together, an intense, mesmeric ballad called 'Don't Cry', and an even older, more throwaway ditty dating back to Axl's last days in Lafayette, which he wrote with Paul Huge, called 'Back Off Bitch'.

By the end of 1985, the band wrote and refashioned more than a dozen original songs, with almost a dozen more quickly taking shape as the months passed. So quickly were the songs coming, Duff said, that the band wasted no time in making a demo, and less than two months after they'd returned from Seattle they talked a well-known local figure named Black Randy into fronting them the cash to make a tape 'at this little punk rock studio'.

Black Randy – real name John 'Jackie' Morris – had once been the frontman for an LA band called the Metro Squad who released one album in 1980 called *Pass The Dust, I Think I'm Bowie* (the cover featuring a headshot of Randy spoofing Bowie's famous slicked-back *Hunky Dory* pose, ciggy dangling from his over-rouged lips), and before that, an affectedly 'controversial' 1978 single called 'Idi Amin'. Randy then co-founded Dangerhouse Records, the first indie label in LA, putting out seven-inch singles by local punk luminaries like X, the Weirdos, and The Avengers. By 1979, however, with LA punk now established as a viable form with the major labels, Dangerhouse fell into abeyance and Black Randy contented himself with reactivating Metro

Squad (whose 'punk revue' style show briefly included Belinda
Carlisle as a 'Blackette' on backing vocals) and becoming one of
those sub-Kim Fowley-type figures who populated the Strip scene,
now more famous for the colourful West African dashikis he
liked to wear than his music.

By the time Duff ran into him in the summer of 1985 Randy
was ill, having been diagnosed HIV-positive some time before.
What he hoped to achieve by helping out Guns N' Roses has
never been fully established – beyond some vague idea about
'supporting new talent' – since he died within months of the
original demo being made. It's likely that the band saw Randy's
help as a one-off occurrence anyway.

In fact, this was how they viewed anyone who offered to help
them out in the early days. With the exception of fellow 'street
rats' like Axl's friends West Arkeen, a twenty-five-year-old self-
taught musician from San Diego who had moved to LA in 1981,
and Del James, a displaced New Yorker who met Arkeen and
subsequently Axl and the band during his first weekend in
Hollywood in 1985, almost everybody else that came into
contact with them was seen first and foremost for how 'useful'
they might be, providing either money, sex and drugs or career
advancement.

One victim of this cavalier attitude was club promoter and
would-be GN'R manager Vicky Hamilton. 'I met Axl and Izzy
when they were Hollywood Rose. I was a booking agent at a
place called Silverlining Entertainment. Axl called me and said
could he come by and play me some songs. I said yes and he and
Izzy came down with a ghetto-blaster and played me a tape of
three songs. I loved it, and started booking them right away. I
booked them a couple of shows before I even saw them live.'

The band were not the easiest of houseguests. Axl was quoted
boasting in their first interview with *Kerrang!* in 1987 that they
had once 'destroyed her apartment' for fun. Speaking almost
fifteen years later, Steven Adler was somewhat kinder in his
recollections of Hamilton. 'Vicky was very sweet, very motherly,'
he said. 'We were pretty much living in her house, having sex
with strippers on the roof. We destroyed it.'

More recently, he added that Vicky was a 'wonderful lady'

and an 'awesome woman' and that he very much regretted 'her not being a part of the band after we got signed, because she got us signed'. The destruction of her home, he says in the interview, largely occurred on 'the last day we stayed at her apartment' after he and Axl 'got in a fight, and just destroyed it.' Axl 'threw me into the fire extinguisher thing, and then I pushed him onto the glass coffee table. And you should've seen that fucker blow up.' But then, Axl and Steven always 'got into good fights man'. Afterwards, 'We'd hug and kiss each other.' Axl would say, 'Dude, sorry, man. Hey, it's just you know . . .' And Steven would reply, 'Hey, dude, I love you too, don't worry about it. Let's go do our show.'

Deep down inside it may be that Axl resented the defiant remarks and snide comments Steven sometimes made about him, treating him like the out-of-towner he'd worked so hard to eradicate. Especially as Steven never bothered to hide his feelings to the rest of the band whenever he disagreed with something Axl said or did. While Slash, Izzy and Duff would do almost anything to avoid confrontation with Axl, Steven would plough in. Axl decided that Steven didn't know when to shut up. If he wasn't careful, he reportedly told friends, Steven would talk himself right out of the band one day.

Meanwhile, whatever difficulties Vicky Hamilton went through with Axl and the band, she was one of the main people who helped keep them all alive throughout this period. She booked most of their important gigs, not to mention feeding them, letting them crash at her small one-bedroom apartment when they had nowhere else to stay, allowing them to stash their clothes and equipment there, picking up the drinks tab occasionally at the Rainbow, letting them use her phone. At one stage, Axl recalled, 'There was eight people living there, and a dog. It got really crazy . . . really rude.'

The problems came after the band signed their deal with Geffen Records, when Hamilton sued them for repayment of approximately $100,000 she claimed she had spent on their behalf during their association, as well as a cut of all future royalties, saying the band had accepted her offer to manage them. Speaking to *RIP* magazine in 1989, Axl was quoted disputing this: 'She managed the band? We – Slash, Duff, Izzy, Steven and Axl – managed the band. A year later she sued us for one million dollars . . . We settled out of court for $30,000, [half] of which Geffen paid.'

All this, however, was in the future. For now, the band were living a virtual hand-to-mouth existence, scraping along as best they could, and one thing about Hamilton none of them could disagree on was that she championed them to all and sundry during this period. Speaking in 2003, she ignored the subsequent jibes to recall how the 'Hollywood scene was very much alive' back then. 'All the people of that big-hair scene knew each other and supported each other's bands. Then they would go to the Rainbow Bar and Grill and hang out. Guns N' Roses were simply the best band of that era and had real talent as songwriters, players and performers. It's not surprising that [they] were the band that everyone loved.'

Their fame having now spread beyond the confines of the Troubadour, the band began a regular circuit of shows at venues such as the Whiskey A Go-Go, the Roxy, the Water Club, Scream and the Radio City in Anaheim, where they put on a special Halloween show in October 1985. Word was finally out and it was around this time that the first of several A&R scouts from the major labels began trekking along to their shows to see what all the fuss was about.

By now the five band members had moved into a converted garage just off seedy Hollywood Boulevard, which they nick-named the Hell House: a single room that measured just sixteen feet by ten that Izzy later described as a 'fucking living hell'. Originally rented as a rehearsal space, one by one they all began sleeping there too when they had nowhere better to go. Part crash pad, part rehearsal space, they also hosted endless parties in order to get people to bring food, money, booze and drugs, though rarely in that order. 'A lot of crabs were transferred in that place,' Slash shrugged. 'There was a lot of indoor and outdoor sex,' Axl added.

Or as Duff put it: 'It was a place where the whole sleaziness of the band could fester.' Luxuries were few: no shower, holes in the roof where the rain leaked in, and no beds either, so they

Ian Tilton / Corbis

Slash and Axl at the Marquee Club, London, 28 June 1987.

Welcome to the Jungle: Guns N' Roses after the release of *Appetite for Destruction*, 1987.

'A brutal band for brutal times', 1989.

Axl with Erin Everly,
the inspiration for
'Sweet Child O' Mine'.
They married in 1990.

HEADLINING ROCK IN RIO, 1991

Neal Preston / Corbis

Axl and Izzy Stradlin on stage in 1991. Izzy would leave Guns N' Roses later that year.

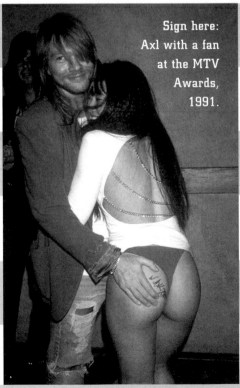

Sign here: Axl with a fan at the MTV Awards, 1991.

Axl in 1991 with then girlfriend Stephanie Seymour, who appeared in the 'November Rain' and 'Don't Cry' videos.

built a makeshift loft in which they slept above their equipment. Del James told me he remembered how Izzy used to sleep 'in the tiny space between the back of the couch and the wall. He'd be behind there for days sometimes. You'd just see this head appear over the back of the couch occasionally, to check out what was going on, then disappear again. I'd say, "Izzy, you okay, man?" And he'd go, "Ah, yeah . . ."'

'But God, did we sound good in there,' Slash said. 'We'd bash away with a couple of Marshalls in this tiny room, and it was cool because all the losers from Sunset and all the bands would come over and hang out there every night. We used to rehearse in there and sleep in there. It got hectic. But at least we didn't get fat and lazy. Basically, it's just down to a poverty thing, that's where that kind of "fuck you" attitude comes from, because you're not showering, you're not getting food or nothing, you do what you have to, to survive.'

Three years later, I drove with Slash down to the street where the Hell House used to be. Now living in a large rented house in the Hollywood hills and relieved to have come so far in such a short space of time, he remained nostalgic for the days when, as he said, 'we really didn't give a fuck. It was kinda desperate but in other ways they were great times, the only time we were ever really close as people, when even me and Axl got along.' We went for dinner at a nearby Mexican restaurant called El Compadre where he said they would persuade girls to take them to in the Hell House days. The food was 'lousy', he admitted, 'but the drinks were always strong and the waiters left you alone'. It was, he added with a smirk, 'a great place for getting blowjobs under the table'.

By the start of 1986, interest in the band was starting to get more serious. They saw the new year in with a typically over the top show at the Troub on 4 January, which they advertised with a flyer that read, '*Get Yourself Together, Drink Till You Drop, Forget About Tomorrow, Have Another Shot. Happy New Year! From the boys who brought you the most chaotic shows of 1985.*' A few weeks later they got their first good review in a mainstream newspaper, when the *Los Angeles Times* music critic Steve Hochman named Guns N' Roses in his top ten list of local acts destined to be 'stars of the future'. They were now perceived as heading a burgeoning club scene. Wise to the possibilities such a scenario offered music writers and local taste-makers, the band encouraged other LA bands like Jetboy, Faster Pussycat and the now reactivated LA Guns to open for them. 'It kinda created this scene,' said Axl, 'and in that crowd we were pretty much the top draw.'

Less interested in the big picture, and less practised than Axl at turning any situation to his advantage, Slash epitomized the rest of the band's attitude to such scene-stealing when he told me how he always saw Guns N' Roses as 'totally apart from all that. I never really saw us as part of that whole shitty LA scene. I mean, my attitude is, basically, fuck changing clothes to go on stage, I'm just gonna put on my jeans.' Most of the bands they got lumped together with (in the media's eyes) had a different attitude. 'It's like they went out and bought the clothes first and then decided to start thinking about the music. That's what we were really against. I know it's a cliché but there [were] bands out there whose roots [went] back about three years, you know what I'm saying? It's ridiculous, there's no soul in it, there's no dynamics in the music or anything. It's just bland. But they look good.' All Guns N' Roses needed to do, he suggested, was 'just hammer our amps and just go out and play'.

Which is essentially what they did, guided by Axl's controlling vision. Their live set now evolved into more of a showcase for their own material like 'Welcome To The Jungle' and 'Paradise City' and less the superannuated bar band version of the rock classics most club acts thrived on. Kicking off with an intro tape of 'What's That Noise' by the Stormtroopers of Death, the lights would flash on and the band would jump straight into 'Reckless Life', reworked from the Hollywood Rose-era 'Wreckless'. Still built around familiar cornerstones like 'Mama Kin' and 'Nice Boys . . .' the rest of the set featured new stuff like the punk-nasty 'It's So Easy' and 'Nightrain' (the latter named after the dollar-a-bottle gut-rot wine they drank), punctuated by more adventurous new songs like the dark and slithering, semi-acoustic 'You're Crazy' and Axl's hair-tuggingly overwrought ballad 'Don't Cry'. The inclusion of so much original material also helped distinguish

the band from the countless others who wore the same clothes
and affected similar 'bad' attitudes but possessed none of the
same substance to back it up. By the start of 1986 the band had
a discernible fan-base, kids who would turn up at every show,
singing along as though they already owned the records.

'Their audience,' says Vicky Hamilton, 'suddenly went from
150 to 700 almost overnight. And it was all word of mouth.'
Which was all the encouragement the West Coast-based record
companies needed to suddenly start filling up the guest lists at
Guns N' Roses gigs. 'The buzz got out,' says Slash. 'And we kept
getting invited out to meet these idiots from record companies.
One label we were talking to, I was saying, "It sounds kinda like
Steven Tyler," and the chick goes, "Steven who?" All of us just
looked at each other and went, "Uh, can we have another one of
those drinks?" '

Record company figures even started turning up at the Hell
House. 'They would come over to the studio and come in the
alley and see drunks,' says Slash. 'There'd be one guy sittin' there
with a bottle on his head – and the next thing you know we're
being taken out to lunch. At first, I didn't really know what to
think. I'm pretty naive about all this stuff. I try to keep my wits
about me in most things. But in this whole band there's a certain
naivety in the way we approach this whole business . . . Our
attitude was, well, fuck 'em. We're only gonna sign to the one
who gives us what we want.'

'The Chrysalis fuckin' brains came along and said we'll give
you guys $750,000,' Duff told me, 'and we just said, yeah, but
have you ever heard us play? And they were like, "No, but . . ."
So we were like, "See ya!" Suddenly there was this little label
war, everybody trying to get us to sign – we had a lot of great
lunches, I tell ya! Finally we went with the record company that
really wanted to put something into us and believe in us. And it
worked. Everybody was into the kind of record we were making,
and everyone dug in and did a good job.'

Whatever Slash, Duff and Izzy may have thought of all the
attention the band was now getting there was clearly only ever
going to be one person in the group who decided something as
momentous as which record company they signed to. Suddenly

imbued with the newfound confidence a rapidly swelling audience brings, Axl viewed the approach of the major label dudes with a commendably cool head. Inside, as he would confide to friends like West Arkeen and Del James, he knew this was an incredibly important decision for both himself and the band, though he was determined to put on a suitably unimpressed front and tough out the negotiations. Having learned early on in LA the value of playing one admirer off against another, he now proceeded to try and do the same with the record companies. Helped in this by the fact that in a relatively small but intensely close-knit industry environment like LA, when one major label becomes openly interested in an act, it's usual for all the others to immediately register their interest too, at the end of the first round of lunches, brunches and pitchers of Margarita at El Compadre, Axl shrewdly judged there to be only two labels prepared to open their chequebooks in a big way: Chrysalis and Geffen.

As Duff suggests, Chrysalis seemed the most intent on secur-ing the band's signatures, offering $750,000 in advance against future royalties. Finally, however, it was the Geffen Records A&R team of Tom Zutaut and his assistant Teresa Ensenat who beat Chrysalis to the prize after Zutaut went out of his way to convince the band, and Axl in particular (who he shrewdly delivered his pitch to personally), that they would be allowed total freedom to do things their way, whatever that might eventu-ally mean in practical, artistic or financial terms. According to Axl, Zutaut was 'the first major record person we were able to talk openly with, and he's the main reason our record happened'.

According to Joseph Brooks, the influential KROQ radio DJ and former owner of the hip Hollywood record store Vinyl Fetish, it was he who first interested Zutaut and many other label executives in the band. 'I dragged A&R people to their gigs and played the "Welcome To The Jungle" demo on my [KROQ] show,' he says. It's a memory Zutaut shares, 'Joe at Vinyl Fetish was like, "There's this new band called Guns N' Roses – you should check them out." I went to see them at the Troubadour and there were a lot of A&R people. So I left after two songs – I didn't need to see any more to know they were going to be the biggest band in the world. On my way out I said [to one of the other A&R people], "They suck – I'm going home," knowing full well I was going to sign them to Geffen come hell or high water.'

In March 1986, having caught the band at the height of their Troubadour success – the same club, in fact, where David Geffen himself had discovered and signed so many acts to his Asylum label a decade before – Zutaut was obsessed with signing Guns N' Roses to the Geffen label, later telling friends that he'd become hooked after witnessing just two numbers, 'Welcome To The Jungle' and 'Nightrain'.

A short, thickset twenty-five-year-old from the Chicago suburbs, Zutaut had been lured to the Geffen label a year before from the A&R department of Elektra Records, where he had scored a major success as the man who convinced the label to sign Mötley Crüe. Signing Guns N' Roses, he felt sure, would not only cement his new professional relationship with Geffen himself, but drag the label out of the sales doldrums it had been experiencing throughout the latter half of 1985. Moreover, he simply *believed* in the band. When he'd signed Mötley Crüe three years earlier, they'd been the loudest, most exciting band on the Strip. The one thing they patently lacked, however, was hit songs; a gap in their repertoire Zutaut filled by persuading them to cover material like 'Smokin' in the Boys Room'. Guns N' Roses were similar to the Crüe in that they were now the band everyone on the Strip was talking about. Despite the frequently inserted profanities, the difference was they had the tunes to back it up. Zutaut was excited. So excited he was prepared to give them anything they wanted – and more.

The day after seeing the Troubadour show, Zutaut called Axl and arranged to meet him at the Hell House. He cut straight to the chase and offered him a contract. With the offer from Chrysalis still ostensibly on the table, and the business cards of at least two other record company executives in his pocket from the night before, at first Axl did his best to play it cool and told Zutaut he would need to talk it over with the rest of the band. The more they talked, however, the more Axl warmed to the Geffen exec. According to Zutaut, 'Axl didn't strike me as being particularly savvy or into his career. He was more like a wild animal from the African jungle.' Only two years older than the singer – unlike most record company A&R people who tended to be in their thirties – Axl was also more than a little impressed by the fact that this was the guy who had signed Mötley Crüe. He eventually made Zutaut a bravura counter offer. 'If you can get us a cheque for seventy-five thousand dollars by Friday night at six p.m.,' he said, 'we'll sign with you. Otherwise, we're going to meet with some other people.'

This was a most unusual request, even for an out-there LA rock singer, and certainly not one that would be considered normal business practice, even for an exec as experienced at dealing with outré Sunset Strip vagabonds as Zutaut. Furthermore, even if his bosses at Geffen went for it, he strongly doubted they could come up with the money in time. The days of the fat guy in the sharkskin suit, smoking a cigar and writing out cheques were long gone, even in Hollywood. Nevertheless, Zutaut agreed to Axl's proposal and told him to wait by the phone and talk to no one else until he got back to him. Then he drove to his office wondering how on earth he was going to pull this one off.

Sure enough, despite noting his genuine enthusiasm for the deal, Zutaut's immediate superior, label president and de facto number two to Geffen himself, Eddie Rosenblatt, proved highly sceptical. But, Zutaut blurted, 'This is gonna be the biggest rock'n'roll band in the world!' He *had* to have that cheque by Friday.

'Tom, the wheels just don't move that fast here,' Rosenblatt responded.

'In that case,' Zutaut said, 'we have to defeat the system. Once the band goes into play, we're never gonna get them.'

But Rosenblatt, a music biz veteran since the late-1960s, had heard it all before. 'You know they say that, but they won't really do it.'

This may have been true with all the other artists he and Rosenblatt had dealt with before, thought Zutaut, but this guy, this Axl Rose, he was definitely something else. 'No,' he said, 'this guy is nuts. If he says it, he'll do it.'

With Rosenblatt still throwing his hands up, a now frantic Zutaut took the unprecedented step of asking for the chance to put his case to David Geffen personally. Exasperated but sensing this was strictly a one-off for the label's promising young A&R whiz, Rosenblatt agreed to arrange the meeting. Putting his case all over again, reiterating that this was going to be 'the biggest rock'n'roll band in the world', Zutaut watched helplessly as Geffen laughed out loud at his pronouncement. How many times had he heard that one before?

'So, really,' Geffen chortled, 'the biggest rock'n'roll band in the world? You're serious?'

'David, I swear to God,' Zutaut insisted. 'I have no doubt about it, and you have to make this happen. I have to have this cheque for seventy-five thousand by Friday at six.' Perhaps recalling his own days as an impetuous young executive trying to convince the world of the importance of discoveries like the Eagles, Geffen stared out of the window for a moment, then glanced back at the anxious, fit-to-burst figure of Zutaut. Geffen nodded his head. Zutaut exploded with joy, thanking his boss profusely, even as he was being shown out of the door, promising he would never regret his decision.

After he'd gone, Geffen personally put a call through to the business affairs department at Warner Bros Records, the umbrella corporation that funded Geffen in those days, directing them to cut through the red tape and issue a cheque for $75,000 to be delivered to Tom Zutaut at the Geffen office by Friday afternoon.

There was still one last hurdle for the over-eager Zutaut to overcome before he finally got the name Guns N' Roses on a signed Geffen contract. Two days before the deal was to have closed, Axl called him at his office and said, 'I've done something stupid.' Zutaut recalls: 'He said, "Look, man, we told the A&R person at Chrysalis that if she walked naked down Sunset Boulevard from her office to Tower Records, we'd sign with her." He was dead serious.' Zutaut's office in the Geffen building happened to be on the stretch of Sunset Boulevard directly opposite the Chrysalis offices. He remembered thinking, 'I'm going to have to watch [out the window] until Friday at six o'clock, because if she does the nude walk, I'm going to lose the band.'

Again, this was hardly a normal request for an unsigned band to make as a prerequisite for getting their first major deal. But Zutaut feared that if the Chrysalis A&R person had the same high opinion of Guns N' Roses as he did, she might just take off her clothes and streak down the street. Once more, he found himself in panic mode. 'Axl, I already went to David Geffen. We're making the deal here. You can't do this.'

But Axl had, and for the next two days Zutaut watched nervously from behind the blinds in his office to see if Chrysalis would trump him. When, after sweating throughout the final afternoon, the digital clock on his desk at last reached 6.01pm, and a naked Chrysalis employee hadn't appeared in the street below, Zutaut gave a whoop of triumph and picked up the phone to call Axl.

Later that same night, Axl, Slash, Izzy, Duff and Steven dutifully showed up at his office and signed the official papers Zutaut hurriedly shoved across his desk. By midnight it was a done deal: Guns N' Roses had signed a major, long-term recording contract with Geffen Records. Kim Fowley, who had rubbed shoulders with the band, as he'd done with almost every promising new club act that hit the Strip in those days, later recalled Axl swanning into the Rainbow that Friday night brandishing a photocopy of the Geffen cheque. 'He said, "Look, we got our deal." I said, "Congratulations," and he said, "Buy me a drink – I don't have any money."'

All Guns N' Roses had to do now was fulfil Tom Zutaut's outlandish predictions about becoming the biggest rock'n'roll band in the world. Something not even Axl in his wildest dreams had ever really thought possible. Big, he had no doubt they would be, but the biggest? Fuck you, dude. Don't tell me what to do . . .

Part Two

YOU'RE IN THE JUNGLE, BABY

I am extraordinarily patient,
provided I get my own way in the end.

MARGARET THATCHER

Chapter Four

SUCK ON THIS

In March 1986, having signed his first major contract with Geffen Records, Bill Bailey could now afford to make another long-held dream a reality: the legal changing of his name to W. Axl Rose. The acronym it formed – WAR – was purely coincidental he insisted, yet it summed up perfectly his attitude towards the journey he was fully embarked on with Guns N' Roses. As he told me in 1990, brandishing a copy of the then recently published Mike Tyson biography, *Bad Intentions*, 'I relate what I do to what Tyson says about when he punches someone in the head. He says he imagines hitting 'em so hard his fist knocks their nose bone right back into their brains. He says when he goes in the ring he does it with bad intentions. Well, that's like me getting ready to start something, like going onstage. And you gotta make sure when you knock 'em down they stay down.'

Of course, it wasn't only onstage that Axl would appear to carry this idea in his head. Over the next few years the figurative list of bruised and battered opponents he left in his wake would grow staggeringly long. For now, however, it was an attitude that served both him and the band well as they struggled to establish a musical identity for the first time in the recording studio. Things didn't go well at first when they couldn't find the right producer. 'People were very afraid of this band,' Teresa Ensenat says. 'There were a couple of people who dissed us hard,' Slash recalls now. '[People] who were just assholes about it,' Zutaut remembers, 'managers, other record companies, who said, "They'll never make it, Tom Zutaut, you're a fucking idiot." Even people in our own record company were like that.'

Among the array of producers originally contacted was Kiss's Paul Stanley, who had expressed an interest in working with the band then cried off when he realized their lifestyle was more than just an image they projected. Bob Ezrin, producer for Alice

Cooper, Lou Reed, Kiss and Pink Floyd's *The Wall*, was also approached by Geffen but decided to 'steer well clear' for the same reasons. Spencer Proffer, a well-known local producer who had helped propel proto-LA metal quartet Quiet Riot to stardom in the early 1980s, agreed to go into the studio but quickly fell out with the band once it became obvious that, unlike Quiet Riot or even Mötley Crüe, this was one LA band intent on not playing the hits-by-numbers game.

Out of desperation and the it-takes-a-thief-to-catch-a-thief principle, Zutaut even turned to Nikki Sixx of Mötley Crüe, the band he had signed to Elektra five years earlier. But Nikki, though flattered, was still wrestling with his own demons. As he later explained: '[Zutaut] wanted me to produce their record and see if I could give the punk-metal they were playing at the time a more commercial, melodic edge without sacrificing credibility. They were just a punk band, he told me, but they were capable of being the greatest rock'n'roll band in the world if someone could help them find the melodies to take them there. I was too much in agony trying to slow down my drug intake to consider the idea . . .'

Still high on the Geffen advance – modest though it was by the standards of bands with a high-profile management team behind them, which they didn't yet have – and unused to the rigours of working to a deadline in a professional studio, the whole process threatened to unravel before it had begun. In fact, early sessions eventually had to be postponed while Slash and Izzy took time off to try and rid themselves of the bad habits they had been recklessly nurturing. According to Steven, 'drugs and drink' had already begun 'to take their toll as Slash [was] secreted away by the label to dry out'.

'There was a point where I stopped playing guitar and didn't come out for three months,' Slash told me. What snapped him out of it was, he says, a phone call from Duff. 'He said, "You've alienated yourself from the band." Since they were the only people I'm really close to, that really affected me, and I quit.' Izzy underwent a similar catharsis, taking action only when he sensed his place in the band was under serious threat. It was a pattern both men were doomed to repeat more than once over the coming years. As Izzy later told me, 'When you're on that stuff, you're always either quitting or starting again . . .'

The arrival of manager Alan Niven at least gave them a bridge between their shambolic working practices and the increasingly worried executives at Geffen, many of whom were beginning to wonder if Zutaut hadn't bitten off more than he could chew this time. A number of better-known rock managers had already been approached by Geffen but all of them turned the band down, including Iron Maiden manager, Rod Small-wood, then involved in the early major-label days of Poison, whose debut album that year, *Look What The Cat Dragged In*, was on its way to going platinum. 'There was already a huge vibe building around them,' he told me a decade later, 'I saw them, but at the end of the day I passed. There was just something about them I wasn't quite sure of. The singer did most of the talking but it wasn't anything he said, so much, that put me off. Just something about them that wasn't quite right, some vibe that was just . . . wrong.' (Ironically, years later Smallwood's organization, the Sanctuary Group, spent several million dollars buying out Axl's management contract, taking stewardship of his career some fifteen years after originally passing up the opportunity.)

Aerosmith manager Tim Collins was another established music business figure that Geffen – who Aerosmith was also signed to – originally approached. Zutaut invited him to a specially arranged showcase gig at the Roxy on Sunset, and afterwards they and the band went to Collins' hotel suite for a late dinner and an informal discussion about where the band saw their future heading. Everything seemed to be going reasonably well, thought Zutaut: Izzy stayed awake, Axl wasn't rude. But when Collins retired to the adjoining room to get some sleep the band carried on drinking, running up a $450 drinks bill on Collins's room tab. In the morning, the incensed manager – then going through a very heavy scene trying to get members of Aerosmith off drink and drugs – decided it was more than he could handle and announced that he, too, would pass on the deal. 'David Geffen asked me to manage Guns and I thought about it for ten seconds and declined,' he later commented.

It wasn't until August, the same month they finally began work in earnest on their debut album, that Axl and the band signed with Alan Niven's Stravinsky Brothers management company, who also oversaw the career of another soon-to-be-platinum LA act called Great White. They sealed the deal with a special showcase gig at the Whisky A Go-Go on 23 August, which Niven and his team attended. But, in a spectacularly prophetic harbinger for the sort of cliffhanger relationship he would enjoy with his new manager, Axl turned up late for the show.

Niven remained undeterred, perhaps because, as he later confessed to me, he had taken the band on 'more as a favour than because I really saw their potential'. He made no bones about the fact that, certainly in the early days of the relationship, Great White was not only his first priority but obviously the band with greater commercial potential. 'When I signed [Guns N' Roses], I didn't know what to expect,' he told me. 'When I heard the first album, I thought we'd be doing well if we sold 200,000 copies. If you'd told me there was a hit single on it I would have laughed in your face.' For Axl, being late for such an important gig may have been his way of exerting his authority. As though he were saying, 'This guy may be our new manager, but that doesn't make him the boss of me.'

What he wasn't prepared for was Niven's sheer insouciance. Very little that Axl said or did would ever faze him. New Zealand-born, he'd been groomed by his father for a career in the military, before he fell in love with rock music and rebelled. He learned to play guitar and began writing his own songs but never got as far as forming his own successful group. Instead, he arrived in LA in the early 1980s, as a trader in antiques. It was only after he became friendly with Robert Plant sound-alike vocalist Jack Russell and guitarist Mark Kendall – with whom Niven would share a number of songwriting credits in Great White – that he finally began making a name for himself in the music business.

In person, his studiedly urbane personality put one in mind of Spinal Tap's cricket bat-wielding guardian Ian Faith. On the surface, a most unlikely match as manager for the practised guttersnipes of Guns N' Roses, but he provided the unruffled presence they would most benefit from in their earliest wildest days. 'From the very beginning, my relationship with Axl was often strained,' Niven later recalled. 'His failure to show for the very first gig after signing a management contract rather set the tone. There were aspects to his behaviour that I found excessively abusive of others, even considering the difficulties of whatever might have occurred in his childhood.' In the end, though, Niven 'believed that if I could keep some kind of discipline in place, we could sell half a million records.'

The only really sensible move the band made after receiving their $75,000 Geffen advance was to move out of the awful Hell House, putting a down-payment on the rent of a small, beaten-up wooden bungalow off Santa Monica Boulevard, in the more upmarket Griffith Park neighbourhood, where they got down to the serious business of writing and rehearsing songs for their debut album. According to Steven, 'the band [wrote] the music together while Axl [supplied] the lyrics.' Axl, he said, was 'definitely a great lyricist. But the thing people forget is that Slash, Duff, Izzy and I wrote the music – sometimes Axl wasn't even at rehearsal and we just gave him a tape. For the longest time I had no clue what he was singing.'

It was a statement Axl would later refute, claiming he was responsible for a great deal of the 'bitchin' riffs and melodies' that comprised the first Guns N' Roses album. The likelihood is there were some tracks on the eventual album that Axl had almost nothing to do with writing. Duff and Axl's friend West Arkeen were mainly responsible for the brutal music and harsh lyrics of the bands first single in the UK, 'It's So Easy'.

Two years older than Axl, West was also more worldly. Born in the Parisian suburb of Neuilly-sur-Seine, he grew up in San Diego, where his talent for music first manifested itself when he was fourteen, when he learned to play guitar while he sang. Self-taught, at twenty-one he moved to LA where he spent the next five years struggling to get into the music biz, often meeting the rent by busking in the street. His luck changed, however, when he hooked up with a like-minded musician by the name of Bill, who often crashed on his floor. Bored and penniless, they often wrote 'joke songs' to keep each other entertained (one of which, 'One In A Million', would cause even more controversy on the next GN'R collection). When Axl signed the record deal, he was determined to get his old street pal in on the action. It was a favour he would repeat in the future with other fondly regarded pals such as Paul Huge and Dana Gregory.

Other tracks Axl had little active role in writing were 'Mr Brownstone' – built on a staccato riff Slash came up with, fleshed out by some brash Izzy barre chords and a clearly autobiographical Izzy lyric based on the experience of seeing himself and Slash succumb to the deadly lure of junk for months at a time, and 'Think About You', a fairly innocuous filler written more or less solely by Izzy.

A more typical example of the way they worked back then may be gleaned from the story of how they wrote the track, in the summer of 1986, that would take them to number one in the charts two years later: 'Sweet Child O' Mine'. Others could take the credit for writing the cartwheeling central guitar riff and the wonderfully insistent melody because it was Axl who first identified it as a key musical moment for the band. 'I was fucking around with this stupid little riff,' Slash recalled. 'Axl said, "Hold the fucking phones! That's amazing!"' Within a matter of minutes, he says, the rest of the band expanded on Slash's nagging little riff with some chords and the suggestion of a chorus. All they needed were the words. Enter Axl, who based the surprisingly sensitive verses on a poem he had recently penned for his new girlfriend, a pretty eighteen-year-old brunette model named Erin.

Erin Invicta Everly was the eldest daughter of Don Everly – one half of the legendary early 1960s pop duo the Everly Brothers – and the actress Venetia Stevenson, famous in America in the late-1950s for her appearances in such TV shows as 77 *Sunset Strip*. (The famous American soap star Anna Lee – last seen as Lila Quartermaine in the late-1990s *General Hospital* spin-off *Port Charles* – was Erin's grandmother.) Axl met Erin just a few weeks before recording on the album began, after being introduced at a gig. Gregarious, educated, open-minded and from a wealthy, middle-class background, Erin was completely unlike any girl Axl had previously been involved with, and he was instantly smitten. At first he felt like he'd been reborn. Overnight, he swore-off groupies and instead found himself writing love poetry to his newfound muse. Some of the breathlessly romantic lines were later adapted for 'Sweet Child'.

However, the rest of the band took some convincing that the new song Axl was so keen on was the sort of thing they should be doing. Not least Slash, who began to regret he'd ever started the ball rolling, describing the process of writing and rehearsing the song as 'like pulling teeth. For me, at the time, it was a very sappy ballad.' Duff agreed, calling the new song 'a joke. We thought, "What is this song? It's gonna be nothing."'

'It *was* a joke,' Slash still says now. 'We were living in this house that had electricity, a couch and nothing else. The record company had just signed us and we were on our backs. There was a lot of shit going on. We were hanging out one night and I started playing that riff. And the next thing you know, Izzy made up some chords behind it, and Axl went off on it. I used to hate playing that sucker.'

But Axl didn't agree. For him it was an anthemic rocker more akin to something redneck Southern rockers Lynyrd Skynyrd might have done in their yee-haw, mid-1970s heyday. 'I'm from Indiana, where Lynyrd Skynyrd are considered God to the point that you ended up saying, I hate this fucking band,' Axl later explained. 'And yet for "Sweet Child" I went out and got some old Skynyrd tapes to make sure that we'd got that heartfelt feeling.' It was an instance where Axl's refusing to take no for an answer paid off, and a significant turning point on various levels for both singer and band. When the song later became the biggest hit of their career, it was enough to convince Axl he should not be put off by what anyone else had to say about one of his songs – including Slash.

Meanwhile, the band was finally getting down to working on their first album. Booked into Rumbo Studios, in the LA suburb of Canoga Park, the producer they eventually chose to work with was Mike Clink, a Baltimore-born studio-hand who began his career as an engineer at New York's Record Plant studios, often working with producer Ron Nevison on hit albums by soft rock giants such as Jefferson Starship, Heart and, most notably, Survivor, on their 1982 worldwide hit single and album, *Eye Of The Tiger*. Clink's main attributes, according to Slash, were 'incredible guitar sounds and a tremendous amount of patience'. He was also smart enough to understand that what Guns N' Roses wanted was something much harder-edged than the albums he usually found himself producing. 'Those were pop records,' he says of his previous credits. 'But I knew what to do with Guns. They played me records they liked. Slash had Aerosmith [albums]; Axl had Metallica's [second album] *Ride The Lightning*.'

Nevertheless, Clink admits he had serious doubts about the characters of these new kids he was getting involved with. 'I'd never come into contact with guys like that. During our first meeting, they were spitting over each other's heads! They really were living on the street, that reckless life. But I pushed them hard and had a rule: no drugs in the studio.' Outside of the studio, however, there was no controlling them. Slash may have stuck to 'Jack Daniel's and coffee and Marlboros' in the studio, but most nights he would 'be out until three a.m., carousing. I had a van that I crashed after passing out. I woke up sitting in the middle of the road with this chick.'

Originally the home of plain-folks 1970s husband-and-wife team Captain and Tennille, on the surface Rumbo Studios was an incongruous choice of venue for the making of a Guns N' Roses album, situated largely off-the-beaten track for Hollywood studios and sharing a parking lot with the Winnetka Animal Clinic. But it was relatively cheap and had the added benefit of forcing the band to live nearby. Not that that in itself caused them to amend their bad habits. 'I put them in an apartment when we were making the record,' Clink recalls, 'and they destroyed it. One night they locked themselves out, so they put a boulder through a window. They thought it would look like somebody had robbed the place. When they finally got kicked out, there wasn't one thing left intact. It looked like somebody was remodelling and had knocked down the walls.'

Unimpressed, Clink agreed to ignore such destructive behaviour as long as it didn't interfere with their work on the album. Even when the band fell into their familiar pattern of working mostly at night, Clink kept his cool as long as they were still delivering the goods. 'He kept us at arm's length,' says Slash. 'We partied really hard, but when we were in the studio, we were pretty much together. There was no doping and all that stuff.' As Clink says, he was intent on 'capturing the band's essence, not beating it into the ground', all the tracks were initially recorded as live, with the aim of recording the song with a minimum number of takes, and with overdubs kept to an only-when-absolutely-necessary minimum.

That said, it soon became clear that Axl had his own ideas about the recording process, and that while he was happy to try and do whatever his producer deemed necessary to capture the band's live energy on tape, left to his own devices he would demand endless revisions of his own and the band's performances. As Axl later told me, what people didn't understand 'is that there was a perfectionist attitude' to the making of that first Guns N' Roses album. 'I mean, there was a definite plan to that. We could have made it all smooth and polished. We went and did test tracks with other producers and it came out smooth and polished – with Spencer Proffer. And Geffen Records said it was too fuckin' radio. That's why we went with Mike Clink. We went for a raw sound, because it just didn't gel having it too tight and concise.'

Even the fact that the record sounded so 'live' was down to simple planning, he said. ''Cos Guns N' Roses on stage, man, can be, like, out to lunch. Visually, we're all over the place and stuff and you don't know what to expect. But how do you get that on a record? But somehow you have to do that. So there's a lot more that's needed on a record. That's why recording is my favourite thing, because it's like painting a picture. You start out with a shadow, or an idea, and you come up with something that's a shadow of that . . . And then you add all these things and you come up with something you didn't even expect. Slash will do, like, one slow little guitar fill that adds a whole different mood that you didn't expect. That's what I love . . . You use the brush this way and allow a little shading to come in and you go, "Wow, I got a whole different effect on this that's even heavier than what I pictured. I don't know quite what I'm on to but I'm on it," you know?

' "Paradise City", man,' he continued, 'that's like, I came up with two of those first vocals – there's five parts there – I came up with two and they sounded really weird. Then I said, look, I got an idea. I put two of these vocal things together, and it was the two weirdest ones, the two most obtuse ones. And Clink's like, "I don't know about that, man . . ." I'm like, "I don't know either, why don't we just sleep on it?" So we go home and the next day I call him up and now I'm like, "I don't know about this." But he goes, "No, I think it's cool!" So now he was the other way. So then we put three more vocal parts on it and then it fit. But the point is that wasn't how we had it planned. We don't really know how it happened.'

Typically, Slash saw the whole thing rather differently. As far as he was concerned, most of the tracks had been 'easy to record'. The hardest part for Slash was that guitar intro to 'Sweet Child O' Mine'; the same one that had originally come to him so easily. 'It took me all afternoon to time it out and be at the right place when the drums came in.' However, once it was finished, Clink agreed with Axl that they had captured something special, claiming the song had 'made the hairs on my arms stand up. It was magical.' The rest of the material tended towards the same auto-biographical content. 'Welcome To The Jungle', which would become the band's calling card – Slash's opening guitar refrain echoing like hurried footsteps down an unlit alley, Axl sighing 'Oh, my God . . .' before Steven brings the hammer down with a deafening thud and the rest of the band throw their shoulders hard into the teeth-grinding riff – was another track, like 'Sweet Child', that began life as a little mongrel riff Slash was tinkering with one day as he sat on the bed in his room, messing around on the acoustic. Again, Axl happened to overhear what he was doing and immediately picked up on it, writing the lyrics – loosely based on his own experience of first arriving in LA – then and there. 'I think it took maybe an hour,' Slash shrugged.

'My Michelle', which opened side two of the original vinyl version of the album, was ostensibly a ballad that quickly becomes a tirade. It was yet another true story about Slash and Steven's old high school friend Michelle Young, whose father, as the song says, worked in the porn industry and whose mother died of a drugs overdose. Slash and some of the others had complained when Axl first sang them the lyrics that they were too close to the bone and that 'poor sweet Michelle, she'll freak out.' Axl's retort was that he'd tried writing 'this nice sweet song about her and then I looked at it and thought that [it] really doesn't touch any basis of reality, so I put down an honest thing. It describes her life. This girl leads such a crazy life with doing drugs, or whatever she's doing at the time, you don't know if she's gonna be there tomorrow. I showed her the lyrics after about three weeks of debating and she was so happy that someone didn't just paint a pretty picture. She loves it.'

According to Michelle Young (who had dated Axl briefly before he met Erin), he was still occasionally sleeping over at her apartment 'because he had nowhere else to go. After they got famous, there were better places to stay – and go shopping. They would call and say, "I got this. I got that. I got a new car."' As for the song, she admitted she found it strangely flattering, explaining that she'd been driving Axl to a gig in her car when 'Your Song' by Elton John came on the radio. It was a mutual favourite. 'I said that I wished somebody would write a beautiful song about me.' Of course, 'My Michelle' hardly compares to Elton's tender ballad but, nevertheless, she says, 'I didn't care because I was so fucked up, but what it says is all true. My dad does distribute porno films and my mom did die.'

Much would also be made of the fact that the word 'fuck' appeared in the lyrics of the album's twelve songs at least a dozen times; a ratio of once every track. Given the conformist nature of big league rock music in the mid-1980s, it came as a shock to hear a band purportedly aiming for that same league indulging itself so freely; or more to the point, for their record company to allow it. 'The record company knew what they were doing,' Slash later told me. 'In fact, they kinda encouraged us to go further. It was like they knew we weren't going to get any radio play so we might as well just go for it.'

And they did, not least on the track chosen a year later as their first British single, 'It's So Easy', a ferocious punk-metal hybrid so uncompromising in its relentless unashamed misogyny that by the time Axl screams out the words 'fuck off!' at the end of the fourth verse, one is inured to it. Metallica drummer and co-founder Lars Ulrich, no stranger to controversy when it came to song lyrics, later recalled listening to the track for the first time on a flight to San Francisco unable to believe what he was hearing. 'It just blew my fuckin' head off.' It wasn't just the use of the expletive, 'It was the way Axl said it. It was so venomous. It was so fucking real and so fucking angry.'

In this case, of course, Axl couldn't claim the credit for the lyrics, co-written as they were by Duff and West. Axl's main contribution to 'It's So Easy' was the full use he made of his impressively eclectic vocal range, from the deep, languid, almost spoken-word first verse and chorus, building through the gently crooning roué of the middle section, climaxing with the hysterically whining punk misfit spitting hate at the finale. As Axl explained, 'I sing in about five or six different voices that are all part of me, it's not contrived.' In fact, it was a trick he'd perfected during his years in his father's church. 'I'm like a second baritone or something. I used to take choir classes and stuff and I'd always sit there and since I could read music, I'd try to sing other people's parts and see if I could get away with it. We had this teacher who was pitch perfect, or whatever you call it. He had ears like a bat, man, like radar. So in order to get away with singing someone else's part, you'd really have to get it down. Or else he'd know.'

The frantic, paranoiac bustle of 'Out Ta Get Me' was another autobiographical number inspired by Axl's time in various correction centres and what he called 'weekend jailhouses' back in Lafayette. Then there was the equally self-explanatory 'You're Crazy', at Clink's urging, recorded at twice the speed of the semi-acoustic original they'd sketched out at their gigs, but no less menacing, the perspiring narrator of the song searching forlornly for love in a world that was much too dark.

Not all the songs were so full of doom and gloom, though. 'Nightrain', a paean to the ephemeral joys of the cheap 'bum's wine' it was named after – the only drink the band could regularly afford in the days before they were signed – was comparatively light-hearted, while tracks like 'Sweet Child' and, less grandly, 'Think About You' – though played at the tempo of an insult, a surprisingly pretty song, Axl poking a small tentative smile through the clouds – were clearly love songs.

After 'Sweet Child', perhaps the most glorious moment on an album apparently busting at its seams with venom and depravity, was 'Paradise City', the song Slash had already worked into shape from the careless line Duff brought with him from Seattle. Full of nostalgia for a place and time that probably only ever existed in newspapers and bad movies, 'Paradise City' was also the best-crafted anthem to an all-American rock aesthetic since Lynyrd Skynyrd's 'Freebird', Slash pumping out the breaks with his knee, Axl as theatrical as the Stars and Stripes itself. 'When you watch the news and you see what's going on everywhere else,' said Slash, '[LA] *is* fucking paradise . . . You can get away with murder here. I'm just waiting for this place to self-destruct and the record companies to drop off into the ocean and everything will mean nothing.'

The only weak moment came on 'Anything Goes', the sole survivor from Axl and Izzy's Hollywood Rose days, albeit refurbished with a more incandescent riff and better, more knowing lyrics. Nevertheless, compared to the immaculately dishevelled material surrounding it, the song never quite matches up, sounding exactly like what it is: a filler. But it was the ultimate track, 'Rocket Queen', that fittingly brought the first Guns N' Roses album to its fraught and dazzling climax; the last ace in an already loaded deck, the band simply playing out of their skins. Again, it came from the seemingly fathomless file of Axl's sordid true-life tales. 'I'm singing as if it's me, but it's about this girl I know,' he said. 'I'm singing as though I was in her shoes, and then at the end of the song I'm singing the song to her. The girl it's written about, her life is history now,' he added melodramatically. What did he mean? 'I mean, she's alive but there's not much left of it. Since I've been in LA I've lost five or six friends that I used to hang with every day. It's a fucked thing.'

Which 'five or six friends' has never been documented and he may have been exaggerating. Nor did Axl ever explain why he felt the need to augment the track with the sounds of him having sex with a stripper. As respected engineer Steve Thompson, who mixed the finished tapes with his regular partner back then Michael Barbiero, later claimed, 'Axl wanted some pornographic sounds in "Rocket Queen" so he brought a girl in and they had sex in the studio. We wound up recording about thirty minutes of sex noises. If you listen to the [guitar] break on "Rocket Queen", it's in there.' More used to working with classy pop artists like Whitney Houston and Simply Red, Michael Barbiero was less sanguine about the whole process. 'I didn't want to be around for recording a girl getting fucked. That wasn't the high point of my career. So I set up the mikes and had my assistant record it. If you look at the record, it says, "Victor 'the fuckin' engineer' Deyglio". So it's literal.' Axl and the band simply thought it was funny. Or as Duff later put it, 'She was a goer. She knew how to work a microphone.'

When, in December 1986, all the tracks had finally been recorded, Mike Clink says he felt certain both he and the band had excelled themselves and that the album would be a success, despite its obvious commercial deficiencies. 'I said to Tom Zutaut at Geffen, "This is going to sell two million copies." He said, "No, it's gonna sell five million!"' According to Barbiero, 'Sweet Child O' Mine' had 'sounded like a hit to all of us. So much so that I remember Axl asking me when we were finished if I thought the album would actually sell. I told him that, despite the fact that it was nothing like what was on the radio, I thought it would go gold [500,000 US sales]. I was only off by twenty million records.'

All the finished album needed now was a title. It was Axl who came up with the perfect suggestion, lifting the title from a cartoon-like painting by legendary LA imagist artist Robert Williams (which the singer owned a postcard of), titled *Appetite for Destruction*. Axl liked the picture so much he would also try and use it as the album's cover art. Depicting a robot standing over an apparently sexually assaulted woman, her shirt torn, scratch marks on her exposed breasts, her panties around her calves, while above the scene hovered an avenging vision of hell with red claws and dagger teeth, it perfectly summed up for Axl what the album's content was all about.

Born in Albuquerque, New Mexico, where he grew up on a diet of EC Comics and his father's stock car racing, Robert Williams is now recognized as one of the most controversial American painters of the twentieth century. He began his career in the late 1960s as part of the groundbreaking Zap Collective comics artists, along with other underground cartoonists such as Robert Crumb and 'Bid Daddy' Ed Roth, mixing up images of Californian car culture, future-shock apocalypticism and 'outsider' art to create a new genre of psychedelic imagery defiantly unbeholden to the strictures of mainstream 'fine art' – a world which Williams openly abhorred. His earliest 'canvasses' were the hot rods, motorcycles, billboard ads and T-shirts he grew up surrounded by. The fact that his later painting *Appetite For Destruction* was destined to become his most famous work was a double-edged sword. While it brought him new levels of fame and notoriety, it also obscured the seriousness of much of his art. These days, however, his oil paintings are shown in smart galleries and command fees of tens of thousands of dollars.

Anxious not to lose the momentum gathering around the band, Geffen came up with the idea of releasing a live vinyl EP as a stop-gap until they were ready to release the first Guns N' Roses recordings proper, in six months' time. Entitled *Live?!*@ Like a Suicide*, it was released on Christmas Eve in a 'strictly limited edition' of 10,000, ostensibly on the band's own Uzi Suicide label (in reality, a simple marketing device from Geffen who pressed and distributed it). The EP featured four of the numbers from their current live set not intended for inclusion on the forthcoming album: two of their older compositions, 'Reckless' and 'Move To The City', plus covers of Aerosmith's 'Mama Kin' and Rose Tattoo's 'Nice Boys Don't Play Rock'n'Roll'.

Recorded one hot and overwrought night at a club date in Hollywood earlier in the year and 'produced' by the band themselves – i.e. taken straight from a cassette recorded on the live mixing desk – as a first bruised statement of intent, *Live?!*@* *Like a Suicide* announced the presence of Guns N' Roses to the rock world. A year on from Live Aid, the biggest-selling rock album in the world in 1986 was Bon Jovi's breakout hit, *Slippery When Wet*: clean-cut, radio-friendly and about as controversial as a glass of milk; the apotheosis of everything the safe dollar-conscious music scene of the mid-1980s had come to represent.

From the dumb, squalling announcement of a drunken roadie at the start of side one, 'HEY, FUCKERS, SUCK ON GUNS N' FUCKIN' ROSES!' *Live?!*@* *Like a Suicide* was everything the 1980s were not supposed to be about. From the way Steven machine-guns the band into the riff to 'Reckless Life' to the grungy power-chords Slash loosens the teeth with on 'Mama Kin', Axl berating the audience, 'This is a song about your fuckin' mother!', it was clear Guns N' Roses, unlike most of the self-styled bad boys then crowding Sunset Strip, really were working without a safety net; and even preferred it that way. Dedicated on the sleeve to 'all the people who helped keep us alive', all 10,000 copies of the *Live?!*@* *Like a Suicide* EP, only a few of which made it across to Britain and Europe, quickly sold out. As Izzy commented, maybe somewhat disingenuously at the time, 'We felt that all the people who saw us from the beginning should have a chance to get our early stuff on record. It's like an expensive dedication to all the kids who helped us get going when we had no money.'

Be that as it may, the cumulative effect of the EP was to attract the attention of rock critics on both sides of the Atlantic, which it did spectacularly. Particularly in the UK where it was regarded as the choicest slice of lowlife rock'n'roll to emerge out of LA since Mötley Crüe's self-consciously sleazy debut, *Too Fast For Love*, four years before. It was inevitable, given the inclusion of 'Mama Kin', that comparisons with 1970s-era Aerosmith were also rife. The band, however, took any mention of themselves and one of their great heroes in the same sentence as a huge compliment. 'What I always liked about them was that they weren't the guys you'd want to meet at the end of an alley if you'd had a disagreement,' said Axl. 'I always wanted to come out of America with that same attitude. They were the only band that the people who lived in my city in Indiana would accept wearing make-up and dressing cool. These people thought the Stones were fags. But everybody liked Aerosmith.'

Their signing to Geffen, then becoming one of the most powerful rock labels in America, also brought the band their first headlines in the national music press. Early quotes included such typically self-aggrandizing gems from Slash as: 'I don't care if you think I'm big-headed about it, but this is the only rock'n'roll band to come out of LA that's real and the kids know it.' Or Axl's own equally strident proclamation that: 'They haven't seen anything like us in the last ten years!'

Meanwhile, life offstage continued as before. On 18 March 1987, just ten days short of the anniversary of their signing to Geffen, three LAPD squad cars pulled up outside the crumbling two-story building in West Hollywood that the band, along with their ever-expanding coterie of friends, hangers-on and groupies, still called home. Inside, bags of trash piled up, empty bottles and overflowing ashtrays littered the floors, a terrible stink rising from the stained carpets. This was hardly the first time an LAPD squad car had been called to the scene, either by exasperated neighbours or concerned passers-by. Either the party had gotten out of hand or the cops were on a 'fishing expedition', knowing it was a likely venue for drugs. Already well known in the 'hood, Guns N' Roses spelled trouble.

When the cops arrived on that particular spring afternoon, the band was gathered on the front porch for a photo session with Axl's friend Robert John. Axl had persuaded Geffen to commission the photographer to take some suitably evocative portraits for the inner sleeve of the forthcoming album, a rough mix of which was thundering in the background as they stood around posing. One of the cops stepped over the broken furniture on the front lawn and demanded the band either turn the music down to a level more tolerable for their put-upon neighbours or find themselves accompanying him downtown. They dutifully turned the music down. 'The West Hollywood sheriffs have got to be the biggest fucking pig-faces I've ever known,' grumbled Izzy as the squad cars eventually pulled away.

With the final mix of the album – now officially titled *Appetite*

For Destruction – complete, Geffen pencilled-in a mid-summer release date and plans were put in place for the band to go on tour for the first time. Shrewdly, they decided to preface their first full-scale US tour with three dates in England, at the famous Marquee Club on London's Wardour Street, scheduled for 19, 22 and 28 June. Not only were these the band's first shows in the UK, but with the exception of the British-born Slash it was also the first time any of them had travelled outside America. Well versed in rock history and iconography – 'We were excited because we all knew about the Marquee,' said Slash, 'and all the bands that had played there like Zeppelin and Bowie' – for Axl especially, the trip to London would be a major source of self-validation. London was where Elton John and Queen were from. The city where nearly all the rock music he most loved had originated. If he could make it there, that really would be something to write on a postcard and send to the folks back home.

Strangely, considering they hadn't even released their first album yet, the UK music press lost no time making the most of the bad-boy reputation the band had spent so long nurturing back home in LA, and ran with it to an almost unprecedented degree for an act barely known to their readers. Aided by a series of press releases similar to the ones Geffen had issued in America – 'They'll make it if they survive!' etc. – their imminent arrival in Britain brought on a rash of dubious press stories. Everything from a rumour that the band had already broken up (a tale which would be repeated ad infinitum over the next few years until, finally, it came true) to, most disturbing of all, a news report that Axl had been admitted to LA's Cedar Sinai hospital where he'd undergone electro-convulsive treatment after being arrested in a brawl outside a club in Hollywood. 'It just happened real quickly,' he was reported as saying. 'I got hit on the head by a cop and I guess I just blacked out. Two days later I woke up in hospital.' None of it was true, but it proved useful in helping to shift tickets for those three upcoming Marquee dates.

Never slow to jump on a bandwagon, Britain's notoriously scandal-mongering tabloid press also got in on the act. 'A rock band even nastier than the Beastie Boys is heading for Britain!' shrieked a June headline in the *Star*. According to the accompanying story, 'Los Angeles based Guns N' Roses are led by the outrageous W. Axl Rose, who has an endearing habit of butchering dogs . . . He is on record as saying: "I have a personal disgust for small dogs, like poodles. Everything about them means that I must kill them."' It's said that Axl laughed the first time he heard the story, but saw less of the funny side as he read on: 'The other two [*sic*] members of the group are as sleazy as their crackpot leader. Guitarist Slash and bass player Duff McKagan claim they have been on a boozing binge for two years. Says Slash: "When we get up in the morning our hands are shaking like windmills . . ."' Preposterous though the stories were they had the requisite effect and by the night of the band's first Marquee show the line outside the club stretched all the way to Oxford Street. 'It was hilarious!' Duff laughed. 'But we knew our rock history. We knew how these things worked.' They understood, too, that 'people were getting turned off with all the stories that came out about us in the press even before our first record came out. Hell, I don't blame 'em,' though he added they 'were very confident about the record' they were about to release.

To coincide with the dates, on 15 June Geffen rush-released two tracks from the forthcoming album – 'It's So Easy' and 'Mr Brownstone' – as a double A-sided single. Strewn as it was with expletives, Geffen knew the record would have no chance of being played on radio or TV (hence the lack of accompanying video at that stage). But as Jo Bolson, then working for Geffen in London, later told me, 'We knew the music press would pick up on it, which they did, and that it would reinforce the band's reputation as being wild and out there, so it did its job. It also sold quite well. We only pressed up about 10,000 copies initially anyway.' All of which would sell out, turning the original pressing into a collector's item. Certainly, by the staid standards of the time both 'It's So Easy' and 'Mr Brownstone' stood out as wilfully obnoxious, totally without hope of commercial success, and yet all the more thrilling for that. Clearly, Bon Jovi or Whitesnake – the two biggest-selling rock bands in the world that year – this was not.

'It's great to be in fuckin' England, finally,' Axl told the audience from the stage that first night, as Slash wrung the life out of the closing, snarling chords to set-opener 'Reckless Life'. At first the capacity Marquee crowd failed to respond in kind and a hail of spit and plastic beer glasses rained down on the stage as the band moved quickly into 'Out Ta Get Me'. Losing patience, Axl brought the number to a premature close and addressed the hecklers directly. 'Hey, if you wanna keep throwin' things we're gonna fuckin' leave,' he yelled, his eyes wide with anger. 'So whaddaya think?' he challenged. Another glass clattered noisily into Steven's drum kit. 'Hey, fuck you, pussy!' Axl screamed, pointing his finger angrily at the drunken culprit and yelling more obscenities out of the microphone's range.

It was an inauspicious beginning and the set went downhill from there. By the end of the third number, the aptly titled 'Anything Goes', the barrage of abuse from the audience slowed to a trickle but the damage was done, Axl's concentration broken by the over-impatient Friday night crowd. Though he didn't walk off, the way he surely would have just a year later, Axl felt the show was a disaster on every level, for the band and the fans who had queued to see them do their best, but most of all for him personally. He had dreamed all his life of playing in London. Now he was actually here doing it, and it had been 'a total nightmare'.

A fact reflected in the uniformly dreadful reviews that appeared in both *Kerrang!* and the *NME* a few days later. The *NME* review, written by future editor Steve Sutherland, the band largely shrugged off as it seemed to be less about the show and more an excuse for the writer to make fun of them. Showing his characteristic absence of humour when it came to such things, Axl took it upon himself to phone the recalcitrant Sutherland. As the writer later wrote, having been informed that the singer 'would like to call round for a frank exchange of opinions', he hastily vanished from the *NME* office and took 'an early lunch'.

Much more upsetting for Axl was the review that appeared in *Kerrang!*, in which Xavier Russell, the same writer who had previously heaped praise on the *Live?!*@* Like a Suicide* EP, wrote that 'Guns N' Roses blew it, pure and simple.' He did add, presciently, that the forthcoming *Appetite for Destruction* album was 'truly wonderful' and that he blamed the band's poor performance at the Marquee on 'those beer cans that were hurled at Axl'. It was a view the band themselves shared. The *Kerrang!* review also hurt more because, as Axl himself would tell me when they returned to tour the UK a few months later, 'It was the first magazine that really came out and supported us big time. When you said we were good, I believed you guys. So if you say a gig sucks, I believe that too.'

Kerrang! certainly went out of its way to nurture a relationship with the band in the early days, to the point of commissioning a second review, this time of the third and much better show at the Marquee on 28 June. The magazine described it as 'raw, savage, furious, emotional, dangerous, rebellious, vibrant, hungry, intoxicating' and concluded by placing the band firmly in the tradition of 'the Stones, Aerosmith, Rose Tattoo, Sex Pistols, Motörhead [and] AC/DC.'

Still stinging from the original review, Axl sardonically dedicated 'Out Ta Get Me' that night to 'all the critics at the back'. Wearing a 'Fuck Dancing, Let's Fuck' T-shirt, he then went on to lead the band through a genuinely enthralling performance. Slash, his face buried in his mop of dark curls, kick-starting the riff to 'It's So Easy' as Axl swayed like an angry rattlesnake getting ready to strike, eyes slitted, voice growling, Izzy, Duff and Steven leaning into the beat, teasing out the riffs then nailing them. For the encores they cranked out a white-hot version of 'Whole Lotta Rosie' to rival even that of AC/DC's splendidly hoary original, Slash and Duff bringing the number to a calamitous end by stage-diving into the audience. They then raised eyebrows by doing the same with Bob Dylan's 'Knockin' on Heaven's Door', the first time they had ever played the song live.

Naturally, their week in London was not without its share of incidents. Slash got drunk and caused a furore at a party to celebrate the release of *Hearts of Fire*, a new movie starring Rupert Everett and Bob Dylan. Axl had trouble with in-store security guards on the steps of Tower Records at Piccadilly Circus. He went there with Alan Niven and Tom Zutaut but was feeling weak from the combined effects of jet-lag and an antihistamine pill he'd taken earlier in the evening to relieve congestion. The security guards became agitated when they found him sitting on the steps of the entrance, head in hands, clutching an Eagles tape he had just purchased, and they demanded that he move. Fortunately Niven and Zutaut were on hand to smooth things over.

All in all, that first trip to England was looked back on by the band as a good time in their lives, a grand adventure. All three of the shows were recorded and several of the numbers ended up as B-sides and bonus tracks on a variety of twelve-inch singles and picture-discs released over the next two years. More than anything, it was a relief to get out of LA, and certainly for Axl. 'In LA, you look out at a crowd of 700 people and you know 300 of them. This person loves you, this one hates you and this one's mad at you because you owe him five bucks. You're mad at another 'cos he owes you twenty-five . . .' He shook his head. 'When I'm onstage, that's when I get to take what I'm worth to the public. When I'm singing a line, I'm thinking of the feelings that made me come up with the song in the first place. At the same time, I think about how I feel singing those words now, and how those words are gonna hit people in the crowd.' Maybe, he added, that was why 'I might be known as histrionic, 'cos I go full out.' Maybe . . .

What drove him, he said, wasn't just the headlong plunge into hedonism the publicity blurb always suggested. 'The truth,' he said, was that when he watched MTV it was 'hard not to throw shit at the TV set because it's so fuckin' boring. Even the bands in LA, the whole music industry . . . It's new to us, this business and we meet people and they say do this, do that, and we say, fuck it, fuck you. Because it's just not us; we do whatever we want to do.'

As planned, the three Marquee dates also proved the ideal media launch-pad for the release of *Appetite* the following month. Before the Marquee shows, Guns N' Roses had been just another tragically glammed-up LA band, their legend extending only as far as the narcissistic environs of the West Hollywood club scene that spawned them. After the Marquee, as Izzy put it: 'Everything just took off. Word spread and we had a platform at last.'

The former *Sounds* journalist Peter Makowski, who hung out with them at the crowded Kensington apartment they rented during their ten-day stay in London, recalls: 'There wasn't much to judge them on musically yet, just the EP and a single that came out the week of the shows. The excitement came more from their image and the way they instantly connected with an audience. Rock was going through a very safe phase, Bon Jovi were the big sensation, Iron Maiden still ruled. Guns N' Roses appealed to the fans left cold by that stuff. The disaffected punk and metal fans that were hungry for something a bit more real, and suddenly here it was at last.'

Offstage, he says, the band 'seemed like a fairly normal bunch of people. I took Izzy to Ladbroke Grove to buy some reggae albums, and got to know Axl a little bit. He was the quietest of the bunch, almost shy, I thought, if you can imagine that now. In terms of drugs, there was a fair bit of drinking but I never saw them use anything heavy. Then, a few days after the first show, Slash phoned one night to ask if I could get him "anything". I thought he meant hash and I said I'd see what I could do. Then Izzy rang and said, "Whatever you do, don't get Slash any gear" – meaning heroin. "He's only just stopped and it's too risky." That was the first time I realized they might have a problem.'

The Marquee shows led to their first extended press exposure outside the US, with *Kerrang!* again leading the way, writer Sylvie Simmons describing them neatly as 'The nearest thing to a street band in a city where there's nothing but boulevards and freeways . . . Guns N' Roses stalk through your every silk scarf fantasy and rub you raw like Piranhas in a Jacuzzi.' Asked for their musical influences, Axl talked about how they all had *Never Mind The Bollocks* by the Sex Pistols and Aerosmith's *Rocks*, and that right then they were listening a lot to *Exile On Main Street* by the Stones and that Duff was 'a real big Johnny Thunders fanatic', while Slash was big into Motörhead. 'We have pieces of everything in our band,' Axl boasted. 'We try and find a way to bring it all out rather than limit ourselves into one frame. You don't see a lot of that any more – Queen used to do it, and Zeppelin, but nowadays people tend to stay in one vein.'

Prompted to explain what would-be fans could expect on the forthcoming album, Axl talked about how he sang 'in about five or six different voices' and how there was a ballad on the album and one song which he bafflingly described as 'like Black Sabbath goes to Ireland'. But then, he added, 'there's two guitar players that play very different from each other – one plays an '80s blues electric guitar and the other guy's completely into Andy McCoy and Keith Richards – and they've figured out a way to fit it together.' Axl would later trot out similar quotes in other interviews from that time. 'We're a bad-boy band,' he would say with a straight face. 'We're not afraid to go to excess with substances, sexually and everything else. A lot of people are afraid to be that way. We're not.' What about their apparent glam influences – the make-up and big hair that they shared with other LA-based bands like Poison? Axl was having none of it. 'We don't want to associate ourselves with glam,' he said. 'And the main reason is because that's what Poison associates themselves with.' None of the band liked Poison, he said. Far from sharing anything with them, they had virtually copied their whole act from Guns N' Roses: 'They used to come to our shows before they ever played a gig.' But the 'big' hair, surely he couldn't claim all the credit for that? It was more of a 1980s Hollywood thing? Again, he wasn't having it. 'The only reason I put my hair up,' he said exasperatedly, 'is because Izzy had these pictures of Hanoi Rocks and they were cool, and because we hung out with this guy who studied *Vogue* magazine hairstyles and was really into doing hair.'

The animosity that existed then between Guns N' Roses and Poison was fuelled further, Slash said, when guitarist C.C. DeVille took to wearing a top hat on stage. Even though Poison beat them to it in terms of releasing an album and having a big hit, he felt C.C. had stolen the idea from him. 'Listen, I'm not saying I was the first rock'n'roller to wear a top hat onstage,' he told me. 'But look, man, C.C. is the type of guy who probably didn't even know what a top hat was until he saw me wearing one. You know, I caught up with him one night in the Rainbow, and I just told him quietly, "If I ever see you wearing a top hat onstage again I'm gonna shoot you!" He freaked, man! But sometimes you just gotta draw the line for people.'

The feud with Poison may have been merely a side-issue but it was also a portent of the way Axl's relationships would all

eventually distil into those who were either for or against him –
and the very public way he had of dealing with such issues.

Any serious comparisons with Poison or indeed any other LA
band of the time went out the window, however, once *Appetite
For Destruction* was officially released in America on 31 July
1987. Axl was ecstatic. Here was the proof he needed that the
folks back home had been wrong all along. As he put it in the
final sentence of the fifty-lines worth of dedications on the original
vinyl sleeve: 'Guns N' Roses would like to thank . . . the teachers,
preachers, cops and elders who never believed.' However, there
were also thank yous buried in the middle to both his stepfather,
L. Stephen, and his mother, Sharon, though again the likelihood is
that he was merely making a sardonic point. The only encouragement he'd ever received from these quarters, he would tell
friends, had been to get out of town and never come back. If
Appetite For Destruction had sold only a handful of copies, it
would at least prove that he hadn't been kidding around when he
said he was going to do things his way, and fuck what the rest of
yous thinks.

Musically, however, most people agreed that *Appetite* showed
that here was one LA band whose talent was bigger than the
heels of their cowboy boots. Inevitably, the reviews it attracted
tended to focus on the band's all-too-convincing ability to look
and sound mean. 'This is attitude music through-and-through,'
crowed *Kerrang!*, describing Axl and the band as 'real raunch
rebels'. But while that was certainly true on one level, such
reviews failed to capture the real essence of what the album was
all about – the very thing that actually made it interesting. Indeed,
to this day the music press will explain how it was the band's
unfalteringly street-tough approach that attracted so many fans,
moths left powerless by the intense heat of their flame. In fact,
that was only the starting point for the band's popularity.

The media always fall for a tough-guy image because that's
what tends to sell newspapers and magazines. But thirty-five
million people don't buy the same album because of anything as
dispensable as 'attitude'. It certainly wasn't why so many millions
would buy Nirvana's *Nevermind* album four years later, or why
Oasis became so massively popular in the years that followed

Kurt Cobain's suicide. In fact, people will only buy an album in the multi-millions when it is packed full of top-drawer pop hits. Especially if there's a top-drawer ballad or love song included.

In the same way that Led Zeppelin will always be remembered first and foremost for the haunting 'Stairway To Heaven', and why the Beatles' most superlative moments are still regarded as tracks like 'Yesterday' or 'A Day In The Life' – and arguably why the Rolling Stones, authors of so many classic uptempo rock songs but few similarly momentous ballads, are not held in the same critical regard as the Beatles – *Appetite* would owe its elevated place in rock history not to flagrantly provocative tracks like 'It's So Easy' or 'Rocket Queen' but to the golden light shed by 'Sweet Child O' Mine', 'Paradise City' and 'Welcome To The Jungle'. Indeed, if the band had had the foresight to ditch a few of the clearly less important songs like 'Anything Goes', 'Think About You', 'Out Ta Get Me' and the needlessly speeded-up 'You're Crazy', in favour of the four acoustic-driven tracks they recorded soon after for the expanded 1988 reissue of their live EP – the sublime 'Patience', the so-hurtful-it's-funny 'Used To Love Her', the original lengthier, utterly hypnotic 'You're Crazy' and the plainly incendiary but undeniably compelling 'One In A Million' – they would arguably have released one of the greatest debut albums of all time, ready to stand alongside comparably titanic debuts such as those by Led Zeppelin or the Velvet Underground.

As it is, *Appetite* suffers because it puts all its eggs in one basket. The band was perhaps trying too hard to live up to that spuriously flattering 'most dangerous band in the world' tag. Much sense of quality control was slung out the window, and it tended to obscure the fact that along with it went any attempt to fit in with the prevailing commercial trends of the existing 1980s 'hair' metal scene which the band is still, to this day, unfairly considered figureheads for. Certainly, if you were judging the book by its cover there would be plenty to put off the casual observer, including the sight of Robert Williams' disturbing vision of a post-coital robot and its aghast victim causing several major US retail chains to refuse to stock the album, even though 30,000 copies had already been pressed and shipped to their stores.

'All that people saw was a girl with her knickers pulled down – not the karmic retribution in it,' Alan Niven claimed. But Robert Williams himself had foreseen the problems the band would have by using his painting. 'I told Axl he was going to get into trouble,' he says now. As soon as they'd asked him if they could use the title of the painting, he says 'I knew there'd be a problem.' Although he admits he was thinking more of the trouble it would cause him, his main concern was that, 'None of the guys in this band were too articulate, so [I knew] they would direct the media to me to defend the cover.'

In the event, Geffen circumnavigated the problem by moving the image on new pressings of the album from the front cover to the inside, while the front was freshly adorned with another cartoon-like image – a plain black sleeve featuring Axl's tattoo of a death's-head cross studded with five skulls, each of which represented a different member of the band. The alternative 'black sleeve' was also made available to record retailers in Britain after W.H. Smith banned the original cover from their shelves and Virgin Megastore in London refused an in-store display.

Of course, the critics that bothered to review it – neither *Rolling Stone* nor any other high-profile mainstream magazine in the US saw fit to comment – took the whole thing at face-value, either lavishing praise or dismissing it completely. This was 'heavy metal' after all, wasn't it? Not the sort of thing the big boys of the music press took seriously, which was a shame because they missed a unique opportunity. Whatever one's take on deliberately outré tracks like 'My Michelle' or 'It's So Easy', the album as a whole so defied the conventions of rock in the 1980s that, like the Sex Pistols before them and Nirvana soon after, the sudden arrival of the sleazy Guns N' Roses single-handedly redrafted the rock map. It was the first truly potent chronicle of urban street life that existed outside of the realms of hip-hop and rap since the decade began, a genuine return to the raw, untamed, visceral values of rock in its pre-MTV heyday.

Post the advent of AIDS and Reagan, and into the third-term of Thatcher, rock was a shiny, happy, big-haired thing that apparently no longer needed drug dealers and groupies to sustain it. Stars like Jon Bon Jovi, Def Leppard's Joe Elliot, and even that notorious ladies' man David 'Whitesnake' Coverdale, were all married and drinking mineral water. Almost every rock band I interviewed avoided the subject of drugs completely, whatever the reality I had witnessed behind the scenes. Instead, they were now into working out, they said, along with cosmetic surgery, liposuction, hair-weaves and getting a good night's sleep. Marketing was more important than A&R; videos more 'market penetrative' than tours. Frankly, the whole thing bored me to tears. I hadn't begun writing about rock to find myself discussing demographics with people too uptight to take a drink.

Then came Guns N' Roses, and how refreshing it was to find a band that not only let it all hang out but appeared talented enough to make it mean something too. Ever since Live Aid two years before, rock had become obliged to embrace a new orthodoxy, encompassing political correctness and a more global effort to tackle such issues as famine relief in Africa, AIDS and Nancy Reagan's self-aggrandizing 'Just Say No' campaign. Leading the way for rock's concerned elite were the worthy U2, closely followed by do-gooders like Sting, Peter Gabriel and keen-to-get-in-on-the-act 'pop-rockers' like Bon Jovi. In that context, it felt extraordinarily liberating to hear a band like Guns N' Roses openly complaining of how rock had 'sucked a big fucking dick since the Sex Pistols', as Izzy put it, and whose heroes were supreme drug-monsters like pre-rehab Aerosmith and the permanently-stoned-Keef-era Rolling Stones. How marvellous it was to have a new kid in class like Slash stand there and announce that Mick Jagger 'should have died after *Some Girls*, when he was still cool'.

The outer limits of rock may have been working on its own bad-tempered renaissance with the parallel rise of bands like Metallica and the thrash-metal aesthetic they embodied then quickly abandoned, but Guns N' Roses was the first new rock band to engage mainstream pop tastes that openly derided everything that mainstream appeared to stand for. The first that openly talked of sex and drugs since the decade began. Bands like Def Leppard and Bon Jovi didn't sing songs about shooting heroin and fucking porn stars. Axl Rose did. And that was tremendously courageous, and at that time a breath of foul air in the air-conditioned nightmare that rock had become by 1987.

'What this industry's about in the 1980s is pretty obvious,' said Slash, 'trying to polish everything up. We go against every standard of the industry.' Or as future Nirvana drummer Dave Grohl saw it, 'They were considered fucking outlaws. They were bringing the grit back into rock'n'roll.'

Suddenly everybody wanted to know what they would do next with it . . .

Chapter Five

WAR ALL THE TIME

Not everybody got it straight away. In fact, such deliberate 'outsider' attitudes as the band affected – not least their propensity for swearing in practically all of their songs – threatened to keep them firmly outside of everything, including TV, radio and, by direct correlation, the top forty charts. Indeed, the position they voluntarily put themselves into seemed so impossible even Tom Zutaut began to despair of the album selling enough copies to justify his faith in signing them. David Geffen himself was heard to openly express his doubts, having finally listened to *Appetite For Destruction*, only to find it 'unpleasant'.

Zutaut resolved to work harder at making the whole thing a success, if only a moderate one, encouraging Alan Niven to book a month-long US tour, as well as a return visit to Britain, where the audience relied less on radio and TV exposure and more on the music press, which had been generally warmer than at home in the US. It was a simple plan: the band would have to get their message across in the time-honoured rock style by taking their show direct to the people. Meantime, Zutaut did everything he could to present a brave face to the Geffen promotions department, as if a complete lack of TV and radio exposure was all part of his cunning plan, never missing an opportunity to inform head of promotions, Al Coury, and his staff that Guns N' Roses were going to be huge and that *Appetite* was merely a 'slow-burner'.

Coury remained unconvinced. Despite his team's best efforts, nobody could convince any of the radio stations they routinely approached to take a chance on the band's next single – their first in the US – 'Welcome To The Jungle'. Even MTV, until recently considered by the music industry as the virtual home of 'hair metal', turned its nose up at the 'Welcome To The Jungle' video, shot at the Park Plaza Hotel on Saturday 1 August, the day after the album was released. It wasn't only Guns N' Roses, the programme directors at MTV told Coury; they were cutting back on air-time for all such bands in the belief that the trend had already peaked with Mötley Crüe and Poison. Besides, as Coury told Zutaut after viewing the 'Welcome To The Jungle' video for the first time, 'They're certainly never gonna play this one in church.'

Axl wasn't the kind of person to be assuaged by such arguments. He thought the video was 'killer' and began to pester Alan Niven about why he wasn't doing more to get it aired on national TV. Niven in turn leaned on Zutaut. Why wasn't the A&R man doing more to ensure the video was played, thereby increasing album sales? Zutaut didn't want to unsettle the band by revealing that MTV thought their music was uncommercial but did tell Niven that MTV were 'nervous' of playing the video because of its 'gritty' scenes depicting Axl tied up in a straight-jacket while strapped to an electric chair, violently convulsing in front of several TV screens like Alex in *A Clockwork Orange*, forced to watch endless images of war and brutality. MTV was 'afraid' that if they put such a video into rotation some of the crucial local cable systems that carried their signal would throw the switch and take them off the air. Axl took this as a back-handed compliment and was momentarily placated.

The video was in fact fairly innocuous, opening with a shot of a country bumpkin (Axl) getting off the bus in LA for the first time. Dressed in old-fashioned flared jeans and a backwards baseball cap, Axl is then seen wending his way past drug-dealers and hustlers, looking around with an expression of wide-eyed disbelief as he walks unsteadily towards his fate. He then stops in front of a TV store window, behind which we catch our first glimpse of Slash sitting around slurping from a Jack Daniel's bottle. The rest of the video cuts between the band performing the song in a sweaty club, Axl in full glam mode, his face made up and hair back-combed into a flaming red halo, marching back and forth to the microphone while the others buzz and spin around him, interspersed with more semi-autobiographical scenes of Axl ensnared in the pulsing neon light of the LA half-life.

Given its limited budget and the timorous times in which it was made, it was a good video. With the band touring the US with The Cult, it should have been enough to shoot them several significant rungs up the ladder of success. It was a pity no one who watched MTV in America would get to see it – not yet anyway. It was a different story in Europe, however, where MTV didn't yet exert the same stranglehold on music television. While it was true that most mainstream pop shows would not consider airing it without the record already being in the charts, existing rock shows on the pan-European cable and satellite stations lapped up the chance to show a video by America's most controversial new rock band, and immediately put it on regular rotation. As a result, demand grew for the band outside America and dates were hastily put together, including plans for them to make a return trip to Britain.

Meanwhile, they began promoting the album in America via the only route left open to them – a six-week tour, in August, opening for British rockers The Cult, whose singer, Ian Astbury, had offered them the gig after seeing one of their Marquee shows in London. 'He spent more time in our dressing-room than his own,' Axl said. It was a shrewd bill for the times and Guns N' Roses went down well with The Cult's punk-metal crossover audience. Not that it stopped Axl from getting into trouble again. This time in Atlanta, where police arrested him onstage during the second song for attacking one of the arena security guards who Axl claimed had beaten up the band's friends in the audience. He was held for questioning backstage while the rest of the band was left to get on with their forty-five-minute set as best they could. A roadie was hurriedly hauled on stage and helped out with some of the vocals, while Slash contributed a fifteen-minute guitar solo and Steven managed a longer-than-usual drum solo to fill in the gaps. After the show, Axl was incandescent with rage, claiming he was the victim of trumped-up charges. 'In Atlanta I dived in and I had police saying I hit them,' he was later quoted claiming in *Musician* magazine. 'I never did, but I had to plead guilty because we didn't have any money at the time. Lie? Yes, I guess I did lie once. I lied and said that I hit four cops. I guess we should re-open the case and take me to trial for perjury. But I didn't have $56,000 to pay them off under the table.'

When the dates were over, the plan was to return to Britain, this time for a proper tour opening at theatres and concert halls for Aerosmith – 'a bill made in hell' as Slash gleefully described it. But when Aerosmith pulled out at the last minute and the band was suddenly left with an empty date-sheet, the bold decision was taken to go ahead with some of the dates anyway, with Guns N' Roses headlining their own shows. Even though *Appetite* had barely sold 10,000 in the UK and few of the shows would sell out, Alan Niven talked Axl into seeing the trip as an opportunity to rake in some valuable PR. 'It didn't matter whether we sold out any of the shows or not,' Niven told me, 'I knew the fans would just be grateful that – unlike Aerosmith – Guns N' Roses had actually showed up.'

Fellow LA scene-makers Faster Pussycat, who had also just released their first album, were roped in as support and in October Guns N' Roses arrived in Britain for five dates, beginning at the Rock City in Nottingham and ending seven days later at the Hammersmith Odeon in London. As far as Geffen were concerned, the hope was that in Britain – where sales were fractional compared to the US and therefore it was easier, in theory, to achieve a chart placing – 'Welcome To The Jungle' might just break through, thereby kick-starting a wave of interest back home in the US.

The had tour started on 29 September with a sold-out show at the Markethalle in Hamburg. From there they had played a further club date in West Germany before crossing the border into Holland for a one-nighter at the Paradiso Club in Amsterdam on 2 October. Even though none of them had ever been to Continental Europe before, Axl was already in full flow. Before 'Move To The City', the second song at the Paradiso, he went into a rap about how 'some older generation rock stars' had 'a lot of shit to say' about him and the band. No one was sure what he was talking about, the only clue coming at the end of his tirade when he concluded: 'People like Paul Stanley from Kiss can suck my dick! And some of these old guys that say we're ripping them off, maybe they should listen to some of their earlier albums and remember how to play them!'

Behind the scenes, the Paradiso show was also significant for Steven Adler who now claims it was the first time he succumbed to heroin. 'Let me say for the record that I was no angel,' he told me years later. 'I drank – no, scratch that – could outdrink any of the other guys in the band, including Slash (which is saying a hell of a lot). I once swallowed thirty-two kamikazes and lived to tell about it ... But I never shot smack until we arrived in Amsterdam during our first European tour ... It made me sick to see Slash shoot up. I wouldn't let him do it in front of me.'

After the show in Amsterdam, he says, 'we were bumming around the Red Light District, amazed that hookers actually advertised it in store windows. We stopped by a hash bar, ordered off a menu – I could not believe this! – and got high. On the way out, this Dutch dude recognizes us and invites us to a party. We follow the stranger to his townhouse on one of the canals. Everything's cool until Slash and Izzy disappear into another room. I know what they're doing – and I'm tired of being left out. I walk in and Izzy and Slash are already flying. I turned to Slash and said, "Do me". He ties up my arm and stabs me. Halfway through the syringe, I was already freefalling and told him to take it out. This would be the night I most regret in my life. But at that moment it felt so damn good.'

By the time they arrived in Nottingham the following day, the tour was in full swing. On the flight over, Slash accidentally set fire to his seat with his cigarette, while Faster Pussycat drummer Mark Michals fell asleep on Duff's hotel bed that night, for which his punishment was to be stripped naked, tied up in gaffer tape, bundled into an elevator and sent down to the lobby.

At the Apollo in Manchester the following night the venue was barely half-full, with so few tickets sold in advance that the management ordered the balcony section to be closed off. Even so, the stalls were hardly full: good seats down the front were easy to find and most people stood around as they would in a club. Arriving on stage to scattered applause, interest was slow to build as the band thundered through a truncated sixty-five-minute set. Despite the low-key vibe, it was clear they had progressed considerably since the three high-profile dates at the Marquee back in June. In London they'd gone from ramshackle and disappointing on the first night to quite brilliant by the last, now they immediately made their presence felt as they owned the stage, unafraid of anything or anyone.

Coming on straight after Faster Pussycat, who had seemed fun, this was clearly something else. Not fun. Or certainly not the same kind. This was Bad Fun. Like smoking your first joint or having sex with someone you shouldn't. Axl was clearly in charge, the charismatic ringmaster leading the circus animals out of their cages. To his right, Duff, the tall, bottle-blond whose clean-cut good looks belied his Seattle punk past to the left, Slash, one boot resting on a monitor, firing off riffs with the exuberant abandon of a man pissing his name into the snow. Behind them, sweating and shirtless, Steven, the quintessential blond himbo who liked to 'hit things and get high'. And then – last as always, but hardly least – Izzy, who never really found a permanent place for himself onstage the way the others did, ghosting around at the sides and the back, scaring away crows.

The posturing was familiar, yet what immediately came across was how little this music had to do with the more nonsensical forms that rock and metal had twisted itself into by the late-1980s. In Guns N' Roses' songs there were no dungeons or dragons, no armies of marching men. In their place staggered junkies and sluts ('Mr Brownstone', 'Rocket Queen'), thieves and outcasts ('Welcome To The Jungle', 'My Michelle') – 'mother-fuckers', one and all, as Axl was quick to point out. Even more intriguing, there were also tales of loved ones and lost dreams buried in the dark chaos. 'Paradise City', with its overwhelming sense of yearning, was instantly appealing, right up there with 'All Right Now' and 'Brown Sugar', as one of rock's most uplifting anthems. 'Sweet Child O' Mine', too, suggested a sub-merged vulnerability not immediately obvious in other songs. It was this more transcendent aspect to their music that would eventually enable Guns N' Roses to rise above the tawdry LA scene they sprang from and get them noticed by fans and critics that wouldn't have been caught dead listening to lightweight metal misfits like Mötley Crüe and Poison.

Just as Nirvana would do four years later, Guns N' Roses eschewed contemporary musical mores in favour of what they saw as a more meaningful seventies mien, taking their inspiration as much from Elton John and Freddie Mercury as they did Led Zeppelin and the Rolling Stones. 'We didn't have any defined goals,' Slash says now. 'We just didn't want to be lumped in with the LA scene. We were dying to get away from that. The Who, the Stones, Aerosmith . . . that's what we grew up with. The decadent seventies shit.'

Which was another reason why, in an era when most rock bands more or less copied whatever was already in the charts, hiring the same producers, the same video-makers, even the same songwriters, Guns N' Roses and their remarkably unfriendly approach stood out like a sore thumb. It was a statement that said: this band is different. And 'different' was a quality in despairingly short supply right then. Standing in the dressing-room after the Manchester show, it seemed as though the clock had been turned back fifteen years. It wasn't just the way they were dressed – the pimp hats, polka-dot bandanas and buttonless shirts, the scuffed leather jackets, skull-and-crossbones tattoos and lurid, mock-crucifixion jewellery – it was the way they *were*.

'Hey, man,' Steven said, spying strangers. 'Where can I score some loods?' referring to Quaaludes, drugs du jour for early-1970s American concert-goers; heavy-duty tranquillizers that made walking into walls seem fun.

'You can't get loods in England,' I replied.

'What!' he cried. 'You're fuckin' kidding me! What *can* you get then?'

'Mandrax,' I said. 'Mandies. Or reds – Seconal. That's probably the nearest equivalent.'

'Cool,' he said, 'so how can I get me some red Mandies, dude?'

The guy was clearly on a mission. Then Izzy ambled over. 'Hey, man,' he drawled, 'I smell pot. Who has pot?' Someone passed him the joint and he clung to it like a drunk steadying himself against a lamp-post. I turned to speak to Slash, the only one I'd actually been introduced to. He looked like he'd just stepped off the album cover: black top hat pulled low over a waterfall of dark curls deliberately obscuring his soft brown eyes, holding on tight to a Jack Daniel's bottle like a toddler clinging to its teddy.

'I bet you go to bed with that thing,' I joked.

'Sure,' he said, 'I like to wake up to it, too. It's the only way . . .' He paused and glanced around, '. . . I can handle *this*.'

I was introduced to Axl as we passed on the stairs. Utterly unlike the manically pumped-up banshee that had just bossed the stage, up close he looked surprisingly small, his pinched freckled face and upturned nose giving him a vulnerable quality the stage-lights had kept hidden. Definitely something of the badly mis-treated dog about him, avoiding eye contact, glancing at you warily when he thought you weren't looking. It was hard to believe this was the same guy who had just been arrested for attacking a burly security guard in Atlanta. Controversy was more than just part of the act, it seemed. And yet, of all of the band he seemed to be the most self-contained and most certain of who he was and what he was trying to achieve. The only one who took his time when speaking to you, even if he couldn't quite look you in the eye. 'I wanna thank you and the magazine you're from for everything you've done for this band,' he told me, gripping my hand firmly. 'And I wanna tell you how much it means to me, 'cos I read your shit, man. I know who you are. You coming to see us in London, too?' he asked. By that point, wild horses couldn't have dragged me away.

By contrast, the show at London's Hammersmith Odeon a few nights later was only two hundred tickets short of a sell-out. Onstage, Axl dedicated 'Knockin' On Heaven's Door' to the memory of his friend Todd Crew, bassist in Hollywood band Jetboy, who had also occasionally roadied for Guns N' Roses over the years – that is, when he wasn't working on his heroin habit. Todd went with them to London for their Marquee shows four months before when, unable to score, he drank himself into unconsciousness and missed the whole of the first show. Back in LA, before The Cult dates, they had tried to persuade him to seek professional help for his problems. But between then and their return to Europe, he died from a heroin overdose. Two years later, Axl told *Rolling Stone* that not talking to Todd before he died was one of the biggest regrets of his life. 'I felt a massive need to talk to him out of concern for his well-being. But I wasn't aware enough to realize I didn't have the time I thought I did. I thought I'd have time later . . .'

As Axl was fast discovering, 'later' was a concept fame did not necessarily recognize. There was only the interminable now, and as the band's reputation for danger spread, so the expectations placed on them grew disproportionately. Returning to the US, on 24 October, they made their first appearance on MTV's weekly rock show, *Headbanger's Ball*. Encouraged by the show's producers to smash bits of the set as a prank, Axl and the band took the joke seriously and systematically tore down the whole set. The following week they were back on the road, replacing Whitesnake as the opening act for Mötley Crüe.

In terms of the prevailing Hollyweird rock scene, if Guns N' Roses were the new bad boys in town, Mötley Crüe were then at the height of both their infamy and commercial appeal. Their latest album, *Girls, Girls, Girls*, had reached number two in the US charts and given the band their first significant worldwide hit. Now the relentless drug abuse that had long been part of the Crüe touring experience was reaching its nauseating peak. Putting GN'R on the same bill as the Crüe for weeks at a time was obviously somebody's idea of a good time. It was also the height of irresponsibility.

As drummer Tommy Lee later recalled, 'We had a huge-ass jet, we had endless cash, and we could do whatever the fuck we wanted. *Girls, Girls, Girls* was the raddest time I ever had in my life, or at least I think it was, because nothing stands out but a blur of fucking insanity. We partied like clockwork, bro. You could check the clock in whatever time zone we were in and figure out exactly what kind of shit we were into. For a while, we even had this drug king-pin following the tour bus in an exotic Excalibur with a license plate that said "DEALER". Whenever we got out of the bus, he would suddenly appear with his diamond-packed Rolex, gold chains and a token couple of bitches on each arm, throwing bindles of coke to everyone in the band and crew. He was the pimpest fucking drug-dealer ever and he always had his party hat on. But the record company flipped out and told us he had to go because he was a magnet for cops and trouble. We were sorry to see him leave, but fucking dealers and pimps and partied-out freaks were a dime a dozen on that tour.

Every day was a battle between a band bent on destruction and a record company determined to keep us in check.'

Every night after the show the two bands would hang out together. A particularly unholy alliance was formed between Slash, Nikki Sixx and Steven Adler, who went out together every night and caused mayhem in the clubs and bars of whatever unfortunate Midwestern town the tour happened to be in. The trio broke up only after Steven fractured his hand, apparently in a nasty bar-room brawl (Cinderella drummer Fred Coury was hastily drafted in for the remainder of the dates), and Slash was officially warned by the Crüe's management that his band would be off the tour if he didn't curtail his carousing with the wayward Crüe leader. Which he did – for almost forty-eight hours. The real break-up occurred after Nikki overdosed after shooting-up smack one night. Slash and Steven discovered him comatose on the floor of his hotel room. Slash called the paramedics while Steven pulled the needle out of Nikki's arm and dragged his unconscious body into the shower, turned on the cold water and began slapping him in the face trying to bring him around. The only trouble was Steven's arm was still in plaster at the time, and when Nikki rang him the next day to thank him for saving his life, he asked: 'Dude, what happened? My face is killing me.'

The 'fun' continued long after the tour was over. On New Year's Eve, Slash again found himself embroiled in another near-death experience involving the unrepentant Mötley bass player. Killing time back in LA after a spate of December shows supporting Alice Cooper, the band – now officially homeless, having given up the rented shack they'd been living in before the tour started – was staying at the Franklin Plaza Hotel. Axl immediately went back to hanging out with the same circle of friends, while Duff and Steven busied themselves 'chasing pussy'. Izzy and Slash also returned to doing what they did best: scoring smack and getting fucked up.

When Nikki called him that night Slash, as ever, was ready to party. As Nikki recalled fifteen years later in *The Dirt*, he turned up that night in the back of a silver limousine, along with Rätt guitarist Robbin Crosby. Having already snorted a gram of coke between them, Nikki threw up on the way over. 'I wiped the chunks off on an antique beaver-hair-covered top hat I had bought for Slash and gave it to him at his door along with a bottle of whiskey,' says Nikki. 'Some of the guys in Megadeth were also staying at the hotel, so we all piled into the limo. Robbin scored some junk from his dealer, who wasn't too happy about the conspicuous limo outside his house, and we did drugs until our minds went blank.'

They spent the rest of the evening club-crawling. Back at Slash's hotel later that night, things took a turn for the worse. As Nikki relates, 'Back at the Franklin, Robbin's dealer was waiting. He said he had gotten some sweet Persian heroin while we were gone, and asked if I wanted some. "Yeah", I told him. "But you do it." By that point in the evening, I was too sloppy fucked up to get myself off . . . He rolled up my sleeve, tied off my arm with a rubber tube, and plunged the Persian into my veins. The heroin raced to my heart, exploded all over my body, and in an instant I was blue . . .'

Details of what happened next are understandably hazy. Nikki later recalled waking up in hospital to overhear a paramedic saying, 'We're losing him . . .' Slash, meanwhile, had gotten the hell out of Dodge – with a little help from a guardian angel in the form of an older lady friend who always allowed him to crash in the spare room at her condominium when he didn't have anywhere else to stay. Freaked out at finding Nikki comatose on the floor of his hotel room – again – a barely coherent Slash had phoned his friend and begged her to come and get him. Sizing up the situation immediately, the friend rushed downtown to the hotel, grabbed Slash, dialled 911 for an ambulance for Nikki and speedily drove off again. By the time they got back to her place, however, the rumour was already doing the rounds among the Hollywood cognoscenti that Nikki was dead.

Fortunately, Nikki hadn't died, he'd just stopped breathing for a couple of minutes – an incident later immortalized in the Mötley Crüe song 'Kick-Start My Heart'. But the situation had been so desperately close to disaster that it briefly shocked Slash into swearing off heroin. A promise that lasted about a month – or the time it took for him and the band to get back on the road, now headlining the same venues they had performed in as support on The Cult's tour five months earlier.

Current UK flavour of the month Zodiac Mindwarp was signed on as special guest, with German sheet-metallists Udo booked as the opening act. Looking for ways to keep the band out of trouble before the tour started on 31 January, Alan Niven booked them into Rumbo Studios again with Mike Clink to cut various acoustic-based numbers they'd been messing around with for years: 'Patience', 'One In A Million', 'Used To Love Her', 'Corn Chucker' and the slower more sinister original of 'You're Crazy' from the *Appetite* album. These were recorded mostly 'as live' in the studio, and were intended to be used as 'future B-sides, or possibly an EP', as Axl explained whenever anybody asked.

The only real concern was that the *Appetite* album had already peaked, with US sales tapering off at approximately 200,000. Not bad for a debut – especially since there was virtually no TV or radio support – but hardly scintillating. Tom Zutaut had to admit he was disappointed. He continued to harass the promotions department, but even Geffen president Eddie Rosenblatt told him he thought the album had done all it was going to, and to concentrate instead in building these new acoustic recordings into the basis of a follow-up album. Zutaut refused to listen. 'No way, this record's just beginning,' he told Rosenblatt. 'We haven't even scratched the surface yet. There's a number-one single that is buried on the second side of the album. The promotion people have not even listened to it!' Zutaut was referring to 'Sweet Child O' Mine', but by then neither Rosenblatt nor anyone else at the company was prepared to listen to him.

Exasperated, Zutaut did what he'd done when signing the band and appealed directly to David Geffen. Unconvinced, yet sympathetic to his star A&R man's plight, Geffen asked: 'What is the one thing that I could do to help you?' Zutaut instantly replied: 'It would help if you could get the "Welcome To The Jungle" video played on MTV.'

Geffen said he would do what he could and after Zutaut left his office, he put a call through to his old friend, MTV chief executive Tom Freston. Geffen was one of the few record company executives to have foreseen the impact MTV would have in its earliest days, and Freston had never forgotten the invaluable support he'd received from him. So he agreed, as a personal favour to Geffen, to air the 'Welcome To The Jungle' video. However, there was one proviso: MTV would play it only once, at 3:00 a.m. on the East Coast, midnight on the West Coast. After that, all bets were off.

However, moments after the video aired a week later, the switchboard lit up at the network as their system overloaded with calls for repeat plays from over-excited fans. Within a month, 'Welcome To The Jungle' became one of the most-requested videos on MTV that year. And just as Zutaut had predicted all those months ago, the album finally began to sell with sales leaping to more than 500,000 units almost overnight, thereby earning the band their first gold record.

Although he tried to act cool in front of his friends, Axl was overjoyed. He had already lived so much of the dream he could hardly believe the rest of it might actually come true too. But it did and he had the gold record as proof. The mere thought of it was enough to do strange things to his head. Slowly but surely he was beginning to feel less out of control. Destiny started to feel like something you made into whatever shape you were clever enough to think of. It was a feeling he liked – a lot. Suddenly, he decided, there was to be no stopping him.

With *Appetite* now steadily moving up the US album charts – it was now top twenty – almost all the dates for the January–February tour had already sold out by the time the band went back on the road, where controversy continued to trail after them. With his video now on TV and his album in the charts, Axl was feeling famous for the first time, as well as vindicated. As a result, his behaviour was worsening as he became more and more belligerent, storming offstage in the middle of a song if he didn't think the audience was 'appreciative' enough.

Then Slash and Duff were arrested for brawling in a bar in Seattle, resulting in another postponement. And then, just when they thought they'd seen it all, a fortnight before the end of the tour, according to an article in *Spin Magazine*, Axl refused to leave his hotel room before a show in Phoenix, causing the band to play an ad hoc instrumental set without him. Understandably furious, when the band – led by Steven – got back to the hotel they told Axl he was fired. Refusing to accept his punishment, Axl said he'd already decided he was leaving anyway. He walked out and got a car to the airport. It wasn't the first time anything like this had happened – nor would it be the last – but it had never happened at such an important time for the band. At first the other members were stricken, as the implications of their front man's departure began to sink in. 'For about three days, it really did look like the band was over,' Alan Niven later told me.

But not even Axl was wound up enough to blow the whole deal just as things were starting to cook. Three days later, following a lengthy heart-to-heart on the phone with Slash, he was back in the band. Like a couple that announces their separation to all and sundry then gets back together the very next night, both Axl and the band were mostly embarrassed and refused to say any more about it in public. In private, however, heads were shaken with resignation and the well-worn expression, 'Well, you know Axl . . .' would once again sum up their feelings.

As Steven says now, those early days, when the band's success was just beginning to gather momentum, were 'the greatest time of my life, but one of the guys – I don't need to name him – made it so difficult for us all. Quite often he made the best and most exciting times I'll ever experience feel like a complete pain in the ass. Besides the loneliness and sadness I felt when I was excluded, the worst thing was to play in front of [thousands of] people and have the guy storm offstage in the middle of the first song. With no warning, he'd throw the microphone to the floor then leave. And not come back. Quite rightly, the audience would boo, and it was an awful feeling to know there was nothing the rest of the band could do about the situation. You'd go backstage and get in a fight with the guy. He'd say, "Fuck you" and get on a plane and you'd have to cancel a lot of other shows. It's all coming back to him now because he's the one who looks bad. But at the time it reflected badly on all of us.'

As ever, Axl felt his actions were entirely justifiable. 'I guess I get mad because of some form of fear about my own weaknesses,' he was quoted as saying in *Rolling Stone*. 'Everybody has theirs, and mine happen to be in what I do. And what I do is sing and run and get my picture taken. I've always needed high maintenance to keep my act together. Nothing really comes naturally to me except the desire to sing. I used to jump ship every three days. And I wasn't crying wolf. It would usually come down to, I was leaving but there was no place to go. What am I gonna do, go to Paris, do poetry? Look at art museums and hope that not going after what I set out to do didn't eat me alive? Go pump gas? I was leaving to pump gas a few times, and ready for it. Then, I don't know, something in me would go, "You can deal with this now." It just took time to be able to deal with it.' Ultimately, he reckoned, 'A lot of my anger came from people not understanding that I needed that time.'

With the tour due to begin again in May, when they were to return to the US arena circuit as the 'special guests' of former Van Halen star and now solo singer David Lee Roth, Geffen promotions man Al Coury began agitating for the company to release 'Sweet Child O' Mine' as the next single. Now that MTV's regular rotation of 'Welcome To The Jungle' had proved how popular the band was, Coury and his team felt confident that 'Sweet Child' stood a good chance of being played on mainstream daytime radio.

Zutaut and Rosenblatt agreed and the band hurriedly shot a video to go with it, taking over a room at the Ballroom in Huntington Park for two days in early April and inviting all their friends and girlfriends along for the ride – most especially, Axl's girlfriend, Erin. It was the first of three occasions when Axl would put his girlfriends in a GN'R video.

A simple, straightforward document of the band performing the song, albeit mimed, 'Sweet Child' is a near-perfect rendition of everything that made W. Axl Rose and Guns N' Roses so captivating in their original incarnation. From the second Slash's hand nonchalantly plugs the buzzing lead into his guitar, to the final quivering moments as the camera focuses on Axl clenching his hands into fists, everything in the 'Sweet Child' video, from Axl's cobra-swaying dance to the cigarette dangling from Izzy's thin lips, to Slash coaxing then bullying his trusty Les Paul through the guitar solo, this is Guns N' Roses at their dizzying seductive peak. Even now, nearly twenty years later, whenever they show the video on MTV its power remains undiminished. It's a great song, of course, and you certainly don't have to be a Guns N' Roses fan, or even a rock fan, to appreciate it. But it's also an era-defining video, shot half in black-and-white half in colour, as though symbolic of the transitional phase it found them in. The fact that their girlfriends are also briefly glimpsed – all now consigned to the heartbreak pages of history – adds a delicious poignancy to what is, after all, a song about the ephemeral nature of young love.

A month later the band was back on the road and all such notions were quickly forgotten. Somewhere among the din of clashing egos the idea of the David Lee Roth tour was eventually abandoned. Instead, in May Guns N' Roses began opening the show for Iron Maiden. To coincide with the dates an edited, radio-friendly version of 'Sweet Child O' Mine' was released as a single on 3 June and immediately slammed its way into the US top forty.

But the Iron Maiden tour wasn't going as well for Guns N' Roses as expected. The main problem was that Maiden had difficulty selling tickets for some of the earlier dates. By contrast, *Appetite* had entered the US top ten for the first time on 23 April, receiving its first platinum record – for over a million US sales. As a result, once the band joined the ailing Maiden tour, they were suddenly starting to play to packed houses again and the feeling grew inside the GN'R camp that it was them and not Iron Maiden who should be headlining the tour. So unimpressed were the band by their new tour-mates that Duff took a week off to fly back to LA and marry his long-standing girlfriend, Mandy, leaving his pal, former Cult bassist Kid Chaos – these days known as Haggis – to fill in for him.

I had planned to see Guns N' Roses opening for Maiden over two nights at Irvine Meadows in Long Beach, California, but by the time I caught up with the tour in June things had degenerated to the point where the two bands were barely speaking to each other. The brace of Irvine Meadows shows should have been a glorious home-coming for Guns N' Roses. Instead, both appearances were cancelled when Axl succumbed to 'voice problems'.

The rumour-mongers whispered (wrongly) that there was nothing wrong with his voice, that he simply resented opening for a band he now considered smaller than Guns N' Roses. But when shows in Japan and Australia scheduled after the Maiden dates were also cancelled it seemed there might be something really wrong with Axl after all.

Whatever the truth, the sudden break left Slash kicking his heels that weekend. Staying at the Hyatt House on Sunset, under the name Mr Disorderly, he invited me to join him on the Saturday afternoon. I arrived as he was saying goodbye to his father, Tony Hudson. He was a well-dressed, soft-spoken Englishman who looked nothing like Slash, but obviously knew enough about the music business to be concerned about his son's impending elevation to its giddiest heights.

'He was telling me to keep my feet on the ground and stuff,' Slash said as we crossed to the bar. 'I told him, I'm cool. I know what it's all about. I mean, look at me. T-shirt, jeans, boots, that's me, man. That's all there is. Besides we haven't had any money yet. We just get these phone calls – yesterday it was 35,000 sales, today it's 91,000 sales. It freaks my ass out.'

He was, he said, most excited about the next album. The new songs he and Axl were working on would be 'even more angry and anti-radio' than the ones on *Appetite*. 'To prove there's more to us than those bands whose roots go back, like, three years. The ones who bought the clothes first.' It was that same quest for authenticity, he seemed to suggest, that led to incidents like Axl walking off the tour in February. Acknowledging that part of the band's appeal lay in the notion that it might end tomorrow, Slash concluded, somewhat prophetically, 'Actually, I'd *rather* it collapsed. I'd rather be as good as possible in the amount of time that you can do it, and do it to the hilt. Then fall apart, die, whatever . . .'

The band had already written lots of new songs, he said. Two he mentioned were 'Perfect Crime' and 'You Could Be Mine', which they planned to record when they began the next album in October – 'or maybe November'. Whichever it was, 'We plan to have a new album out some time in mid-1989.' Famous last words . . .

In July, the band were on the road in the US again, this time opening for their former idols Aerosmith on their *Permanent Vacation* tour, a jaunt which would take them through to September. However, with 'Sweet Child' now storming up the charts, *Appetite* went to number one on 23 July – almost a year after its release. Suddenly the band was once again in the position of being a bigger act on paper than the one they were opening for – *Appetite* had now passed the three-million mark, while Aerosmith's current album, *Permanent Vacation*, had peaked at that same figure.

As Aerosmith guitarist Joe Perry later recalled, 'Bands like Bon Jovi and Whitesnake were big around then, but Guns N' Roses were different. They had dug down a little deeper into rock's roots. I heard a lot of Aerosmith in them, which meant I also heard a lot of bands that came before us. And I remember being a little jealous, because they were really hitting the nail on the head. Axl knew how to work an audience. They used to have to go out there and tape foam rubber around everything that Axl could touch – from his teleprompter to his mike stand – to make sure he wouldn't break anything, or hurt himself. I think people saw that he was basically just let out of the cage. Part of the thrill was wondering what he was going to do next.'

Aerosmith manager Tim Collins, who had turned down the chance to manage Axl and the gang two years before, later recalled that by the end of the tour, 'Guns N' Roses were huge. They basically just exploded. We were all pissed that *Rolling Stone* showed up to do a story on Aerosmith, but Guns N' Roses ended up on the cover of the magazine. Suddenly, the opening act was bigger than we were. But we felt sorry for them . . . they were so fucked up it was ridiculous.'

In fact, 'Sweet Child' was destined to become the big US rock hit of the summer, slowly but steadily climbing the charts until finally, on the week ending 10 September, it reached number one in the *Billboard* singles' chart, where it stayed for two weeks. As a result, *Appetite*, which had been on store shelves for over a year, was also now on its way back to number one, where it would remain for another five weeks. In fact, the album would eventually stay in the US top forty for nearly three years, as well as becoming a number one hit in Britain and virtually every other record-buying country in the world. The staff at Geffen Records were thrilled, none more so than David Geffen himself, who went out and bought Tom Zutaut a brand new Range Rover as reward for both his hard work and downright persistence. Within eighteen months of its release *Appetite* had sold nine million copies in the US, making it the best-selling record in Geffen history. It earned the company profits of around $13 million, before taxes, and helped turn Geffen into the hottest independent label in music business history.

Meanwhile, back on the road with Aerosmith, the band might have been at number one but they still had to toe the line. Tim Collins had initially baulked at the idea of having 'heroin users and drug addicts' touring with the newly sober Aerosmith. But Geffen Records, to which both bands were signed, 'insisted we find a way to handle this, so we came up with a plan. Guns would play, Aerosmith would arrive then Guns would leave, all their drug scene contained in their dressing-room. At the beginning, it worked so well that the bands had no contact, but it gradually loosened up when the Gunners were respectful, and everyone got along great.'

'What got me was they were us,' says Aerosmith vocalist Steven Tyler. 'Slash is Joe Perry. Izzy is Brad . . . Axl is the same as me, a visionary egomaniac. Sometimes I walked into their dressing-room and it was like looking in the mirror. I talked to them a little about drugs. Aerosmith was upset that the press was giving us a lot of shit about supposedly not letting them drink and smoke and do drugs. That offended us because we never presumed to tell anyone that. Before the first show, I got Izzy – who I once did drugs with – and Slash and maybe Duff to come to my dressing-room. I told them where I came from with drugs and booze and just told them, "Look, if you got any blow, please keep it to yourself. Do it in your dressing-room. If you do it in mine, I'm gonna have to leave my own dressing-room.' But they were okay. They told us we were their idols. [We] had tour shirts printed up with names of the rehabs we had gone through instead of tour dates, and we gave them to the guys in Guns. That was our statement.'

This story was later spun into an unlikely but oft-repeated tale of how Aerosmith had 'handed over the mantle' of their bad-boy reputation by presenting Guns N' Roses with their own custom-made 'Toxic Twins' T-shirts – the toxic twins being the nickname Tyler and Perry had borne with pride in their own drug-addicted days. In truth, there were several occasions when the older musicians found themselves shocked and reproachful at just how out of control their younger versions were. Slash told me about coming into his dressing-room and finding Tyler mooching around. Gesturing to the two bottles of Jack Daniels on the table – one of which was already empty, the other half-full – Tyler asked Slash reproachfully, 'Did you drink all that today?'

Steven Adler now describes the day Tyler caught him taking heroin as, 'the worst moment of my life'. It occurred on the final night of the tour, backstage at the Irvine Meadows arena in LA. Having just injected heroin for what he now claims was only 'the second time in my life', Adler opened his dressing-room door to find the Aerosmith frontman standing in the corridor outside 'just ten feet away, talking with this girl laughing, and he looks up 'cos he noticed my presence. And he has the biggest smile on his face, and then he could just see in my eyes that I did heroin, and he made the saddest face and . . . my heart just dropped, and I wanted to die right there. Because Steven Tyler is the greatest person in this whole world, and I love him, and there is nobody in the world like him, and I . . . hurt his feelings, and it just hurt me so bad.'

Onstage, the Aerosmith/Guns N' Roses tour had become more of a co-headline event by then, with as many fans turning up to see the opening band as the reputed headliners. Having weaved their way from coast-to-coast throughout the summer, the two bands enjoyed an obvious master-and-apprentice relationship which boosted the credibility of both. Behind the scenes, however, for Guns N' Roses things were already beginning to unravel. If the first serious cracks in the relationship had occurred when Axl decided Guns N' Roses had no place opening for Iron Maiden, the after-shocks were now being felt in other ways. As Izzy says, 'Even then, it was like the music was taking a back seat to all the other shit.'

The day after *Appetite* went to number one in the US chart the tour reached the Starplex Amphitheater in Dallas. It was Slash's twenty-third birthday the day before, and before the show started the band and crew presented him with a cake iced with the message: *Happy Fuckin' Birthday, You Fucker*. Slash celebrated by getting stuck into a bottle of Stolichnaya vodka, rather than his usual Jack Daniel's, because downing two bottles of bourbon a day was now 'giving me black stripes on my tongue'.

The only one who didn't seem pleased for him was Axl, who had spent the previous two days alone in his hotel room refusing to answer the phone. While Slash was being given his birthday cake and vodka, Axl warmed up for the show by singing to an excruciatingly loud playback of 'The Needle Lies' by Queensryche. Slash wondered if he was being paranoid or whether Axl was making a veiled reference to the guitarist's ongoing drug problems. Axl was also now travelling in his own tour bus, away from the others. He needed the 'space', he said. 'We all used to live together, but we've outgrown being crowded in together. Not because we don't like each other, but because we have different lifestyles.' The main reason he now travelled alone, he later reportedly admitted, was that, like Aerosmith, Axl didn't want to be around while the others were getting 'annihilated'.

On 15 and 16 August, during their two-night stint at the 65,000-capacity Giants Stadium in New Jersey, video footage was shot for what would be their next single, 'Paradise City' – directed entirely by phone and headset by the English videomaker Nigel Dick (who had also directed 'Welcome' and 'Sweet Child'). The single was the band's third top ten single in the US and first major hit in Britain. Two days later, the band left the tour briefly to fly to England for their appearance at Castle Donington Monsters of Rock festival.

By then *Appetite* was sitting pretty at number one in the US charts and the band jetted to London on Concorde. Given their escalating American success and despite being only fifth on the bill – above Helloween and below Megadeth, David Lee Roth, Kiss and headliners Iron Maiden – Guns N' Roses was now indisputably the biggest rock band in the world. Backstage, Alan Niven was the personification of bonhomie. 'If you'd told me a year ago that this album was going to be number one I'd have laughed in your face.' He laughed anyway as he went off to fetch more champagne.

In the 1980s, Donington was the biggest and most prestigious outdoor event in the British rock calendar. Everybody in the band was looking forward with enormous enthusiasm to returning to England, especially Axl, whose favourite rock artists had always been British and for whom the place still held a special meaning. The day of the show was blustery and cold, dark storm-clouds looming ominously – traditional Donington weather, one might have said. The first really serious downpour saved itself, with immaculate timing, for the moment the opening act, Helloween, took to the stage at 1.00 p.m. sharp. Rain continued to sheet down mercilessly throughout the duration of the hapless German outfit's set, the fierce wind blowing one of the fifty-foot side-stage video screens from its moorings. Luckily, the screen fell harm-lessly onto empty ground and no one was hurt, but a shudder of foreboding swept through the crowd.

Though official figures put attendance that day at 97,559 (the largest in the festival's history) later unofficial estimates put it at well in excess of 100,000. However, the crowd was only around 50,000-strong when Guns N' Roses came on at 2.00 p.m. and hammered full-pelt into 'It's So Easy'. The torrential rain that had lashed down for the past twenty-four hours, turning the site into a mud-bath, briefly subsided but the wind was still howling. At first, applause for the band seemed scattered, most of the crowd subdued by the chilly conditions. The band ploughed gamely into their next song, 'Mr. Brownstone', and the atmos-phere started to pick up, Axl wheeling from one side of the stage to the other in white cowboy boots and a custom-made white leather jacket with the GN'R logo emblazoned on the back, the scarf tied around his waist flapping wildly in the wet wind.

Halfway into the third number – the slowed-down 'You're Crazy' – Axl stopped the show as a commotion broke out at the front of the crowd as fans were being dragged out by security. 'Back up! Back up!' he shouted angrily. After what seemed an age Slash began peeling out the riff to 'Paradise City', but fans were still being pulled from the crowd and Axl stopped the band mid-song a second time. 'Look!' he yelled, 'I'm taking time out from my playing to do this and that's the only fun I get all day.' The situation appeared to ease again and the band edged warily into 'Welcome To The Jungle'. But black clouds reappeared in the sky and another torrential downpour threatened. They tried to calm the mood by playing a ballad, 'Patience', one of the new acoustic numbers, but the crowd seemed distracted. The intro to 'Sweet Child', the last number, received a belated cheer and the band crunched through it as best they could before hurriedly exiting the stage. There was no encore. 'Don't kill yourselves,' Axl said as he left the stage, unaware of the awful truth that was to follow.

There had been a massive surge towards the front of the stage when the band came on, dozens of fans knocked over and trampled into the mud as an ugly scramble ensued and continued right through the set. Tragically, two of the trampled teenagers yanked from the mud – Alan Dick and Landon Siggers – would later die in the emergency tent.

'I saw the whole thing happen,' Maurice Jones, head of promoters MCP, later told Donington chronicler Jeff Clark Meads. 'The problems were created by idiots, absolute idiots. They were pushing stage right and the crowd compressed. They just couldn't go any further. Then about fifteen feet from the stage, a hole in the crowd opened and people went down. I went down to the front of the stage and I saw First Aid people and the doctors working and I felt so useless . . . I can't describe how it felt. I saw five bodies on the ground and I knew somebody was dead.'

Despite the official statement by Chief Superintendent Dennis Clarke of the West Midlands police, in which he described the crowd at Donington that year as 'otherwise superb' and announced that there had been no arrests, reaction in Britain's notoriously tacky tabloid press was predictably over the top. The more scurrilous Sunday editions, published the following day, ran sensationalized and wholly inaccurate stories claiming, among other things, that the stage had collapsed and that Guns N' Roses had refused to stop playing even after being informed about the injured fans. 'We even had very well-known and supposedly responsible newspapers saying the stage had collapsed,' Jones complained to Meads. 'The stage didn't collapse and was never in any danger of doing so.'

The coroner's inquest later recorded an open verdict, concluding there was nothing more that could have been done to ensure the safety of the crowd. Nonetheless, North West Leicestershire District Council placed a crowd limit of 70,000 on all future Donington events, and it was two years before promoters were granted another license.

'We just looked out and it was like, oh fuck!' said Slash when I later questioned him about it. 'You could see that surge when we came on, you could *see* the force . . .' When they were told afterwards that two fans had died, 'It just destroyed the whole thing for me.' Duff seemed even more upset: 'Saw the whole fuckin' event, man,' he told me. 'I saw it going down. And we stopped, man. We stopped and screamed, "Back the fuck up!" 'cos we saw the kids going under. "Back the fuck up! Back the fuck up!" And the mud was *this* thick, it was about a foot deep, and we saw the kids go under and then some other people came over them. They couldn't tell they were stepping on people, they thought it was just mud.'

He pushed his calloused fingers through his lank yellow hair. 'Man, we were like, this is our fault, man . . . I was there and I was watching it and there just seemed like nothing we could do except scream at them. I was ready to jump into the crowd, but I was scared to die myself. Maybe that's chicken shit.'

I said I thought it was a brave and honest admission, under the circumstances. But did Duff blame himself personally in any way for the tragedy of the two fans' deaths? 'I tell you, Mick, it really crushed us all. It really crushed us all. We went back to the hotel that night and we were watching the fuckin' news – they didn't know who the kids were yet but one of them had this tattoo. We were just . . .' He drifted into uncomfortable silence. 'At first I felt that it was totally our fault for months and months. I probably will for the rest of my life.'

John Jackson, booking agent for both Guns N' Roses and

Iron Maiden, had been standing at the side of the stage when the accident happened. 'You could tell fairly quickly that there was a major problem,' he told me. 'When a band's onstage there's always a lot of swirling around, and because it was so muddy, the kids just lost their footing and went down. It's impossible, looking down from stage, to see if people are actually on the floor. But I knew something was going on. The security guys had spotted something, and they immediately relayed that there was a problem to the crew on the stage, who quickly got a message to the GN'R guys, who were fantastic. They were fifteen minutes into a storming set, second band on, and suddenly they were told to stop, which they did. They couldn't have had any idea what was going on, but they cooled the set down completely. They stopped and did some slow, rambling ad lib bluesy thing to calm the audience down, and in effect ruined their own set. But thank God they did.

'The kids were taken into the St John's ambulance unit, but my head told me they were dead straight away,' Jackson continued. 'I can't remember exactly when it was confirmed to me that deaths had occurred but it wasn't long after. Very, very few people realized the extent of the tragedy until later, so it wasn't necessarily discussed that the show should be called off. One of the reasons being the crowd had settled and we didn't want to start more trouble. I've got an aerial photo of the audience actually taken around the time of the tragedy and there was loads and loads of room on the site still, plus you could see people still coming up the roads and through the turnstiles. It wasn't a question of a crush; it was a question of people losing their footing because of the mud.'

None of the bands was informed of the tragedy until after Iron Maiden finally clambered offstage more than eight hours later. The question of whether the festival should have been allowed to continue once the deaths had been made known to the organisers was thus sidestepped. Was cancelling the show considered?

'I don't think so,' Jackson said. 'It would have been very difficult to tell that many people that the show was cancelled. It could have caused an even greater crowd problem. Over 100,000 people turned up that day, and nearly half of them were still on their way at the time of the tragedy. The previous record attendance had been 66,500 for AC/DC, in 1984. So it was a huge crowd. More than 35,000 people just turned up on the day expecting to buy tickets.'

The atmosphere after the show was over and the bands had been informed, he said, 'was horrible, really rotten. There was no after-show party or anything like that, we couldn't. Most of us just sort of hung about for a while and then just drifted off separately. After what happened to those poor kids, or what the families must have been feeling, there's not really a lot you can say in situations like that, is there?'

Backstage, an hour after the show, when I spoke to Axl we were both still unaware of what had happened. But he already looked wasted, thin, his face ashen, his voice barely more than a croak. He admitted he hadn't enjoyed the set, was having a tough time of it on tour generally. 'We're still supposed to be out there until November,' he told me, his eyes sunken, 'but right now I don't know if I can make it.' When Alan Niven later broke the news about the deaths of the two fans, 'he was just short of crying', Slash recalled. 'That changed the whole thing. From such a high to such a low, it was too much. We never felt that carefree again.'

Later that night Axl and Slash could be found sitting side by side at the bar of their hotel, the scale of the tragedy too much for them to take in, chatting to their entourage of friends and press pals, their thoughts clearly elsewhere.

A week later they were back on tour with Aerosmith, Donington and its hideous complications already a dimming memory. They began with three sold-out shows at Great Woods, a new outdoor amphitheatre in Mansfield, Massachusetts – virtually a hometown gig for the Boston-born Aerosmith guys. Almost as if to show his defiance of the no-drugs, no-alcohol rules imposed by the headliners, Axl played the set in an Eat the Worm T-shirt, introduced Izzy as 'the king of beers' and Steven as 'the biggest pot-head I know'. He did make sure to add, however, what a huge influence Aerosmith had been on his own band.

The tour ended in Los Angeles in September. For the final show, Aerosmith's road crew surprised Guns N' Roses by jumping around the stage in gorilla suits during 'Welcome To The Jungle'. Then at the end of Aerosmith's set, Axl and the band joined them onstage for a bit of mutual back-slapping during a long, drawn-out version of 'Mama Kin'. Not that everything was entirely sweetness and light behind the scenes, with Aerosmith manager Tim Collins quoted in the press as saying that Guns N' Roses were a lot like Aerosmith, in that 'They'd have to do $2.5 million worth of dope before they were ready to get help.'

September also saw a re-released 'Welcome To The Jungle' scaling the US chart, eventually reaching number seven. Geffen shrewdly reissued it to tie in with the release that month of the new Clint Eastwood movie in the Dirty Harry series, *The Dead Pool*, which featured the band in a cameo role performing the song 'live' in a Miami club, a sequence they filmed earlier that year before the album had gone platinum. Slash later described the legendary movie star as 'one of the most intimidating people I've met. You'll have to try and picture this: we're on location in a graveyard, all these people and then this funny-looking rock band, totally out of place. And in between takes this nine-foot character comes over and goes, "Uh, nice record", and walked away. And that was it. I bet he never heard it and they're obliged. But he was more Clint in person than he is on the screen.'

The band also performed the song live at MTV's Video Music Awards on 7 September, where they won the award for Best New Artist. Slash and Steven also joined Steven Tyler, Joe Perry, Billy Idol and Tommy Lee for the performance of comedian Sam Kinison's remake of 'Wild Thing' (they had also featured in the video).

There was one final live date to fulfil, on 17 September, when the band appeared on the bill at that year's Texas Jam in Irving, Texas, where the headliner was INXS. And then, with the Aerosmith tour over, Axl and the band were suddenly left kicking their heels at home in LA just as their star seemed to be at its zenith. There was talk about the re-arranged Japanese and Australian dates being rescheduled for November but when I had dinner with Slash in October he said he thought that was 'a long shot'. What were their plans then?

He stared hard at me through his long, corkscrew hair. 'Uh, I don't know. Right now, it's just about getting fucked up . . .'

Chapter Six

NIGGERS, FAGGOTS AND
MR BROWNSTONE

One might have thought the period between the end of 1988, when they finally stopped touring to promote the *Appetite For Destruction* album, and the summer of 1991, when they eventually set out on their next world tour, would have been a marvellous time for the five members of Guns N' Roses, not least their volatile young singer, who could now say 'I told you so' – one of his absolute favourite phrases – with the utmost conviction to all those people on his ever-growing mental check-list who he felt had once tried to do him down. The band he had run away to Hollywood to form had achieved everything they set out to do and more – *much* more – selling millions of albums all over the world and becoming the biggest, best-known rock band of its era. Instead, the two-and-a-half years that Axl and his band spent off the road turned for some into an almost never-ending nightmare of bad drugs, worse sex and very little rock'n'roll. As Izzy Stradlin now admits, 'That was a real dark period for all of us. The drugs and stuff was a big part of the isolation but it was more than that. It was like *self-imposed* and it got worse . . .' But why? What had happened to them?

In November 1988, *Rolling Stone* put Guns N' Roses on its cover for the first time, describing them as 'a brutal band for brutal times' in a report from the Aerosmith tour that focused mainly on subjects like Axl's 'mood swings'. Or as Slash moaned to me afterwards, it was more about the band's 'chemical intake, and violence, sex, groupies and all those sorts of things', than about music. The writer, he said, 'had used quotes that were, like, just made in passing, just bits of conversation . . . It was sort of a drag to read that and see how you can be had so easily.' It also rankled that the photographer who shot the *Rolling Stone* cover had kept them waiting at a New Jersey biker bar until dawn, despite the fact that they had a show to do with Aerosmith later that same night.

Axl, however, said he thought the piece was 'very good from an outsider's point of view, but some of the things were exaggerated'. Specifically, he disapproved of the fuss the story made of the fact that by the end of the Aerosmith tour he was travelling in a separate tour bus to the rest of the band. 'First of all, it was Izzy's idea to get a separate bus,' he insisted, 'and secondly, after shows I can't afford to party out like the other guys. There's been several times when I had to leave the bus because of nerves. It's impossible to sit there completely straight, listening to someone who is annihilated go off about something or another.'

But if it was true that, in print, the band came across as typically spoiled rock star brats spending too much money on drugs and not enough time tuning their egos, in reality it was now almost impossible to put down in words exactly what it was that made Guns N' Roses so special. The context they arrived in had a lot to do with it undoubtedly, and the fact that they had written a couple of killer hit songs obviously helped. But there was far more to it than that. Like all the great rock bands, in many ways their appeal defied description and eluded analysis. Like Zeppelin, the Stones and the Pistols, Guns N' Roses appeared to operate with its own internal logic; any attempt to explain them as some sort of synthesis between punk and hippy, love and hate, sex and anger, failed to grasp the real point – that, ultimately, it worked because it looked right, smelled right, behaved right: which is to say, wrong.

Meanwhile, the rest of the rock world was desperately trying to catch up. Suddenly, even previously clean-cut bands like Bon Jovi and Def Leppard were now letting their stubble show through the make-up, ripping holes in the knees of their designer jeans and allowing themselves to be pictured drinking and smoking, while new dicks on the block like Love/Hate, the Sea Hags and a revamped LA Guns were signing lucrative recording contracts on the basis that they contained some of that same gritty, deal-gone-down GN'R vibe. Watching MTV, Slash said, was like watching 'Axl aerobics'. None of which served to help the band come to terms with the seismic changes now occurring in their personal lives.

At a time when any other band in their position would have been churning out copycat hits and raking in the bucks from their headline arena tours, Guns N' Roses sank back into the quicksand of LA. 'I always used to say the problems only really arrived for us when we came off the road,' Slash says now. 'And it's true. Taking us off the road for so long nearly killed us . . . We should have made another album and just gone straight back out there. We should have done a lot of things. But then it wouldn't have been Guns N' Roses.'

Being in LA a lot at that time, I recall seeing the band around town on a number of occasions throughout the last years of the 1980s. Slash and Duff were habitués of the LA club scene, the sort of rock-steady dudes you'd always run into at places like the Rainbow, the Roxy, the Whiskey and the Cat club. Out of their heads on booze and coke and anything else they could get their hands on, surrounded by sycophants and groupies, at least they looked like they were having a so-called good time. Which is more than could be said for the others. Sightings of Izzy or Steven were rarer and far less conspicuous, owing to the fact that they were both then entering the first melancholy throes of heroin addiction.

As for Axl, he was no stranger to the half-moon tables at the Rainbow either. But he tended to roam alone and separate from the rest of the band. Indeed, when I think back now, the only time I recall seeing Axl with any other member of Guns N' Roses was in the dressing-room before or after a show. Not that he drank alone. Along with his half-brother, Stuart, writer Del James and a gaggle of other floating members of his entourage like Robert John, David Lank, Dana Gregory and Paul Huge, Axl was never short of company. But these were still the days when he travelled without bodyguards.

He already had a major rep for being one bad mother to get into a tangle with – a bona fide red-head who never failed to notice when someone looked at him funny – but on the few occasions I happened to share a drink with him I usually found him to be quite mellow. He was intense but talkative, maybe even a little shy. Which is why, I assumed, he'd grown the big red beard he sported throughout 1989. What with the thick horn-rimmed glasses and the old baseball cap turned backwards, it made him virtually unrecognizable from the bouffed-up sex bomb then seen on MTV every day. A perfect disguise which allowed him to wander the streets of LA, free from the kind of hassle the more instantly recognizable Slash and Duff now suffered on an almost hourly basis.

Axl hadn't changed so much as been let loose. He began the New Year in LA by moving into his own luxury, two-bedroom condominium on the twelfth floor of a security-guarded building a couple of blocks north of Sunset Boulevard. He had the walls and ceilings painted black and bought nothing but black furniture – including a black refrigerator, black Persian rug and black marble coffee-table – the only exception being the mirrored walls in the lounge, on which his many gold and platinum records now hung, along with a fast-growing collection of plaques and awards from around the world. Over the next few weeks he also pur-chased a new top-of-the-range (black) BMW and a substantial plot of land in Wisconsin on which he told friends he eventually planned to build his dream house. He liked to live 'in my own little world', he said, privacy being the one thing he now valued above everything else. So much so, not only were his calls now routinely screened, he even claimed not to know his own phone number.

Stacked neatly behind the long L-shaped couch in the lounge he kept an Uzi semi-automatic machine gun, and laid casually on the coffee-table would be a nine-mm pistol. Other weapons – including a sawn-off shotgun – remained concealed in nearby closets. He hadn't bought the guns because he was paranoid, he said blankly. He just liked the 'feeling of security' they gave him. The Uzi caught his eye, he explained, after seeing an ad in *Soldier Of Fortune* magazine with the strapline: '*When the going gets tough, the tough get an Uzi*'. 'Let's get tough!' he laughed.

In fact, guns had been an obsession since he was a child and his stepfather had allowed him to handle a shotgun. Not because he fantasized about shooting people, he insisted, but because he liked 'the sport'. As he told MTV, 'The first time I shot my shotgun was the first time I'd shot a shotgun since [I was] a little kid, and the first thought in my mind was what this would do to a man. And it was so gross of a picture, it's just . . . you know, most people's actions, no matter how much they infuriate you, are definitely not worth what it's going to do to their human body if you shoot them – it's pretty horrible. I think about the beer can I'm shooting and my accuracy. I think about the target, I don't think about shooting people.'

At the same time Axl had decided to seek help in dealing with his feelings.

'I'm very sensitive and emotional, and things upset me and make me feel like I'm not functioning or not dealing with people, the band or anything. I went to a clinic thinking it would help my moods,' he was reported telling Del James for an interview in *RIP*. 'The only thing I did was take one 500-question test – you know, filling in these little black dots. And all of a sudden I'm diagnosed manic-depressive! Let's put Axl on medication.' Except the medication didn't work. 'The only thing it does is help keep people off my back 'cos they figure I'm on medication,' he was quoted as saying.

In the midst of this he found himself in the absurd situation of having to deny his own death on what for a while felt like an almost weekly basis. Slash complained to me that even MTV were getting in on the act. 'They ran these pictures on the screen: "Axl – not dead". "Jimi Hendrix – dead". Then a picture of me and the band: "not dead". Then, "Jim Morrison – dead". Then they showed a picture of Elvis – "dead?" – with a question mark. It was a classic!' he scoffed. 'I mean, when it gets to that level, you just can't take it seriously any more.'

Axl himself put it down to the fact that he periodically liked to unplug the phone and vanish for days and weeks at a time. He said that people presumed that if he wasn't constantly in the public eye, 'something must have happened'. Instead, he said, 'I'll be right in Hollywood, laying low, not calling or wanting to deal with anybody; so no one knows exactly what happened to Axl. I just have to get away every so often to digest and understand all that's going on around me.' When he couldn't get away, he would encourage friends from the old Lafayette days to come and stay with him, paying for their plane tickets and sending cars to meet them at the airport.

Dana Gregory ended up staying in LA semi-permanently with Axl, sleeping in the spare room at the new West Hollywood condo and placed on a monthly retainer as one of Axl's growing retinue of 'assistants'. Years later, when pressed about what he actually did during his time working for Axl, Dana shrugged. 'His condo had these giant mirrors going all around it,' he recalled in GQ. 'And every now and then, he'd take that space-man statue they give you when you win an award on MTV and smash up the mirrors with it. Well, he slept till four o'clock in the afternoon every day. Somebody had to let the guy in when he came to fix the mirrors.' Dana's job was to do 'shit like that'.

On a more upbeat note, Axl had also recently announced his engagement to twenty-one-year-old Erin Everly. Not that it appeared to cause any revision in his schedule, often spending days and nights at a time 'up and about' then sleeping for two or three days straight. This was, after all, what he had worked so hard with his band to achieve. As he put it: 'That feeling of freedom to choose to do what I want to do.' Suddenly it seemed nothing was off the menu. He even appeared to be dabbling with heroin again. He later reportedly told Del James in an article for RIP magazine, 'I did it for three weeks straight and had one of the greatest times in my life, because I was with a girl I wanted to be with in this beautiful apartment, and we just sat there listening to Led Zeppelin, doing drugs and fucking. It was great, 'cos at that time I had nothing to do but sit on my ass and make a few phone calls a day. I stopped on, like, Saturday, because I had serious business to attend to on Monday. I felt like shit, sweated, shook, but on Monday I was able to function.'

Slash, meanwhile, had gone back to his bad old ways almost as soon as they'd returned from the Australian tour in December. When, after a two-month break, rehearsals reconvened in LA, he was discovered injecting himself in the stomach with heroin – skin-popping – which resulted in him being put on a plane to Hawaii for a couple of weeks enforced, drug-free R&R. 'Word had gotten out that I was doing junk [again],' he says now, 'and at the time, I guess I was.' The next thing he knew 'they were putting me in a car, I was off to the airport and I'm in Hawaii! It gave [tour manager] Doug Goldstein a great excuse to play golf. But I caused a lot of trouble in Hawaii. I've ruined many a fuckin' golf game for Doug . . .'

'We used to basically kidnap them every now and then and take them to Hawaii to clean up,' Alan Niven says. 'We'd call Slash and say, "Interview tomorrow with *Guitar Magazine*, midday". He'd arrive at the office, we'd put him in a car, drive him to the airport and take him to the island. Steven Adler was the worst. He became quite tragic. I remember one time in San Francisco when Steven was rushed to hospital with an overdose. The road manager was literally running up the streets with him on his shoulders.'

While Slash resented these 'intrusions into my personal shit', he grudgingly agreed to clean up. Over the next few months, however, hunkered down in his newly bought house in the Hollywood hills, playing with his seventeen snakes and 'sinking deeper into my hole', his habits would grow steadily worse again – as would Izzy's. Driving down the 101 Freeway one day in March 1989, with 'a head full of coke and a gun in the glove compartment', Izzy says he was startled to see it snowing outside. 'I thought, gee, I never knew it snowed in LA.' But then, he'd been 'staying with this coke dealer and I'd been up for five fucking days', which may have had something to do with it. 'I didn't even know I was in trouble until someone pointed it out to me.' That someone happened to be Aerosmith's Steven Tyler, who had stayed in touch by phone with the errant guitarist since their tour together. 'We were talking on the phone and I said, "Steven, I've got this hole that goes through the middle of my sinuses. I've got like one nostril now." He goes, "Oh, yeah – deviated septum." He knew all the terminology. I was like, what? Let me write this down . . .'

To begin with though, Izzy's main obsession – apart from getting loaded – centred on the not unreasonable inquiry, 'where all the fuckin' money had gone, man.' With US sales alone for *Appetite* then tipping ten million it didn't take a genius to work out that Guns N' Roses were now generating zillions of dollars worldwide. 'Paradise City', the fourth single from *Appetite*, had just become their third top ten hit in the US (and their first in Britain, where album sales were also now into seven figures). Yet none of the band was millionaires – yet – and Izzy damn well wanted to know why.

'I'm out of my fuckin' gourd, right?' he shakes his head now. 'I'm at the fax machine and I've got, like, a hundred faxes strung across this room. I've got a loaded pistol on the desk, 'cos I keep hearing people walking on my roof, and I'm snorting coke, doing smack, reading through this stuff just trying to grasp what had happened to us. All I knew was we left [to go on tour] broke and we came back and suddenly there's loads of money but we can't get to it. I'm yelling on the phone going, "I know it's there somewhere, motherfucker! Where the fuck is it?"'

In fact, the money was already starting to filter through – all five members of the band had recently been handed cheques for $850,000 – but Izzy was so thoroughly out of it that he walked around with it crumpled in his jacket pocket for weeks. When it fell out of his pocket as he fumbled for cigarettes one night while we sat chatting together over drinks at a mutual friend's house, he joked that he had no bank account to put it in. 'Give it to me,' I kidded. 'I'll take care of it for you.' He staggered to his feet, appeared to consider the possibility for a moment, then folded it up and put it back in his pocket. 'Later, man,' he said.

Steven also spent most of his time, he says, 'sitting in some big fuckin' empty house I'd bought, shooting dope twenty-four-seven'. He was, he admits now, 'very naive to the dangers of heroin. The first times I did it were two years apart. It made me so sick. Then the third time I did it, it didn't affect me that way. So I did it every day for a month.' At first, he'd been 'so fucking happy, driving my Mercedes around with my fucking stereo on, and the top down'. He remembers driving down Sunset Boulevard 'and people just yelling, "Hey Stevie, what's happening?" That was great.' Soon, though, the smack had taken over and he was spending most of his days 'never going nowhere, never seeing no one, just out of my fuckin' mind . . .'

Though he'd tried it, smack wasn't Duff's bag at all. When it came to drugs he preferred coke and weed. More often, he stuck to legal highs like booze and cigarettes – what he called 'social drugs'. Despite his over-eagerness to buy into the Sid Vicious myth (hence the padlock neck-chain and lop-sided sneer he always affected in pictures in those days), Duff couldn't help his affability. Nevertheless, even his puppy-dog enthusiasm would become subsumed as his year-old marriage to Mandy started to break down once the touring stopped and he began to spend more time at home.

But if the wheels were starting to come off the band's personal lives, professionally they were thrusting into overdrive. On 30 November, with *Appetite* still at number three, Geffen issued the first new Guns N' Roses recordings since its release fifteen months before: a mini-album that the band originally planned to call *Lies! The Sex, the Drugs, the Violence, the Shocking Truth*, a parody of the British tabloid press, replete with the album cover as a newspaper and all the song titles mocked up into the kind of trashy headlines that had greeted them on their first trip to London the year before.

But Geffen vetoed the idea at the last minute, opting instead for the snappier abbreviation, *GN'R Lies*. Comprised of the four tracks from the original *Live?!'@ Like A Suicide* EP two years before, plus the four acoustic tracks the band recorded with Mike Clink at the start of the year, *GN'R Lies* immediately crashed into the US album charts at number two, making Guns N' Roses the first band for fifteen years to have two albums in the US top five simultaneously. It was certified platinum before Christmas. By the end of 1990 it had sold more than five million copies worldwide.

As *Rolling Stone* pointed out in its review, 'Given that Guns N' Roses could probably release an album of Baptist hymns at this point and go platinum, it would be all too easy to dismiss *GN'R Lies* as a sneaky attempt by the band to throw together some out-takes and cash in on the busy holiday buying season . . . The good news is that *Lies* is a lot more interesting than that.' The four-song side two acoustic set was where the main interest lay. Opening with Duff lazily counting in the beat, 'Patience' was the first song Guns N' Roses had ever recorded that didn't have razor-edged electric guitars and bludgeoning

NIGGERS, FAGGOTS AND MR BROWNSTONE

two-fisted drums all over it. In fact there were no drums at all, or electric guitars. Instead there was just the sound of Izzy, who wrote the song, and Slash and Duff on sweetly jangling acoustic guitars, Axl charmingly whistling the melody, the collar of his coat turned up, cigarette in hand, before stooping before the mike to croon.

'We did this [album] for the same reason as we did the first live EP,' Slash told me. 'It's material that we wanted to get off our chests but without taking up too much space. And it's real simple, real sloppy. You can hear us talking, there's guitar picks dropping. Real off-the-cuff stuff.'

The next track, 'Used to Love her', was a tongue-in-ear slice of misogynistic black humour worthy of Lou Reed at his most reactionary for its enviable ability to make you laugh out loud. As Axl wrote on the liner notes: ' "Used to Love her" is a joke, nothing more. Actually, it's pretty self-explanatory if you ask me!' Slash agreed. 'I think it's pretty fuckin' funny. I don't know anybody who hears it and doesn't find it funny, except for the people that never find jokes funny.'

There was little to laugh about on the next track, 'You're Crazy'. Slowed down from the hysterically pumped-up version on *Appetite*, the new belly-crawling version was far starker and more sinister, detailing Axl's claustrophobic search for love in a dark world. For Slash, it was simply 'a lot bluesier, which is the way me and Axl and Izzy originally wrote it. I think I prefer the slower version, it's got something. We've never done it the same way twice.' Axl, however, said he thought it 'sucked'. The band played superbly but his singing was 'shit'. He did allow, though, that it was 'a very special, magical song. Every time we record "Crazy" something happens. When it's really on, the band goes into a trance-like state.'

It was the final track that would deliver the storm of protest and controversy promised by the album's pseudo-provocative sleeve. A vicious piece of gutter-talk from Axl called 'One In A Million', in which homosexuals are depicted as immoral disease-spreaders and blacks as a bunch of gold-chain-wearing 'niggers', it left a lot of people – including many of their own fans, most critics, even David Geffen and members of the band – deeply disturbed. Originally titled 'Police And Niggers', its lyrics drawn from the same autobiographical experiences Axl had previously described in songs such as 'Move To The City' and, most memorably, 'Welcome To The Jungle', most people were shocked by what they saw as a racist, homophobic attack on two of the most stigmatized minority groups in America.

Before *GN'R Lies* was released, Axl was warned the song was certain to provoke an almost unanimously negative reaction. But, as was increasingly the case, he was confident he knew best and insisted the track remain on the album.

Privately, Geffen was concerned that the song might prompt criticism of him personally. The arrival in the 1980s of AIDS had spawned the creation of a highly active, sometimes reactionary gay press that, in an effort to force the US government's hand in doing more to finance the fight against what was then too often seen as a 'gay disease', canvassed for famous but closeted homosexuals like Geffen to come out in public – an idea that was anathema to the over-sensitive record company doyen. More than anything, Geffen feared being outed in retaliation for allowing such an incendiary song to be released on a label bearing his own name. He was also deeply embarrassed when offence over the song caused the band to be unceremoniously – and very publicly – dumped from an AIDS benefit in New York, where they were to have represented the interests of the Gay Men's Health Crisis, one of the organizations involved with the show and that Geffen had personal connections with.

Even his own band condemned Axl for his stubbornness in keeping the song on the album. Not least Slash, whose mother Ola is black and who felt particularly distressed by the situation. As he told me, 'There's a line in that song where it says, "Police and niggers, get out of my way" that I didn't want Axl to sing. But Axl's the kind of person who will sing whatever it is he feels like singing.'

Slash did make a half-hearted attempt to defend it – 'He wasn't talking about black people so much; he was more or less talking about the sort of street thugs that you run into' – but it was clear he was deeply uncomfortable with the subject. 'That kind of thing does bother me. I mean, I'm part black. I don't have anything against black individuals. One of the nice things about Guns N' Roses is that we've always been a people's band. We've never segregated the audience in our minds as white, black or green, you know? But with the release of 'One In A Million' I think it did something that I don't think was necessarily positive for the band. It's definitely something to attack us with. It's a bona fide, real thing that they can actually say, you know, "Well, what about that?"'

Presumably, I enquired, Axl would argue that it was okay to make a statement like that on the grounds of 'artistic licence'? 'I guess . . .' But Slash didn't agree? 'Personally, no, I don't think that that statement served any good. I think that should have been kept at bay altogether. But Axl has a strong feeling about it and he really wanted to say it. But then, God forbid that any of us should get arrested and end up in county jail. Can you imagine?' He shuddered. He said he asked his mother at the time if she'd heard the song yet and that she said she hadn't. But his little brother, Ash, later told him she had heard it and 'was so shocked that she didn't know what to say to me'.

Duff tried to shrug it off when I spoke to him about it some months later, explaining that he had 'black blood' in his own family – his sister had married and had children with a black man. None of the other guys in the band were prepared to stand up and defend the song in public either. Says Steven now: 'When I first heard "One In A Million" I asked Axl, "What the fuck? Is this necessary?"' Izzy just shook his head and smiled ruefully. 'That's a song that the whole band says: "Don't put that on there. You're white, you've got red hair, don't use it." You know? "Fuck you! I'm gonna do it 'cos I'm Axl!" Okay, go ahead, it's your fucking head. Of course, you're guilty by association. [But] what are you gonna do? He's out of control and I'm just the fucking guitar player.'

Such was the commotion caused by the song that Axl was even persuaded to go on MTV and defend it. 'There's a lot of different meanings to that word,' he began, referring to his use of the word 'nigger'. 'But a lot of people just take the time to assume that when a white person uses the word "nigger" it's meant [as] derogatory and you're a racist. I don't think people took the time to listen to the third verse and figure that one out. It says "radicals and racists don't point your finger at me". You know? Which is exactly what happened. We had the Ku Klux Klan saying we were promoting shows and backing the Ku Klux Klan, and they immediately got a letter from my lawyers. 'Cos that is not true.'

As for some of the other words that caused such offence, such as 'faggot', as he later reportedly told *Interview* magazine in 1992, 'A lot of people have used the word "faggot" and they're not getting told they're homophobic.' He did admit, however, that 'maybe I have a problem with homophobia.' Adding, 'Maybe I was two years old and got fucked in the ass by my dad and it's caused a problem ever since. But other than that, I don't know if I have any homophobia.' That said, he did admit that the revelation about his childhood sexual abuse had only become apparent to him at least four years after he wrote the song. He first suspected it, he said, in about 1990, when 'all of a sudden the thought crossed my mind'. He had been driving at the time, he was reported as saying, and had to pull over to the kerb, where 'I just broke down crying. Such an outpouring had never come out of me . . .'

It was a theme he had already suggested when speaking to *RIP* in 1989, explaining how he had had 'some very bad experiences with homosexuals'. Not that he was actively anti-homosexual, he said, more that he was 'pro-heterosexual', before adding provocatively, 'I'm not into gay or bisexual experiences.' Though he did admit he'd 'rather see two women together than just about anything else. That happens to be my personal, favourite thing.' As for being dropped from the AIDS benefit in New York, he merely shrugged. The band was 'in no way associated with the Gay Men's Health Crisis, except that David Geffen is on the board of directors for the concert and he's the owner of our record company.' Turning the responsibility back on the organization, he added, 'I don't feel they have the right to deny the money and attention they would have gotten from us playing. It's pride, it's ignorant and it's childish.'

Attention shifted back to the music, briefly, in the new year when 'Patience' was prepared for release as the next Guns N' Roses single. On 30 January, the band performed the song live at the American Music Awards at the Shrine Auditorium in LA, with former Eagles frontman Don Henley joining them on drums. Then on 18 February, they shot a video for the single, using the Record Plant studios for the performance footage – the band pictured playing amid draperies and pillows, Axl stealing glances at his lyric sheet – and rooms at the Ambassador Hotel for the offstage material, including shots of Slash lolling around on a bed playing with his snakes while a line of semi-clad *Playboy* models climb into bed with him before disappearing like ghosts. Meanwhile an angry-looking Axl stomps around in an adjoining room, destroying his strangely glowing telephone. In a final scene, a bemused Axl sits watching the 'Welcome To The Jungle' video, seemingly older and – the suggestion being – a great deal wiser.

When the finished video and single were issued in May it became their fourth consecutive top ten hit in the US and their first top five hit in the UK. As a result, by June 1989, combined sales for both *Appetite* and *GN'R Lies* had reached in excess of fifteen million copies in America alone. The same month, *Rolling Stone* gave the band its second cover in seven months, though only Axl's picture appeared on it this time. It was the first major interview Axl granted that year, but in order to get it *Rolling Stone* had to agree to allow Axl's friends, Del James and Robert John, to submit the only story and pictures the magazine would be allowed to use. It was an extraordinary concession for a magazine of *Rolling Stone*'s status but Axl was adamant. As even his own band was finding out, either you played by Axl's rules, or you didn't play at all.

In the published story, presented in a largely question-and-answer format, Axl was quoted talking about how much he had been 'hating' the success when he first got off the road at the start of the year, but now that he had his own place to live and everything was 'coming together' he realized that he had, in fact, 'wanted to be here my whole life'. Though he had 'thought about it a lot' he had never dreamed it was possible that his first album could actually sell so many millions of copies. 'Everything was directed at trying to achieve the sales without sacrificing the credibility of our music,' he said. 'The album wasn't just a fluke.' Ultimately, though, the way he looked at it, he had 'escaped from one group where I was looked down on for being a poor kid that doesn't know shit, and now I'm like, a rich, successful asshole.'

He also refuted any suggestion that he was a recreational drug-user, claiming his comments about heroin in the *RIP* article of just a few months earlier referred to the time before the first album came out. Lately, he said, he had been getting his highs from 'drinking champagne' and having 'a few beers'. Drugs would only 'get in the way of my dreams and goals . . . they just don't fit in with my life right now. Then again, I could be out on tour for six months and a blast might be what cheers me up that night.' Most astounding of all, he hinted at some sort of reconciliation with his stepfather, who he claimed 'likes "Welcome To The Jungle". Ten years ago, if a song like that was caught in our house, man, it was over. But I can't hold how he once felt against him.' On those rare occasions when he went back to Lafayette now, he couldn't enjoy himself at all. 'I just go to my friends' houses, but people I don't know show up wanting autographs. People that I used to go to school with, people that used to hate my guts want me to invest money in this and that. People say shit like "Axl thinks he's too cool to party with us." But those people never wanted to party with me before . . .'

He saw his own musical education as ongoing, he said, adding that lately he'd been listening seriously for the first time to Derek and the Dominos, the Bar-Kays, the first Patti Smith album, *Horses*, and was 'just starting to discover The Cure. I keep trying to find things to open myself up to.' He also name-checked a new Seattle band called Soundgarden, whose singer, Chris Cornell, he said, 'just buries me. The guy sings so great.'

Getting back in touch with his old friends and family may have been high on his priority list but the rest of the summer of 1989 found Axl drifting further and further apart from his band mates; the writing of new songs was made practically impossible since all five of them were almost never in the same room anymore. In order to try and get the band away from the distractions of LA and back working together again, it was decided to reconvene in Chicago, where a three-month stint was booked in a large rehearsal complex on the outskirts of town. They had the bare bones of several songs they'd already begun working on – 'You Could Be Mine', 'November Rain', 'Pretty Tied Up', 'Civil War', 'The Garden', 'Dust And Bones', 'Yesterdays' and one or two others – and the time in Chicago was meant to be spent paring them down and moulding them into shape, as well as seeing what else they might come up with together. But while Slash, Duff and Steven turned up on the first week of July ready for work, Axl put in an appearance only a couple of weeks before they were all due to go home in September – and Izzy never turned up at all!

In Axl's case, the reasons for his non-appearance were never fully explained; no more than his frequent disappearances, either from the stage or from public view. Instead of flying with the rest of the band to Chicago at the start of July, Axl and his old pal West Arkeen got up onstage at the Scrap Bar in LA and performed early makeshift versions of 'The Garden' (co-written with Del James) and 'Yesterdays' (written by Izzy) which MTV were there to film as part of a Guns N' Roses documentary they were putting together. Then in August, Axl flew to New York to make a cameo appearance in a video shoot for the first solo single by former Hanoi Rocks frontman, Michael Monroe, a piece of sub-GN'R swagger entitled 'Dead, Jail Or Rock'n'Roll'. A few days after that, Axl joined Tom Petty onstage at the New York State Fairgrounds in Syracuse, where they performed current Petty hit, 'Free Fallin'' and a version of Dylan's 'Knockin' On Heaven's Door'.

Meanwhile, back in Chicago, Slash, Duff and Steven were slowly churning away, doing what they could on the songs without their singer or rhythm guitarist. Slash admitted he didn't mind working without Izzy – if he'd had his way, he said, that would have been the normal state of affairs. But trying to get by without not only Axl's vocals but his input, was proving intolerable. According to Steven, Axl showed up in Chicago 'on like the last day. Axl shows up and all he wanted to work on was "November Rain". So that set back the recording process.' According to Duff, however, talking to me a few months later, Axl had merely been 'waiting for us to do our trip as musicians'. Izzy, he said, was 'having a hard time with life at that point and was just travelling the world. So we sat in Chicago for three months, the three of us, and kinda got suicidal. But at that point we also got a lot of shit done.'

As Axl later told me, when he did finally show up in Chicago – having driven himself there from LA, a journey that took over two weeks, including various 'pit stops' along the way – it was to a hostile reception. 'We got into these fights in Chicago. I was, like, just into fuckin' everybody's music – getting into Slash's stuff, getting into Duff's stuff. Our timing schedules were all weird and we kept showing up at different times. But when I would show up, I'm like, okay, let's do this, let's do that, let's do this one of yours, Slash. Okay, now let's go to this one and Steven needs to do this . . . And then they decided I was a dictator, right? I'm a total dictator and I'm a completely selfish dick. I was like, fuck, man. And we were on a roll, man! You know, we were cranking. Slash is like, "We're not getting' nothin' done". I was like, "What do you mean? We just put down six parts of new songs in, like, a couple weeks!" He was like, "Yeah, but I've been sitting here a month on my ass." This was while I was driving across country in my truck, you know. Like, yeah, let's party! Shoot guns!' He laughed it off.

The real reasons why Izzy didn't turn up in Chicago would have a much more serious long-term affect on the future of the band. On 27 August, he was arrested on a domestic flight from LA to Phoenix for urinating in the aisle of the first class section, verbally abusing the aghast stewardess who remonstrated with him, and defiantly smoking in the non-smoking section.

'Ah, I was drunk, man,' he says now. 'Then waking up in jail . . .' He shook his head and smiled wryly. 'Not cool, man.' In fact, the first Izzy knew about it was when he woke up hung over in Phoenix County Jail. His lawyer had to fill him in on the grisly details. He'd been arrested at Sky Harbor airport as the plane landed the day before. Although the charges were dismissed in a press statement simply as 'Izzy's way of expressing himself', the damage was done. Because it happened in 'federal airspace' the US authorities were rather less amused. Taking into consideration a prior arrest for marijuana possession, Izzy was put on probation for a year and – irony of ironies – subjected to random urine tests for the next twelve months. Now he really had to stop: the law demanded it. 'Suddenly, I can't use drugs anymore or I'm going to jail,' he told me. Then shook his head, 'Wow . . .'

Back in LA in September, the band attended the annual MTV Video Music Awards show where they were presented with the gong for 'Best Heavy Metal/Hard Rock Video' for 'Sweet Child O' Mine'. Axl's new friend Tom Petty was also booked onto the show and Axl and Izzy joined him onstage for 'Free Fallin'', followed by a ferocious run through Elvis's 'Heartbreak Hotel'. Unfortunately for Izzy, Mötley Crüe singer Vince Neil was also in attendance backstage and used the occasion to pay Izzy back for what he saw as a slight against his wife. Catching him by surprise as the guitarist walked offstage Vince punched him in the face. Izzy toppled over, his lip badly gashed, but otherwise completely unabashed by the whole thing. Newly sober, 'I wasn't in the mood for fucking around with Vince.' Axl, however, had other ideas, and chased after the Crüe singer to exact his own revenge.

According to Vince, in *The Dirt*, Axl had a sudden change of heart the moment Vince turned to face him. He recalled how Mötley Crüe 'had taken that fucking band on tour as an opening act' in the days when 'nobody believed in them [and] they were nice.' Back then, Vince said, 'Axl was a shy, humble guy who was a lot of fun to be with. But now they were starting to believe their own press clippings.'

As Vince made his way to the exit after decking Izzy, he recalled, 'Axl came snarling after us like an overdressed Doberman. "Come on, motherfucker, I'm going to fucking kill you!" he yelled . . . I twirled around. His face was sweaty and twisted. "Let's fucking go!" I said to him. And I meant it. The blood was still pumping into my fists. [He said] "Just don't fuck with my band again, okay?" And he walked away.'

The biggest flashpoint of the year for Axl was still to come. In keeping with Mick Jagger's penchant for inviting the most talked-about groups of the day to open for the Rolling Stones on their tours, both Guns N' Roses – as the most commercially successful rock band in the world – and Living Colour – as the most commendable, given their singularity as an all-black rock band in an almost exclusively white music genre – were invited to share the bill with the Stones when, between 18 and 22 October, they headlined four sold-out nights at the 70,000-capacity Los Angeles Coliseum football stadium.

With controversy over 'One In A Million' still raging, Living Colour vocalist Vernon Reid had voiced strong concerns in the press over the efficacy of releasing a song as apparently ill-intentioned. In order to avoid any awkward moments at the Coliseum shows, Axl and the band were allotted their own separate area backstage. Living Colour were also placed in their own special area on the opposite side of the dressing-rooms, while the Stones and their entourage occupied the largest area in the middle, surrounded by a virtual army of private security men. However, Reid, who had a reputation for his own outspoken views, managed to get his point across most forcibly when speaking from the stage the first night. He gave a short speech to the effect that he felt anybody who called somebody else a nigger – whatever the situation, but particularly in the mass-media context of a popular song – was promoting racism and bigotry, no matter how hard they tried to explain it away. The inference was obvious and large sections of the Coliseum crowd stood on their seats and applauded loudly, whistling and cheering their approval.

'We went out with a mission,' Reid admits now. 'I made a statement about "One In A Million" onstage, and I remember afterward Keith Richards made it a point to come over to the dressing-room and shake my hand.' Ultimately, he says, 'When I heard that song, I was probably more disappointed than anything, because I liked the band. [But] I thought the objectification was wack, like I'm somehow standing in the way of this guy.' When word got back to the GN'R dressing-rooms about Reid's put-down, and that it had received a standing ovation, there was concern over how Axl might react to so public an attack. According to Colleen Combs, then Axl's personal assistant, he was already so 'paranoid' about the reaction to his first major appearance onstage since the controversy over 'One In A Million' started, 'he really thought someone was going to take him out. He thought someone was going to kill him.'

There was possibly a further reason why Axl was in such a

strange mood that day. Recently, his real father, William Rose, had tried to contact him. He later confessed to *Rolling Stone* that someone purporting to be his birth-father's brother had phoned him 'right around the Stones shows'. Axl refused to take the call personally, leaving it to his half-brother, Stuart, to speak to his putative uncle. 'I needed to keep that separation,' Axl explained. The likelihood, however, was that he was probably worried about what his real father – if indeed it was him trying to get in touch – might want with him after all these years. He may also have resented the fact that, if it was him, he was only getting in touch now because his long-lost son was famous – and rich. After all, he had never been in touch before – why now?

In the event, Stuart fielded the call, asking to take a message, and Axl never heard any more about it. Straight after the Stones show, he confronted his mother, Sharon, about it and she told him that as far as she and the rest of the family were concerned, William Rose was dead – and had been for a long time. 'It looks pretty much to be true that he is,' said Axl. 'He was pretty much headed for that anyway. A very unsavoury character.'

As for 'One In A Million', if Axl was feeling any remorse over what he saw as the misconstruing of his intentions, you'd never have known it as the band followed Living Colour onstage that first afternoon. Perhaps as a way of dealing with his own guilt and fear over what Reid – and others – were saying about him, Axl sublimated his anger, as usual, by lashing out at what he now considered the more pressing problem threatening him; he announced mid-set that this would be his last appearance with the band as too many of its members had been dancing with Mr Brownstone. His actual words were: 'I hate to do this onstage. But I tried every other fucking way. And unless certain people in this band get their shit together, these will be the last Guns N' Roses shows you'll fucking ever see, 'cos I'm tired of too many people in this organization dancing with mister goddamn Brownstone!'

Axl was referring specifically to Slash and Steven, both of whom seemed smacked out for the Stones' shows. Izzy, who was also still in the throes of heroin addiction, was at least making an attempt to clean up his act after his arrest in Phoenix. Both Slash and Steven were horrified. Slash, whose mother was at the show and knew exactly who Axl was talking about, told me afterwards that he had briefly considered walking off when Axl came out with his shock announcement. However, there was no denying that he was, as he put it, going through another 'really bad phase'. He said he even avoided meeting any of the Stones, who were among his idols as a teenager, because he was so 'high out of my gourd'. He added: 'That was during my real wasted days, and basically when you are high like that you don't care who it is; nothing was more important than getting on with what I had to get on with.'

Steven, who was by then shooting up on a daily basis, was even more appalled by Axl's tirade. '[Axl] said to me, "Just start playing 'Brownstone',"' he recalls. 'So I'm playing "Brownstone" and he comes out and says everybody's fucked up on dope. He was so gone that I'm hiding there behind the drums thinking, I don't know this guy . . .'

As a result, the scene backstage after the show was one of utter pandemonium. Like the boy who cried wolf, nobody was really sure if Axl would carry out his threat. But then, nobody was really sure he wouldn't. According to Duff, everyone 'was pissed off at him for that. But I can say I was pissed off with Axl for doing that because I was not one of the guys that he was talking about. I mean, I just walked into that thing. So I was furious, of course. But the next day we were on the phone together, and, you know, it was okay, he explained his reasons for doing it. [Axl] was blowing off a lot of steam about a lot of shit. A *lot* of shit . . . That's what happens with this band, we don't bottle shit up. We just let it out.'

A few weeks later, when I got the opportunity to ask Axl for myself, he was adamant. 'That was definite and that was serious,' he said. 'I mean, I offered to go completely broke and back on the streets, 'cos it would have cost, like, an estimated $1.5 million to cancel the shows, okay? That means Axl's broke, okay? Except [for] what I've got tied up in Guns N' Roses' interests or whatever. But I didn't want to do that because I wouldn't want the band to have to pay for me cancelling the shows. I don't want Duff to lose his house 'cos Axl cancelled the shows. I couldn't live with that. But at the same time I'm not gonna be a part of watching them kill each other, just killing themselves off. It's like, we tried every other angle of getting our shit back together and in the end it had to be done live. You know, everybody else was pissed at me but afterwards Slash's mom came and shook my hand and so did his brother.'

He said that Elton John sent flowers to his dressing-room after the first show with the Stones. 'Yeah, it was great. He sent these flowers and a note. He didn't mean it against the Stones. It was meant towards the press and anybody else who was against Guns N' Roses. It said: "Don't let the bastards grind you down! I hate them all too . . . Sincerely, Elton John." That was just the greatest.'

It was only after extracting firm promises from Slash and Steven, he said, that they would clean up their acts straight after their stint with the Stones, along with the condition that Slash make an announcement from the stage saying as much – which he did, somewhat red-faced but courageously, the following night – that Axl agreed not to walk out permanently. Had it worked, though? Axl nodded his head vigorously. 'It way worked, man! 'Cos Slash is fuckin' on like a motherfucker right now. And the songs are coming together, they're coming together real heavy.'

For Slash, the real turning point, he says now, came not after Axl's headline-making speech, but three months later, after he followed his tour manager, Doug Goldstein, to an exclusive luxury resort in Phoenix where he was vacationing. 'This was when I was in my worst drug period,' says Slash, 'and actually what ended up getting me to clean up. [Doug is] on the golf course and all of a sudden the fuckin' police come looking for him saying, "We've got a naked guy in handcuffs. He assaulted a maid." I'd smashed up my room, there was glass. I was all bloody. I'd showed up in Phoenix the night before. I'd done all [my drugs] and mentally had a trip-out scene. I took off running naked out of the shower – went through the glass shower windows. Ran out naked onto the resort, into one of the rooms, ran over this maid and kept running. It was a big scene.' Narrowly avoiding arrest, he flew back to LA and checked into a hotel. 'I passed out and woke up to what they call an "intervention". I ended up going for the first and only time to rehab, which lasted for all of about three days. I said, "I'm not that fucked up." So I got out and took myself to Hawaii – on my own this time – and dried out. I've never had that serious a problem since then.'

By then Izzy had also quit for good, following his own 'turning point' when he was arrested and placed on probation. 'That was my wake-up call,' he says. 'That was the point where I said, this has got to fuckin' stop. I didn't wanna wind up dead or, worse, in prison.' Suddenly the band's enforced lay-off had an unforeseen positive side. With the time and the motive to clean up his act properly, Izzy went into rehab and began professional counselling. What really made him stop, though, he thinks now, 'was I *wanted* to. 'Cos I figured, at some point your heart's just gonna pop, or your mind's gonna snap, right? Eventually, that shit will kill ya, and it does. It kills people all the time. Once I got maybe like a week of sobriety, like actually going a whole week without a drink, I thought, oh god, if I can just keep this up . . .'

It wasn't easy. 'I'd been straight for a long time before some of the others even noticed. They'd offer me a line. I'd say, "Uh, no thanks, I don't anymore, remember?" But these were like the only friends I had. Those first five years we were together, the band was like our little family. Dysfunctional as hell but everybody had each other, you know?' Indeed, 1989 had ended on an upbeat note for both Axl and Izzy, who had accepted an invitation to join the Rolling Stones onstage at their show, on 17 December, in Atlantic City, New Jersey, for an extended version of 'Salt Of The Earth'. They showed up and did it all again at the next two Stones shows as well, on 19 and 20 December. The only downside for the headliners was that Axl had kept them all waiting for the initial rehearsal. Even the naturally phlegmatic Keith Richards was put out. 'Fucking kids,' the exasperated guitarist was overheard saying afterwards. 'What ya gonna do, you know?'

The mess and confusion over 'One In A Million', however, would continue to dog both Axl and the band for years to come. Speaking to me at length about it in January 1990, during our interview at his blacked-out West Hollywood apartment, Axl began by making light of what Vernon Reid had said about the song. 'Vernon Reid was talking about how people make racial jokes, but that it was kind of sad. Because you'll laugh but then, after all, when you think about it, it *is* sad. But humour and comedy, you know, everybody makes fun of everybody and everything. It's kind of like you go, well, I can't find a way to be happy, maybe I can find something to laugh at for a moment and take my mind off things . . .'

Was that all 'One In A Million' was, then, a joke? He nodded thoughtfully. 'The whole song coming together took me by surprise. I mean, yeah, I wrote the song as a joke. West [Arkeen] just got robbed by two black guys on Christmas night a few years back. He went out to play guitar on Hollywood Boulevard in front of a bank at, like, Highland and Hollywood . . . he's standing there playing and he gets robbed at knife-point for seventy-eight cents. A couple of days later we're all sitting around, we're watching TV, there's Duff and me and West and a couple of others. And we're all bummed out, hungover and this and that. And I'm sitting there pissed off with no money, no job, feeling guilty for being at West's house, sucking up oxygen and stuff. And I got hold of this guitar – and I can only play, like, the top two strings, right? But I'd been fuckin' around with this little riff for a while, little by little. It was the only thing I could play on the guitar. So all of a sudden I wanted to write some words as a joke, right? We'd just watched Sam Kinnison on the video, you know, so I was gonna make my jokes, too. So I started writing this thing. And when I said "Police and niggers / That's right . . ." that was to fuck with West's head. 'Cos he couldn't believe I would write that, right? And it came out like that, okay?' Maybe it was one of those jokes you had to be there to find funny, I said. He shrugged and lit another cigarette. He said it was true that he had underestimated the scale of the reaction the song would provoke. 'I used a word, it's part of the English language whether it's a good word or not. It's a derogatory word, it's a negative word. It's not meant to the entire black race, but it was directed towards black people in those situations.' He shrugged.

'I was robbed, I was ripped off, you know? I had my life

threatened, okay? And it's like, I described it in one word. And I wanted to see the effect of a racial joke. I wanted to see the effect that would have on the world. Slash was into it.' Now it was my turn to shrug and look confused. 'It wasn't contrived so much as we were trying to grow with it,' he insisted. 'Now after getting beat up over it in the press we're like, hey, fuck you! It says: "Don't wanna buy none of your gold chains today." Now a black person on Oprah Winfrey who goes, "They're putting down black people" is going to fuckin' take one of these guys at the bus stop home and feed him and take care of him and let him babysit their kids? They ain't gonna be near the guy, okay? And it's, like, I don't think a black person is a nigger. I don't care. I'm like, they're whatever, you know? I consider myself, like, green and from another planet or something . . . I never felt I fairly fit into any group, so to speak. But it's like . . . a black person has this three hundred years of whatever on his shoulder. I don't got nothin' to do with that! It bores me, too.'

He knew plenty of black people that felt the same way, he said. 'Like, a black chick came up to me when we were in Chicago and goes, "You know, I hated you 'cos of 'One In A Million'. But I ride the subway, and I looked around one day and I know what you're talking about. So you're all right." I've got a lot of that.' He went on, 'Ice T sent a letter, wanting to work with me on "Welcome To The Jungle" if I ever did it as a rap thing. And I got the word to Ezee E that I'm interested in having him be a part of it too, if we ever do it. I mean, I don't think it'll be on this [next] record now, there's already too much material. But we ended up having this big heavy conversation about "One In A Million", and they could see where I was coming from. And those guys know more about that shit than most.'

He began to tire of talking about it, sensing the circles he knew he was going in. 'I don't defend it,' he growled. 'I just record it.' I asked him instead to talk me through the rest of it. He said the chorus – where he sings about 'Trying to reach you/ But you were much too high' – came about 'because I was getting, like, really far away, like "Rocket Man" Elton John, you know, like in my head; getting really far away from all my friends and family in Indiana. I realized those people have no concept of who I am any more, even the ones I was close to. Since then I've flown people out here, had 'em hang out here. I've paid for everything. But there was no joy in it for them. I was smashing shit, going fuckin' nuts, and yet trying to work. And they were going, "Man, I don't wanna be a rocker any more if you go through this." But at the same time, you know, I brought 'em out and we just hung out for a couple months, wrote songs together, had serious talks. It was almost like being on acid, 'cos it would just get to serious talks about the family and life and stuff. And we'd get really heavy and get to know each other all over again. Just trying to fuckin' replace eight years of knowing each other every single day, you know, and now all of a sudden I'm in this new world . . .'

Back in Indiana he had been just 'a street kid with a skate-board and no money who talked about being in a rock band. And now all of a sudden I'm here, you know? And they're kind of amused, freaked out and all kinds of stuff by their friends putting up Axl posters, and it's just weird to them . . . they ask, why don't I call? It's like, well come out here and watch how many times my phone rings.' We both looked at the phone, which had rung just once since I'd arrived a couple of hours before. 'It doesn't ring that much tonight,' he said, reading my thoughts, 'because nobody thinks I'm here. So anyway, all of a sudden I came up with this chorus: "You're one in a million." And then: "We tried to reach you but you were much too high."' A deliberate 'drug analogy' he said, because 'the language is always the hippest language.' Mainly, though, he was simply 'picturing 'em trying to call me if, like, I disappeared or died or something.'

Ultimately, however well Axl defended the song or found new ways to explain it away, the after-effects of 'One In A Million' would continue to reverberate around him for years. That wasn't his fault, though, he said. He wasn't the one to blame. It was everyone – and everything – else. Not least his own band, whose shaky defence of the song he deeply resented. Why, when he needed them, hadn't they backed him up more? If 'One In A Million' had any real consequences for Guns N' Roses, it lay in Axl's newfound desire never to find himself in that position again. Looking back now it's easy to see it as the beginning of his move to become the all-powerful leader of the group; one whose decisions would never be questioned again, however wayward they might seem to the rest of the world. It was in that sense the beginning of the end, for both Axl Rose and Guns N' Roses . . .

As we spoke that night, Axl sat with his back to the balcony window, an undraped glass wall, the lights of the city twinkling behind his head like some vast dark garden of fireflies. I sat opposite him, with an impressive art deco glass coffee-table planted solidly between us. 'This is the third one I've had,' he remarked, running a hand lovingly across its surface. What happened to the other two, I asked politely? 'I got pissed and smashed 'em,' he replied matter-of-factly. At different times, he said, he had also smashed every mirror in the place and thrown his piano off the balcony. What drove him to such extremes, he said, were the same simple desires he walked off the bus with when he first arrived in LA seven years ago. The simplest things still amused him; but the ugliest things were what enthralled him. 'I've got this little psycho-ball. It's just the thing at times like this,' he said, his voice as deep as a well. 'Where did it go?' He rummaged around among the empty Coke cans, cigarette packets, magazines and ashtrays that littered the table – then found what he was looking for: a small, apparently harmless rubber ball. He squeezed it and a terrible wheezing scream filled the room. Axl immediately cheered up. 'It's supposed to be for helping to relieve tension,' he smiled. Then gave it another squeeze. Another long, nerve-jangling wail filled the room. 'I use it all the time . . .'

It was January 1990, a few days after the New Year's holidays. I asked him how his Christmas had been and he pulled a face. 'I had the worst New Year's and Christmas in my fuckin' life, man, as far as I was concerned. I'm in a good mood tonight 'cos it's fuckin' over and I fuckin' lived through it.'

He had 'fuckin' hibernated,' he said, 'didn't see anybody. People say that's wrong. But it wasn't wrong, it worked out really good for me. Then last night I had, like, eight people here and I was in shock. Eight people that were all close friends. Like, whoa! Immediately it was like . . . all heavy talk. This happened with my family, oh yeah, this happened with my girlfriend, dah dah

dah. It was just heavy. Heaviness all around.' He began talking about West again, who he said had just had his nose broken in a fight. 'He went down to a bar, or a liquor store, really drunk and some guy said something and got in West's face. West said something back and the guy just smashed a beer bottle in his nose.' He scrutinized the walls. 'That's fucking unreal, huh?' Axl sat there for a moment, skipping TV channels with the remote, gazing at several screens at once, all of them silent, like a scene from the 'Welcome To The Jungle' video – minus the bouffant hairdo, a contemptuous smile on his face.

Just prior to the October shows with the Stones, the band had shot a video for 'It's So Easy' at the Cathouse club in LA, directed once again by Nigel Dick. I asked him why, as the song had already been a single over two years earlier: were they thinking of re-releasing it, perhaps? A strange idea since no radio station would be able to play it.

'We always wanted to do a video for that song,' he said. 'We're gonna have a home video at some point, so we wanted to do some videos that were, like, completely no holds barred, uncensored type of things. Just live shooting, instead of worrying about whether MTV is gonna play it. Just go out there and do a fuckin' blown-out live, real risky video.' It was during the Cathouse shoot that Axl apparently got into an altercation with David Bowie, who he had taken umbrage with for supposedly flirting with Erin. 'Bowie and I had our differences,' he shrugged. 'And then we went out for dinner and talked and went to the China Club and stuff."'

Axl recalled how at the Stones' shows Mick Jagger and a visiting Eric Clapton had cornered him about Bowie at the soundcheck. 'I'm sitting on this amp and all of a sudden they're both right there in front of me. And Jagger doesn't really talk a lot, right? He's just real serious about everything. And all of a sudden he was like [doing a Cockney accent] "So you got in a fight with Bowie, didja?" I told him the story real quick and him and Clapton are going off about Bowie in their own little world, talking about things from years of knowing each other. They were saying that when Bowie drinks he can turn into a Devil from Bromley! I mean, I'm not even *in* this conversation.

I'm just sitting there and every now and then they would ask me a couple more facts about what happened, and then they would go back to bitchin' like crazy about Bowie. I was just sitting there going, wow . . .'

Bowie, though, was 'really cool', he said. 'We started talking about the business and I never met anybody so cool and so into it and so whacked out and so sick in my life . . . And Bowie's sitting there laughing. Then he starts talking about, "One side of me is experimental, and one side of me wants to make something that people get into. And I don't know fucking why! Why am I like this?" And I'm, like, thinking to myself, I've got twenty more years of *that* to look forward to? I'm already like this! Twenty more years? It was heavy, man . . .'

I asked Axl if he saw himself as the leader of Guns N' Roses? He certainly seemed to act that way. 'Listen, after working with Jagger it was like, don't ever call me a dictator again, man.' He smiled wanly. 'You can go and work for the Stones and you'll learn the hard way.' Jagger, he said, was the one who 'makes it happen. With the looseness that those guys have and the amount of people around them you need somebody being the general, you know? And he does it. He has to do it. 'Cos the frontman . . . you don't plan on that job. You don't want that job. You don't want to be that guy to the guys in your band that you hang with and you look up to. But somebody's got to do it.'

I remarked that it was two years since the band last recorded anything new in the studio. What had been delaying them, I wondered – the drug habits that Axl had referred to onstage at the Stones shows, perhaps? 'Partly,' he acknowledged. 'But another reason things have been so hard in a way is this. The first album was basically written off Axl coming up with maybe one line and maybe a melody for that line or how I want to present that line, how I'm gonna say it or yell it or whatever, okay? And then we'd build a song around it. Or someone came up with one line, okay? On this, Izzy's brought in eight songs – at least. Slash has brought in an album. I've brought in an album. Duff brought in one song. He said all his in one song. It's called "Why Do You Look At Me When You Hate Me?" and it's just bad-assed. I wrote a bunch of words to that, but Duff brought in the song . . .'

As far as the next album was concerned, he said, 'If we can pull this thing off, if we do this right, it'll be five years before we have to make another album. And we can have five years to . . .' What? 'It's not so much like five years to sit on our asses. It's like, five years to figure out what we're gonna say next, you know? After the crowd and the people figure out how they're gonna react to this album, and then the mental changes we will go through . . .' He tailed off.

'This record will have seen us grown a lot,' he said eventually. 'There'll be some childish, you know, arrogant, male, false bravado crap on there, too. But there'll also be some really heavy, serious stuff.' Musically, he said, 'You have a choice, man. You can grow or die, you know? And it's like, that's what we have to do. We *have* to do it. We have to grow. You know, we can't do the same sludge. I can't play sludge, man, for fuckin' twenty years!'

He said he saw himself as 'reaching some sort of peak'. He spoke earnestly of a couple of songs he was working on that 'if they come off like I want them to, are going to be the biggest things this band has ever done. I was working on, like, writing these ballads that I feel have really rich tapestries and stuff, and making sure each note in effect is right. [Because] it has to be the right note and it has to be held in the right way and it has to have the right effect, you know?' He was referring specifically to a ballad he'd written called 'November Rain', a song he'd begun as a child, he said, but had only now brought to the band. 'If we get that right,' he said, 'I can walk away from this . . .' Walk away? Why would he want to do that? 'Because I've done it, man. I can work a *stadium* now, you know? I've done it. So if I wanted to . . . I could walk away.'

He said that ultimately he preferred the whole business of recording to touring. 'If I'm psyched for the gig, great. Nine times out of ten, though, before the gig I'll always not wanna do the fuckin' show and hate it. I mean, I love it when I'm psyched, you know, let's go! But most of the time I'm, like, mad about something, something's fuckin' going wrong . . . I'm nervous. I'm like, "I'm not playing for these fuckin' people!" Not the crowd so much. But, you know, situations are always different before a show. Something always fuckin' happens. And I react like a motherfucker to it. I don't like this pot-smoking mentality.' He sucked in his cheeks. 'I feel like Lenny Kravitz. Like, peace and love, motherfucker, or you're gonna die! I'm gonna kick your ass if you fuck with my garden, you know? I like that attitude more.'

Had the overwhelming fame thrust on him bolstered that attitude? 'What do you mean?' he asked suspiciously. You know, forced you to be larger than life, I prodded. Obnoxious because you knew there would always be somebody there to take care of it?

A long pause. 'No. I've always been that way,' he said, eyes narrowed. 'But now I'm in a position to just be myself more. And the thing is people allow me to do it whether they like it or not, you know?'

Did he take advantage of that situation, though, to use the heights to which the public had elevated Guns N' Roses to shit on those he despised below? Another long pause. 'No,' he eventually decided. 'No, usually I'm just an emotionally unbalanced person.' He sniggered. 'Maybe it's chemical, I don't know. 'Cos maybe emotions have something to do with chemicals in your brain, or whatever. So then it's a chemical imbalance. I'm usually an emotional wreck before a show anyway, because of something else that's going on in my life or whatever. I mean, something weird will happen in my family. Like, I finally found William Rose, okay? He was murdered in '84 and buried in seven miles of strip-mining in Illinois. I found that out, like, two days before a show and I was whacked, right? It was fuckin' gnarly.'

He claimed he was disappointed not to have made the old man's acquaintance again. 'I was trying to uncover this mystery since I was a little kid, you know? 'Cos as a kid I was always told that it was the Devil that made me know what the inside of a house looked like that I supposedly never lived in. But I knew I did. I knew I'd lived in this house when I was a little kid. Weird things like that happen. So I've been trying to track down this William Rose guy. Not like, I love this guy, he's my father. I just wanted to know about my heritage and what my hereditary traits might be. You know, am I gonna have an elbow that bugs the shit out of me in, like, three or four years. Is that a hereditary trait or what? I wanted to know.'

I asked if he knew exactly how his father had died. 'No. But it was probably, like, at close range, man,' he deadpanned. 'Wonderful family, man. Just wonderful . . .' I wanted to return to what he said earlier, about 'walking away'. Could Axl now really leave all this behind, I wondered? Not just financially, but artistically, spiritually, emotionally, even? If he wanted to, could Axl really turn his back on Guns N' Roses and just walk away?

'If I wanted to badly enough,' he asserted. 'This is all right, in bits and pieces. But whether it'll take up all the chapters in the book of my life, I don't know. But I'll write in bits and pieces – whether I ever compose it into a book or not – for the rest of my life. I'll always do that. But I would also like to record for a long time. And . . . I have to make this [next] album. Then it doesn't matter. This album is the album I've always been waiting on. Our second album is the album I've been waiting on since before we got signed. I mean, we were planning out the second album before we started work on the first one. This is the thing, okay? But as much as it means to me, yeah, if it bombed or whatever, if that would happen, yeah, I'm sure I'd be bummed business-wise and let down, or whatever. But at the same time, it doesn't matter. It's like, I got it out there, you know. So what? That's the artistic thing. And then I could walk away.'

What about the money, though? 'I'd like to make the cash off the touring,' he said. 'I'd like to walk away knowing that, like, I can support my kids for whatever they want for the rest of their lives off my interest rates, you know? I'd like to have that security. I've never known any security in my whole life, you know? Some people are like, oh, why don't you give money to this or that? You know, you have all this money. I'm like, well, no, I got a certain interest rate and I bought my security. You bought your house, didn't you? I worked for my livelihood too, you know? I have that in the bank now and I'll keep it, you know? What I can spend off interest and shit like that, I'll do. But I don't wanna give away my security unless I'm like . . .'

Forced to? 'Yeah.'

The only thing he really cared about now, he said, was 'this damn album, man. It's like, Guns N' Roses doesn't fully function, nothing ever really happens to its utmost potential, unless it's a kamikaze run. Unless it's like, this is it, man! Like, fuck it, let's go down in fuckin' flames with this motherfucker . . . you know?'

I wasn't sure that I did, actually. Instead, I watched him draw another cigarette from the pack. Light it, inhale . . .

Part Three

RINGSIDE

Holding on to anger is like grasping a hot coal
with the intent of throwing it at someone else;
you are the one who gets burned.

BUDDHA

Chapter Seven

THE RED-HEADED DICTATOR

Despite Axl's best efforts to get the band moving forward again, for Guns N' Roses the 1990s began just as the 1980s had ended: dissolute, distracted, no nearer to starting work on their next album. Attending the same Hollywood party as a surprisingly subdued Slash and a spectacularly drunk Duff, we saw the New Year in together by sharing a bottle of Dom Perignon and counting in the chimes on MTV. Axl was also supposed to be there but it was no surprise when he didn't show up. As he later told me, he had been 'hibernating' all through the Christmas and New Year's holidays. Izzy had spent the night in alone with his new girlfriend Anneka, glad not to have to fight temptation. Newly sober but still on probation, as he says now, this was the period when he was at his most fragile. 'I'd come in for rehearsals and there's one of the guys on a road case with a big line of coke. "Hey, Iz – you want some coke?" Ah, no thanks, I just got back from my probation officer, you know? To get sober is really [tough] but to do it like that, in a situation where everybody's still using . . .' He shook his head.

Steven, meanwhile, was still living life at the opposite end of the drug spectrum. Speaking to *Classic Rock* magazine in 2005, he recalled how his habit had grown significantly worse throughout 1989, 'until after a month of doing heroin every day this one day came along when I didn't do heroin and I was sick as a dog. I couldn't understand it, so I called the manager [Doug Goldstein], who took me to a doctor that gave me an opiate blocker. I didn't know that you couldn't take opiate blockers with opiates in your system. It only made me worse. I literally had to crawl to the bathroom.'

Nevertheless, seemingly without trying, controversy and public outcry kept their names consistently in the news. On 22 January, Slash and Duff attended the American Music Awards, a staid music-industry event held annually at LA's Shrine Auditorium and televised live across America. Staggering up to the podium to accept the first of two awards they'd been nominated for, each clutching a bottle of wine, Slash had the buttoned-up patrons tut-tutting loudly when he uttered the word 'shit'. Then, when he began his speech with the words, 'I want to thank fuckin' – oops!' the invited crowd grew visibly agitated. As if to rub it in, he continued by thanking Alan Niven and Doug Goldstein 'for fuckin' getting us there'. At which point the TV director panicked and cut to a commercial break. ABC, the network that aired the show, logged hundreds of complaints and the following morning the story made the front pages of both the *Los Angeles* and *New York Times*.

Inevitably, while such shenanigans may have irritated the LA music industry establishment, it only deepened the band's popularity with their ever-growing audience. With sales of *Appetite* and *Lies* now topping twenty million worldwide, Guns N' Roses was officially not only the most successful rock band in the world, they were now, suddenly and against all odds, the most fashionable. Other artists clamoured to work with them – Michael Jackson, Bob Dylan, Iggy Pop, Alice Cooper and Lenny Kravitz would all invite either Axl or Slash to contribute to their next albums – while artists as diverse as Elton John, Bono, George Michael and Queen guitarist Brian May now declared themselves fans. Similarly, a titillated media intelligentsia lined up to see who could portray them in the most outrageous terms: Herb Ritts wanted to photograph them; Doors biographer Danny Sugarman declared Axl to be the veritable inheritor of the 'Dionysiac spirit of Jim Morrison', seeking enlightenment through oblivion.

Not all these approaches were appreciated by the band. Slash, who had enjoyed playing on Jackson's and Kravitz's albums, described working with Dylan as a disaster, having been asked to 'strum like Django Rheinhardt' on one track that the singer later wiped from the finished album. While Axl, in thrall to Sugarman's famously hagiographical portrait of Morrison, *No One Here Gets Out Alive*, had been unduly flattered by the writer's hyperbole, he later publicly dismissed Ritts as one of those people that needed 'to get the fuck out of my ass'.

Musically, however, the band was no closer to getting it together. It was common knowledge that they were back in Rumbo Studios, working on a spectacular new song Slash and Duff had concocted called 'Civil War', for which Axl had penned some of his best lyrics yet. It was equally well known that the sessions were fraught with problems. Rumours suggested that most of the problems surrounded Steven, who was still struggling with smack addiction. It was so bad that a close friend of the band told me they were on the point of firing the drummer.

'Was it true about Steven?' I asked Axl when we spoke on the phone in February. Had he been fired? 'No,' said Axl. 'He is back in the band.' 'Back' in the band? So he was out for a period, then? 'Yeah,' he said. 'He was definitely out of the band. He wasn't necessarily fired. We worked with [former Sea Hags drummer] Adam Maples; we worked with [former Pretenders drummer] Martin Chambers. Then Steven did the Guns N' Roses thing and got his shit together. And it worked. He did it. And Steven plays the songs better than any of 'em. He's just bad-assed and he's GN'R. And so, if he doesn't blow it, we're gonna try the album with him.' He paused then added, 'You know, we worked out a contract with him. He's going to do the album and, if he doesn't blow it, then he's going to do the tour. Then if he doesn't blow that he's fully reinstated.'

'Fully reinstated' – what did that mean? Steven's position was sounding weaker by the moment. Axl wasn't in the mood to explain any further, his thoughts on his own future. The plan now, he said, was to reconvene in the studio in May, when they would be joined by a new member, he added almost matter-of-factly: a keyboardist named Dizzy. (Real name: Darren Reed.)

I expressed surprise. None of the others had ever mentioned the possibility of adding someone to the band. As it transpired, the appointment of a new member had been a decision taken by Axl on the spur of the moment. Dizzy was a twenty-six-year-old from Hinsdale, Illinois, who had like Axl migrated to LA in the early-1980s, playing in a succession of small-time club bands like The Wild, Hairy Bananas, Bootleg and Johnny And Jaguars. According to Axl he'd first been asked to join Guns N' Roses in 1986. 'But the very same day,' said Axl, 'he was in a car wreck and had his hand smashed, so he had to get pins and stuff put in it. Then he came into rehearsal a few months ago and played three songs that he'd never heard before, songs that we didn't even plan having piano in, that were heavy metal. But he put heavy metal piano into it, you know? And it was amazing.' When he discovered Dizzy was about to be evicted from his apartment Axl called Alan Niven and said, ' "Secure this guy, hire him. Write up the contracts. Put him on salary and give him an advance so he can get an apartment." So now we have a piano player.'

Dizzy's first gig with the band – and as it turned out, Steven's last – occurred just a few weeks later on 7 April, when they appeared – along with Bob Dylan and event co-organizer John Cougar Mellencamp – at the fourth annual Farm Aid concert in Indianapolis. The set included a first performance of 'Civil War' – the first new song added to the set for over two years, for which Axl donned a ten-gallon hat and shades – and an unrehearsed stab at 'Down On The Farm' by the UK Subs, during which Steven, who had never even heard the song let alone played it, found himself covering up by jumping up on the drum riser 'and almost breaking his fucking neck', Slash recalls. True to form, the band never did make it into the studio in May. Instead, according to Erin in an interview for *People* magazine, exactly three weeks after the Farm Aid show, Axl drove over to her house at 4.00 a.m. and threatened to kill himself if she didn't marry him that very night. She dressed and jumped into his black BMW and they drove to Las Vegas and were married at Cupid's Inn the same day. Less than a month on, Axl filed for divorce – then forty-eight hours later changed his mind again.

Axl's relationship with Erin had always been turbulent but this was a new low, even for them. Erin periodically moved into the West Hollywood apartment with Axl, but it always ended the same way: rows, fights, mirrors smashed, bottles broken. At one point, Axl even bought a house for them in the Hollywood Hills, which they redesigned and furnished together, installing a grand piano and having two topiary elephants helicoptered into the grounds. But when it was ready they rowed again and never moved in. Accordingly to Erin's deposition when they later divorced Axl was so furious he spray-painted a picture of a gravestone on the garage door and wrote underneath: 'Erin Rose: RIP Sweet Child O' Die. Slut. You Were One Of Many, Nothing Special.'

Axl blamed a lot of his anger with Erin on his own difficult beginnings. Kim Neely quoted him in *Rolling Stone* in 1992 explaining how he had recently uncovered childhood memories of 'being sexually abused' and 'watching something horrible happen to my mother when she came to get me'. As a result, he now said he suffered physical reactions that manifested themselves in the form of 'problems in my legs and stuff from muscles being damaged then'. He had grown up to believe 'sex is power and sex leaves you powerless'. Views he now realized were 'distorted' but which he'd had 'to live my life with'.

It wasn't all one-way traffic in the relationship, though. According to friends, Erin could be a flirt. She thought it hardly likely he had been faithful to her while he was on the road with the band, and this was her way of paying him back. 'She knew how to push his buttons,' says one friend. Others simply saw it as Erin's doomed attempt to try and exert some small element of control over Axl's uncontrollable moods. A view concurred by Michelle Young: 'Erin would call me and say, "Axl's crazy – he's throwing things around." She pushed his buttons, but I know that he loved her.' Yet others say that she may have been spoiled and liked to get her own way. 'Erin has never worked a day in her life, except the modelling gigs she gave up when she met Axl.'

Whatever the truth, it was after another fight that one of the defining moments in Axl's relationship with both Erin Everly and Steven Adler occurred – the flash point being Axl's belief that Adler gave Erin heroin. According to Steven, he'd been hanging out at his house one afternoon when Erin arrived. She was clearly ill already and he now insists that he was the one who tried to help her. 'I'm the one who carried her and put her in my bed and called the ambulance and saved her life.' He is adamant he did not give her heroin. 'For one, I only [had] a little bit left, and if you've ever been a heroin addict, you ain't giving away your last bit. Two, this was Axl's fucking girl.'

All hell broke loose, according to Steven, when Axl was told he had given Erin heroin, news which Axl (according to Steven's version of events) reacted to with fury, immediately phoning Steven and threatening him.

Axl never showed up. In fact, giving his own version of events two years later, he claimed he forgave Steven 'after he nearly killed my wife', even though Axl had been forced 'to spend a night with her in an intensive care unit because her heart had stopped thanks to Steven. She was hysterical, and he shot her up with a speedball. She had never done jack shit as far as drugs go, and he shoots her up with a mixture of heroin and cocaine? I kept myself from doing anything to him. I kept the man from being killed by members of her family. I saved him from having to go to court, because her mother wanted him held responsible for his actions.'

Instead, it was announced a few weeks later that Steven was no longer in the band. As far as Axl was concerned, Steven had been 'fucking up' almost since the band's inception. The incident with Erin was the last straw. Even the official press announcement made no bones about why he'd been fired: he was a heroin addict. He'd been warned that if he didn't clean up he would be fired. Now he had been. 'Ah, man, it was fucked up,' says Slash now. 'Izzy and I went through great pains to get our shit cleaned up [but] we never could fuckin' pull Steven back in, and we really tried.'

Steven doesn't deny that Axl had already given him one official warning, but even then, he says, it was under heavy manners. Alan Niven's assistant Doug Goldstein had called him into the office and given him contracts to sign that stipulated the drummer would be fined $2,000 every time he was found to have taken heroin. According to both Axl and Slash, the turning point was Steven's flawed attempts to record his drum parts for 'Civil War' in Rumbo Studios back in January. Speaking to *RIP*, Slash claimed they had been forced to abandon the sessions because 'Steven would nod out to the point where he would be on a stool, but his head would be touching the floor. He'd say, "I'm tired. I'm sleepy" and he couldn't play. That was basically it. We gave him so many chances to turn around . . .'

But Steven claims his timing had been 'so up and down'

because he was 'sick from the opiate blocker I got from the doctor that Doug Goldstein took me to . . .' So that when 'Slash called me on a Thursday, knowing that I was sick, and said, "We're going in the studio this weekend," I said, "Dude, you know I can't go, I'm sick from this bullshit medication." He said we can't waste the money, and I said don't even tell me about wasting money, we know somebody who [has] wasted plenty of fucking money!' referring to Axl's no-show in Chicago the previous summer. 'If one of them was sick,' Steven says now, 'it would have been postponed. We just weren't a team any more.'

Fair or not, Steven was out. His replacement was twenty-six-year-old Matt Sorum. Born in Long Beach to English-Norwegian parents, Matt's mother was a music teacher who had initiated an early appreciation of classical and opera. His path to becoming a drummer began with a childhood fascination for Ringo Starr and the influence of his older, Hendrix-loving brothers. Having joined his first band in high school, by fourteen he was playing Sunset Strip haunts such as the Starwood and the Whiskey A Go-Go. After graduating, he met guitarist Gregg Wright at a gig at the Central Club (later the Viper Room, co-owned by Johnny Depp) and began travelling. By nineteen, he was in New Orleans playing in well-known French Quarter dives like Jimmy's and Ol' Man River's. Returning to LA in the mid-1980s, he played various gigs and sessions with artists including Shaun Cassidy, Belinda Carlisle, Solomon Burke, Tori Amos and the Jeff Paris band, who he recorded his first album with in 1987.

Matt got his big break the following year when he joined British rockers The Cult, then on the verge of their commercial breakthrough in America with the Bob Rock-produced *Sonic Temple* album and attendant hit singles 'Fire Woman' and 'Edie'. Touring in The Cult with bands like Metallica and Aerosmith, Slash saw the band when they headlined the Universal Amphitheater in LA in the summer of 1990 and 'figured I'd steal him'. Which is exactly what he did.

The first song Matt recorded with Guns N' Roses was a new version of Dylan's 'Knockin' On Heaven's Door' for the soundtrack to the forthcoming Tom Cruise movie, *Days Of Thunder* (a typically 'high concept' Hollywood blockbuster about motor racing described as '*Top Gun* on four wheels'). Large and muscular and a player of tremendous natural power and precision, Matt was in many ways the perfect replacement for the drug-enfeebled Steven, although, as he admits now, he was hardly drug-free himself at the time. There was one crucial difference, however: 'Here I was replacing the drug addict drummer, right? But he did heroin and I had cocaine.'

Having finally dealt with Steven Adler, Axl spent the summer of 1990 working on fixing his disintegrating relationship with Erin. Their systematic reconciliations never lasted long, though. She may have been a flirt, but for her his mood-swings were becoming more out of control. According to her sworn deposition, which was quoted in *Spin*, she said that once, while she was walking ahead of him, he stubbed his toe and immediately flew into a rage, blaming her 'because he was coming to tell me something'.

Yet for all his oddball moments Axl was always deeply sorry afterwards. Speaking two years later, he said he still cried 'every time I think of how horrible we treated each other. Erin and I treated each other like shit. Sometimes we treated each other great, because the children in us were best friends. But then there were other times when we just fucked each other's lives completely up.'

It was also during one of their periodic live-ins, in the summer of 1990, that Erin fell pregnant. Although he acted cool about it in front of his friends, Axl was secretly delighted. In October Erin suffered a miscarriage that affected him more deeply than he could ever have imagined. Despite the rebel-rousing image, friends of Axl had been reported as saying that he desperately wanted to have children and start a family of his own. To make things worse, on 30 October, the day after Erin's miscarriage, Axl was arrested on a charge of 'assault with a deadly weapon'. The 'deadly weapon' was actually an empty wine bottle. According to his next-door neighbour he threatened her with it after she threatened to call the police if he didn't turn down the music blaring from his apartment. Axl claimed the neighbour was an obsessed fan who swung a bottle at him before he took it from her. He was released on $5,000 bail, and the case was eventually dismissed six weeks later.

According to Erin, unable to live with the strain of being with him, by the end of 1990 she walked out on Axl for good. In January 1991, their marriage was officially annulled, one consequence of which was that Erin didn't receive the hefty financial settlement she would have been entitled to if the marriage had ended in divorce. At first, this hardly mattered. Exhausted and depressed by the experience, she was, she told friends, just glad to be rid of him. But over time, once the worst of the wounds had healed, she began to think differently. Despite the emotional cuts and bruises, Erin Everly wasn't quite done with Axl Rose yet.

Meanwhile, work on the new Guns N' Roses album finally began in earnest in September 1990 in Studio One at A&M Studios in Hollywood. With Matt Sorum replacing Steven Adler on the drums and Axl leaving the band to get on with it, the backing tracks to almost forty new songs were all recorded in less than a month. Once that was done, recording continued at The Record Plant, where at one stage Axl had a bed installed so he could literally work round-the-clock on getting his vocals done. He also had a boxer's punchbag brought in for him to work out his frustrations on, as well as two customized Kiss and Elton John pinball machines. 'There was no heat in that room,' he later recalled. 'It was a cold, lonely place, but it was the only place I could stay to keep myself in the work. It was cool-looking, but it was dark, cold and weird.' The other reason he'd moved into the studio, he said, was because 'I couldn't go back to my condo because of my neighbour. That was a nightmare . . .'

'None of us had anything to say about the music at that point,' Matt Sorum recalls. 'Axl had this vision he was going to create. We'd start [recording] at noon, the work ethic was cool. There was a lot of alcohol around, but the heroin thing had definitely subsided at that point – Slash had quit, Izzy had quit. We were dabbling in cocaine and partying rituals.' By the end of the sessions, however, 'it was later nights. We'd start at six or seven. Axl would want to do "November Rain" and "Don't Cry", his songs.'

Axl also took to inviting some of his newfound friends down

to the studio when drugs were off limit. 'It was candlelight in the studio,' Matt remembers. 'You'd look and there's Sean Penn and Bruce Springsteen hanging out, and supermodels like Naomi Campbell. It was like a Fellini movie! But it was never really cool to do a lot of drugs in front of Axl. I did some coke with him once and he talked for about fuckin' ten hours! I never did coke with him again . . .'

There were also guest star performances. Alice Cooper, who sang vocals on 'The Garden', was staying in LA at the Sunset Marquis hotel when Axl called him out of the blue. Not really familiar with the band's work, Cooper was pleasantly surprised to discover how hard-working Axl could be. 'When you're in the studio one-on-one with him, he's really amazing – the guy can really sing. I did my bit maybe three times, but Axl was a perfectionist – almost to the point where you want to say, "At some point, Axl, it's gotta be good enough." '

The band had already agreed to allow an early version of 'Civil War' – perhaps the most ironic flag-waver since Hendrix's wilfully misshapen version of 'Star Spangled Banner' twenty years before – to appear on the *Nobody's Angel* compilation album, a fund-raiser organized under the aegis of George Harrison, with the proceeds going to the Romanian Angel Appeal (a charity set up to aid the children left orphaned by the Romanian Uprising of December 1989). In July 1990, a rough-hewn studio out-take of 'Knockin' On Heaven's Door' found its way onto the soundtrack album to the *Days of Thunder* film. The resultant video – itself an out-take of a performance filmed at the Ritz club in New York in 1988 – quickly shot to number one on the MTV most-requested charts, despite Axl's swearing throughout the song being bleeped out.

With Axl insisting he wanted all the material the band was recording to be made available more or less simultaneously, the problem he presented Geffen was how to package it all in some coherent form that made sense to both them and the singer. Axl pushed for a release of one massive quadruple box-set, but Geffen baulked at such an extravagant proposal. As an alternative, Axl suggested they release two double-albums simultaneously. Geffen were understandably sceptical. Tom Zutaut suggested a compromise: the release of a double album, followed a year later – halfway through what already promised to be a two-year world tour – by a more conventional single-album release, with the added prospect of at least one EP of the various cover versions Axl was also insisting the band record. These included 'Down On The Farm' by the UK Subs, 'New Rose' by the Damned (with lead vocals from Duff), 'Don't Care About You' by Fear, 'Attitude' by the Misfits, 'Jumpin' Jack Flash' by the Stones, 'Black Leather' by the Sex Pistols (featuring Pistols' guitarist Steve Jones) and, most surprisingly of all, a heavyweight version of 'Live And Let Die', Paul McCartney's hit theme tune to the 1974 James Bond movie of the same name. There was even talk of a series of EPs – one punk-themed, one funk, one rap, one rock – and the probability of a live album at the end of the tour.

Always a band of extremes, it was as if Axl was determined to make up for all the lost time since *Appetite* had hit pay-dirt. Original titles included Duff's 'Why Do You Look At Me When You Hate Me' and 'So Fine' (his 'ode to Johnny Thunders'), which he sang punk-lead on; a new, even more full-on recording of 'Civil War'; Axl's beloved epic, 'November Rain'; another classic Elton John-style autobiographical Axl ballad called 'Estranged'; the swaggering, Stonesy 'Shotgun Blues', allegedly written about Vince Neil; yet another ten-minute epic co-written by Axl and Slash about a real-life overdose, called 'Coma', replete with the sound of a defibrillator hired in for the occasion and authentic ECG beeps; Izzy's self-explanatory 'You Ain't The First' and 'Pretty Tied Up', about a dominatrix he knew on Melrose; 'Dust And Bones' and 'Double Talkin' Jive' (both featuring lead vocals from the guitarist); Slash and Izzy's 'Perfect Crime', and a clutch of sneering Izzy and Axl rockers 'You Could Be Mine' and '14 Years' (again, featuring Izzy on vocals); the more usual handful of full-on Slash and Axl work-outs like 'Don't Damn Me' (also featuring some lyrics by Axl's old Lafayette pal, David Lank), 'Garden Of Eden' (Axl's tirade against organized religions) and the Zeppelinesque 'Locomotive'; plus a handful of 'joke songs' in the 'One In A Million' mould called 'Back Off Bitch', 'Bad Obsession' and 'The Garden' (the last co-written by Axl,

West Arkeen and Del James and featuring the duet between Axl and Alice Cooper).

There were also two new versions of 'Don't Cry', the maudlin Axl and Izzy ballad from the demo-tape they first gave to Tom Zutaut – now featuring on backing vocals another Indiana escapee named Shannon Hoon, younger brother of Axl's high school friend Anna, and soon to become famous in his own right in Blind Melon – plus an updating of an unusually sentimental West Arkeen tune called 'Yesterdays' (with additional lyrics by Del James). Musically, the tracks roamed widely across the borders of the rock and pop spectrum, from Axl's intricate piano-led balladry to the jaunty banjo with which Slash introduces one track, to the remarkably adept sitar playing Izzy utilizes in the intro to another, and the affectedly futuristic synthesizers and electronica Axl fiddles with on the track that would provide the esoteric finale to the collection, 'My World'.

Of nearly forty different tracks recorded – aside from the originals and various covers, there were also some older songs that were re-recorded but didn't make the cut, such as the anthemic 'Ain't Goin' Down' and the more throwaway 'Just Another Sunday' – thirty would make the finished track-listing. Of these, twenty-one had already been mixed when Axl, unhappy with what he saw as the too generic 'rock radio' sound from engineer Bob Clearmountain, moved to have him replaced by British producer Bill Price, whose work with more tendentious UK rock acts like the Sex Pistols, Roxy Music and the Pretenders Axl greatly admired.

As Axl told me, 'When you're writing off your life and not fantasy you have to, like, have gone through these different phases. And now I think there's enough different sides of Guns N' Roses that, like, no one will know what to think, let alone us. Like, what are they trying to say? I don't fuckin' know!'

He said the band was still writing even as recording was taking place. One of the new tunes he was sure would be on the album was called 'Right Next Door To Hell', about his ongoing battle with his obsessive next-door neighbour. Then there were others he hadn't even finished yet.

'It's like, I wrote this thing today . . .' He closed his eyes and began to recite. 'It goes, ah, "Call us violent / I say we're a product of our environment / Call us hostile / Babe, we gotta survive / You call us heartless / Before we had the money nobody gave a damn / You call us deadly / All my life you been killing me . . ." ' His eyes snapped open again. 'So the mean stuff is there at the same time as the ballads are now. And then Izzy's got his sense of humour in there, too. Like, "There were lots of other lovers / Honey, you weren't the first," then something, something, then, "But you were the worst / Yes, you were the worst' . . . He dissolved into peals of laughter. 'I'm gonna try to get him to sing that one 'cos Izzy sings it the best. But, like, there'll also be West playing on "The Garden", because West plays that song the best. And Slash wants to do the solo. He's like, "I'm gonna nail that motherfucker this time!" He's been trying to nail the solo for "The Garden" for the last three years . . .'

Axl said the main thing he was after was 'to give a broader picture of Guns N' Roses' and that he was looking at the new recording as 'like a trilogy – *Appetite*, *GN'R Lies* and this, okay? That those three albums were kind of like, Guns N' Roses can do whatever the fuck they want. It might not sell, but like, it will break our boundaries. The only boundary we're keeping is hard rock. We know that's a limitation, in a way. But we want to keep that because we don't want it to die, you know? And we're watching it die. At least we were before Guns N' Roses formed. We were watching it just kind of being obliterated. By radio – by, like, all the stations not playing heavy metal any more, and all this crap. And so we decided, okay, we like a lot of guitars, we wanna keep it.'

Another last-minute recording Axl instigated involved a fairly drastic reworking of Duff's 'Why Do You Look At Me When You Hate Me', which he retitled 'Get In The Ring'. The first I heard of it was when Lonn Friend, then editor of *RIP* magazine, tipped me off during a trip to Hawaii to see Megadeth play. 'I don't know what you've done to him but he's majorly pissed at you,' Lonn, who like most journalists always revelled in bad news, told me delightedly. By now, however, I was starting to understand how little it took to get in Axl's bad books and merely shrugged it off as a storm in a teacup. The way Axl was still tinkering with the album, I wasn't even convinced the track would make the final cut. Even the title of the album was constantly changing. The last time we spoke, Axl had told me: 'There's all kinds of titles for the record. There's, like, *GN'R Sucks*. That's one of our favourites. There's *B-U-Y Product*, like, *Guns N' Roses – BUY Product*.' While Duff told me with a straight face that he favoured calling the album *Girth*, in honour of West Arkeen's penis, which was 'only about this long but it's like *this wide*, man! So he's got the girth, right? We even wrote a song about it.'

Eventually Axl plumped for a far more portentous title: *Use Your Illusion* – named after a painting of the same name by modern American artist Mark Kostabi. According to Kostabi, 'Axl wandered into this gallery and saw the *Use Your Illusion* painting. The next day, one of his representatives called and asked if he could use it on the cover of his next record. He said that he had been writing about illusions, so it made sense.'

Early in January 1991, Guns N' Roses began rehearsing for their first major gigs as headliners in their own right: two nights at the Rock in Rio festival in Brazil, a ten-day event held at the giant 170,000-capacity Maracana football stadium that brought together such diverse acts as Prince, George Michael, Billy Idol, Megadeth, INXS, Faith No More and New Kids On The Block. Taking over the stage at Long Beach Arena in preparation, the plan was to get the newly augmented band into shape for what would effectively be their comeback, in May, when their first world tour for three years would commence with three months on the road in America. With only the mixing of the near-forty tracks left to complete, Tom Zutaut felt sure the new album would be ready for release by then.

The band arrived in Rio on Thursday, 17 January – three days before their first show – and checked into the Intercontinental Hotel, high on a cliff overlooking Ipanema beach and several miles from where most of the other acts were staying, at the Rio Palace Hotel on Copacabana beach. 'I remember getting off the plane and feeling like we were in the fucking Beatles,' Matt says. 'We had to send a decoy through the airport – a guy dressed like

Slash and a guy dressed like Axl. We went out the back of the airport and still the kids found us.'

Privacy and seclusion had now replaced sex and drugs as the tour's watchwords. Certainly for Axl, who hadn't travelled with the band. He was still working – and sleeping – in the studio in LA, recording and re-recording his vocal tracks. When he did show up on Saturday afternoon, the day before the first show, he went straight to his hotel suite and wasn't seen again until he was ready to hop in the limo for the show. Even then he was surrounded by a posse of menacing-looking bodyguards. Axl, it soon became clear, wasn't interested in talking to anyone at that moment. Certainly not to the journalists for whom he had introduced contracts to sign before he would allow the band to consider giving interviews, nor to any of the other musicians on the bill (including Dave Mustaine of Megadeth, an old buddy of both Axl's and Slash's, who had cleaned up his act); nor even to some of the band members, judging by the grim expressions on some of their faces whenever they were glimpsed, huddling behind their bodyguards.

The whole atmosphere surrounding the band seemed hopelessly, unnecessarily tense. The contracts were two-page documents guaranteeing the band total control over all aspects of the interview and resulting story, including copyright ownership and approval rights, on pain of a $200,000 damages claim if violated. Similar contracts were also handed out to any photographers, including ownership of all resulting pictures to be given directly to the band.

Though impossible to enforce in practical terms, the contracts naturally proved immensely unpopular with all sections of the media in Rio. A host of important magazines refused to sign them, including *Playboy*, *Rolling Stone*, the *Los Angeles Times*, *Spin* and *Penthouse*. Axl merely shrugged. As Geffen Records publicity chief Bryn Bridenthal commented: 'In twenty-five years of doing publicity I've never dealt with a press contract before, but when you deal with this band, you deal with a lot of firsts.' Although the contracts would later be revised, dropping the $200,000 penalty, they would become a source of ill-will throughout the forthcoming world tour.

The Rio shows, on 20 and 23 January, were strangely low-key affairs, distinguished only by spot-on soloing from Slash, grandstanding by Axl and a band doing their damnedest to pretend everything was going to plan. Axl ended the first show twenty minutes earlier than planned when the crowd failed to rouse itself to his satisfaction, unfamiliar as they were with some of the new numbers like the interminable 'November Rain'.

Controversy continued to surround them. When five audience members died on the day of the second show on 23 January, although the tragedy occurred hours before the band arrived at the site, the subsequent news reports tied it to their appearance at the festival, the real causes of death seemingly swept under the carpet by surly local authorities. During one of my visits to the festival site there was also an alleged rape, as well as several reported episodes of bullying and violence from the various 'security men' present. But again, local police either ignored the incidents or acted as though the journalists questioning them were making an undue fuss. It was unnerving, trying to deal with the same uniformed thugs you knew were also engaged in 'cleansing the streets' of the gangs of kids who routinely mugged and pick-pocketed the tourists along Copacabana beach.

What the band must surely have some responsibility for was the way the media was treated during their two performances. Photographers, journalists and other perceived 'problem makers' were routinely rounded up and 'escorted' from the venue before the band set foot onstage; never mind what access their backstage passes said they were entitled to. Singer Rob Halford, whose band Judas Priest were second on the bill to Guns N' Roses at the second show, complained bitterly to me that they had been forbidden from using their full show, depriving them of their pyrotechnics and props and cutting their allotted stage time by some twenty minutes. 'If anything, being treated like that only made us more determined to put on a really hard show,' Halford told me immediately afterwards. 'But I still can't understand that kind of attitude problem. It just doesn't make sense.'

Speaking some months later in an interview with *Musician*

magazine, Axl utterly refuted any suggestion that he or the band had acted inappropriately in Rio, blaming the corrupt local police for at least one of the deaths there, which he maintained had been 'caused by the police shooting the fire marshal for not allowing 20,000 people with tickets in the show when they allowed 20,000 people *without* tickets in the show and were taking the money for themselves.' He also claimed there were eighty bootleg Guns N' Roses T-shirt booths in the venue, which were 'run by the police. The other deaths happened during Megadeth's show. We went onstage early because Judas Priest had pulled off on their own accord . . . We had told Judas that they could play as long as they wanted, they could have whatever they wanted. The only thing they couldn't have, which the fire marshal wouldn't allow, was their pyro.' He said 'there was no way' they had been stopped from doing 'whatever they wanted', and that Rob Halford was 'one of the major influences on my singing'.

Following the mixed success of the Rio shows, Axl returned to LA more determined than ever to do things his way. He no longer wanted Guns N' Roses to be seen as competing with the grisly likes of Mötley Crüe or the yeomen of Iron Maiden. He wanted to put the band on the same elevated level as his heroes Elton John, Led Zeppelin and Queen. It was now that he conceived the idea of releasing two double-albums simultaneously, to be titled *Use Your Illusion I* and *Use Your Illusion II*. After all, why wait to release material that represented exactly where the band was at. A year from now there might be more or even better songs to talk about releasing. And besides, he couldn't bear to wait, or worse still, have Geffen apply pressure to drop some of the songs – 'You Ain't The First', maybe, or 'Back Off Bitch' and 'The Garden' – that even Tom Zutaut privately agreed were not as substantive as the album's obvious cornerstone moments like 'Estranged' and 'November Rain'.

Axl knew that if he was ever going to get his way about this it was now. And so he laid down his terms, the same ones he routinely offered anyone he perceived as a threat – all or nothing, take it or leave it. Two double-albums, each containing more than seventy-five minutes of music, to be released on the same day. Wiping the sweat from their palms Geffen reluctantly agreed, then immediately began pumping up the press by talking in terms of 'history in the making' while privately reassuring themselves by looking at it as 'a marketing first'.

Alan Niven, meanwhile, shrugged and described the project as 'a cross between Led Zeppelin's *Physical Graffiti* and Pink Floyd's *The Wall*. It's a record that's gonna amaze and frighten at the same time.' It was virtually the last statement he would make on behalf of Guns N' Roses. What Niven didn't know was that while plans were going ahead for the band's comeback with a monumental album-release, there were moves to ensure Niven had absolutely nothing to do with it, by replacing him in the managerial hot-seat with Doug Goldstein, Niven's former junior partner in his Stravinsky Brothers company. The announcement was made in May, just days before the band's US tour. Goldstein, it was explained, would now front his own management company, on behalf of Guns N' Roses, to be called Big Fuckin' Deal (BFD).

'Everybody has a lot of good and bad, and with Alan, I just got sick of his fucking combo platter,' was Axl's explanation to *Rolling Stone* for Niven's leaving. When Niven accepted a rumoured $3 million pay-off in exchange for signing a confidentiality agreement prohibiting him from publicly discussing the inner-workings of the groups' activities, the matter was over.

When I met Niven in LA later that summer I detected no animosity towards his former charges, only frustration at not being there 'to reap the rewards of all the hard work we put into making the band happen'. And also a certain sadness over losing touch with Slash and Izzy. 'I actually really miss those two,' he said. 'Beneath the tough exteriors they're both real sweethearts, and I do miss them.' But 'not the red-headed dictator though'. When I asked him to elaborate, he puffed out his cheeks and threw me a baleful sideways glance that said you-know-what-I'm-talking-about. 'I can't say I'm sorry I don't have to deal with that kind of day-to-day madness any more. It's exciting, but it's also a lot of pressure.'

One of the many side-effects of Niven's departure was to delay the new album still further, with Axl and Doug Goldstein negotiating a new contract with Geffen before allowing it to be released. As a result, it would remain unavailable throughout the first three-month leg of the US tour; commercial suicide in almost any other situation but one that Axl was prepared to risk until he was satisfied that not only was the material finished to his own increasingly high standards but that his business was too.

'There are no delays on our record,' Axl told one reporter defiantly. 'There have never been any delays on our record.' Geffen could announce as many release dates as they liked but nothing would be released 'until we're done with it. What do you mean delaying the record? It's my record! Delaying it? Do we want another *Godfather III*? No. We don't want *Godfather III* with our record. We want it to be right!'

It wasn't only the release date of the album that was under threat. The other initiative Axl instigated once Niven was out of the way was his plan to wrest sole control of the Guns N' Roses name. Still smarting over the perceived slights he'd suffered in his battle to convince both the public and his own band that 'One In A Million' was not a bigoted 'joke song' that no one outside Axl's own circle found funny, but a valid artistic statement, he also became progressively agitated with what he saw as a lack of 'back-up' when he made unilateral decisions such as going public with their drug problems at the Stones' shows, challenging Vince to a fight in the press, hiring Dizzy, choosing the album title or deciding on the simultaneous release of the two albums (a decision no one in the band except Axl was really sure about until the albums were actually released). It is possible Axl was determined his authority would never be questioned in the same way. According to Tom Zutaut, and reported by *Spin*, he declared he would not go on tour again – thereby losing tens of millions of dollars – until they signed over their rights to the name. Convinced Axl wasn't bluffing the band reluctantly did as instructed.

With the tour back on, Slash, Duff and Izzy contented themselves with the fact that they could now get on with rehearsals. They hired a fenced-off compound at an airport in the Los Angeles valley where a sound stage was erected in one of the disused aircraft hangars and a small area divided off as a band hang-out decked with candles, incense and scarf-draped lamps, and the band – minus Axl, who now routinely skipped rehearsals – set to work.

It was also around this time that someone new arrived in Axl's life and he began a relationship that would have unexpected long-term effects on both him and the band. Her name was Stephanie Seymour. A dark-haired, blue-eyed, twenty-two-year-old Victoria's Secret model from San Diego then dating Holly-wood legend Warren Beatty, Stephanie's impact on Axl was immediate. As he told his assistant Colleen Combs, 'I've been hit by a Mack truck and the license plate said "Seymour".'

Axl met Stephanie through another new friend, Josh Rich-man, a young actor then best known for his guest appearances as Ronnie Seebok in the hit TV show *21 Jump Street*. Axl had hired Josh to help make videos for Guns N' Roses that would be 'more out-there than Michael Jackson's'. Stephanie was one of several professional models Josh invited out to the valley compound to audition for the lead part in the 'November Rain' video. According to Richman, it was love at first sight – at least for the singer. 'Axl desperately wanted Stephanie Seymour – period,' he says. 'That night they went to the set, which was being built in an airplane hangar out in the Valley. That was their first date.'

Stephanie was certainly a step up from the cutesy teenager Erin was when Axl first met her. A model since she was fifteen, when she was spotted by Elite Models president John Casablan-cas at the Elite Look of the Year Talent Contest Stephanie's career had taken off spectacularly. She fell in love with little-known blues musician Tommy Andrews, who she married in 1989 and had a son with a year later, named Dylan Thomas Andrews. The marriage did not last long. None of this fazed Axl when he first started going out with her. To begin with, Axl was sure she was the one.

With the album being mastered in New York, as a warm-up for the tour three 'secret' club dates were arranged, all of which would be plagued by aborted songs, delays and Axl's intermin-able costume changes. 'Live rehearsals,' Axl called them. The first, on 9 May, was at the small Warfield Theatre in San Francisco. *'Here and now and going to hell'* it said on the tickets, by way of offering a clue. The second warm-up show was at the Pantages Theater in LA two nights later, with the third at the Ritz in New York on 16 May.

No more eighteen-wheel tour buses, the band now travelled exclusively by private plane, chartering the luxurious MGM Grand. Getting on the plane for the first time, 'I felt like someone in Led Zeppelin,' smirked Matt Sorum. The only one who didn't enjoy the experience was Izzy, who elected not to travel with the band, travelling instead with his girlfriend, Anneka, and dog, Treader, in his newly purchased tour bus, towing his Harleys behind. Having earned the nickname Whizzy, following his arrest for urinating on a plane, Izzy spent most of his rehabilitation period travelling anonymously with Anneka, visiting Germany, Spain and England, with stops along the way in Paris and Amsterdam. The thought of having to start travelling again with the band was too much for the newly sober guitarist. Wherever possible, he even stayed in separate hotels from the band. 'There's nothing worse than waiting on somebody,' he said. 'Their jumbo jet would sit on the runway for three hours while Axl blow-dried his hair.'

All three warm-up shows went well, the band looking and sounding better each night. After the show in LA Axl hosted a party where he was joined by his new girlfriend, Stephanie, plus Shannon Hoon from Blind Melon, as well as several other older friends like Dana, all rubbing shoulders with newer pals such as Josh Richman, Johnny Depp and Sean Penn. But it was the final warm-up show in New York that really caught fire. Billed as 'An Evening With The Doors', the band previewed an array of new material, including a blistering version of their next single, 'You Could Be Mine', which they'd just learned was to be used as the title music for the new Arnold Schwarzenegger movie *Terminator 2*. Hoon joined the band for 'Don't Cry' (also ear-marked as a future single) and Axl dedicated the final number of the night, 'Welcome To The Jungle', to the 3rd Street Hell's Angels, a half-dozen of whom were present.

The only worrying moment occurred when Axl injured his left ankle toppling from an onstage monitor. However, the long-faced vocalist was eventually fitted with a specially constructed shin-splint put together by a sympathetic group of Milwaukee medics in consultation with a hastily drafted-in sports-shoe designer from New Balance. It meant he wouldn't be able to do his trademark sashaying little dance throughout the early shows of the tour but at least he could do the tour, prompting relieved sighs from nervous record company execs, concert promoters and, most especially, the band.

The relief, however, was replaced by tension – and fear. Of all the most outrageous rock tours – the Sex Pistols' nightmarish trek through the American south in 1978; the Stones' ill-fated 1969 US tour which ended in Altamont – none was so gruellingly long or incident-filled as the outwardly successful but inwardly solipsistic road trip Guns N' Roses undertook between 1991 and 1993. By the end they were not only the biggest rock band in the world, they were also the deadest. Indeed, Axl would never perform with any of the original members again. By then that was neither here nor there as far as Axl was concerned. He owned the name, he ran the game, and the song would remain the same whatever the others had to say about it.

Nobody could have guessed at the outcome when the tour finally got underway with two sold-out nights at the Alpine Valley Music Theater in East Troy, Wisconsin, on 24 and 25 May. Even the rain, which began early in the morning and was still falling by the time the band came on onstage, didn't dampen Axl's spirits. All 40,000 tickets for the shows sold in a day (a feat equalled only once before, by The Who), and American pro-moters had gone into a feeding frenzy at the news, offering the band multiple nights everywhere they played. 'We're gonna end the States leg in LA, at the Forum,' Duff said, where they were scheduled to play four consecutive nights. 'They wanted us to do eight!' he shook his head. 'Eight fucking nights!'

An unusually happy Axl returned from the second East Troy show and began cracking open bottles of champagne in his hotel suite, where the party went on until 5:00 a.m. The reason the tour had started in Wisconsin, he revealed, was because 'I wanted to be buried here. I bought land here specifically for that reason.' For a guy from a small Midwest town like Lafayette LA would never be home, he said. He'd since changed his mind about wanting to be buried there, and he was considering selling the land. 'There were reasons why I bought that particular piece of land, with those particular trees and that particular smell and that particular vibe,' he was reported as saying in *Rolling Stone*, then added enigmatically: 'These reasons don't exist any more.' He said he had enlisted the help of his stepfather to buy the land, after he'd first become rich, but had now changed his mind about having him so closely involved in his affairs.

It was a feeling only reinforced by the unfortunate events surrounding the next stop on the tour, in Noblesville, Indiana.

Arriving onstage at the 17,000-capacity Deer Creek Music Center more than two hours after support band Skid Row finished their set, this was Axl's first performance in front of friends and family from Lafayette for three years. He wasn't going to let the occasion pass without comment and straight after set-opener 'Rocket Queen' he motioned for Slash to hold fire. 'You fuckers been waitin' a long time tonight, huh?' he growled.

Pissed off about a county-wide curfew that required all 'large gatherings' to be completed by 10.30 p.m., Axl compared the local authorities to Nazis. 'I grew up in this state,' he began. 'It seems to me there are a lot of scared old people in this fucking state, and basically, for two-thirds of my life they tried to keep my ass down.' He gazed forlornly at the crowd. 'I got a lot of cool prisoners here in Auschwitz,' he told them. He gave Slash the signal and the band ploughed into a furious 'Out Ta Get Me'. It was already past 10.30 anyway and the next day they were duly fined $5,000 for their trouble. The Auschwitz comment also made headlines across America. 'I wanted to tell them that they could break away, too,' an unrepentant Axl told the *Los Angeles Times*.

He was also feeling more anxious than usual that night as he had taken the unprecedented step of inviting his family to the show, sending a stretch limo to pick up his parents, his half-brother and -sister, and even his grandmother. The latter, described by friends as 'a female version' of Axl, particularly enjoyed the occasion, singing along to all the words and generally making her presence felt backstage.

The video for 'You Could Be Mine' – a performance piece featuring a cameo appearance from a robotic Arnie, whose behind-the-eyeballs computer humorously decides that blowing Axl away would only constitute 'wasted ammo' – received its official premiere on MTV on 19 June. The band was in New York at the time, where two days before they had headlined another controversial show at the Nassau Coliseum in Union-dale. Having kept everybody waiting until almost midnight before he arrived at the hall, Axl was already in a strange mood when he stepped off the specially chartered helicopter (the rest of the band had been driven). When Skid Row singer Sebastian Bach asked him where he'd been, he replied tersely: 'Taking a shower.'

Axl's mood took a downturn after Slash failed to show up for a band dinner the singer had organized on the spur of the moment the night before. While Axl played gracious host to the band and its ever-growing entourage of tour advisors and personal assis-tants at the Old Homestead steakhouse in Manhattan, running up a $3,000 bill on champagne alone, Slash decided to stay in his suite at the Royalton Hotel. According to Axl, it was meant as a come-if-you-please invitation. But that wasn't the way Slash construed it, seeing it more as a summons to the court of King Axl. As a result, he deliberately didn't turn up. Now someone would have to pay.

'Yeah, I know it sucks,' Axl nonchalantly informed the 18,000-strong Nassau crowd when he eventually took to the stage. 'If you got any real complaints, you could do me a favour though. You could write a little letter on how much that sucked and send it to Geffen Records . . . Tell those people to get the fuck out of my ass!'

The band then launched into 'Mr Brownstone' but Axl wasn't done yet. When the music died down he told the crowd: 'There's a *Rolling Stone* coming out with us on the cover. Do me a favour. Don't buy it. And if you want to read it, steal it.' He then went on to complain about not only *Rolling Stone* but the editors of the *Village Voice* and John Pareles of the *New York Times*, all of whom Axl said had been 'fucking with my mind'. He went on: 'The new record will be delayed again. Geffen Records decided they wanted to change the contract and I'm deciding fuck you. And since I don't have time to do both – go back there and argue and bitch with them or be on tour – I guess we'll just be on tour and have a good time and fuck them. It's a shame but . . .' He looked out at the barely comprehending audience. 'So we'll play a lot of the new shit tonight and it really doesn't matter, does it?' Several voices yelled encouragement but most of the crowd simply stared in silence. One or two began to throw things. By the end of the set, it was almost 2.00 a.m. and the Geffen Records executives present had long since left, having been advised by Doug Goldstein that it would probably be unwise to try and talk to Axl that night.

As the tour continued, Axl's onstage rants would become an almost nightly occurrence, his targets anyone that had upset him that day, including the audience if they weren't 'rocking enough', as happened in a show in Salt Lake City where he ended the set abruptly with the words, 'I'll get out of here before I put anybody else to sleep,' before walking off and refusing to return.

Axl's unfortunate predilection for not wanting, as he'd put it to me, to do 'the fuckin' show and hate it' led to countless more such incidents over the next two years – dozens of shows either cancelled or re-arranged, halted midway, or begun hours late. His boastful claim to me that 'People allow me to do it whether they like it or not' rang horribly true.

The rest of the band didn't like it but there wasn't much they could do, concerned that the slightest provocation would result in yet more cancelled or delayed shows and possibly even the premature end of the tour itself. Slash had always been able to 'hide behind my hair' as he put it, self-medicating with Jack Daniel's and cocaine. Duff, who fell off the wagon almost as soon as the band returned from Rio, also began a familiar retreat, putting away as much as two bottles of vodka a night. While Matt and Dizzy were still hirelings, doing what they were told, the novelty of having been parachuted into the world's biggest band having inured them against the worst of Axl's excesses.

The worst affected was Izzy, who began to retreat even further into his shell. Regular tour members joked that they saw more of his dog between shows than they did of Izzy. But as he later told me, 'Things just weren't the same any more. The music had taken a back seat completely, there was nothing new coming from us. We didn't sit around and play acoustic guitars any more. It was like, oh, time to go on – where's the singer? The singer walked off? Now what do we do? We'd started out as a garage band and it became like a *huge* band, which was fine. But everything was so magnified – drug addictions, personalities, just the craziness that was already there anyway. It just became . . . too much. Plus, my friends, these guys . . . I'm basically watching them kill themselves. Not so much Axl, but Slash and Duff, man. These guys were on my top ten of guys that might die this week. And I'm thinking, you know what, I just don't want to be part of it. It didn't feel like it was good.'

Izzy's worst fears were realized on 2 July, when nearly 3,000 people rioted at the newly constructed Riverport Performing Arts Center, fifteen miles west of St Louis in Maryland Heights, Missouri, after Axl brought the show to a premature halt after ninety minutes by storming off stage. The trouble started during 'Rocket Queen', when Axl began to shout, 'Take that . . . take that . . . take that away from him!' to the security guards at the front of the stage, referring to a camera someone in the audience was holding. When his pleas were ignored he announced 'Then I'll take it from him' and dived into the crowd, making a grab for the fan with the camera. A brief scuffle ensued during which Axl punched one security guard and was punched several times by other members of the venue's security staff. When he was eventually dragged back onto the stage by his own roadies, he grabbed the microphone. 'Thanks to the lame-ass security,' he said, 'I'm going home!' He then threw down the mike and walked off. The others played on for a few moments then sheepishly followed suit, as confused as the looks on the faces of the audience.

The house lights remained off for twenty minutes before it became obvious the band wasn't coming back, at which point sections of the crowd started chanting, 'Bullshit! Bullshit!' When the house lights eventually came on and roadies began removing equipment from the stage, fights broke out as audience members started to go crazy, throwing bottles, destroying seats and band equipment, even setting fire to the building. Earl Gabbidon, Axl's head of band security, came out and tried to calm the crowd by announcing the band would come back on if the fighting stopped, but it was too late.

The carnage continued for over an hour. A 'Code 1000' riot call went out to every major police department in St Louis County and more than 500 officers in full riot gear arrived to try and take control, turning fire-hoses and CapStun (an aerosol cayenne pepper similar to Mace) on the unruly mob. At the height of the mayhem police lashed out with their nightsticks at anyone who came near them, and fans fleeing the venue smashed ticket-booth windows and anything else they could get their hands on. It was reported that tear gas was eventually used to disperse rioters but that was later denied by local authorities. In all, more than sixty people were injured and sixteen arrested, resulting in an estimated $200,000-worth of damage to the venue, as well as the loss of most of the band's gear, causing them to cancel subsequent shows in Illinois and Kansas City.

The story made headlines all over the world, with Axl unanimously condemned for his actions. He blamed a series of events, not just the camera incident, stemming from the lax venue security. 'I could see bottles, I could see cameras, and I could see that security really didn't have a clue what they were doing,' he told *Rolling Stone*. 'I remember watching this one security guy shove somebody around and then beam up at me like "Look how powerful I am."'

Within twenty-four hours the promoters, Contemporary Productions, in conjunction with the venue's owners, filed lawsuits against the band. Three days later a warrant was issued for Axl's arrest on five misdemeanour charges of 'assault' and 'property damage'. In the meantime the band's lawyers were already feverishly counter-suing the show's promoters. 'I was concerned that people didn't get more of a show,' Axl said. But there were 'a lot of people not taking responsibility for the damage that they did at that place.'

It was almost the last straw for Izzy. 'When something like that happens,' he says, 'you can't help but think back to Donington. Like, what's the point? What are we getting at here?'

Axl did eventually concede that the riot in St Louis 'wasn't a good time for us. I wasn't Mother Teresa that night.' But the fan with the camera was a member of the Saddle Tramps, he explained, a local Hell's Angel gang that had been 'yelling and driving me nuts the whole night. It had nothing to do with us playing. They were like, "We know Guns N' Roses and we're going to prove we're his best friend and we are his biggest fan" and so on. I was like, "Shut up!" I don't care about people screaming, but this guy kept on waving his motorcycle card for his gang . . .' Until finally he snapped. 'I just didn't care about it.'

When the tour resumed six days later at the Starplex Amphitheater in Dallas, Axl once again turned up over two hours late for the gig. Stressed out at the prospect of facing 20,000 Texans who'd heard nothing all week except that this was the guy who'd just incited a riot, he almost didn't show up at all. Then when he did finally take to the stage, he began by telling the crowd, 'It's hard to figure out why we get up onstage to do this, because sometimes it's fun, but other times it takes all the physical fucking energy we've got to get up here and do what we do for a living. For the last few days, I'm watching CNN and reading this shit in the St Louis papers about how I incited a riot, and they're talking about "and in the band, they have a recovering heroin addict, and once, Axl Rose was seen driving down the street in a Jeep yelling obscenities at his former wife". What the fuck does that have to do with St Louis?'

He paused to allow the fervent to yelp and scream their approval, then continued: 'And I had to realize that no matter what we did tonight and how good or bad we played, there'd probably be one person in the press here that for some reason didn't dig it, and he'd write about something else and write some lies. Now, at the same time that won't have an effect on Dallas, and it shouldn't affect me [but] it fucks with the entire thing called rock'n'roll in general. Because who are the main people that watch these news things and read this shit? They're all in their forties to fifties, sitting there eating their bran flakes and drinking their coffee.' Cue more whoops of approval.

'I ain't knocking getting old,' he continued, 'it's a fact of life. Unless you die before you get there, you're gonna get old. But just because you're old doesn't mean you have to deny young people their humanity. And so now there's a lot of people reading these negative things about Guns N' Roses, and if their kid likes Guns N' Roses, he's gonna get smacked in the head or something, because the paper said it was an evil thing. And that really makes me go, "Fuck, what's the point?" But I'll tell you what the point is. We're up here and what we are doing is something that is dying in America. It usually stays at an underground level and doesn't get as successful as Guns N' Roses. And that's freedom of expression. And basically, that's all we fucking are. Guns N' Roses is just a prime fucking example of freedom of expression . . .'

By now the crowd was on its feet, half of them impatient for the show to begin, and just as many applauding the sentiment. Less than twenty-five minutes later, however, Axl stopped the show again, and this time he was angry. 'Stop! Stop! Stop!' he yelled, waving an empty whiskey bottle over his head. 'Some selfish, stupid, idiotic motherfucker just threw this onstage! I want to make it real clear that if you throw stuff onstage, we will leave. This is not about us being badder than you or anything, it has to do with being responsible – both to the band and to yourselves. I got my philosophy on this,' he added sombrely, 'from Lemmy of Motörhead . . .'

The band exchanged knowing looks then ploughed manfully into the next song, praying silently that no one else would be stupid enough to do anything that might catch Axl's increasingly irate eye . . .

The tour ended on an up note with the four shows between

29 July and 3 August at the Forum in LA, where Axl announced onstage on the first night that he and Slash had 'finished the record yesterday'. He grinned broadly. 'The motherfucker is done,' he said proudly to enormous cheers. The final show of the four was the longest of the tour, with the band playing for over three-and-a-half hours. Even then, Axl couldn't resist one final dig, dedicating 'Double Talkin' Jive' 'to CBS News'. Afterwards, Axl deigned to hang out backstage with the band as a soundtrack of AC/DC, Led Zeppelin and Queen blared in the background and he sat cross-legged on the floor while Stephanie gave him a back-rub.

Things were back to normal the very next day when Axl was made aware that Vince Neil had responded to his interview with me by appearing on MTV and challenging him to 'put the gloves on' and fight it out in public 'in the ring'. Even Steven Adler emerged blinking from the half-light to see his name making headlines again as he filed suit against the band, accusing them of 'defrauding' him and 'defaming' his character. On the advice of lawyers, Steven decided to sue the band for damages in the region of $2 million, claiming that during his five years with them the others had encouraged him to take heroin – then callously snatched away his livelihood at the very moment he was attempting to seek a cure for his addiction. 'I was their scapegoat,' Steven said in a press statement. 'They were doing it, so was I, and I didn't think I was doing anything wrong.' It seems safe to assume that Axl was not pleased by this development though he said nothing publicly, possibly on the advice of his lawyers.

Nine days later, the European leg of what was officially dubbed the 'Get in the Ring Motherfucker' tour began when Guns N' Roses arrived in Helsinki for two shows on 13 and 14 August at the Jäähalli arena. For once, Izzy flew in with the rest of the band. But if he was hoping that getting out of America might throw some cold water on Axl's temper he was sorely disappointed when, an hour into the first show, Axl walked off without explanation just as the band launched into 'Welcome To The Jungle'. Not knowing what was going on, the band carried on with an instrumental version. When Axl didn't reappear for the next song they quickly covered by having Izzy sing '14 Years', followed by an improvised drum solo from Matt and, when Axl still hadn't returned, a lengthy guitar solo from Slash. Finally, after twenty-five minutes, Axl returned, again without any explanation, and carried on where he'd mysteriously left off as though nothing had happened.

Four nights later, during the second of two sold-out performances at the Globen Arena in Stockholm, the show was delayed for nearly three hours. According to rumours, at 9.00 p.m., when he should have been onstage, Axl was in the casino at the Sheraton Hotel, playing roulette, where he stayed for over an hour and a half. When he left the casino, rather than jumping in the car waiting to take him to the venue, he disappeared to his suite for another quarter of an hour. Finally, on the way to the show, he told the driver to stop while he took in the firework display at the nearby Vattenfestivalen. There is no evidence this rumour is true.

Arriving at the Globen, nobody in the band even bothered to ask him where he'd been or why he was so late. But their troubles weren't over yet. Upset that so many of the crowd seemed restless and unresponsive, he introduced 'Knockin' On Heaven's Door' by telling them: 'Now on this one maybe you people that have been falling asleep the whole fuckin' show . . . could sing along too.' He ignored the whistles and catcalls to add: 'If you're bored, you should've saved your money and gone and seen the fireworks tonight.'

The pattern for the tour was set. Two nights later, during the show in Copenhagen, he responded to a firecracker landing onstage by announcing that the band would not continue playing until 'the idiot who did it turns himself in'. After a nervous fifteen-minute break during which no one came forward, the show finally continued. Axl left the venue still unhappy, so much so that he refused to get on the plane for the next day's gig in Norway. Izzy had to explain to the production manager at the Spektrum arena in Oslo that the show might have to be cancelled as no one knew where Axl was. Sure enough, Axl's new personal assistant, Blake, phoned later that evening to inform everyone that she and Axl had flown to Paris – Axl's newly self-proclaimed 'favourite city' – for a much-needed 'break' and that he would meet up with the band at their next gig on 24 August at an outdoor stadium show in Mannheim, Germany (where all 38,000 tickets sold in two days, faster than Madonna and the Rolling Stones the year before).

A week later, on 31 August, came their biggest date yet: a sold-out show at London's 72,000-capacity Wembley Stadium – their first show in Britain since their ill-fated Donington appearance three years before. Before he even set foot inside the venue he was already aggravated by the Wembley Borough Council's demand that the band refrain from making any public profanities during the show – an inevitable red rag to Axl's raging bull – so the singer responded by demanding a poster campaign be peppered across all available London billboards and advertising hoardings, with the following message: 'Guns N' F____g Roses, Wembley F____g Stadium, Sold F____g Out!!!'

Arriving on the Wembley stage seventy minutes late, Axl sported a red tartan kilt and shirt over a white T-shirt emblazoned with the declaration: *No Martyr*. The show was another strangely subdued affair, dominated by Axl's petulant dedication of 'Double Talkin' Jive' to '*Sky* magazine, to *Time Out*, and to something I respected years ago, but now I'd rather wipe my fuckin' ass with – *Kerrang!*' Once again, I was left in no doubt as to whom this last barbed comment was directed at, and once again, I marvelled at how petty seemed the concerns of a singer who could stand before more than 70,000 people and make such a big deal out of . . . what?

Sadly for the fans the show never really recovered from that. The most tedious moment, however, was the unforgivably boring seventeen-minute drum and guitar solo sequence, during which Axl again left the stage while the vast Wembley crowd stood around fidgeting uncomfortably and wondering what exactly was going on.

While they were in London, the band stayed at the luxurious Conrad Hotel at Chelsea Harbour – rather hilariously, in the same suites that Mötley Crüe had occupied just a week before, information that was withheld from Axl for fear he might overreact.

Indeed, when the DJ hired for the post-Wembley party back at the hotel played a Mötley Crüe number, Axl was not impressed.

Everyone – not least the band – was now bending over backwards to keep Axl happy. Despite the success of the tour, the atmosphere on the road was suffocatingly tense. Insiders whispered that Izzy was on the point of walking out. The day before the Wembley show no one was even sure if he'd arrived in London yet. While Axl hid away in his hotel suite, obsessively working out on the state-of-the-art exercise equipment he now took with him everywhere, Izzy was staying with Anneka in a different hotel. Slash, who also had his new girlfriend, Renee, with him, still affected to see things from both sides.

'I spend so much time with Axl,' he shrugged, 'I realize what he goes through to do that and to be able to sing every night.' He said Axl had given him an analogy. 'I've got replacement guitars, more strings. It's not as harsh for me to go through my personal situations onstage as it is for him. I've got something to hide behind.' Whereas for Axl, 'being out there you're bigger than life. They don't want to see any fucking faults at all! And Axl's a very sensitive guy, and a lot of shit does go down onstage. There's always a bottle flying here, a bomb going off there . . .'

Not just onstage, either. In fact, when the band returned to LA for a short break after the Wembley show, Izzy quietly handed in his resignation. Apparently nonplussed, Axl and Slash initially discussed offering his job to Jane's Addiction guitarist, David Navarro. But then Izzy changed his mind and the Navarro idea was dropped. A month later, however, just as the band were preparing to return to the road, Izzy changed it back again, re-hired Alan Niven as his manager and announced plans for a solo album.

As Izzy later told me, it was the thought of going back out on the road that did for him in the end. 'The shows were completely erratic. I never knew whether we'd be able to finish the show from day-to-day, 'cos [Axl] would walk off. I said to Duff and Slash, we gotta learn a cover song or something, for when [Axl] leaves the stage. They were like, "Ah, let's have another beer . . ." They didn't care.'

The final straw, he says, came after he reversed his initial decision to leave, and Axl issued Izzy with a contract to sign. 'I was like "Fuck you! I've been there from day one, why should I do that? Fuck you! I'll go play the Whiskey." That's what happened. It was insane.'

By then, he says, the control issues seemed to have completely taken his old school friend over. 'And I never saw it coming. I mean, this is my side of it, he'd probably say I'm completely fucking crazy, but I think he went power mad. Suddenly he was trying to control *everything*. The control issues just became worse and worse and eventually it filtered down to the band. He was trying to draw up contracts for everybody! And this guy – he's not a Harvard graduate, Axl. He's just a guy, just a little guy, who sings, is talented. But man, he turned into this fucking maniac! And I did, too, but it was a different kind of maniac. I was paranoid about the business aspect – freaking out going "Where's all the money?" '

'For [Axl] the money wasn't as big a deal. But he had this power thing where he wanted complete control. And you can say, well, it goes back to your fucked-up childhood, and he had no control, so now he's getting it back. But it's like, it's still kooky, you know? You don't have to have everybody signing stuff.'

In fairness, Axl gave an interview to *Rolling Stone* not long after Izzy's departure in which he acknowledged the part Izzy had played, not just in the band but as a friend. 'If people think I don't respect or acknowledge his talent, they're sadly mistaken,' said Axl. 'He was my friend. I haven't always been right. Sometimes I've been massively wrong, and Izzy's been the one to help steer me back to the things that were right.'

Izzy's departure was announced officially in November 1991 and his replacement, a little-known LA boy, formerly of the band Kill For Thrills, named Gilby Clarke, drafted in for the remainder of the band's touring commitments. Looking back at the cuttings, nobody made much of a fuss about it. As Izzy had feared, the downsizing of Guns N' Roses to the Axl & Slash Show had begun long before that.

While Izzy was deliberating his future, the *Use Your Illusion* albums both finally came out, released in America simultaneously on 17 September (16 September in Britain and Europe). Preceded by the 'Don't Cry' single, both albums debuted at number one and two on the *Billboard* Hot 100 chart. Marking the first time a major contemporary rock artist had released two separate albums on the same day, the critical response to both was mixed. Most jumped on the band-wagon, determined to accent the positive of what was a most peculiar double collection. 'Axl Rose has stopped teasing his hair, taken a few of the chains off his cowboy boots, left the pink lipstick to Skid Row's Sebastian Bach and gotten a bit of perspective,' the predictably circumspect review in *Rolling Stone* reassured us, with songs 'which range from ballad to battle, pretty to vulgar, worldly to incredibly naive.'

Others, like the *Village Voice*, shot more from the hip, declaring that 'What we're left with is not four albums' worth of firm decisions, but weak compromises', and mocking the band's so-called rebellious stance, branding them 'capitalist tools' that 'the marketing geniuses at their record company [knew] how to package'. It concluded: 'All that they seem free to do is say "Fuck you" and they say it a lot.'

In truth, if *Appetite* had taken the LA sound to another dimension, following it up four years later with two double-albums was a genuine history-making event, almost regardless of the merits or otherwise of the contents. It's often been suggested since that a scaled-down version of both *Illusions* would have produced perhaps the greatest rock album of its era, but that misses the point entirely. Here was a major band showing off all its tricks while operating at the very height of its crooked powers, both albums characterized as much by their throwaway moments – the effete 'The Garden'; the ludicrously offensive 'Back Off Bitch' – as they are by towering heights like 'Estranged', 'Coma', or Axl's much-cherished 'November Rain'.

'Since we put out *Appetite For Destruction*, I've watched a lot of bands put out two to four albums, and who cares?' said Axl. 'They went out, they did a big tour, they were big rock stars for that period of time. That's what everybody's used to and the record companies push that. But I want no part of that. We weren't just throwing something together to be rock stars. We wanted to put something together that meant everything to us . . .'

Chapter Eight

INSIDE THE COURT OF
KING AXL

In September 1991, just as *Use Your Illusion II* was on its way to number one in the US charts, Axl Rose was on the cover of *Rolling Stone* again. The major theme of the interview this time was his disclosure that he'd begun therapy in February that year – undergoing five-hour sessions five days a week, he claimed – in order to try and deal with the depression that had at times made him almost suicidal. He was quoted as saying, 'For over two years I lived in a black room.' He was referring to the infamous West Hollywood apartment he'd now abandoned. 'Blackout curtains, black floors, black walls. It's what I always thought I wanted, and sometimes it was really cool and sometimes it was a nightmare. And for two years, I worked on trying to put my head together, and find answers, because I couldn't find a reason to stay alive.' Now he was 'finally starting to settle into my life', though touring was an area he still regarded as the 'combat zone'.

Certainly, as the band geared up to begin the second leg of their US tour that year, Axl saw himself more as 'a soldier' than a musician, taking several hours each day to ready himself – physically, mentally, emotionally, even spiritually – for the stage. Preparations would begin in the late afternoon when he'd spend an hour on mainly cardiovascular exercises – running, stepping, bicycling. Working out on the StairMaster with his chiropractor-trainer, he said, 'enables me to breathe and move better on stage'. He would follow this with an extensive massage from the tour masseuse, Sabrina Okamoto. After taking a shower and grabbing a light meal – often a specially prepared salad of fresh vegetables, fruit, nuts, grains, white meat or fish – he would begin his daily vocal exercises either alone or with his vocal coach, Ron Anderson. This could take up to an hour, after which he'd disappear to his hotel suite to watch TV, read or listen to music.

He often used this time to call his LA psychotherapist, a beautiful Victoria Principal look-alike named Suzzy London, who he eventually invited to join him on tour, allowing her to supervise her own secluded area backstage for herself and Axl. According to a *Spin* magazine interview with Colleen Combs, who Axl insisted accompany him to his earliest sessions with London, she billed herself as a 'past-life regression' therapist. 'I only went twice,' Combs says. 'She told me that I didn't have any past lives and later told Axl that I was a 50,000-year-old being that put a hex on him.' Combs ceased working as Axl's assistant a short time later.

Once Axl was ready to go to the venue, he would get his new assistant Blake to phone his bodyguard Earl and tell him to have the limo ready for departure, at which point Axl would either be ready to leave immediately or might take another hour or so dawdling in his suite before coming down in the elevator, depending on his mood that evening. Once he finally arrived at the venue, he would sequester himself in his private dressing-room, away from the rest of the band, and summon the chiropractor to begin taping up his ankles to help prevent him twisting them onstage, as he'd done in New York. This was something that happened more often now; he said his ankles were still weak from his days as a cross-country runner at high school. He would then spend another forty-five minutes or so working again with Sabrina Okamoto, concentrating on getting his lower back into shape.

By then it was usually gone 10.00 p.m., sometimes as late as midnight, but no matter how bored or restless, the audience – and band – would still be waiting for the signal that the star of the show was finally ready to 'go to work'. Slash and the others tended to fill these yawning gaps with booze and drugs, flipping through copies of *Penthouse*, *Raw Sex*, *Hot Split*, *Big Boobs* and other magazines fanned out for them backstage like in a dentist's waiting-room. 'I remember thinking, "Fuck, man, this is nuts,"' says Matt Sorum. 'Subconsciously, down deep inside, I had a lot of fear initially going into Guns N' Roses. Before the beginning of each leg of every tour, I would get myself a nice pile of drugs. The machine of Guns N' Roses was scary. And not knowing what Axl was going to do was even scarier. So I'd just numb myself down.'

Axl, however, had entered a newly austere period and he almost completely renounced drugs – with the exception of marijuana, which he reportedly told *RIP* he still smoked to help him mellow out after a show – in favour of protein shakes and endless bottles of still mineral water. Over the course of the tour he also began to experiment with different kinds of herbal remedies and potions, most especially an echinacea elixir. Also known as Snake Root because it grows from a thick black root Native American Indians used to treat snake bites, herbalists consider echinacea one of the best blood purifiers and natural antibiotics in the world, good for stimulating the immune system, helping stave off diseases from the common cold to serious fevers. There are no known side effects associated with its use, other than the evangelical zeal with which its users tend to advocate its 'magical' properties to others. Axl was no exception. Try as he might, he couldn't interest Slash or any of the others in trying it. They had their own preferred stimulants.

By the start of 1992, when the band was ready to leave for shows in Japan, Axl's personal life began to overlap alarmingly with his professional life in other ways, too. 'Don't Cry', the second single from the *Use Your Illusion* sets, was accompanied by the band's most bizarre video yet. Written by Axl and Josh Richman, and making full use of a budget that allowed them to build an entire movie set, it tells the story of a rock star whose personal demons are beginning to devour him, specifically his relationship with his girlfriend. Intercut with footage of the band performing live on top of a skyscraper, circled by helicopters with searchlights, representing a band at the height of its success, the most explosive scenes involve Axl – in character but in effect playing himself – fighting over a gun with Stephanie Seymour – playing the part of a fictionalized Erin. 'In real life that happened with Erin and myself,' Axl reportedly confessed to *Metallix* magazine. 'I was going to shoot myself. We fought over the gun and I finally let her win. I was kind of mentally crippled after that.'

Having to play the scene with Stephanie added a strange twist to it for him, he said. It was 'a very touchy thing to do'.

The scene in which he's depicted drowning was also 'a real mind trip because that's how my life had felt for I don't know how many years, especially in my last relationship [with Erin]. I've always felt like I was drowning and being pulled down.' After he finished shooting the scene, he went back to his trailer and 'all of a sudden, I broke down for a bit because I was experiencing that [feeling of] "okay, now that's over, and you've expressed it, got it out of yourself". It was so close to how I really felt, it was really disturbing and hard to do, but by doing it, it helped me heal and get over certain things.'

Other pivotal scenes included a heavily sedated Axl in a hospital bed while two further Axls look on – representing, he later explained, his split personality. He also cast Suzzy London in a cameo role – as the therapist – looking sultry in a black mini-skirt. In the climactic scene Axl visits his own grave – bearing the inscription on the headstone: 'AA Rose – 1962–1990'. It was a symbol, he later explained, of the fact that as far as he was concerned he was 'a walking dead man' at the time the song referred to. 'I was, like, for two months recording the record, smoking pot because any other drugs just screwed me up. That was the only thing I could do to, like, sedate me and keep me contained enough to not freak out on how depressed I was. I was doing it almost medicinally. I was too depressed. I'd just flip out.' He also claimed in another interview that the gravestone was there to depict his anger over his childhood, which he had 'buried . . . for too long. I watched almost everyone in this church's lives go to shit because their own hypocrisy finally consumed them.'

Finally, a green 'demon' spirit appears to rise from beneath the grave, an allegory he said for what 'people call my demon voice, so I wanted to put that into an actual character. I feel like it's a part of me. It's also to do with reincarnation, whether anyone believes in that or not. It's to symbolize that if you didn't get it right, you get to try again, or you might *have* to try again.'

The one development Axl had no control over whatsoever was, ironically, an entirely musical one: the arrival of a new breed of rock band that, like punk before it, threatened to raze to the ground everything that immediately preceded it, including the now loftily placed Guns N' Roses. The critics even had a name for it: grunge. Its leaders were a three-piece from Seattle called Nirvana whose breakthrough album, *Nevermind*, was released under the aegis of the same Geffen label as Guns N' Roses' only weeks after *Use Your Illusion I* and *II*, and would by January 1992 replace both albums at the top of the US charts. Spear-headed by the most iconic rock single – 'Smells Like Teen Spirit' – since Guns N' Roses' own 'Sweet Child' three years before, so all-consuming was the sudden success of Nirvana and their fragile-looking singer, Kurt Cobain, that rock entered a new year-zero. Overnight, bands like Mötley Crüe and Poison were effec-tively finished. Even mainstream rock favourites like Bon Jovi and Def Leppard only survived the cull by cutting their hair and repositioning themselves as mature, adult-oriented balladeers.

Inevitably, Guns N' Roses' image also took a battering. Compared to the elegantly stripped-down pop-punk sound of *Nevermind*, the idea of two double-albums released simul-taneously quickly came to be seen as the folly of a band now straying dangerously close to self-parody. The Led Zeppelin to Nirvana's Sex Pistols, Guns N' Roses, until then the coolest, baddest band on the planet, now became distinctly unfashionable. But if releasing thirty tracks across two CDs was a folly, it was a brave, monumental one. True, there is nothing there that antici-pates Nirvana – what did? – but they certainly kicked down the doors for edgy, passionate rock that blithely ignored the rules. Much as Kurt Cobain may have despised the fact, it was no coincidence that many of the nine million Americans who bought *Nevermind* were also Guns N' Roses fans. The rest of the band were largely indifferent to their new rivals, but Axl was swift to grasp that Nirvana now had the edge musically. As Slash recalls, 'The only person that the encroaching '90s music scene had an effect on was Axl. I didn't really give a shit at the time.' Axl insisted Slash accompany him to see the new band when they played in LA in October 1991. 'One of the few times Axl and I ever went out in public together was to go and see Nirvana at the Palace here in Hollywood,' Slash said. 'I didn't think much of it at the time. We went on doing our thing . . .'

Cobain's wife, Courtney Love, remembers Axl standing next to her at the Nirvana show 'doing that dance he did in the "Sweet Child O' Mine" video. He said to Kurt after the show: "You're everything I could've been."' Later, Axl told one journalist how much he'd love to hear Nirvana do a version of 'Welcome To The Jungle' – 'their way, however that is'. He even put in a request to have Nirvana perform at the thirtieth birthday party he was planning in February 1992 (an offer Cobain rejected out of hand). Axl was such a fan early on that he even put a Nirvana baseball cap on one of the characters in the 'Don't Cry' video.

For Kurt Cobain, though, Guns N' Roses represented everything he most despised about rock stardom, seeing them as unforgivably self-indulgent and out of step with the times. 'I knew we were a hundred times better than fucking Guns N' Roses – or any of that shit,' he remarked matter-of-factly. Worse still, because of 'One In A Million', he considered them racist and homophobic. A view he did nothing to hide in subsequent interviews. 'They're really talentless people,' Cobain told one writer, 'and they write crap music.' The only thing he had in common with Axl, Cobain told his biographer, Michael Azzerad, was that they both came from small towns 'and we've been surrounded by a lot of sexism and racism. But our internal struggles are pretty different. I feel like I've allowed myself to open my mind to a lot more things than he has. His role has been played for years. Ever since the beginning of rock'n'roll, there's been an Axl Rose. It's just totally boring to me. Why it's such a fresh and new thing in his eyes is obviously because it's happening to him personally and he's such an egotistical person that he thinks that the whole world owes him something.'

Axl was deeply hurt by such remarks, not least because he thought he'd found a potential ally in the angst-ridden singer, going so far as to offer Nirvana the support slot on the summer 1992 leg of the 'Get In The Ring' tour that also included Metallica. Cobain dismissed the offer with a haughty sneer. Again, Axl was deeply affronted. This time, though, he hit back. 'They would rather sit home and shoot heroin with their bitch wives than tour with us,' he sniped in an interview with *Metallix*.

Instead, when the US tour reconvened with a show at the

Spectrum theatre in Worcester, Massachusetts, on 5 December, Nirvana's Seattle rivals Soundgarden opened the show. But even they would find being patronized by the world's biggest band a strangely surreal experience. According to *Blender* magazine Soundgarden vocalist Chris Cornell later described the experience as like living 'in a comic book'. He claimed that neither he nor anyone else was allowed to be in the same hallway 'or anywhere Axl might see you when he was walking between the dressing-rooms and the stage. So one day I see a security guard walking him down this long corridor where there's no one except for me, and it's like they want me to see him. He's wearing his Axl Rose tennis shoes that say "Axl Rose" on them and these teeny-tiny, painted-on red shorts, a backwards baseball cap and a fur coat that goes to the floor. He just walks by and goes, "Hey, bro!" And that was it. At that point, it's one of those moments where you think about your life as a comic book.' Cornell also recalled with puzzlement the various teleprompters Axl had set up at the end of the catwalks which connected to the stage, just in case he forgot any of his lyrics. 'I thought [that] was a little weird because they only had two [*sic*] albums.'

By now Guns N' Roses had positioned themselves about as far from the garage-punk-grunge ethic as was possible, their six-man line-up doubling in size, at Axl's insistence, to include keyboard and harmonica player Ted Andreadis, backing vocalists Diane Jones, Roberta Freeman and Tracy Amos, and a three-piece horn section dubbed the 976-Horns, comprising: Lisa Maxwell, Cece Worrall and Anne King. On 9 December, the new twelve-man band headlined the first of three shows at New York's Madison Square Garden, where they not only managed to make it onto the stage more or less on time each night but the critics bent over backwards to write rapturous reviews. The year ended on a suitably triumphant note, with a special New Year's Eve show at the massive Joe Robbie Stadium in Miami.

The tour continued without a break right through January. By now, Axl was into wearing kilts onstage along with T-shirts variously depicting such diverse figures as the famously alcoholic LA writer Charles Bukowski, a suitably saintly looking Jesus and a typically demonic-looking Charles Manson. He said the idea of the kilts came in an effort to 'try to make my own unorthodox moves' and went back to the Rock in Rio shows a year before when he'd worn tight, red, white and blue cycling shorts. 'I wanted to wear something different,' and the shorts and then the kilts meant 'I could move around better, because what I do is pretty athletic.'

In February, the band left for Japan and three sold-out shows at the new Tokyo Dome. After that there was a short break in LA before they set off on the road again with a show in April across the border in Mexico. Their next high-profile appearance occurred in London, on 20 April, where, despite objections from gay rights groups, the band returned to Wembley Stadium to take part in a special commemorative concert for Queen singer – and lifelong Axl hero – Freddie Mercury, who had died of AIDS-related causes the previous November. Billed as the Freddie Mercury Tribute Concert for AIDS Awareness, the whole band performed two songs – 'Paradise City' and 'Knockin' On Heaven's Door' – before Axl joined Elton John for one of the highlights of the event, a stunning duet performance of 'Bohemian Rhapsody'. Wearing a Union Jack leather jacket and a T-shirt with the slogan 'Kill Your Idol' beneath a picture of Christ, Axl hopped around the stage waving his arms. For the encores, he sang 'We Will Rock You' with Queen, who Slash also joined onstage for a flat-out version of 'Tie Your Mother Down'. At the end of the show, Axl, Duff and Slash joined the rest of the performers for 'We Are The Champions'. Gilby Clarke recalled the show as 'The best experience I had in the band.' Axl, he says, 'was awesome – he really respected Freddie Mercury. We went on, on time, we played great together, and everybody got along. I thought it was very moving.'

For Axl, the Queen gig 'was the most humbling experience of my life. It was fucking intense.' Brian May was 'one of the nicest people I've met.' Indeed, it was May who suggested the duet on 'Bohemian Rhapsody'. 'I spoke to Elton before the show,' Axl said, 'and he was kind of uneasy about meeting me, you know, I'm supposed to be the most homophobic guy on Earth.' Once he explained his long-standing admiration, though, 'he was like, "Whoa!" Onstage, I was trying to be as respectful to him as I could. I was purposely vibing out, and if you look close, you can see it at times, how much love and respect I have for Elton. There was some heavy eye contact going down. It was amazing.'

The same month, in a new interview with Kim Neely, in *Rolling Stone*, Axl was quoted announcing that his recent therapy sessions had helped him recover memories of the sexual abuse he'd suffered as a very small child at the hands of his birth-father, William Rose, as well as helping him to come to terms with the strict upbringing he went on to endure under the tutelage of his stepfather. He insisted that, as far as he was concerned, it wasn't about forgiveness, it was about having 'to re-experience it and mourn what happened to you and grieve for yourself and nurture yourself and put yourself all back together'. All of which he was painfully aware would take a long time, possibly the rest of his life. 'You find out your mother and father had their problems and their mother and father had problems, and it goes back through the ages.'

The therapy hadn't cured him of the extremes he perennially experienced, he reportedly admitted, 'but it is a lot better because of this work'. He said his 'growth' had 'stopped at two years old', so that when the media talked 'about Axl Rose being a screaming two-year-old, they're right'. Further he had found solace in the work he'd done for child-abuse organizations, offering support, both financially and in person, even dropping into one centre where he was encouraged to speak to 'a little boy who wasn't able to accept things that had happened to him and to deal with it'. According to *Rolling Stone* Axl said the boy saw something of himself in his hero. 'He said, "Well, Axl had problems, and he's doing okay."' At which point he 'started opening up' to the singer. 'And that's more important to me than Guns N' Roses, more important to me than anything I've done so far.' He said he could relate because of the hatred he still felt for his father, for women in general and, ultimately, 'yeah, myself'.

Spending time with Stephanie Seymour's three-year-old son, Dylan, often left his head 'spinning because of the changes it's putting me through'. Stephanie had been 'very supportive in helping me deal with all this'. The romance in their relationship was 'a plus', but it was their friendship that was 'the most important thing'. He added that being with Dylan, taking responsibility for such a young child, 'scares me. It's like they could break at any time.'

When Neely, changing the subject, asked why he seemed so unable to start a show on time, he apparently bridled. 'I pretty much follow my own internal clock and I perform better later at night. Nothing seems to work out for me until later at night.' He was said to insist that the wait was worse for him. 'That time period that I'm late going onstage is a living hell, because I'm wishing there was any way on earth I could get out of where I am and knowing I'm not going to be able to make it.' He added that he was 'late to everything' and joked that he was going to have it written into his will that when he died 'the coffin shows up a half-hour late and says on the side, like in gold, "SORRY I'M LATE."'

Turning serious again, he was quoted concluding: 'We're out there to win at what we do. And if that means going on two hours late and doing a good show, I'm gonna do it. I take what I do very seriously.' The constant lateness proved how much he cared about his fans. 'If I didn't give a fuck about them, I'd come out and do a shitty show.' It was 'confusing to me that people go, "Well, I have to work in the morning." If you were getting laid, you wouldn't be so worried about what time it was. I know it's complicated, but so is getting onstage.' He admitted, though, that he did act like a spoiled rock star sometimes. 'I've spoiled myself. I'll get better at dealing with that, though. I mean, it's still new. Then again, there are a lot of things I complain about that everybody else complains about but won't do it publicly. Like having somebody thrown out who is causing a commotion and basically obstructing the show. Most performers would go to a security person in their organization, and it would just be done very quietly.'

Trying to pin him down on the real reasons why Izzy left the band, Axl had, according to *Rolling Stone*, 'talked to Izzy for four-and-a-half hours on the phone. At some points, I was crying, and I was begging. I was doing everything I could to keep him in the band.' He apparently admitted to giving Izzy a contract to sign, though – making what he called 'stipulations'. The main one being, 'If he was going to do like the old Izzy did he wasn't going to make as much money. It was like "You're not giving an equal share." Slash and I were having to do too much work to keep the attention and the energy up in the crowd. You're onstage going, "This is really hard, and I'm into it and I'm doing it, but that guy [Izzy] just gets to stand there."' He was said to have objected to Izzy 'riding bicycles and motorcycles and buying toy airplanes – donating all this energy to something else, and it's taking a hundred per cent of our energy to do what we're doing on the stage.' Axl was to said to feel this meant 'we were getting ripped off.' The fact that Izzy subsequently went back to working with Alan Niven was also said to have pissed him off. 'He put his trust in people that I consider my enemies. It's like, "If you're involved with these people, we can't talk to you."'

Just before the *Rolling Stone* piece was published, however, Axl gave a phone interview to Andy Warhol's *Interview* magazine, in which he talked about happier things, like his blossoming love affair with Stephanie Seymour. Indeed, the accompanying pictures – taken by fashion iconographer Bruce Weber – featured not the band but shots of Axl and Stephanie French-kissing. 'Steph and I have a really good time talking with each other,' Axl was quoted as saying, 'and we want to try to see if we can have that, in our lives, for our lives. We don't know, but we're definitely trying to communicate as much as we can.' He went on: 'Sometimes your friends are your lovers, or have been at one time, or are at some time or are at different times. Maintaining the friendship and taking the responsibility of being a friend and also helping the other person be a friend to you, and expressing your feelings about your friendship . . . Stephanie and I do that with each other. It's a good thing.'

Again he was quoted referring to his therapy in terms of improving his mental attitude to his relationships with both men and women. 'I reached a point where I was basically dead and still breathing. I didn't have enough energy to leave my bedroom and crawl to the kitchen to get something to eat. I had to find out why I was dead, and why I felt like I was dead. I had a lot of issues that I didn't really know about in my life and didn't understand how they affected me. I didn't realize that I felt certain ways toward women, toward men, toward people in general, and toward myself. The only way to get through that was to go back through it and find it and re-experience it and attempt to heal it. I'm still working on that but I'm a lot further along than I was.' Meanwhile, he apparently likened his relationship with the band as 'kinda like a marriage and a half, or a marriage and a household.' Especially his relationship with Slash, which was 'definitely a marriage'.

He was also quoted speaking openly about his changing views on the whole rock'n'roll lifestyle; specifically, the drug-taking and heavy drinking he and his band had openly advocated. 'But I would also like it to be known that I'm not a person to be telling the youth of America, "Don't get wasted."' Too many bands that had publicly cleaned up 'talk about things they did and how they were wrong. I don't know if it was necessarily wrong. It helped them survive. At the time they weren't given the proper tools to do the proper healing. I personally don't do any hard drugs any more, because they get in the way of me getting to my base issues, and I'd rather get rid of the excess baggage than find a way to shove it deeper in the closet, at this time in my life.'

In that context, he was said to have admitted the overwhelmingly negative critical reaction to 'One In A Million' had also helped him change. 'I went out and got all kinds of video tapes and read books on racism. Books by Martin Luther King and Malcolm X. Reading them and studying, then after that I put on the tape and I realized, "Wow, I'm still proud of this song. That's strange. What does that mean?" But I couldn't communicate as well as I do now about it, so my frustration was just turned to anger. Then my anger would be used against me and my frustration would be used against me: "Look, he's throwing a tantrum."'

On 12 May, at a press conference held at The Gaslight in Hollywood, Slash and Metallica's Lars Ulrich appeared together to announce that Guns N' Roses and Metallica would tour the US together that summer. Ulrich began a mutual appreciation society with Axl as far back as Donington 1988, when the two hung out together backstage, and both bands were enjoying their biggest success – combined sales of the *Use Your Illusion* albums were topping ten million and Metallica's self-titled album, featuring the breakthrough single 'Enter Sandman', was also number one in 1991 and on its way to selling its first ten million copies. Guns N' Roses and Metallica on the road together was Ulrich's brainwave and promised to be the biggest concert-draw of the year. It would also be one of the most incident-filled and controversy-ridden tours in the history of rock, a joint expedition that would see the bands fall out with each other so spectacularly that even the Axl-besotted Ulrich was forced to admit the tour became 'out of control'.

Before that, Guns N' Roses spent another two months touring Britain and Europe, commencing on 16 May with an outdoor festival at Slane Castle in Dublin, where they arrived via private jet forty-eight hours previously. A year into the tour, this was one of their happiest nights so far. With Axl's smiling face splashed across the front page of the *Irish Independent*, the band were delighted to find a crate of forty-year-old Black Bush whiskey and a barrel of Guinness waiting for them backstage, courtesy of U2, who were also touring Europe that summer. Despite the presence of over 800 police patrolling the Castle site, the show went off without a hitch.

Four nights later they were in Prague for a sold-out show at the Strahov Stadium, where Soundgarden and Faith No More opened for them and a crew from MTV waited to interview them. In line with the newfound light-heartedness that seemed to characterize this leg of the tour, Axl had Del James (now travelling with the band) start the show by yelling into a mike, 'Okay, you ex-Commie bastards, get ready to rock!' Two nights later, at the Nep Stadium in Budapest, Axl stopped halfway through the set to perform the Hungarian folk song 'Tavasziszel', giving the third verse over to the emotionally charged crowd to sing for him – the same song he'd been told Queen shrewdly performed there in 1985.

The following night at the Donau Insel Stadium in Vienna, U2 (who were due to play there the next night) were Axl's honoured guests. Later that evening, Axl joined Bono at a restaurant party to celebrate the birthday of U2 tour accountant Osmond Kilkenny. The next night, with U2 now headlining the Donau, it was Axl's turn to be Bono's guest, joining him onstage for an acoustic version of 'Knockin' On Heaven's Door' which the U2 singer introduced by describing Axl as 'someone the song could have been written for'. Flattered beyond belief, Axl gave 'the performance of his life' of the song, according to one eyewitness.

The tour continued in similarly high spirits as it racked up sell-out crowds in Germany (40,000 at the Olympic Stadium in Berlin and more than 75,000 at the Cannstatter Wasen in Stuttgart, the biggest crowd of the tour so far, where Del introduced the band with: 'Okay, you beer-swilling, Merc-driving mugs . . .') and Paris, where they performed a special televized pay-per-view show to 58,000 people at the Hippodrome in the Bois de Vincennes on 6 June.

Staying at the impossibly luxurious Hotel De Crillon overlooking the Place de la Concorde, Jeff Beck, Lenny Kravitz and Aerosmith's Steven Tyler and Joe Perry all flew in to appear with the band as special guests at the Paris show. Axl nearly ruined everything when, after a row over the phone with Stephanie earlier that day, he embarrassingly dedicated 'Double Talkin' Jive' to Warren Beatty. Jeff Beck, however, pulled out at the last minute, claiming Slash's playing was so loud at the previous day's rehearsals that he'd developed tinnitus. Kravitz stayed the course, though, helping the band through a blistering 'Always On The Run' (the track Slash had played on from Kravitz's album *Mama Said*), as did Tyler and Perry who joined the band onstage for an extended encore knockabout through 'Train Kept A-Rollin' and 'Mama Kin'.

Four days before the Paris show, the band released their latest single, 'November Rain', replete with a cringe-making video: a $1.5 million farce in which Axl got to 'marry' Stephanie, with Slash as 'best man'; 'taste' and 'sanity' were distant members of the family who couldn't make it. Previewed as the second part of a trilogy that began with 'Don't Cry' and would be completed later that year with the video for 'Estranged', each was self-contained but would eventually form a broader, overall story. All three were directed by Andy Morahan, who had made video-features for Elton John, George Michael and Michael Jackson. 'Andy puts up with more shit and handles the disorganization of Guns N' Roses, all the time changes and scheduling changes, and stuff, so easily,' said Axl. 'He's just so into the project.'

Unlike 'Don't Cry', which was an almost entirely autobiographical scenario, the video for 'November Rain' was loosely based on a short story, 'Without You', written by Del James, which in turn was inspired by the true-life tale of Axl's tortuous relationship with Erin. Ostensibly, it was about a rock star called Mayne who dreams while in a 'drug-and-alcohol-induced coma' of a girl whose 'innocence was enchanting' and 'beauty breathtaking', yet the dream always ends the same way – as a nightmare in which the girl shoots herself in the head while dancing to one of his songs. The portrait James draws is clearly based on Axl, from the 'silver and gold bracelets' he wears to the 'long blond hair and tattoos' he sports and his 'scraggly beard' and 'emerald eyes'.

There's even a nasty neighbour who starts banging on the wall, complaining about the noise, although in this scenario the Axl figure shoots the neighbour with a .357 Magnum. When Elizabeth, the 'real-life' girl of his dreams, kills herself while listening to the song he wrote for her – the 'Without You' of the story's title – he's devastated. The story continues: 'He removed the pistol from her hand and put it against his temple. He was going to join her. CLICK. It was empty. Elizabeth had known she would only need one bullet.' In the end Mayne gets what he wants when a forgotten cigarette starts a fire in his apartment that overwhelms him as he sits at his piano, playing one last song.

James later explained how the inspiration for the story came from an incident one night in 1989, when Axl phoned him at 4.00 a.m. and asked him to come over. When he got there, Axl poured out his heart about his unhappy relationship with Erin. Some months later, after James showed the story to Axl, the singer called him again late at night, this time to tell him he'd written the theme song to the story, also called 'Without You'. 'I'd never planned on that, never even thought of that,' said Axl. It just 'ended up fitting together' with a song he was already at work on. Later on in the recording process, the song reverted back to its original title – 'Estranged'.

Where the video for 'November Rain' fitted into this scenario is harder to explain, apart from the very beginning where we see Axl in bed in a darkened bedroom, taking pills to help him sleep. After that, though, the video dramatically diverts from the short story as we follow the lead character into a concert hall, the band onstage backed by a full orchestra and conductor, while Axl sits dolefully at a piano, playing the intro to the song, intercut with images of a bleeding crucifix.

Various scenes ensue in which Axl marries his beautiful bride – played by Stephanie – Slash then celebrates by performing a back-arching solo outside the church while a helicopter swoops around him. Climbing into a white Bentley convertible, the bride looks away, as if unsure about what she's done. Then, at the wedding party, it starts to pour with rain and the guests scatter, sending tables flying and knocking over a bottle of red wine which spills its contents over a white tablecloth like blood.

Another solo from Slash, perched atop the piano, with the orchestra sawing away behind him. (Even though you can't hear it in the video, Axl insisted the orchestra indulge him and play live so he could hear what it would sound like to have one of his songs properly orchestrated.) Like 'Don't Cry', the video concludes with a graveyard scene, this time with the bride lying in a coffin while Axl sits listening to the funeral service. (To Axl's great annoyance, Stephanie fell asleep while this scene was being shot.) Then the coffin is carried to the cemetery for burial as the rain pours and the mourners leave. Finally, we return to Axl in his bed, as if waking from a nightmare, only to be suddenly transported back to the bride's open grave, which he is crouched over as her wedding bouquet lands on the coffin.

The final part of the so-called trilogy – the video for 'Estranged' – wasn't completed until the very end of the world tour over a year later, to accompany what would be the final single from the *Illusion* albums. A nine-minute epic featuring the band playing live on Sunset Strip, which was sealed off by police, the video also contains a baffling sequence in which Axl throws himself off an oil tanker into the ocean, where we then see him swimming underwater with a group of dolphins (an encounter that led to him sponsoring an environmental group dedicated to protecting marine wildlife). Again, quite what this has to do with the original Del James story is impossible to say. With Stephanie out of the picture in real life by then, she is nowhere to be seen either, despite the fact that the pearly-white Malibu mansion he bought for them both to live in features in the video.

Indeed, with the new down-and-dirty orthodoxy introduced by grunge overwhelming every aspect of rock music in the summer of 1992, everything about the 'November Rain' and 'Estranged' videos smacked of a band whose giant collective ego was teetering dangerously out of control. (British comedy duo French & Saunders sent the whole thing up beautifully with a wonderful parody of the 'November Rain' video; the blonde Jennifer Saunders hilarious as an uptight and irony-free Axl and the more rotund Dawn French absolutely spot-on as a derisive Slash soloing like King Canute trying and failing to command the rising tide.)

Meanwhile, back in Paris, unaware of the critical derision their latest 'high concept' video was stirring in Britain and America, the band enjoyed a couple of days off. Axl had hoped Stephanie would fly out to join him and was deeply distraught when she phoned to cancel because she had to 'work'. Fearing the worst – that she was spending time again with her former beau, Warren Beatty – it was this disappointment that sparked his sardonic dedication to Beatty at the previous night's show. Instead, a dour-looking Axl made a very public visit to the Louvre to see *Winged Victory of Samothrace*, aka *Nike of Samothrace*, a marble sculpture of the Greek goddess Nike (meaning victory). Discovered in 1863 on the island of Samothrace by the French consul and amateur archaeologist Charles Champoiseau, it's one of the great surviving masterpieces of sculpture from the Hellenistic period, despite the fact that it's missing its head and outstretched arms.

That evening a doctor hastily summoned to the Hotel De Crillon diagnosed 'complete physical exhaustion' and recommended the singer take thirty-six hours' rest. The next show at Manchester City's Maine Road football ground – tickets for which had already sold out – would have to be postponed. In a gesture meant to placate the British press, ready to go to town on the show's last-minute cancellation, the no longer needed production crew catering was given free to a local hospice, while fans were told their tickets would be valid for the rearranged gig to be held on 14 June, the day after their next Wembley Stadium show.

On the day of the announcement, 9 June, Axl remained in Paris while the rest of the band travelled to London and checked back into the Conrad Hotel, where fellow guests included Prince (in town for his Earl's Court shows) and INXS (who seemed to spend most of the time in the bar with Slash and Matt).

Axl finally flew in two days later, while everybody else took part in a softball game at the Bank of England sports ground. The day of the Wembley show did not begin well, with Axl adamant that he be flown by helicopter from the Conrad to the stadium, despite being told there was nowhere for it to land. As a result, the agitated singer was forced to disembark from the helicopter even further away from Wembley than he had been at the hotel, and was driven the rest of the way by road. The show itself, however, was reckoned to be one of the best of the tour, with Brian May joining them onstage for 'Tie Your Mother Down' and 'We Will Rock You'. Axl found something to bitch about, stopping the show to remonstrate with security for not removing a drunken, trouble-making fan from the crowd quickly enough. He stopped the show for a second time later on in the set, however, to allow security men to lift a young girl clearly in distress from the suffocatingly tight crowd gathered around the stage.

By comparison the rescheduled date in Manchester the next day and their show at the Gateshead International Stadium in Newcastle on 16 June went without a hitch, although the Manchester show started more than two hours late, while the Newcastle performance was briefly interrupted by Duff who got into a slanging match with a fan which Axl eventually broke up by telling the fan: 'I wouldn't mess with him, he's not had a drink in two weeks!' After Newcastle, the band boarded a private plane and flew back to London.

On the afternoon of 19 June they resumed the tour in Frankfurt. The journey was made especially aggravating for Axl when he was singled out for special attention by an over-zealous security guard at Heathrow Airport, who appeared to take great pleasure in painstakingly inspecting every item of his luggage while grilling him thoroughly about his travel plans. Having received similar treatment earlier in the year when he arrived in London for the Freddie Mercury tribute show, Axl predictably blew his top, instructing his record company to issue the following press statement, cheerfully reported in all the newspapers the following day: 'Having just given what I consider to be the best performance I am capable of at this point in my career, I totally understand why someone in the UK would want to needlessly harass me in this way. I don't expect to be treated any differently from anyone else travelling in and out of Britain and I understand these people have a job to do. However, to be singled out by someone who just wants to score a few points and have a story to tell his friends over a beer is really out of order.'

The last half-dozen shows of the European tour did not pass by without incident, either. The show at the Feyenoord Stadium in Rotterdam almost turned into another riot when, yet again, the band was over two hours late arriving onstage. On this occasion, however, there was some justification behind the delay as both Axl and Duff were obliged to seek medical treatment for influenza. Duff was in bed for two days and Axl was given further medication by a doctor waiting for him at Rotterdam airport when the band's private plane touched down on the evening of the show. They finally got onstage at 10.00 p.m., but as there was an 11.00 p.m. curfew at the venue the best the local authorities could offer was to extend the curfew by thirty minutes. Made aware of this just before he went onstage – absolutely the wrong time to give Axl any news that wasn't wholly positive – he walked on in such a temper he told the 48,000 crowd: 'You have a right to a complete show. You paid for it.' He glared at unseen figures in the wings, before concluding: 'If they cut the power, be my guests, do what you want.' With the crowd in uproar, the on-duty police hastily decided to allow the show to continue until well after midnight.

With Duff feeling decidedly worse afterwards, the following night's show in Ghent, Belgium, was cancelled. Instead Axl flew direct to Milan, where to his immense relief he was met at the hotel by Stephanie, who took him to visit the showrooms of top Italian designers Gianni Versace and Giorgio Armani. Two nights later, with Duff still confined to bed, Axl and Stephanie had dinner with Versace's sister, Donatella, and her model husband Paul Becak. Also at the dinner party was supermodel Naomi Campbell. Stephanie agreed to stay on the road with Axl for the final clutch of dates: a show in front of 65,000 of the Della Alpi Stadium in Turin on 27 June and yet another football stadium in Seville, Spain, on 30 June where, with no curfew to contend with, on Axl's orders the start of the set was delayed until after dark so that the light show could be enjoyed in full. The show itself ended in the early hours of the morning.

The very next date, at the Alvalade Stadium in Lisbon on 2 July did not go well. With the band not coming onstage until almost 11.00 p.m., the crowd were without entertainment for nearly five hours (the time between support act Faith No More finishing their set and Guns N' Roses starting theirs) and were in no mood for fireworks. As soon as Axl led the band on, the crowd started throwing empty water bottles. Halfway through the opening number, Axl slipped on one of the bottles and fell flat on his back. Refusing to move, he lay there and sang the rest of the song as well as the following number on his back. Duff eventually went over to see if he was all right, at which point he got back on his feet and told the crowd that if they didn't stop throwing bottles he would walk off. Then he did, taking the rest of the band with him. 'I didn't come here to get hurt!' he cried as he left.

A short while later the band meandered back on again, but now the crowd began to hurl fire-crackers and lighters around the stadium. Once again, Axl stopped the show, this time during 'Civil War', and ordered them to stop – or else. A member of the Portuguese organization then came on to try and calm the situation but failed. Eventually the band found their own solution to the problem by playing the aptly named 'Patience', after which the crowd finally appeared to settle.

There was supposed to be one last show after that, at the Vicente Caldaron stadium in Madrid on 4 July, but that, too, had to be cancelled when it was discovered that the concrete fabric of the building had been disastrously affected by aluminosis. In a short press statement, Axl expressed his regrets: 'We were looking forward to this last date in Europe, as we love the Spanish audiences and we were planning on a wild night to end the tour. We hope that we will be able to return soon and make it up to our fans.'

Making the most of the situation, while the road crew and most of the band flew straight back to the US, Axl and Stephanie stayed on for a few days longer, staying at a luxury hotel resort in San Remo.

A year on from the dreadful riot in St Louis, friends said they had never seen Axl so happy and relaxed. But his newfound good humour was instantly shattered on his arrival back in the US on 12 July when the ghosts of St Louis came back to haunt him. Stepping off the plane with Stephanie at JFK airport in New York, Axl was arrested as soon as he cleared customs when police issued him with 'fugitive warrants' – apparently on assault and property damage charges relating to the St Louis riot – on the basis that he had effectively ignored all previous efforts to turn himself in. Even though his own legal team was standing by in New York, it was not enough to prevent him suffering the ignominy of being led from the airport to a waiting squad car with his hands cuffed behind his back.

Two days later he stood before the judge at a courthouse in Clayton, Missouri, and pleaded innocent to four counts of misdemeanour assault and one count of property damage. Ushered into the courthouse through a basement entrance, in order to avoid the hundreds of waiting fans and reporters outside, Axl was warned that if convicted of all charges, he could face up to four-and-a-half years in jail and a total of $4,500 in fines. After a nine-minute hearing, a trial was set for 13 October, though St Louis County Court Judge Ellis Gregory ruled that Guns N' Roses could begin its American tour as scheduled, on pain of a $100,000 bail bond which Axl agreed to put up. In an interview he gave to MTV straight after the hearing, Axl called the St Louis County Prosecutor Robert McCulloch 'a liar', to which McCulloch's office responded by saying they would drop any plans for a negotiated plea agreement. When the case eventually

came before the courts, Axl was found guilty of property damage
and assault. His sentence, though, was comparatively light: he
was given two years' probation and ordered to pay $50,000 to
community groups.

Exactly a week after his arrest in New York, Guns N' Roses
began their twenty-five-date tour with Metallica at the RFK
Stadium in Washington, where all hell was about to break loose
– again.

By now, Axl had assembled an even larger and more elaborate
support team for the road: his usual retinue of chiropractor,
masseuse, vocal coach, bodyguard, driver, personal assistant,
PR, manager and gaggle of friends like Del James and Dana
Gregory regularly augmented by his brother Stuart and sister
Amy, his psychotherapist Suzzy London and a new, even more
influential figure in his life: a professional psychic named Sharon
Maynard.

The head of a non-profit organization based in Sedona,
Arizona, called Arcos Cielos Corp (from the Spanish for 'sky
arcs'), describing itself as an 'educational' enterprise specializing
in 'channelling' past lives, extraterrestrial intelligence and the
power of crystals, Maynard was a short, middle-aged Asian
woman who would start to take a central role in Axl's life that
continues behind-the-scenes to the present day. Operating out of
her countryside home where she lived with her husband, Elliott,
a kindly grey-haired man, 'Dr Elliott and Sharon Maynard' were
thanked in the *Use Your Illusion* liner notes. Known to the rest
of the band and touring crew as Yoda (after the goblin-like
mystic in *Star Wars*), Maynard's role on the road was less specific
than London's though Axl's reliance on both grew equally
important. Axl was now spending more time with them than he
was with his own band. Every major decision he now made was
deeply influenced by Yoda's opinions. 'It's, like, I have a pit
crew,' he said. 'And it's, like, I'm a car.' The chiropractor also
stood at the side of the stage each night so that Axl could get
adjusted between songs. And for a while he was taking up to
sixty vitamins a day. 'We do muscle testing and kinesiology,' he
explained. 'We do chiropractic work and acupuncture. We do

Take a bow. Guns N' Roses at
the Sports Palace in Mexico City
in April 1992, part of the
Use Your Illusion tour.

Axl and Elton John performing 'Bohemian Rhapsody' at the
Freddie Mercury Tribute Show, Wembley Stadium, 1992.

Axl was arrested on 12 July 1992 at Kennedy airport, after failing to appear in court
on charges connected to the St Louis riot in 1991.

And the winner is . . . Guns N'Roses accepting the Michael Jackson Video Vanguard
Award for 'November Rain' at the MTV Video Music Awards in Los Angeles in
September 1992.

Axl and friends in December 1992, the day before the band's first performance in Argentina, as part of the *Use Your Illusion* tour.

The case of Axl Rose versus Stephanie Seymour, August 1993.

Axl and Bruce Springsteen
performing 'Come Together' at the
Rock and Roll Hall of Fame Awards
in January 1994. It was his last
performance on a public stage
for six years.

A pensive Axl photographed at
the same event.

On 11 February 1998, Axl was arrested again again after an argument with a security guard at an airport in Phoenix, Arizona. Shown here in a Maricopa Sheriff's booking photo.

Axl spotted out shopping with Beta Lebris, his assistant, cook and housekeeper, in September 2002.

The mysterious Brian Carroll, better known as Buckethead, who played with Guns N' Roses from 2000 to 2004. Photographed performing during Primus' set at Ozzfest, Vancouver in October 2006.

The Sopranos Sixth Season Premiere after party at the Museum of Modern Art in New York in March 2006. Seen here (left to right): 'Little' Steve Van Zandt; Axl Rose; James Gandolfini; and Chuck Barris, TV producer and author of *Confessions Of A Dangerous Mind.*

Get in the ring! Tommy Hilfiger
appeared to start a fight with Axl
at Rosario Dawson's birthday party
in New York in May 2006.

'Do you know where the fuck
you are?!' Axl introducing
The Killers at the 2006 MTV
Music Awards in New York.

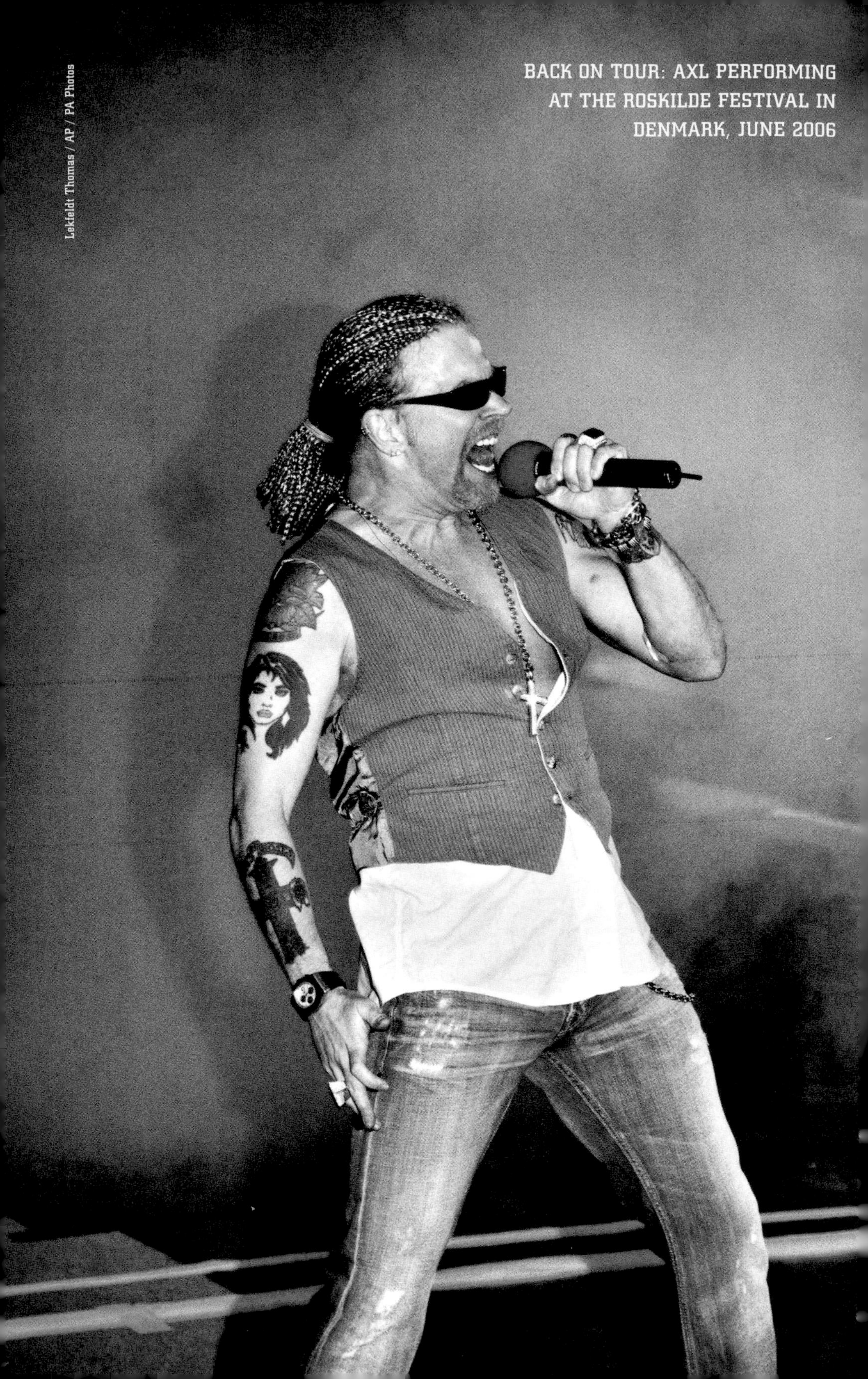

BACK ON TOUR: AXL PERFORMING
AT THE ROSKILDE FESTIVAL IN
DENMARK, JUNE 2006

Lekfeldt Thomas / AP / PA Photos

cranial adjusting. Oh, yeah. On a daily basis. I'm putting my life back together, and I'm using everything I can.'

Everybody – from the lowliest bag-carrier to the loftiest record company executive – was now forced to sign confidentiality agreements forbidding them from commenting publicly on any aspect of the tour without Axl's express permission, and then only in writing. Whatever 'regression therapy' he was undergoing, Axl was more determined than ever to exert as much control as he could over any situation he now found himself in.

For all their efforts behind the scenes, the one thing Maynard, London and co. could not protect Axl from was random acts by his own fans. Ten days into the tour with Metallica, at Giant Stadium in Rutherford, New Jersey, on 29 July, during the last song, 'Knockin' On Heaven's Door', swaying back and forth in his white spandex shorts, white buckskin jacket and white cowboy hat, Axl was hit in the genitals by a cigarette lighter thrown from the audience. Doubled-up in pain, he turned his back on the crowd, threw his microphone into the air, tore off his hat and staggered to the side of the stage to try and catch his breath while Duff took over on vocals. The crowd began chanting, 'Axl, Axl, Axl!' But there was no way he was coming back and when the house lights came on the crowd just stood there for a while before filing out, dejected. The next day an announcement was made explaining Axl had sustained 'severe damage to his vocal chords' and that the next three shows – in Boston, Columbia and Minneapolis – would all have to be rescheduled.

The most disturbing incident of the tour occurred on the night the tour resumed, on 8 August, at Montreal's Olympic Stadium, when Metallica were forced to abandon their set midway after their singer James Hetfield badly burned his left arm after a mistimed pyrotechnic explosion. Given the unforeseen nature of Metallica's abrupt departure, it was hoped that Guns N' Roses would pull out all the stops and deliver a lengthy, compensatory set for the many thousands of disappointed fans. Instead, Axl walked offstage after just nine songs. The problem, he later explained, was with the onstage monitors that weren't loud enough for him to hear his own voice. Before 'Double Talkin'

Jive', he also made the inexplicable comment that this would be 'our last show for a long time'. Then at the end of 'Civil War', which turned out to be the last song of the night, he growled: 'Thank you, your money will be refunded, we're outta here.' As a result of the truncated programme, while traipsing disgruntled from the venue, more than 2,000 fans fought with police, who were barely able to control the mob, leading to more than a dozen injuries.

Once again, the tour had to be interrupted, with the next seven shows all rescheduled. Doug Goldstein observed that the tour had become 'like people who go to watch the Indy 500. They don't go to watch the race, they go to see the crash.' To make up for lost time Axl ordered the band back to LA, where they shot the video for 'Estranged'. When the tour did finally get going again, with a show at the International Raceway in Phoenix, Arizona, on 25 August, Axl again got some people's backs up by resuming his habit of not coming onstage until almost midnight. Then when he did finally walk on, he told the restless crowd, 'Maybe I was just too fuckin' bummed out to get my ass up here any quicker.' Or as he put it afterwards, 'Maybe I couldn't move any faster than I was because it was a bitch.'

By now the band had been on the road for so long that the backstage ostentation had gone into overdrive. 'We'd spend $100,000 a night on parties,' says Matt. 'For two and a half years, there was something every night.' One night would be 'Greek night – four greased-up, muscle-bound guys [carrying] in a roast pig.' Another might be a 'Sixties Night', with lava lamps on all the tables and slogans spray-painted on the walls: 'Acid is groovy'; 'Kill the pigs'. There were also limos on-call twenty-four-hours-a-day. 'The first night we played Giants Stadium,' Matt says, 'there was one pinball machine and a few bottles of booze backstage. Axl came in and said, "This isn't the Rolling Stones!" So the next night there's a full casino, tons of lobster, and champagne flowing everywhere.'

While Metallica were out there sweating beneath the boiling late summer sun, Guns N' Roses were still at their hotel. As if following Axl's lead, none of the band now got to bed much before 7.00 a.m. Axl now spent so little time with the other members of the band he began to take on the persona of a god surrounded by acolytes and servants. Lemmy of Motörhead, for so long one of Axl's heroes, whose band opened the show when they played the Rose Bowl in Pasadena on 3 October, recalled how 'they were already fragmenting. Axl was on his own. It didn't feel like they were thinking as a band any more.'

Once they managed to stagger onstage, the show was the most spectacular they would ever deliver: 250,000 watts of power and a completely over the top fireworks display, featuring no less than twenty explosions, twenty-eight sparkles, fifteen airbursts, twenty flashes, twenty-five waterfalls and thirty-two fountains. Ever the perfectionist, Axl was still using the teleprompter for his lyrics and changed his clothes almost every other song, from spandex shorts to leather kilt to Jesus/Bukowski/Manson T-shirts, to another that read: *Nobody Knows I'm A Lesbian*. The really big moment was saved for 'November Rain', which he sang while seated at a grand piano that rose into the middle of the stage, with the piano designed to look like a motorcycle seat. Slash usually climbed on top of Axl's 'motorcycle' for his guitar solo. 'Knockin' On Heaven's Door' ended the set, the band exiting to a big red sign flashing the words: GUNS N' ROSES, GUNS N' ROSES, GUNS N' ROSES ... If Axl allowed an encore, they would all troop back on and run through a frenzied 'Paradise City', the whole twelve-piece band returning one last time for a bow, arm-in-arm looking for all the world like the cast members surrounding the star of a major theatrical production, right down to the moment when Axl would toss roses into the crowd. It was followed by more fireworks and the red lights now flashing: THANK YOU WE LOVE YOU, THANK YOU WE LOVE YOU ... The very last thing the crowd saw each night was a cartoon of a butcher chopping off his thumb and yelling, 'Son of a bitch!' before chopping off his arm and then his head, which was left twitching in a pool of blood. What the significance of this was supposed to be no one knew but it made Axl laugh.

After each show there was the usual 'themed' party, the only constant being a free bar, several pinball machines, pool tables, hot tubs and strippers, many dancing on the tables as Axl and others took pictures with their Polaroid cameras. The party usually broke up at about 5.00 a.m., splintering into smaller group sessions back at the band's hotel or other places. Roddy Bottum, keyboardist for Faith No More, who played second string on the tour warming the crowd up before Metallica came onstage, later characterized the backstage milieu in an interview with *Spin* as 'excess, excess, excess. There were more strippers than road crew.' Reprimanded for 'laughing about the absurdity of the touring environment in the press' the band tried to explain where they were coming from but the effort seems to have been wasted as they they were then led to a trailer where two naked women strippers were having sex.

On 9 September, Guns N' Roses was booked to perform 'November Rain' live at MTV's annual Video Music Awards, held that year at UCLA's Pauley Pavilion. Elton John agreed to join the band on piano and backing vocals and Axl was desperately excited about it. But the occasion was destined to be remembered for entirely different reasons. Nirvana were booked to open proceedings by performing 'Lithium', but immediately stole the show when they busked a few bars of a completely different song, the as yet unreleased 'Rape Me' (which the MTV organizer's had expressly forbidden them from doing), only segueing into 'Lithium' as MTV vice-president Judy McGrath was about to order the director to cut to a commercial break. It caused a major frisson backstage and set a precedent for confrontational behaviour that Axl found impossible to match with his much more saccharine and overblown duet with Elton. To make matters worse, as Nirvana left the stage Cobain spat on the keys of the piano he believed belonged to Axl but which actually belonged to Elton.

The coup de grâce, however, was delivered by Cobain's wife, Courtney Love, who called out to Axl as he wandered past with Stephanie, surrounded by his usual bodyguards, 'Axl! Axl!' holding up her baby daughter, Frances Bean, 'Will you be the godfather of our child?' Embarrassed, Axl strode over to where she and Cobain were seated and pointed his finger in his face: 'You shut your bitch up,' he ordered, 'or I'm taking you down to the pavement!' The Nirvana entourage burst into laughter. All except for Cobain who pretended to be affronted, glaring at Courtney and telling her, 'Shut up, bitch!' At which point his band and friends all burst into laughter again. In an effort to take the sting out of the situation Stephanie sweetly asked Courtney, 'Are you a model?' but Courtney regarded her coldly. 'No,' she replied. 'Are you a brain surgeon?'

Humiliated, Axl stormed off, trailed by a baleful Stephanie. It didn't end there, though. When Nirvana returned to their trailer after the show, waiting for them was a posse from the GN'R camp. Cobain ran into the trailer to check that Frances was all right, but Nirvana bassist, Krist Novoselic, was immediately surrounded. A lot of pushing and cursing ensued but as a crowd of industry onlookers began to gather the situation was eventually resolved without anyone getting hurt.

Nirvana were the darlings of the music press – early on, the *NME*, then still Britain's most influential music weekly, pronounced Nirvana 'the Guns N' Roses it's okay to like' – and the story of Kurt and Axl's confrontation was gleefully reported around the world, with Axl looking like the sad out of touch rock monster he was fast becoming and Kurt the daring punk upstart who had exposed him. It was one more nail in the coffin of Guns N' Roses' credibility, a process begun with the onset of grunge and only accelerated by the indulgent 'November Rain' video.

With a sense of irony not even Kurt Cobain could have dreamed up, the final show of the Guns N' Roses–Metallica tour on 6 October was at the King Dome in Seattle, the veritable home of grunge's biggest stars, from Pearl Jam and Nirvana to Soundgarden and Alice In Chains. After it was over, *RIP* published one of Axl's most revealing interviews yet, in which he was quoted owning up for the first time to feelings of inadequacy. 'I'm a difficult person to deal with,' he admitted, 'I'm a pain in the ass to understand, and I've had my share of problems.'

The article continued with the revelation that he didn't take drugs any more though, and even the pot-smoking was almost totally eradicated. Instead, he was 'on very specific, high-tuned vitamins'. He was also involved in 'extensive emotional work to reach certain heights with myself that doing hard drugs would interfere with', undertaking several detox programmes at once, in order to 'release trapped toxins that are there because of trauma'. This was one of the reasons why he was so often late onstage, he said. He didn't mean to 'inconvenience the crowd' but he was 'fighting for my own mental health, survival and peace'. The work he was doing was 'so I can do my job'. He had learned that 'when certain traumas happen to you, your brain releases chemicals that get trapped in the muscles where the trauma occurred. They stay there for your whole life. Then, when you're fifty years old, you've got bad legs or a bent back.' That wasn't going to happen to him. 'But as soon as we release one thing and that damage is gone, some new muscle hurts. That's not a new injury; it's a very old injury that, in order to survive, I've buried.' Every day he was on the road he received some form of either 'muscle therapy' or 'kinesiology, acupuncture . . .' He wasn't about 'escaping through drugs and sex any more', he insisted. 'I've reached a point where I can't escape. There *is* no escape . . .'

He was said to have also admitted that he was basically the leader of the band now. Matt Sorum, Gilby Clarke, Dizzy Reed, even Duff were 'all members of this gang' but 'the business is basically run by Slash and myself. Then we run whatever it is we're discussing by Duff and see if he's cool with it. Guns N' Roses is basically Slash, Duff, Doug Goldstein and myself.'

Asked what came next for the band, he was quoted answering prophetically: 'We've pretty much stayed within the parameters of rock'n'roll music as we know it. I'd like to see if we could add anything to GN'R, possibly bring in a new element that hasn't been there before . . . There was a certain focus we all wanted to keep for *Illusion I* and *II*, but when I did "My World" everyone dug it and wanted it on the record. By the next record I think we can branch out a lot further . . . I don't feel now like I did when I wrote "Estranged". I'm not as bummed out as I was then. I've grown past that.'

During November and December, the band completed their first headline tour of South America, beginning with a show to more than 45,000 people in Caracas, on 25 November – reportedly the biggest show ever staged in Venezuela – and concluding at the giant Autodromo stadium in Rio de Janeiro on 13 December.

Needless to say, the tour was marred by incident and controversy, although none of it was Axl's fault. The band and their entourage left Venezuela just hours before the country was thrown into turmoil by an air-based military coup. In the ensuing chaos, only one of the band's cargo planes was able to take off and over half their equipment and several crew members were left stranded. This meant the following two shows, scheduled for the El Campin Stadium in Bogota, on 28 and 29 November, had to be rolled into one as the full shipment of gear wouldn't arrive until the day before the show. Even then a torrential downpour caused the six-tonne stage roof, complete with lighting rig, to crash to the ground the night before. With no time to rebuild the roof, the set was hastily rejigged, with the surviving lights being repositioned to the sides of the stage.

The show was not without incident, either. By 10.00 p.m. the stadium was declared full, leaving hundreds of ticket-holders stranded outside. Fights broke out, several people were injured and nearby cars and property were damaged before police resorted to tear gas to restore order. The band came onstage at 10.30 p.m., but another downpour during 'November Rain' left their equipment submerged beneath half-an-inch of water, forcing them to leave the stage for half an hour while roadies battled to dry and make their equipment safe.

On 2 December, after a sold-out show at the Chilean National Football Stadium in Santiago, local newspapers reported that Axl was drunk prior to the show and that drugs were discovered in the band's hotel rooms. Doug Goldstein had to give a press conference at which he stressed that Axl never drank alcohol before a show and had, in fact, spent the day working out and doing vocal exercises. He did admit that the Chilean Department of Investigation visited the hotel, but denied they found anything.

Following their first ever shows in Argentina, another torrential downpour forced the second of two shows at Anhembi in Sao Paulo, Brazil, to be postponed for twenty-four hours, which Axl apologized for in a press statement reading: 'We hope that everyone who was planning to come to the show tonight can make it tomorrow. As we proved, both here and in Bogota recently . . . none of us are afraid to get wet!'

In the midst of this, December also saw the release of a video of the band's concerts in Tokyo earlier that year, entitled *Use Your Illusion World Tour 1992 in Tokyo*. With combined world-wide sales for both *Use Your Illusion* albums now touching the twenty-million mark, the video collection was another instant hit, topping its respective charts in the US, Britain and more than a dozen countries around the globe. Grunge may have stolen a great deal of the band's critical thunder, but GN'R's popularity continued unabated. With the world tour, now more than eight-een months old, set to continue throughout 1993, the New Year could surely only bring more of the same.

Axl returned to LA with the band on 14 December, looking forward to a four-week break before the tour resumed in January. While he was on the road he went ahead with a long-cherished plan and bought the dream home he had talked about as far back as his days with Erin. Now he made it a reality with Stephanie instead: a four-acre, Mediterranean-style compound in Malibu with a swimming pool and floodlit tennis court. Situated on top of a steep hill a couple of thousand feet above sea level, with a lighted star on the side of the house that could be seen for miles, it would be symbolic, he said, of this treasured relationship.

And why not? The Axl who returned home from Brazil in December 1992 was a millionaire many times over. With the exception of Kurt Cobain, he was also the most famous and highly regarded rock star of his generation. So many of his dreams had come true, and this was the final piece that completed the jigsaw of his emotional, financial and professional life. With Stephanie and Dylan already there to meet him, along with their nanny and housekeeper, Beta, Axl felt like he finally had a loving environment to come home to. Life must have been good at last for the damaged, angry small-town white boy who no one understood.

However, just when he was beginning to feel his luck, things once again began to unravel. The crunch came when he and Stephanie had a major falling-out in front of friends at a Christmas party she arranged for them at the Malibu house.

Rolling Stone reported that according to her sworn declaration in the legal action she later took against him, the trouble began after 'a verbal argument' Stephanie had with Axl, after which he 'announced that there would be no Christmas party'.

She went on: 'Guests began to arrive in the late afternoon [and] at some point in the middle of the party, [Axl] entered the house, slammed the door, was obviously very angry, went upstairs and then came downstairs and left the house again.' Her mother followed him upstairs to try and reason with him but he 'began yelling and screaming at her and ultimately told her in no uncertain terms that she was not welcome in his house. Thereafter, most of the people at the party left.'

The real trouble began once they were alone, she said. 'When I attempted to talk to [him] to address the issues that had upset him, [Axl] started yelling and swearing . . . He then lifted up the kitchen table, knocking off bottles and glasses. I reached for [him] in an attempt to calm him. However, he would not be consoled and he was clearly out of control.'

At which point Stephanie said Axl threw some wine bottles on the kitchen floor, smashing them, then grabbed her by the throat and dragged her barefoot through the broken glass 'while repeatedly hitting [me] about the head and upper body and kicking [me] in the abdomen.' Axl later retorted by claiming Seymour had grabbed his balls and that he was merely defending himself.

Whatever the truth (Axl does not agree with Stephanie's version of events) it was the beginning of the end. Within months, the love affair was over.

Chapter Nine

AFTER THE WAR

The final six months of the two-and-a-half-year world tour that Guns N' Roses began in 1991 was in many ways the easiest. Having returned to Japan, where their eighty-strong entourage arrived on the morning of 11 January 1993 in anticipation the next day of the first of three shows at the futuristic Tokyo Dome, even Axl understood not to delay the band's set. In Japan, concerts – as with so many things – are strictly controlled events that begin and end on time. Unlike in the West, where a certain amount of tardiness is almost expected of the liberal cultural elite's best-known names, in Japan such behaviour is barely understood let alone tolerated. As a result, the final leg of the world tour got off to an unusually organized start, the band arriving for their soundcheck at 2.00 p.m. sharp on the day of the show, with Axl ready to go onstage promptly at 6.40 p.m.

Kicking off with 'Welcome To The Jungle', the band turned in a tight eighteen-song set which they politely concluded with Axl jumping into the crowd to hand out individually wrapped red roses. Despite the heavy-duty emotional traumas back home with Stephanie, he was still looking ahead to a future with her. This final leg of the tour was 'pure gravy', with the band slimmed down to its more natural six-man line-up, enabling them to pick up one huge payday after another as they trotted round the parts of the world that hadn't had enough of them.

Behind the scenes, however, certain things would never change. Axl had his full support team with him, with special areas backstage for Sharon Maynard and her entourage of assistants.

The rest of the band's time in Japan followed a conventional pattern, beginning with a big party after the first show at a nightclub in the Reppongi district called the Lexington Queen, a familiar after-hours drop-in for bands passing through, frequented by Western models currently on assignment in Tokyo. By the second show on 14 January, even Axl was starting to feel more at home, delaying the show for an hour and dedicating the song 'Yesterdays' to his half-brother Stuart. Afterwards he and the band joined Rolling Stone Ronnie Wood, also playing in town that night, at his after-show party at the Lexington Queen. The following night, Axl introduced 'Live And Let Die' as 'Live And Let Stir-fry'. Wood, still hanging out with Slash from the night before, then joined them onstage for a lengthy knockabout version of set-closer 'Knockin' On Heaven's Door'.

Two weeks later they were in Australia where their show in Melbourne at the vast Calder Park Raceway stadium on 1 February broke national attendance records. Three days later they were in New Zealand, where Axl and Duff held a joint birthday celebration in a luxurious restaurant overlooking Auckland harbour. On 6 February, the day of Axl's 31st birthday, they played at Auckland's Mount Smart Stadium. At the climax of 'November Rain' a dozen or so members of the road crew marched onstage to present their leader with a massive birthday cake, at which point Slash and Duff led the crowd in a rendition of 'Happy Birthday' while Axl did his 'Aw, shucks' best to look surprised. A fortnight later they were all back in the US ready to begin the 'Skin And Bones' leg of the tour, as they were now calling it, with a sold-out show at the Frank Erwin Center in Austin, Texas. Shorn of the extraneous horn section and backing singers, the middle of the set now included an acoustic section comprised almost entirely of side two of the GN'R Lies album – minus 'One In A Million', which not even Axl would at this stage perform live.

Of course, the tour still had its unexpected delays and hastily rearranged dates. Four shows were cancelled at the start of the tour due to 'adverse weather conditions', while on 3 April, a show in Sacramento was curtailed after ninety minutes when Duff was hit in the head with what Slash told the crowd was 'a bottle of piss', but which MTV News later reported was a plastic water bottle. Whatever it was, it knocked Duff clean out and he had to be rushed to a nearby hospital. Although it was Axl who announced the show would have to be stopped, Slash came out and faced the audience once it became clear Duff would have to go to hospital. Explaining the situation, he asked that everyone leave peacefully, adding: 'Don't fuck with anyone, don't fuck with the building.' For once, nobody did.

Another show was cancelled in April – this time at the Omni in Atlanta, Georgia – when Axl realized it was the same venue he'd been arrested at after his scuffle with a security guard on the Mötley Crüe tour in 1987. With Axl still technically on parole after the court case regarding the riot in St Louis two years before, he ordered Doug Goldstein to pull the show. 'I'm not willing to be a sitting duck for the police,' Axl was later quoted as saying. He was already too 'familiar with that experience'.

The most dramatic tour incident this time round concerned Izzy's replacement Gilby Clarke, who broke his left wrist in a motorcycling accident on 29 April while practising for a celebrity race in honour of the T.J. Martell Foundation for leukaemia, cancer and AIDS research. It resulted in the final four shows of the US itinerary being cancelled. Gilby's absence also threatened to scupper the band's planned return to Europe that summer for festival shows. But Axl came up with an unusual last-minute solution. He called Izzy and asked him if he'd do the shows – on a strictly temporary basis, of course. Even more unexpectedly, Izzy agreed.

'Izzy and I grew up together and we're like a family in lots of ways – including having our differences,' Axl explained. When I later reminded him of that quote, Izzy smiled and shook his head. 'Well, what else could he say? They were kind of in a spot and if I hadn't agreed to help out they might have missed out on that whole leg of the tour.'

Opening on 22 May at a specially constructed site in Hayarkon Park, Tel Aviv, more than 40,000 fans turned up for what was officially the biggest music concert ever held in Israel. In the middle of the set, the band broke into a surprisingly full-blooded rendition of 'Hava Nagila' which went down a storm, as did comments in the press the next day about the 'Guns N' Moses' T-shirt Axl wore onstage.

From there the tour alighted on 24 May – its second anniversary – at the Olympic Stadium in Athens, where supermodel Claudia Schiffer joined them afterwards for a party at the Mercedes Club. Then on 26 May they performed in Istanbul, where Axl stopped the show after just three songs to berate the audience for throwing lit fireworks at each other. 'Someone will get hurt and the band will be forced to leave the stadium,' he told them. Remarkably, the crowd stopped and the show continued.

On 29 May, the band performed their first gig in the UK for a year when they headlined the first of two shows to 50,000 people at the National Bowl in Milton Keynes. At the end of it, after the final encore of 'Paradise City', Axl threw two dozen red roses into the crowd. For the British fans, Milton Keynes was also a welcome return for one of the original members. For Izzy who'd agreed to come back temporarily, 'it was weird. We toured Israel, Greece, Istanbul, London – I liked that side of it, seeing some places I'd never seen.' But that was the only thing he liked about it. 'Money was a big sore point. I did the dates just for salary. I mean, I helped start this band . . .'

The second show the following day saw the arrival backstage of Gilby and his wife, who flew in especially for the occasion. With Gilby's wrist injury now healed, this was also Izzy's last show with the band. For the encores they were joined by Ronnie Wood and former Hanoi Rocks vocalist and Axl acolyte Mike Monroe. Afterwards, Izzy says he left without even saying goodbye. 'I didn't actually say "see you" 'cos they were all fucked up.'

With Izzy gone and Gilby back in the fold, the tour returned to the Continent with sold-out stadium shows in Austria, the Netherlands, Denmark, Norway, Sweden, Switzerland, Germany, Italy, Spain, France and Belgium. On 21 June, halfway through their five-date German tour, the band released a brace of new video collections: the self-explanatory *Don't Cry – Makin' Fucking Videos Part I* and *November Rain – Makin' Fucking Videos Part II*.

After one last show in Paris, on 13 July, the band flew straight to Argentina, where the final show of the world tour was

scheduled to take place at the 70,000-capacity River Plate Stadium, in Buenos Aires, on 17 July. Though they couldn't have
known, it would also be the last performance by what was left of
the original band. As if to end the tour in the style to which
everyone had become unhealthily accustomed, the night before
the show more than fifty police officers from the city's narcotics
division forced their way into Axl's top-floor penthouse suite,
where he was eating dinner. Having made a thorough search for
drugs they retreated without apology, having found nothing.
'They'd have had better luck trying one of the others' rooms,'
quipped a crew member. 'By then, Axl was about the only one
not doing drugs on a permanent basis.'

Broadcast live on TV in Argentina and Uruguay, for once the
next night kicked off promptly at 9.30 p.m. Starting the twenty-
one-song set with 'Nightrain' and ending with 'Paradise City', by
midnight the band were already back at the hotel, where Axl,
Slash and others remained in the bar until six o'clock the following morning, with Axl at the grand piano for part of it, treating
the assembled throng to one last tune.

Forty-eight hours later, they were back where they'd started,
in LA. It had been the longest tour in rock history: 192 dates in
twenty-seven countries, with ticket sales in excess of seven million, grossing almost $58 million – an almost unheard-of amount
of money for one tour. Not even the Rolling Stones could make
that kind of gross on ticket-sales alone until many years into their
hit-making career. Even the Grateful Dead, who had been touring
successfully for decades, couldn't expect to earn more than $40
million from touring in the early 1990s.

Meanwhile, both *Use Your Illusion* albums were now seven
times platinum in the US alone, with combined worldwide sales
for both *Illusion* albums, plus *Appetite* and *GN'R Lies* now
teetering in excess of seventy million. Indeed, *Appetite* would
eventually sell more than half that amount on its own. To offer
some perspective, that's a million more albums than Bob Dylan
had sold in his entire career up to that point. Even Led Zeppelin
took four albums to reach that sort of plateau. For Guns N'
Roses it had all happened immediately. Little wonder they had
such trouble hanging on to themselves.

Slash now identifies the summer tour of 1992 as the point of no return in Axl's relations with the rest of the band. 'At some point during the Metallica shows, I just lost Axl,' he says. 'I just didn't know where he was at any more. I didn't know where I was at any more! Steven was already gone, and then losing Izzy . . . And it was all nothing we had control of. Everything was kind of . . . out of hand. Then all of a sudden, we got off the road after two-and-a-half years of touring, and everything just kind of . . . stopped. Dead.'

Not quite. Axl, for one, still had a great deal of business to attend to, beginning on 23 August with a date at the Los Angeles Superior Court where he testified against Steven Adler in the drummer's ongoing legal action against the band, repeating his claim that the band were left with no option but to drop the drummer when it became apparent during the recording of 'Civil War' that Steven was unable to perform his duties adequately because of his heroin addiction – insisting that he needed more than sixty takes to get his part right.

Another telling detail that emerged from the court case concerned the way that the original five-man band had agreed to divvy up their earnings in the days before they became so spectacularly successful. After deducting a 17.5 per cent management commission, Axl described how he and Slash had come up with a specific formula for doling out the rest of the money. During pre-production for *Appetite*, he said, 'Slash devised a system of figuring out who wrote what parts of [a] song or part of a song. There were four categories, I believe. There was lyrics, melody, music – meaning guitars, bass and drums – and accompaniment and arrangement. And we split each one of those into twenty-five per cent.' He concluded: 'When we had finished, I had 41 per cent [of overall takings], and other people had different amounts.'

The case came to an abrupt end just six weeks into its hearings when, on 24 September, an out-of-court settlement was reached. It was reported in the press at the time that the band agreed to pay $2.3 million to Adler, who would also receive $200,000 from the band's past and present managers. Steven now says, 'It wasn't [a] pay-off. It was what they owed me. And I got all my royalties back.'

Despite the money, it's still a cause of great regret for him that the original band came to such a messy end. 'I know myself, I know Slash too 'cos we always talked about [how] we could've been like Aerosmith, like the Stones. Dude, they've been together thirty, forty fucking years.' He added that 'the most touching thing' had been how 'at the end of the trial, all the jurors hugged me and said, "Good luck and take care."'

Still resenting to this day the royalty the drummer receives, now referring to the agreement he made with him as 'one of the biggest mistakes I've made in my life,' Axl's view is that, 'In the long run I paid very extensively for having Steven Adler in Guns N' Roses.' One might add that Adler also 'paid extensively' for being in the band in view of his ignominious departure. Within months of his financial settlement he would overdose so badly it induced a stroke, leaving him partially paralyzed. Apart from his own occasional outfit, Adler's Appetite, with whom he performs intermittently these days, he hasn't worked seriously in the music business since being dumped in 1990.

For the rest of Guns N' Roses it was business as usual, with Slash in particular working on a new set of songs. There was also the imminent release of a new album, titled *The Spaghetti Incident?*, which was set to hit the stores in November. It was an incongruous, poorly received collection of ostensibly punk covers intended to establish the band's roots beyond their obvious heavy metal connections, but it had the opposite effect of making them appear even more out of step with the times than the onset of grunge, which was now reaching its zenith with the recent release of the new brutally uncompromising Nirvana album, *In Utero*.

By comparison, *The Spaghetti Incident?* was a confused, unsatisfying collection, from its obscure title to its woefully literal album sleeve – a close-up of a plate of canned spaghetti. As *Rolling Stone* pointed out in its review, 'Punk rock is sometimes best read as a vigorous howl of complaint against one's own powerlessness, but Axl doesn't quite connect to the punk rock material on *Spaghetti* as anything but a conduit for pure aggression. He can't even seem to curse right.'

Mismatching covers of obvious punk bands like the Damned ('New Rose') and the Dead Boys ('Ain't It Fun') and others from groups that had nothing to do with punk, like Nazareth ('Hair Of The Dog') and, most off-kilter, the Skyliners (whose 1958 hit 'Since I Don't Have You' became the next GN'R single), where it didn't miss the target completely, the album simply tried way too hard. Most notably when Axl adopts a cringe-making Dick Van Dyke Cockney accent for a version of the UK Subs' demented bonehead classic 'Down On The Farm', but most disastrously with the final track on the original collection, a version of 'Look At Your Game, Girl', originally written by the psychotic Charles Manson.

Accompanied by his gardener, Carlos Booy, on acoustic guitar, 'Look At Your Game, Girl' was a song Axl recorded on his own late at night. Slipping it onto the end of the album as a 'hidden' additional track not included on the listing printed on the sleeve, it may have been his personal message to Stephanie Seymour, who he had officially broken up with while putting the finishing touches to the mix in September 1993.

Axl often appeared onstage – and in the 'Estranged' video – in a Charles Manson T-shirt, but recording one of the convicted murderer's songs caused even more outrage than the release of 'One In A Million' five years before. Despite the group's hastily made pledge to donate any royalties to the son of one of Manson's victims, the track provoked calls for a boycott of all Geffen products. Of course, Axl was hardly the first rock star to become childishly enthralled by the cult of Charlie Manson. In Britain, self-styled 'art terrorists' Psychic TV sported Manson T-shirts long before Axl had left Lafayette, going so far as to spatter their dressing-rooms with the same gormless slogans left in blood on the walls of murder victim Sharon Tate's home. While in the US, self-anointed grunge godfathers Sonic Youth previously recorded another Manson song, 'Death Valley '69' (featuring punk poetess Lydia Lunch). When the Lemonheads later recorded Manson's 'Home Is Where You're Happy', singer Evan Dando claimed that 'Charlie was just a good symbol of the beginning of my life in America, of how messed up things were getting.'

Recording a Manson song was nothing compared to the lengths Nine Inch Nails would later go to in 'acquainting' themselves with the Manson 'vibe', when frontman Trent Reznor actually moved into 10050 Cielo Drive – the address of the most infamous Manson Family killings – with a mobile studio and recorded his multi-platinum 1994 album *The Downward Spiral* there.

In Axl's case, he initially defended his choice of song by saying: 'The song talks about how the girl is insane and playing a mind game. I felt it was ironic that such a song was recorded by someone who should know the inner intricacies of madness.' It was a decision he would come to regret. Speaking to *Rolling Stone* six years later, he announced he had recently decided to remove both 'One In A Million' and 'Look At Your Game, Girl' from all future copies of their respective albums. Not that he was apologetic, just that he felt they were 'too easily misinterpreted'.

What Stephanie thought of the song, if anything, has never been revealed. But the likelihood is she no longer cared either way. The fight the previous Christmas was the last straw for her, and even though the relationship continued at a distance while the band was on the road throughout the early months of 1993, by the time Axl returned to LA Stephanie had resumed her modelling career and begun dating millionaire businessman and publisher of *Interview* magazine, Peter Brant.

After their split Axl filed a suit against Stephanie, claiming that during their Christmas party she had kicked and grabbed him, and later refused to return jewellery he had given her worth over £100,000. Stephanie, however, had her own ideas about how to deal with Axl, and by 1994 she had countersued, launching a legal action against him claiming compensation for the domestic violence she alleged she had been a victim of. Axl was horrified at this latest turn of events. To add to the pressure he was now under, when Erin Everly found herself subpoenaed to give evidence in Stephanie's lawsuit, she decided to file one of her own, accusing her former husband of assault and sexual battery.

Suddenly it was all starting to get very messy for the singer. It was one thing to be humiliated by a former band mate, as he felt he had been by Steven and, to a lesser extent, Izzy. But to have the grimmest details of his personal life discussed openly in court was too much for him.

This kind of exposure was way beyond anything Axl had bargained for, and even though he denied the allegations he immediately instructed his lawyers to settle the case out of court, which they did: an action which saw the former Mrs Rose walking away with an undisclosed sum, reported to be more than a million dollars by *Rolling Stone*. Axl also ordered his minions to hurriedly gather up the few existing copies of a tape containing the unreleased version of the 'It's So Easy' video from five years before, which featured Erin tied up in bondage gear, with a red ball pushed into her mouth as Axl screams at her: 'See me hit you! You fall down!'

Stephanie's case dragged on considerably longer. Although Axl denied the allegations he was unwilling to let Stephanie publicly sift through the sorry details of their relationship and he eventually settled before the case could come to court. Stephanie's lawyer, Michael Plonsker, would neither confirm nor deny the sum involved, except to say that the suit was eventually resolved 'amicably'.

Neither Erin nor Stephanie pressed for criminal charges. But the damage was done, and the story of their joint actions against Axl hit the front page of *People* magazine in 1994. Coming only a month after the magazine had led with the story of O.J. Simpson's arrest and charge for the alleged murder of his estranged wife Nicole Simpson, most people took a decidedly dim view of this new story of alleged domestic abuse. Ironically, Erin herself still seemed to retain some sympathy for her beleaguered former husband, admitting: 'I felt sorry for him' and 'I thought I could make it all better.' Clearly, though, she couldn't. As for Stephanie, she married her new lover Peter Brant in Paris just a few months later. Adding salt to the wound, Stephanie gave birth to the first of two sons by Brant shortly after, and they remain happily married.

It was the beginning of Axl's withdrawal from the world. According to Stephanie's nanny, Beta Lebeis, who went to work for Axl after the couple split, he had 'adored her'. 'When the band was over, he thought he could have a family,' Beta said in an interview in *O Globo* newspaper, 'he would be married and would have children. This would be the second part of his life. He would have enough money and would dedicate his time to his family. He dreamed of a family, children, everything he never had.'

Losing Stephanie destroyed that dream. 'Axl is a person who wants to do everything right,' observed Beta. He was 'that kind of passionate man a lot of women would like to have in their lives. He was like a charmed prince. He did, for Stephanie, all kind of things you could find in a romantic book. When they were almost breaking up, he went to her house, riding a horse and carrying flowers. The things he did for her could only be read in books of ancient history. What he did doesn't exist in real life any more! I think a lot of women would have loved to be in her place. I would never leave a man like that. But Stephanie is very pretty and sexy; she can have any man she wants.'

Beta added: 'I always told her she could hurt Axl more than she thought. Other men who fell in love with her would never suffer like Axl did. He wanted to do everything right, and he really thought everything was going right. He took this relationship very seriously.'

Certainly the messy end of his relationship with Stephanie Seymour appeared to bring a significant chapter of Axl's life to an abrupt close. On 20 January 1994, he was one of the guests at Elton John's induction into the Rock 'N' Roll Hall Of Fame in New York. Later that night, he sang 'Come Together' with Bruce Springsteen. It was the last time he would perform in public for six years.

Meanwhile, with sales of *The Spaghetti Incident?* tailing off dramatically – another platinum-selling chart hit in the US, it was nevertheless considered a flop compared to the gigantic sales enjoyed by its predecessors – Slash spent the early months of 1994 writing (in anticipation of 'the real next album'), while drawing from a Geffen advance thought to be around $10 million – superstar money.

However, when he presented his new song ideas to Axl, the

singer was decidedly unimpressed. With Axl now in sole charge of the Guns N' Roses name, there wasn't much Slash or any of the others could do to force the issue, so Slash took the songs back and began working on what eventually became, in all but name, his first solo album, *It's Five O'Clock Somewhere*, credited to Slash's band Snakepit – featuring Matt Sorum and Gilby Clarke, along with vocalist Eric Dover (formerly of Jellyfish) and Alice In Chains bassist Mike Inez – which was eventually released in February 1995.

Exactly three years before, Slash had told *Rolling Stone*, 'We really would all feel sorta lost and lonely if it fell apart and we had to go out and do solo records, because it wouldn't be Guns. None of us could reproduce that. Axl's got so much charisma – he's one of the best singers around. It's his personality. He can go out and do something. What freaks me out is if the band falls apart, I'll never be able to shake the fact that I'm the ex-Guns N' Roses guitar player. And that's almost like selling your soul.'

Now, though, both he and Duff – whose solo album, *Believe In Me*, featuring cameos from Slash, Gilby, Matt, Dizzy and Sebastian Bach, was released in October 1993 – found themselves doing just that. The whole band was suddenly beginning to fragment into side-projects. Even Gilby was working on a solo album. As it happened, he was the next to leave when he was fired without explanation in March 1994. When his regular stipend failed to appear in his bank account, he 'pretty much took that as a hint', Gilby says. When the payments abruptly resumed, however, he assumed he had been rehired. When they then stopped again – then started and stopped for a third time, all within a period of weeks – he consulted his lawyer, Jeffrey Light.

'As you are aware, Gilby has been fired at least three times by the band in the past month and has been re-hired at least two times,' Light wrote on 14 April in a letter to the band's then lawyer, Laurie Soriano, and reported in *Rolling Stone*. By June, when Gilby's solo album, *Pawnshop Guitars*, was released, his position was made crystal clear: he was officially off the GN'R payroll, despite the fact that Axl – along with Slash and Duff – made a guest appearance on Gilby's album. When royalties for

The Spaghetti Incident? album then failed to arrive on time, Gilby instructed Light to sue the band. Once again, Guns N' Roses initially fought the action before eventually agreeing to settle out of court with an undisclosed payment to the guitarist.

Watching these developments from a distance, Slash already feared the worst. 'When I first got home, I just put together this funky little studio and just had a good time, you know? Had some fun. I didn't have a thing in my mind about quitting the band, it was just the band wasn't really functioning. Matt was still there, but Gilby had been fired, and Axl was ... off somewhere.'

Where Axl was really at – when he wasn't consulting lawyers over the latest legal action – was a question he had lately become obsessed with. Stung by grunge's wholesale rejection of the precepts he held most dear – laughed at by some for his 'conceptual' videos, ridiculed by others for releasing two double-albums simultaneously, attacked for the elements of homophobia, racism and sexism that polluted his lyrics, however artfully ascribed – he was smart enough to realize how out of step Guns N' Roses suddenly seemed to great swathes of the media.

Presumably concerned more than ever with the damage done to his image by the lawsuits Erin and Stephanie successfully brought against him, not to mention his very public fallings-out with Steven, Izzy, Gilby and his former manager Alan Niven, for the first time since he'd arrived in LA from Lafayette, Axl found himself with things not going the way he was pushing. As well as firing Gilby, he also ordered a halt to the publication of the band biography Del James had been working on, *Shattered Illusion*, which was to have been published by Bantam/Doubleday in June 1995. He withdrew into the same close circle of friends and paid assistants that had supported him on tour – Del, his half-siblings, Stuart and Amy, housekeeper Beta, bodyguard Earl, and the usual chorus of supportive voices, not least Suzzy London and Sharon Maynard – brooding out at his Malibu mansion as he plotted his next move. 'Axl's anger had quadrupled from the person I used to hang out with,' recalls Michelle Young, who bumped into him around this time.

According to Slash, it was around this time that Axl first

considered making his own solo album. Newly obsessed with the electronica of Nine Inch Nails – he told friends he'd love to hear Nine Inch Nails cover 'Estranged' – he planned to write and record with a 'dream team' comprising NIN frontman Trent Reznor, Jane's Addiction guitarist Dave Navarro and Nirvana drummer Dave Grohl. 'Then he changed his mind,' says Slash, 'and thought, why do a solo record if he could do it with Guns N' Roses . . .'

Meanwhile, Axl's obsession with electronic music continued to grow. Metallica drummer Lars Ulrich recalls him eulogizing about Nine Inch Nails long before anyone else. 'He was saying, "This is the coolest thing I've ever heard." And we were all sitting there going, "What the fuck are you talking about?" He had Nine Inch Nails support Guns N' Roses in Europe, and I remember hearing how they got booed off the stage. But he was there when the rest of us were still listening to fucking Judas Priest.'

Slash, who didn't share Axl's new musical preoccupations, filled in the time 'doing, like, a hundred solo gigs, just clubs and shit [with the Snakepit band]. Stuff I never made a dime off of. When I came back, I thought, "I don't really like my day job any more." I was frustrated, 'cos nothing was happening. But I hung in there for a little while, then finally got disillusioned with the whole thing. And that's when I started thinking about doing my own thing again.'

He wasn't the only one. When Axl invited Slash to join him and the rest of the band at LA's Complex studios in August 1994 for the recording of the Rolling Stones' 'Sympathy For The Devil' intended for the soundtrack to the forthcoming Tom Cruise and Brad Pitt movie, *Interview With The Vampire*, Slash was astonished to find that Axl had once again taken things into his own hands, this time hiring a replacement for Gilby – Paul Huge, his old friend from Lafayette.

Put out that neither of them had been consulted about Huge's sudden appointment, neither Slash nor Duff got on with the new guitarist. As one mutual friend later recalled, Huge was a 'nice-enough guy', but, 'they're Guns N' Roses, for God's sake.' Huge simply didn't have 'the chops'. Or as Sash later put it, 'As far as his relationship with [Axl], they're Indiana kids, I can understand he feels comfortable, but I refuse to ever play with [Paul] again.'

Though not even Axl realized it yet, the antipathy towards Huge would become the thread which eventually unravelled the whole band, with Slash putting Axl in the position where he more or less had to choose between his original, and arguably most important musical partner, or his old school pal. Feeling cornered, Axl did what he always did in these situations and simply dug his heels in. He chose his old school pal. Speaking about it almost eight years later, after Huge had also left the band, Axl's recollections of why he brought the guitarist in differed from those of the band-mates the decision alienated. 'At the time,' he was quoted as saying on the official GN'R website, 'Paul was one of the best people we knew who was both available and capable of complementing Slash's style. You could bring in a better guitar player than Paul. You could bring in a monster. I tried putting [Ozzy Osbourne guitarist] Zakk Wylde with Slash and that didn't work . . . Paul was only interested in complementing Slash, laying down a foundation of a riff or something that would accent or encourage Slash's lead playing.'

Slash now claims, however, that he decided to leave the day after discovering Huge in the studio, saying he couldn't even sleep that night he was so distraught. 'I was suicidal. If I'd had a gun with me at that time, I probably would have done myself in. If I'd had a half-ounce of fucking heroin with me, I probably just would've gone. It was heavy. It was a headspace I'd never been in before. Somehow I managed to go back to sleep. Then, when I woke up later that morning, I made a decision.' At which point, 'I felt the whole weight of the world drop.'

It wasn't just Huge, he says now; it was the general malaise Axl had plunged the band into by insisting they pursue a more contemporary, post-grunge, more electronica-centric direction. By then, Axl had ordered a massive soundstage to be constructed at the Complex, along with a pool table, pinball machines and a huge barrage of new equipment. Other than the presence of Huge at these sessions, the main problem, Slash says, was that Axl was openly acting as self-appointed leader. 'It seemed like a dictatorship. We didn't spend a lot of time collaborating. He'd sit back in the chair, watching. There'd be a riff here, a riff there. But I didn't know where it was going.'

After several months, Slash decided he'd had enough. 'There's a certain personal side to it too,' he told me. 'I can't *relate* to Axl. Maybe I never could. I mean, Axl came with Izzy, I came with Steven, and then we all hooked up with Duff.' With Axl now in sole charge, 'I realized I was out alone, and that meant me and Axl had to come to terms with . . . not our animosity, but having a different opinion about everything. And, I mean, you know, Axl works as hard as anybody else but only on what *he* wants to work on, and I . . . I just lost interest.'

Ultimately, though, 'It all comes down to this: if I hadn't quit, I would have died, hanging round with nothing to do, no mutual artistic relationship, nothing. I mean, I tried to hang on in there, but it was like a big revolving door, from really hi-tech equipment, guitar players, all kinds of shit going on . . . I was just waiting for the dust to clear. Eventually, I thought, we'll *never* be able to put this on the right path.'

When Slash did an online interview in October 1996, where he admitted that 'right now, Axl and I are deliberating over the future of our relationship', Axl decided to go public with his side of the story, sending a fax to MTV on 30 October in which he discussed his unhappiness with Slash. He could no longer work with him, he wrote, because the guitarist had lost his 'dive in and find the monkey' attitude.

'Axl had a vision that GN'R should change and Slash had an attitude that Guns N' Roses was Guns N' Fucking Roses and that's who they were,' Tom Zutaut recalls. 'I don't think they could get over their breakdown in communication. It wasn't announced publicly [initially] because nobody wanted to say the band had broken up.'

To Axl, Slash's decision had less to do with loyalty to one side or the other and far more to do with his own stubbornness. Already arguing over the musical direction the next album should take and then rejecting Huge as a replacement for Gilby, Slash had questioned not only Axl's choice but his authority. As so many had discovered before, putting Axl in a position where he was being asked to retreat from a unilateral decision was only likely to result in one possible outcome.

Speaking about the split to the official GN'R website in 2002, Axl was even more forthright on the subject. 'Originally I intended to do more of an *Appetite* style recording,' he explained. 'So I opted for what I thought would or should've made the band and especially Slash very happy. [But] it seemed to me that any time we got close to something that would work, it wasn't out of opinion that Slash would go "Hey, it doesn't work," but it was nixed simply because it did work. In other words, "Whoa, wait a minute. That actually might be successful, we can't do that."'

It was a strange claim to make since success was never something Slash had knowingly shrunk from before. But as Axl added: 'People like to call me paranoid. It has nothing to do with paranoia; it was to do with reality . . . Slash chose not to be here over control issues. Now people can say "Well, Axl, you're after control of the band too." You're damn skippy. That's right. I am the one held responsible since day one. When it comes to Guns N' Roses, I may not always get everything right but I do have a good idea about getting things from point A to point B and knowing what the job is that we have to do.'

The ramifications of Slash's departure would be devastating. As Duff says now, everything started to seriously fall apart after 'Slash turned his back and said, "This is shit." He and Axl didn't talk to each other any more. It had become quite irrational.' In retrospect, Duff says, it was only a matter of time before he followed Slash out the door. The two had always been close, and when Duff broke up with his first wife Mandy over the Christmas holidays in 1989, it was Slash who came to his rescue, allowing him to stay at his house, changing his own holiday plans to be with Duff. As time went on, though, Duff increasingly felt like the arbitrator in Slash's disputes with Axl, 'the one both came to see, and I got the impression I arbitrated little kids' quarrels'. When Slash left, at first Duff reconciled himself to life in the band without his old friend. A year later, when Axl decided Matt Sorum would be the next to go, Duff knew it was the end for him too.

According to Matt, he walked out after a massive argument

with Axl – about Slash. They were talking in the studio when Paul Huge remarked he'd seen Slash play with his band, Snakepit, on the David Letterman show the previous night and that it 'sounded like shit and looked like shit'. Matt says now: 'He was just bagging on Slash. I said, "Listen motherfucker, when I'm sitting in the room, I'd appreciate it if you don't fucking say shit about Slash. He's still my friend. You can't even hold a fucking candle to that fucking guy. He's got more talent in his little toe than you, motherfucker, shut up!" And then Axl got in my face. I said, "You know what, Axl, man? You're fucking smoking crack if you think this band's GN'R without Slash. You're gonna go play 'Sweet Child O' Mine' with fucking Paul Huge? Sorry, dude, it ain't gonna sound right. Fucking 'Welcome To The Jungle' without Slash?" [Axl] says, "I'm Guns N' Roses – I don't need Slash." I said, "You know what? No, you aren't." We got into a big pissy match; it went on to a bunch of other bullshit for about another twenty minutes. And then he finally said, "Well, are you gonna fucking quit?" I said, "No, I don't fucking quit." And then he said, "Well, then you're fucking fired."'

'Paul Huge chased me out to the parking lot and said, "What the fuck, man? Just come back in and apologize!" I said, "Fuck you, Yoko! I'm gone!" And that was it. I went home to my fucking six-level palatial rock star estate with two elevators and my Porsche. I was producing a band called Candlebox at the time, they were living in my house. And I said, "I just got fired." They said, "Ah, fuck he'll call you back," and I said, "No, not this time." 'Cos he'd fired me before but he always called me back. I said, "No, I don't think so." And about a month later I got the letter from the lawyers.'

'Matt was never a full member of the band,' Duff said, 'he was on an ejector seat and Axl said "I'm gonna fire him." I answered that this decision required more than one person since we were a band, that he alone didn't own the majority. All of this because Matt told him he was wrong. The truth is Matt was right and Axl wrong indeed.' But Axl wasn't listening, and hadn't been for a very long time. 'I thought, I never played for money and I'm not gonna start now,' Duff says. 'I've got a house, I'm secure financially.' This 'was the worst moment of my career in

Guns. I went out for dinner with Axl and I told him, "Enough is enough. This band is a dictatorship and I don't see myself playing in those conditions. Find someone else."'

It was now, in 1997, that Guns N' Roses began to evolve into the band that lines up under that name today. With keyboardist and long-time Axl acolyte Dizzy Reed the only survivor of the *Use Your Illusion* sextet and Paul Huge still stubbornly in the frame, the rest of the band was augmented by former Nine Inch Nails guitarist Robin Finck – originally recommended by Matt, advising Axl that he would make a great foil for Slash, who could then be coaxed back, to which Axl retorted: 'No, he would be a great *replacement* for Slash' – bassist Tommy Stinson (whose albums *Tim* and *Pleased To Meet Me* with his former band, the Replacements, inspired a generation of alternative-rock acts) and former Vandals drummer Josh Freese (a native Floridian brought up in LA, also known as 'the Bruce Lee of drums').

It was also around this time that the first really serious work on new material began. Yet Axl still couldn't settle on a working method that yielded the kind of esoteric musical results he was seeking. Having initially tried working with Mike Clink in his usual producer's chair, Axl moved on to techno star Moby, former Killing Joke bassist Youth and, by April 1998, former Marilyn Manson and Nine Inch Nails producer Sean Beavan. But nobody lasted long.

Youth (real name Martin Glover) says he felt that Axl's malaise was 'partly perfectionism. The psychology is that if you have something out you get judged – so you want to stay in a place where you don't get judged.' While Moby recalled 'an emotionally reserved' and paranoid figure no longer sure what he wanted to do. 'He seemed a little bit like a beaten dog,' adding that Axl became 'a little bit defensive when I asked him about the vocals. He just said that he was going to get to them eventually. I wouldn't be surprised if the record never came out, they've been working on it for such a long time.'

Behind the scenes, Geffen execs were starting to panic. They offered Youth a higher than usual royalty rate if he could bring the album in. Working initially in the poolroom of the Malibu mansion, playing acoustic guitar while encouraging Axl to sing, he recalls how eventually Axl just 'kind of pulled out, said "I'm not ready." He was quite isolated. There weren't very many people I think he could trust. It was very difficult to penetrate the walls he'd built up.'

Instructing his studio engineers to keep recording any ideas the various musicians he'd invited into the fold came up with, at one point Axl was being sent up to five CDs a week with different mixes of proposed songs. Eventually, a stack of over 1,000 CDs and DAT cassettes built up, all painstakingly filed and labelled. 'It was like the Library of Congress in there,' says one studio employee.

Axl's personal life seemed equally rudderless throughout this period. If the 1980s had been more than kind to him, the 1990s was the decade when all his chickens came home to roost. He confessed himself to *Rolling Stone* that many of the songs he was now so tortuously trying to complete were directly about Stephanie, and spoke openly of his hope that one day her son, Dylan, would listen and 'hear the truth' about the relationship.

The gradual dissolution of the band he'd worked so hard to build probably also affected Axl far more deeply than he was prepared to admit, even to himself. His separation from Slash, in particular, he viewed as 'a divorce'. When Shannon Hoon died of an accidental overdose in New Orleans in October 1995, Axl took the news personally. He saw himself as something of a mentor to the young singer, and his tragic, unnecessary death convinced Axl that fame was an even bigger trap than the drugs that had snuffed out his young friend's life.

Worse was to come, though, and it was shortly after Shannon's death that Axl received news that his mother was ill with cancer. She was just fifty-one, and though he loved her he still hadn't quite forgiven her for not 'protecting' him against the physical and mental abuses he suffered from both his fathers. Nevertheless, Axl, Amy and Stuart did make a point of flying up to Indiana to visit their mother not long before she died. When Sharon finally passed away in the small hours of 28 May 1996, her eldest son was devastated.

When Axl's old friend and sometime collaborator West

Arkeen died, at the age of thirty-six, exactly a year later, Axl began to think in terms of a curse. West had been working on his own project, The Outpatience, and had just released their debut album, *Anxious Disease* (featuring contributions from Axl, Slash, Duff and Izzy). But his plans had to be temporarily abandoned when an indoor barbecue in May 1997 went horribly wrong and he was admitted to hospital with second and third degree burns over two-thirds of his body. Returning home from the intensive care unit ten days later, he was believed to have 'accidentally' swallowed an overdose of the opiates he'd been prescribed for the pain. The suspicion remained, however, that the singer-songwriter, who had been addicted to heroin on and off for years, had deliberately self-administered a larger than prescribed dose.

As if to add insult to injury, it was also in 1997 that a musical stage-show, ostensibly about Axl and mischievously titled *White Trash Wins Lotto*, was first performed. Written and narrated by former Wall Of Voodoo frontman Andy Prieboy, *White Trash* quickly won a zealous following among the LA in-crowd, where its satirical jokes about money-hungry record moguls and the dim-hick rockers they exploited and thrust stardom upon – based loosely on Axl's story of fleeing the Midwest to find stardom in Hollywood – rang particularly true.

Having started life as a one-man show in the Largo lounge room, where musicians and comedians regularly competed for the spotlight, by the end of the decade *White Trash* had become a successful Broadway production, the West Coast equivalent of *Hedwig And The Angry Inch*, poking fun at the death cult surrounding Jim Morrison while exploring the hollowness of Hollywood stardom, with Sunset strippers as *Gigi*-style chorus girls and parodic Midwestern youths transformed into braces-twanging *Oklahoma*-types. The Axl figure was played with brilliant innocuousness by Brian Beacock, emerging intermittently to belt out another hilarious paean to his own lack of self-awareness. 'I sing to bring a light into this confusion . . .'

In a piece of promotional brio, Axl was invited to attend the show on more than one occasion, but he refused even to acknowledge its existence or his own part in its inspiration. Instead, he took the whole thing as an insult to his intelligence and the hard work he'd put into his real-life journey from small-town obscurity to the heights of international fame – and notoriety. If anything, it only encouraged him to become even more of a recluse, convinced as he now was that only ridicule lay in wait for him out there, in the so-called real world.

According to an LA scene-maker from those days known as Vaginal Creme Davis, it was around this time that Axl began to wear 'those Michael Jackson-type disguises – fake moustaches and Members Only jackets'. Although rarely seen in daylight, occasionally he would get Beta or her son Fernando to drive him to the beach or, more often, to the movies. Even when he was sometimes spotted at concerts, hanging out backstage with Dave Navarro at a Red Hot Chili Peppers show, dropping in unexpectedly to see Radiohead, Axl's appearance had changed so dramatically – he'd cut his hair short and was now stockier and tended to dress down in jeans and plaid shirts – one witness claimed they even saw security personnel patting him down because they hadn't recognized him. According to Moby, 'If you were walking down the street and Axl passed you, you'd never notice. He looks like a regular, decent guy.'

When not obsessed with putting the new band through its paces in the studio or pulling his hair out trying to write lyrics, Axl spent most of his time on his own behind the electric gates of his secluded Latigo Canyon estate either working out – lately, he'd developed a fondness for kickboxing – messing around on his impressive array of state-of-the-art computers or playing pinball. He also began taking guitar lessons for the first time. Indeed, he became so enamoured of the work he was doing with his tutor, former Circus of Power alumni Gary Sunshine, he invited him to take part in some of the sessions at the studio.

Once a year he would invite friends and their families over for a special Halloween costume party. Decorating the swimming pool with pumpkin-lanterns and dangling fake spider-webs from the overhanging palms, he also had special mazes built. Guests at these parties later described him as almost as excited as the children present as he dashed around enjoying himself. Dave

Quakenbush, vocalist with LA punk band the Vandals and a guest at the 1999 Halloween party, recalls Axl wearing a dinosaur outfit. When some kids approached him and asked if he was Barney the Dinosaur, he told them that Barney was a pussy.

Around this time Izzy dropped by. 'I'd moved back out to LA [and] was riding around one day and I thought, fuck it, I'll go by his house,' Izzy recalls. 'Bastard, he lives up in the hills, he's got a big house, I'll go and see what he's doing, you know? And I go up and he's got security gates, cameras, walls, all this shit, you know. So I'm ringing the buzzer, and eventually somebody comes and takes me up and there he is. He's like, "Hey, man! Glad to see you!" Gives me a big hug and shows me round his house. It was great. Then, I don't know, probably a month later, one night he calls me [and] we got into the issue of me leaving Guns N' Roses. I told him how it was on my side. Told him exactly how I felt about it and why I left.' According to Izzy, suddenly the conversation became very one-sided. 'I mean, he had a fucking *notepad*. I could hear him [turning the pages] going, "Well, ah, you said in 1982 . . . blah blah blah . . ." And I'm like, what the fuck – 1982? He was bringing up a lot of really weird old shit. I'm like, whatever, man.'

It was the last conversation Izzy would have with Axl for nearly a decade. 'Every two or three years I'll put a call in to the office and say, "Hey, tell Axl gimme a call if he wants to." But I mean . . . the weirdness of his life. To me, I live pretty normal. I can go anywhere. I don't think people really give a shit. But for Axl, I know for the longest time, because his face was all over the television and stuff, I don't think he could really go anywhere or do anything. And I think because of that he kind of put himself in a little hole up there in the hills. He kind of dug in deeper and deeper and now I think he's gone so fucking deep he's just . . . I mean, I could be completely wrong. But I know he doesn't drive and he doesn't . . . he doesn't do anything. I've never, never seen him in town. Isolation can be a bad thing, but Axl's been at it for a long time now. You know, he always stays up at night . . .' Izzy drifted off, shaking his head, no longer knowing what to say.

Occasionally, a small ray of light illuminated the gloom. In

April 1997, basketball superstar Shaquille O'Neal found himself recording in an adjacent studio and decided to stick his head around the door and see what Axl and the boys were up to and ended up rapping with them. 'They asked me to join them,' Shaq recalls, 'so I started freestylin' over their track. It was the first time I ever performed with a rock group, and it felt good.'

It was reported in *Rolling Stone* that on 6 February 1998, Doug Goldstein organized a 'surprise' party for Axl, to celebrate his thirty-sixth birthday. Held at a Mexican restaurant in Santa Monica, Goldstein had, of course, asked Axl for permission to hold the event. Having given his blessing, Goldstein assembled a sizeable number of people for the occasion, including several friends, old and new, mostly musicians from the same West Hollywood circuit Axl came of age on, mingled with other more senior industry figures in suits munching guacamole and drinking from pitchers of Cuervo margaritas. Everybody in the forty-strong crowd had brought presents, and a garishly large birthday cake sat on a dais in the corner of the restaurant. When the clock turned midnight and Axl still hadn't shown up, a few people started to leave. Goldstein put in a nervous call on his cellphone to Axl. Bad news: Axl couldn't show up after all. It was left, as usual, to Doug to clear up. 'Axl's not going to be coming,' he told the assembled gathering. 'But order whatever you want and have a good time.'

Ironically, Axl's first public sighting for some years occurred less than a week later when he was arrested at Sky Harbor International Airport in Phoenix after getting into an argument with a security advisor who wanted to check his luggage.

Dressed in jeans, a red sweatshirt and a grey cloth cap, Axl was duly carted off to spend a few hours behind bars at the local police station. A year later, he pleaded 'no contest' to a misdemeanour charge of disturbing the peace and was fined $500 and one day in jail – which he was already deemed to have served.

Why was he so upset at having his bags searched? Friends now claim it was because he was carrying some of the birthday presents he'd recently received. (The gifts included a large hand-blown glass sphere Axl was worried might break.)

Meanwhile, on those increasingly rare occasions when he did

show his face, he was always asked the same tedious questions: what had happened to Slash and Duff and the guys? And when would the new album be released?

It was reported in the *New York Times* that when Todd Sullivan, then working as 'talent executive' for Geffen, couriered a sampling of CDs featuring various name producers with a note suggesting he might like to consider one of them for his album, Axl's response (according to Sullivan) was to place the CDs in his drive and run over them in his silver Ferrari. Some time later, the same exec persuaded Axl to play him some of the snippets he'd been working on. He told him: 'Look, Axl, this is some really great, promising stuff here. Why don't you consider just bearing down and completing some of these songs?' To which Axl replied: 'Hmm, bear down and complete some of these songs?' According to the *New York Times* the very next day Sullivan received a phone call from Geffen chairman Eddie Rosenblatt informing him he 'was off the project'.

With costs now spiralling, some senior industry figures wondered aloud why Geffen executives tolerated such behaviour. The truth may have been that Geffen was then riding a wave of uncertainty about its own future. David Geffen had sold the label to its corporate parent, MCA Inc., back in 1989. By 1998, MCA had itself been swallowed up by the giant alcohol-making corporation Seagram, whose chairman, Edgar Bronfman, found it impossible to grasp the reasons why the delivery of a new Guns N' Roses album was proving so difficult. Deciding to throw money at the problem, he authorized a further $1 million 'incentive' payment to Axl, with the promise of another $1 million if he delivered a finished album by March the following year.

With Sean Beavan coming on-board as producer in April 1998 work finally seemed to gather pace. Over the next nine months the band recorded the best part of thirty songs, continually reworking them until Axl could come up with lyrics to titles including 'Prostitute', 'Cock-a-roach Soup', 'This I Love', 'Suckerpunched', 'No Love Remains', 'Friend Or Foe', 'Zip It', 'Something Always', 'Hearts Get Killed' and 'Closing In On You'. A title for the album was publicly mooted for the first time: *2000 Intentions*, the suggestion thought to be that it would be out in time to commemorate the millennium. Axl claimed this was an entirely spurious title, suggested on an obscure fan-site. The real title was to be *Chinese Democracy*.

Two months before the new delivery deadline, in January 1999, Seagram underwent a massive restructuring of its music division, leaving 110 Geffen employees redundant, including long-time Axl supporter Rosenblatt. From here on in, Geffen's affairs would be overseen by the corporation's much larger Interscope Records division; the unfinished GN'R album was now the responsibility of Interscope chairman Jimmy Iovine, a former producer renowned for being 'artist-friendly'.

Axl was said to be appalled by this latest development. With no one left from the original Geffen team that signed him in 1986, he could be isolated. Inevitably, the March deadline came and went without him even acknowledging it. Indeed, on 16 March when the band was made one of the inaugural artists of the new Diamond Award from the RIAA, commemorating sales of over ten million copies of *Appetite For Destruction*, Axl – the only surviving member of the line-up who'd recorded the album – did not attend the ceremony in New York. Neither Slash, Duff nor Izzy agreed to go, either. In the end, it was the solitary figure of Steven Adler who showed up to receive the award and say a few words of thanks.

In a further strange twist, what no one yet knew was that Axl had spent a significant extent of the preceding months rerecording all the *Appetite* songs with his new band. Interscope decided that this re-recording would not replace the original, rightfully fearing it would destroy the credibility of an album still selling upwards of 10,000 copies a week in America. They did allow the 'new' version of 'Sweet Child O' Mine' to be used over the closing credits of the 1999 Adam Sandler movie *Big Daddy*.

By then all the promise of the previous year's activity in the studio with Beavan had reverted to yet more creative chaos followed by another prolonged withdrawal from the studio. Axl's working routine now became so ragged he rarely showed his face at the studio, despite keeping all the musicians and engineers on a monthly retainer reported by the *New York Times* to have totalled some $250,000. (Including more than $50,000 in studio fees, a combined payroll for seven band members of approximately $65,000, plus guitar technicians on about $6,000 per month, a recording engineer earning $14,000 a month and a 'software engineer' paid $25,000 a month.) It was at this point that studio engineer Billy Howerdel and drummer Josh Freese – who quit soon after – found time to start their own band, A Perfect Circle, recording the album *Mer de Noms*, which went on to sell 1.7 million copies in the US. Guitarist Ron Finck also walked out soon afterwards, ostensibly to rejoin Nine Inch Nails but in reality for the same reasons Slash and Izzy before him had eventually thrown in the towel. He had simply grown weary waiting for Axl.

Beavan quit soon after. Suddenly, after nearly five years of trying, it was back to square one for Axl and his 'new' Guns N' Roses. Interscope were understandably furious. In order to try and claw back some credibility with the company, Goldstein suggested a live album from the original band. Keen to recoup some money from their already massive investment, Interscope agreed. In addition, Goldstein told them Axl was now ready to let a little daylight in on the new material he'd been working on by allowing one of the new tracks, a ponderous piece of fiction with the portentous title of 'Oh My God', to be used as the music on a trailer for the new Arnold Schwarzenegger movie *End Of Days*.

Having wiped Finck's guitar parts from the track and brought in Dave Navarro and Gary Sunshine to re-record them for the track's release on 22 September, Axl issued his first official statement to the media for over five years, a missive that proved both pointed (referring to Matt Sorum as a 'former employee') and unexpectedly wry (ending with the phrase: 'Power to the people, peace out and blame Canada'). Mostly it was weighed down by the kind of language one might expect from someone who had been said to be in therapy for almost a decade. Describing 'Oh My God' as a song that dealt 'with the societal repression of deep and often agonizing emotions – some of which may be willingly accepted for one reason or another – the appropriate expression of which (one that promotes a healing, release and a positive resolve) is often discouraged and many times denied', it was a statement that left most fans even more in the dark than they were already. It concluded: 'The appropriate expression and vehicle for such emotions and concepts is not something taken for granted.' Well, obviously.

Premiered during the 1999 MTV Video Music Awards, Axl made such a fuss over the song that Jimmy Iovine and a posse of studio technicians had to work through the night adjusting the final mix. All their efforts proved to be in vain, however, as the critics had a field day making fun of its pretensions and comparing it unfavourably to heyday classics like 'Paradise City' and 'Welcome To The Jungle'.

The live album, a double-CD titled *Live Era '87–'93*, followed in November, and though it was an accurate document of the band's classic live show it fared only marginally better with the critics. While even a flawed Guns N' Roses collection like *The Spaghetti Incident?* was guaranteed to sell in its millions, *Live Era* entered the US album charts at a 'soft' number forty-five and made little more headway over the following weeks. Four months after its release it still hadn't sold enough copies – 500,000 – in the US to go gold. At the same time, the soundtrack to *End Of Days* which included 'Oh My God' barely scraped the US top forty, and the track itself was nowhere to be found on most US rock radio play-lists.

Axl took refuge in the fact that he'd had little to do with the album's production, leaving most of the duties to Slash. The guitarist, who had worked long and hard on it, was philosophical. He told me: 'I figured if it was gonna come out anyway, it might as well be as good as we could get it.' How much it eventually sold was 'not my problem any more'. He and Axl hadn't even spoken about the album directly, he said, communicating only through their respective managers, Goldstein and Tom Maher. 'Suddenly there's lots of faxes and phone calls, everybody avoiding each other.'

As was increasingly the practice with Axl, he was merely sent CDs. Enlisting the aid of former Faith No More producer Andy Wallace, Slash remixed the live tapes 'the way it should be. I worked shoulder-to-shoulder with Andy, then Duff came down, and in the end there were only a couple of fixes where the drums dropped out and we had to bleed the mikes.' And what did Axl make of the new mix? 'I don't know. I didn't ask and nobody said anything.'

When Matt Sorum saw a proof of the album sleeve his heart sank: he was listed only as an 'additional musician'. 'That hurt,' he says.

When Robin Finck and Josh Freese left the band, Axl hired two new musicians – the guitarist Buckethead, a virtuoso who wore a mannequin-like face mask and an empty KFC bucket upside down on his head and only conversed via a small hand-held puppet, and the drummer Brian 'Brain' Mantia, a thirty-five-year-old native Californian previously known for his work with Tom Waits, Praxis, Godflesh and, most recently, Primus, who was brought into the line-up at the suggestion of Buckethead, whose solo albums he'd also played on.

Buckethead (real name Brian Carroll) was a thirty-one-year-old enigma who had grown up in a Southern California suburb a stone's throw from his beloved Disneyland. A shy, nerdy kid obsessed with comics, video games, Kung Fu movies and slasher-flicks, he'd studied music theory at college, and his musical signature was a fondness for incorporating splashy classical influences into his raucous 'shredding' guitar style. Uncomfortable onstage he developed the Buckethead persona, he said, after eating a bucket of KFC one night. 'I put the mask on and then the bucket on my head. I went to the mirror. I just said, "Buckethead. That's Buckethead right there."' Out of this he developed his absurdly detailed chicken fetish, claiming in interviews that he'd been raised by chickens and that his long-term ambition was to alert the world to the ongoing chicken holocaust in fast-food outlets the world over.

Before signing on as Axl's latest replacement for Slash, Buckethead had recorded as a solo artist for almost a decade, going from the 'post-metal psycho-shred' of his 1999 album *Monsters And Robots* to the eerie ambience of his next release, *Electric Tears*. He also recorded under the anagram Death Cube K. He said the only reason he'd joined Guns N' Roses was that when Axl invited him to his house he gave him a rare collector's edition of the Leatherface doll, which he took as a good omen, deciding that Axl 'must understand me somehow'.

In November 1999, Axl gave his first formal interview for six years to MTV's Kurt Loder, who he agreed to speak to briefly by phone. Axl began by explaining that originally he'd set out to make an album that tried 'to get back to an *Appetite* thing or something, because that would have been a lot easier for me to do.' Then he blamed Slash for his failure to do so. 'We were trying to make things work with Slash for a very, very long time . . . about three and a half years.' He also insisted that the *Live Era* album was not a stop-gap but 'something we wanted to give to the public in a way of saying farewell'.

When asked why he'd been re-recording the *Appetite* songs he replied matter-of-factly that 'there were a lot of recording techniques and certain subtle styles and drum fills and things like that that are kind of '80s signatures that subtly could use a little sprucing up.' Questioned about the reasons behind the exits of Slash and Duff, he insisted, 'That was their choice to leave. Everybody that's gone did it by choice. Matt was fired, but Matt came in attempting to get fired and told many people so that night. So it's kind of like everybody left by choice.' He suggested that if anyone had been let down it was himself. They 'didn't want to help really make a record. Everybody kind of wanted what they wanted individually rather than what's in the best interest of the whole.' He said the 'big difference between myself and Slash and Duff' was that 'I didn't hate everything new that came out. I really liked the Seattle move-ment. I like White Zombie. I like Nine Inch Nails, and I like hip-hop . . .'

He said there were now roughly seventy new songs in various states of completion, and that they had already recorded 'at least two albums' worth of material, some of which was 'too advanced' for their fans to enjoy. 'It's like, "Hmm, I have to push the envelope a little too far. We'll wait on that." '

Ultimately, he compared what he was trying to do with his new band as like 'listening to Queen. [They] had all kinds of different-style songs on their records, and that's something that I like. 'Cos I do listen to a lot of things, and I really don't like being pigeonholed to that degree, and it's something that Guns N' Roses seem to share [with Queen] a bit. With *Appe*-

tite, even though it seems to have the same sound, if you really go back, you can pull all the little parts from different influences.'

When asked why he was so rarely seen in public any more, he replied stutteringly, 'You know I . . . I pretty much stay to myself, and that's about it . . . I just, you know, I pretty much work on this record and, and that's about it. It takes a lot of time. I'm not a computer-savvy or technical type of person, yet I'm involved with it every day, so it takes me a while.'

And finally, in reply to why he decided to call the album *Chinese Democracy*, he shrugged: 'Well, there's a lot of Chinese democracy movements, and it's something that there's a lot of talk about, and it's something that will be nice to see. It could also just be like an ironic statement. I don't know, I just like the sound of it.'

When the magazine was allowed access to the studio to conduct a face-to-face interview with him just a few weeks later, they found an Axl that 'looks a bit older and more solidly built than the lean rock god of his "Sweet Child O' Mine" days' dressed in Abercrombie & Fitch 'with his reddish hair intact and cut to a Prince Valiant-ish mid-length'. They also found a less cocksure Axl than his closest friends and employees were used to. Speaking of the new band he conceded that originally 'this wasn't Guns N' Roses, but I feel it is Guns N' Roses now.'

However, when he was asked whether he had considered simply continuing as a solo artist, the scowl was back. 'I contemplated letting go of that, but it doesn't feel right in any way. I am not the person who chose to try to kill it and walk away.'

Listening back to some of the new tracks – which the magazine described as 'like Led Zeppelin's *Physical Graffiti* remixed by Beck and Trent Reznor' – including the first airing of 'Catcher In The Rye', 'I.R.S', 'The Blues', 'T.W.A.T.' (short for 'There Was A Time') and the album's 'almost grungy title track', the most attention-grabbing song (though still only in instrumental form) was something called 'Oklahoma', which Axl said was inspired by one of his court dates with Erin. 'I was sitting in my litigation with my ex-wife, and it was the day after the [Oklahoma] bombing,' Axl recalled. 'It's just ironic that we're sitting there and this person is spewing all kinds of things and 168 people just got killed.'

He also spoke publicly for the first time of his desire for Stephanie Seymour's son to hear the new album one day. 'I hope he'll hear it when he grows up, if he ever wants to know the story, to hear the truth,' he whispered.

As for his reputation as a recluse, he shrugged off the suggestion. He simply didn't 'find it's in my best interest to be out there'. He was 'building something slowly,' at home and in the studio. 'If you are working with issues that depressed the crap out of you, how do you know you can express it? At the time, you are just like, "Life sucks". Then you come down and you express "Life sucks" but in this really beautiful way.' Beautiful – or not – it would be several years before the rest of the world was allowed to find out.

Part Four

CHINESE CURSE

One should not lose one's temper
unless one is certain of getting more
and more angry to the end.

WILLIAM BUTLER YEATS

Chapter Ten

WHERE'S SLASH?

On 22 June 2000, more than six years since his last public performance at Elton John's Hall of Fame induction show, W. Axl Rose climbed back on a stage. The venue, the Cat Club on Sunset Strip, could hardly have been less prestigious. Or the setting more low-key, singing a couple of impromptu numbers with the part-time Thursday night band, the Starfuckers, led by Cat proprietor former Stray Cats drummer 'Slim' Jim Phantom and featuring, somewhat surprisingly, former Guns N' Roses guitarist Gilby Clarke. But for Axl it represented a major step forward. After the wholesale rejection of 'Oh My God' and the unexpectedly limp sales of *Live Era*, the huge cheer prompted by his surprise appearance on the Cat stage provided him with a much-needed fillip. 'He was psyched,' recalls a former employee. 'It seemed like it boosted him [that] people still want to hear him.'

Having arrived at the bar with only Earl his bodyguard for company and sporting a baseball cap pulled down low over his eyes, nobody even recognized Axl before he got up onstage. Spotting a stocky, short-haired figure at the bar that looked liked Axl, but unsure if it was really him, Phantom and Gilby went over and 'tapped the guy on the shoulder', the drummer recalls. 'He turns round and Gilby says, "That's not him." But Axl grins and says, "Hey, Gilby, how're you doin'?"'

Axl and Gilby hadn't spoken to each other since launching their counter lawsuits six years before. Now all that was forgotten as Axl sat and chatted with his former band mate until dawn, at one point even allowing himself to be talked into getting up for half an hour with Gilby and Jim in the Starfuckers, belting out raucous versions of the Stones' tunes 'Wild Horses' and 'Dead Flowers'. 'I guess he ran into some friends of mine at the Roger Waters show at Universal Amphitheater, and they told him that we were playing down there and he came by,' Gilby shrugged. Axl had been in a great mood, 'Maybe he just wanted to have some fun.' He was also 'very, very excited about his new record and the new band.'

Despite saying they would keep in touch, when it was over neither Gilby nor Jim heard from Axl again. When word got out, however, it seemed to signal the end of the silent years. Emboldened, Interscope now suggested that *Chinese Democracy* would be released in 2001 and – even more surprising – UK concerts were announced for the following summer, the first official Guns N' Roses tour for eight years.

First though, there was still the ticklish subject of actually finishing the album. Sean Beavan joined his exhausted predecessors by quitting, so Interscope came up with the ingenious idea of enticing former Queen producer Roy Thomas Baker out of retirement to oversee the project. As insurance, they also rehired Tom Zutaut to come in and liaise personally with Axl. At first, Axl was thrilled by both prospects: working with a genuine musical hero in Baker – who also endeared himself to the moody singer by helping facilitate Queen guitarist Brian May spending a week laying down some guitar parts on the album – and being reacquainted with the man who had originally shown the faith in Axl's talent by signing the band to Geffen. Axl's attitude began to sour again, though, when he discovered that Zutaut had been offered a bonus if he could coax the singer into completing the album within a year. Baker's meticulous recording habits also alienated Axl, and by Christmas 2000 both Baker and Zutaut were off the project.

Interscope then assigned their most senior talent executive, Mark Williams, to the project but it was weeks before Axl would even allow him to visit the studio. Equally troublesome was Axl's relationship with his new lead guitarist, Buckethead, who was also starting to become disillusioned. In an effort to persuade him to stick with the band, Axl treated him to a trip to Disneyland. Asking outright what it would take to keep him involved, the eccentric guitarist claimed he would be more comfortable working inside a chicken coop. Axl immediately ordered one to be built for him in the studio, using wooden planks and chicken wire.

By now the proposed track-listing was more like an over-grown vine. Privately, Axl was telling people the album would contain up to eighteen new tracks, accompanied by an extra CD containing a further ten selections. Titles now included 'Hearts Always Get Killed', 'Today, Tomorrow Forever', 'Cock-a-roach Soup', 'Closing In On You', 'Something Always', 'Catcher In The Rye', 'No Love Remains', 'Strange Disease', 'Friend Or Foe', 'Never Had It', 'This I Love', 'Silk Worm', 'Prostitute', 'This Life', 'Zip It', 'I.R.S.' and 'T.W.A.T.'. But how they would all knit together or when the rest of the world might get to hear them were still taboo subjects. The fact was, not even Axl knew for sure. However, he did seem prepared to go along with Goldstein's plan, as outlined by Doug in an interview with KROQ, to schedule the release of the album for 'possibly as early as June 2001', along with what seemed at the time an even more ambitious plan to put the new line-up on the road.

On 6 December 2000, just as Zutaut and Baker received their marching orders, the first official Guns N' Roses concert for seven years was announced, the date a special New Year's Eve show at the surprisingly small, 2,000-seat House of Blues in Las Vegas. The band, with the exception of keyboardist Dizzy Reed, would all be making their live debut with Axl, and now comprised guitarists Paul Huge, Buckethead and – surprise – a returning Robin Finck plus bassist Tommy Stinson, drummer Bryan Mantia and additional keyboardist and most recent recruit, former Repli-cants member Chris Pitman.

The House of Blues had already booked the Goo Goo Dolls for the New Year's Eve show, but that was no obstacle. Axl said he was happy for the Dolls to do their show first and 'delay' the Guns' set until the early hours of the morning. Given the generally modest aims of the House of Blues, the venue's Senior VP of Entertainment, Kevin Morrow, admits he could hardly believe his luck when Axl's representatives called to arrange the show. 'I thought it was a joke. I said to myself, "There is no way this can be real."'

But with ticket prices ranged between $150 and $250 each, real it was. In fact, Axl saw the Vegas show as the ideal preparation for the band's bona fide return to high-profile action with an appearance at the Rock in Rio festival in Brazil in January. Nevertheless, nobody could quite believe it until they saw it with their own eyes, including the freshly minted band itself. Indeed, when the start of the 1.00 a.m. show ran over by nearly three hours, there were those inside the band camp who doubted Axl would ever give the signal to begin. At 3.35 a.m. precisely, however, almost four hours after the Goo Goo Dolls had said goodnight, he did.

'Good morning,' Axl told the packed house as the first notes of 'Welcome To The Jungle' rang out. 'I've just woke up. I've been taking a nap for about eight years.'

The new band played for almost two hours, having belted out a twenty-one-song set comprising mainly old favourites like 'Sweet Child', 'Patience', 'Rocket Queen' and a new version, more akin to the Dylan original of 'Knockin' On Heaven's Door', followed towards the end of the set by six new numbers. First up was 'Oh My God', which received a friendly cheer though in truth most of the audience seemed unfamiliar with its thrumming semi-industrial feel.

Other new numbers performed for the first time that night were 'The Blues', a ballad featuring a tinkling piano intro before the main guitar riff came cartwheeling in, Axl crooning to his lost love Stephanie; 'Oklahoma', his bitter-sweet tirade against ex-wife Erin; 'Chinese Democracy', a short, punchy rocker, not unlike something one might have expected from the original line-up; 'Madagascar', a ballad somewhat in the 'November Rain' tradition of self-conscious epics, broken up by looped samples of movie dialogue and a snatch from Martin Luther King's famous 'I have a dream' speech, all set off by a portentous keyboard motif.

The last of the new numbers was the most bizarre: 'Silk Worms', a keyboard and synthesizer special-effects showcase 'put together by Mr Dizzy Reed and Mr Chris Pitman,' announced Axl, interspersed with drums and guitar that cut in like a chainsaw, followed by Axl's dissonant vocals, which were hard to follow but full of copious 'motherfuckers' sung in an English punk accent. The number ended somewhat abruptly and the band pumped eagerly into 'Paradise City'.

'I have traversed a treacherous sea of horrors to be with you here tonight,' Axl announced at one point, with a straight face. The crowd lapped it up, applauding everything the singer said almost before he'd finished saying it.

It was the same when he and his new band turned up in Rio de Janeiro a fortnight later. Except this time Axl chose the occasion to address the subject of what he called 'the old band' at much greater length. Dragging his housekeeper Beta onstage to interpret for him, he told the 150,000-strong crowd: 'I know that many of you are disappointed that some of the people that you came to know and love could not be with us here today. [Cue: cheers and screams from the audience.] Regardless of what you have heard or read people worked very hard, meaning my former friends, to do everything they could, so that I could not be here today. I say, fuck that! [Cue: huge cheers.].'

He went on to say how 'hurt and disappointed' he was that 'unlike Oasis' who were also appearing at the festival, the original Guns N' Roses 'could not find a way to all get along'. Instead, he wanted to introduce the new band 'who have worked very, very, *very* hard to come and see you today,' singling out 'my friend Paul Tobias [Huge]' who 'has worked through the darkness underground for the last seven years' and that without whom 'there would be no more Guns N' Roses.' This last elicited the biggest cheer of the night 'Along with Paul, the only man from the old line-up who stayed loyal and worked hard every day is on the keyboards – Mr Dizzy Reed. [Cue: more obedient audience noises.] Well, so much for the past,' he said as the band chugged into 'Live And Let Die'.

He also asked Beta to come out after 'Rocket Queen', when he told the crowd: 'You know, we have only done one show before this and already we have been criticized for playing the old songs. But I have no intention, and I never did, of denying you something you enjoy. And I thought it was only fair for you to see that this new band can play the fuck out of these songs.' He then introduced the rest of the band one by one, concluding with a special mention for 'General Tommy Stinson,' whom he had recently named as the band's musical director, for 'leading us through these rehearsals'.

Both Finck and Buckethead performed brief guitar showcases, Finck's based on a typically crowd-pleasing call-and-response routine, and Buckethead's more synth-heavy, very industrial; the same one, in fact, he was performing as a solo artist on the Ozzfest tour of eighteen months before. Less the polished futurism Axl envisaged, no doubt, and more the space-tripping noodling of Hawkwind in the early-1970s, neither guitar solo matched the inherent cool of Slash's skilful extemporizing of the *Godfather* theme at the same festival a decade before although some of the audience in Rio actually thought briefly that Buckethead was a disguised Slash.

After Rio, Axl and his crew flew to Argentina for a holiday in Buenos Aires. The plan was to do shows there and in Chile but, as he told a local radio station, 'they didn't work out.' While he was still in Rio though, both he and Beta gave interviews to the national newspaper, *O Globo*.

Wearing a basketball shirt and looking surprisingly relaxed while sitting by the pool at the Intercontinental Hotel, drinking caipirinha – a traditional Brazilian drink prepared with cachaça – and tequila, Axl talked for two hours about the end of the original band, his relationship problems and even his former band mates' drug use. 'Everybody hated each other in the band, with the exception of me,' he was reported as saying. The old war story once again trotted out about Steven Adler falling off his drum-stool while they were recording 'Civil War'. There was also no denying the assertion that Slash had been addicted to drugs and alcohol and that he disagreed with the new direction of the band.

Beta's interview, however, was much more eye-opening, and because it was conducted in Portuguese, more accurately rendered. In it she revealed she had been born in Sao Paulo in 1956 and that she was a divorced mother of three grown-up children in their twenties. She described her role in Axl's life as 'his personal assistant, I organize his house, I co-ordinate his personal life'. She also revelled in her role as what she called the 'mother' of the band, bringing home-made meals to the studio. 'I always light candles for them,' she beamed. Axl, she said, had never had the everyday love of a mother, 'like the goodnight kiss' and so didn't know 'how to demonstrate this kind of love, and it is very difficult for a grown-up to deal with this'. As a result, he found it hard to trust people, or even himself, and needed 'someone who listens to what he has to say and I am here for that'.

She explained how she and her eldest son, Fernando, had lived with Axl at his Malibu mansion for the past seven years, although she now owned her own home 'very close to Axl's house'. Even when she wasn't at the Malibu mansion, she never went out without her cellphone and pager, or anywhere where Axl couldn't contact her 24/7.

Asked about his reported interest in past lives, she replied, 'Yes, Axl and I believe.' It was 'impossible', she thought, 'for two people who never met before, to get along this well. When I opened the door and he was there, I felt as if I knew him from ages ago.' She also claimed that although he still drank alcohol 'once in a while' he had 'never drugged' in all the time she had known him. 'He even quit smoking,' she said. Instead, he now worked out 'for four hours a day' including running 'almost eight kilometers every two days'. There was also 'a doctor who tells us what we must eat'. The reason he didn't go out much any more, she said, was because 'he doesn't like bars or clubs'. He and she did 'go a lot to the movies' together though. And of course he was a famous night owl. 'According to his grandmother,' Beta said, Axl 'had never liked the day . . . He writes a lot in the night, because there's no phone or other thing that could interrupt him. He is more creative late at night.'

It all confirmed the picture friends gave. As one says: 'Beta moms him. She's as close as he's ever had to a real mother.' Her son Fernando also helped out on tour. Indeed, Beta's family now appeared closer to the singer than his own. Amy Bailey, who had once run the Guns N' Roses fan club, and Stuart Bailey, who worked on the road as one of Axl's army of 'personal assistants', had also lived at the Malibu house over the years. But only Beta remained a constant companion – the chauffeur, housekeeper and confidante who still stands by his side to this very day. Always there, she said, to 'give him advice when he asks me for it. I know he values my opinion a lot.'

In the wake of the success of Rock in Rio, shows in London, Glasgow, Manchester and Birmingham were announced in March 2001 as part of a fourteen-date summer tour of Europe, scheduled to begin in Nuremberg on 1 June. But, with tickets already on sale, the tour was pulled just two weeks before it was due to begin because, according to official sources, Buckethead had been ordered to rest after suffering 'internal haemorrhaging' of the stomach. The release of *Chinese Democracy* was also postponed from the 'June release' previously suggested by Doug Goldstein, until autumn at the earliest, pending 'adjustments'.

When Buckethead's latest solo album, *Somewhere Over The Slaughterhouse*, was released on 5 June it also led to unsubstantiated suggestions behind the scenes that one of the reasons Axl had cancelled the tour was because he was 'uncomfortable' with the idea of Buckethead promoting his own album on a tour supposedly promoting a Guns N' Roses album that was still unready for release.

The tour was officially put back until December, including Axl's first visit for eight years to the UK – home of the world's most virulent rock press.

However, come November the entire schedule was cancelled, a move which resulted in several promoters – who again had already sold a great many tickets – reacting furiously. Goldstein issued an official statement to the effect that he had 'forgotten' to tell Axl he'd gone ahead and planned a tour, amid barely concealed scoffing from the British press.

The statement, in full, read as follows: 'Following the euphoria of Rock in Rio I jumped the gun and arranged a European tour as our plan was to have the new album out this year. Unfortunately Buckethead's illness not only stopped the tour, but it slowed down our progress on *Chinese Democracy*. As a result, touring right now is logistically impossible. I am very sorry to disappoint our fans, but I can assure them that this is not what Axl wanted, nor is it "another page from the Howard Hughes of rock", as some media will no doubt portray it. I made a plan, and unfortunately it did not work out. The good news is that everyone is ecstatic with the album and we will be meeting with the label to schedule its release, following which we will announce the rescheduled dates to coincide. Guns N' Roses look forward to seeing everybody next year, and once again, please accept my apologies for the way this has played out.'

Goldstein added that Axl had spent 'every waking hour of every day during the last five years' working on *Chinese Democracy* – a statement that even hardcore GN'R fans found hard to swallow. When Axl added he only found out about his own touring commitments while perusing the internet, some wondered what was going on in Axl's organization. 'I was sitting at home on the internet [when] I found out the tour was cancelled,' the singer messaged. 'I had no idea that I [even] had a tour.'

Despite the cancellation of the tour, the band returned to Las Vegas for another New Year's Eve show that year, this time at the Joint, the small venue housed at the Hard Rock Café. They would also 'warm up' with an earlier show at the same venue on 29 December. 'We've been cooped up in the studio for so long, that we have to release some energy,' Axl explained via the official GN'R website, which may have made ticket-holders in Britain and Europe wish he could have dispelled some of that energy three weeks before.

One would-be fan who wasn't able to enjoy the Las Vegas show was Slash. The guitarist, who happened to be in Las Vegas for New year's Eve, decided to check out the new band – but was astonished to be told he was not welcome and would be denied entrance at the door. According to Doug Goldstein, forced yet again into the role of wide-eyed innocent: 'We didn't know what his intentions were. If nothing else, it would have been a distraction. Axl was really nervous about these shows. We decided on our own not to take any risk.' According to Slash, his 'intentions' had been simple: to see the show. 'I was trying to be discreet,' he said, 'but apparently [Doug Goldstein] found out and it was major pandemonium. It was like they sent out an all-points bulletin.'

It was also the last time Axl's buddy Paul Tobias would play with GN'R. Although Axl was loath to admit it, his new band was experiencing the same problems his old band had had with Tobias. The feeling amongst some was that he was only in the band because of his personal relationship with its leader. When Axl finally bit the bullet and agreed to replace him, it was revealing that the guitarist they chose, Richard Fortus, was recommended for the job by 'musical director' and old friend Tommy Stinson.

A thirty-six-year-old former member of the Psychedelic Furs and Ben Folds Five, Fortus had also worked as a session player – most notably with US boy-band N' Sync. He was no GN'R hanger-on, admitting he 'did not grow up a Guns N' Roses fan'. As he explained, 'Guns N' Roses were so LA, and I was a NYC kid. So it wasn't until much later that I really got into the band.' He also claimed he'd first been approached to join in 1999, 'but before that audition happened, Axl saw Buckethead play, and he decided to go with him instead. Fortunately, I got another call the next time they were looking for someone.'

Fortus' first commitment with the band was the August 2002 tour of the Far East, billed as the start of what would have been the band's first full-scale world tour since 1993. With the launch of the tour scheduled for China, there were even raised hopes among fans – and the band's record company – that this might finally herald the release of the *Chinese Democracy* opus. However, yet again, it was not to be.

They arrived in Hong Kong on 12 August in readiness for the opening night of the tour at the Hong Kong Convention & Exhibition Center, after which they would travel to Japan for two shows in Tokyo and Osaka as part of the Summer Sonic Festival, followed by the first Guns N' Roses show in Britain for nine years, at the Carling Festival in Leeds, then a headline appearance at the Pukkelpop festival in Belgium and a final show in London at the newly opened Docklands Arena.

To coincide with the dates, Axl issued another, much fuller statement via the official GN'R website, in which he began by characterizing the show in Hong Kong as, 'A dream come true . . . I guess it's meant to be.' He described the forthcoming dates as 'a warm-up' for the autumn tour of the US they were also planning, which in turn would be 'a warm-up for the Spring ['03] tour. This thing is starting now and much like [the] *Use Your Illusion* [tour] that went for two and a half years, this thing is going to go off and on for the next two or three years and we'll see how it goes.'

Axl also chose the occasion to comment on the replacement of Tobias with Fortus, though he remained typically oblique about his reasons why his 'old friend' was no longer in the band. 'The original intentions between Paul and myself were that Paul was going to help me for as long as it took to get this thing together in whatever capacity that he could help me in. So when he first was brought into this, he was brought in as a writer to work with Slash. Now whether or not Paul was going to be officially on the album or on the tour that really wasn't an actual consideration at the time.'

Ultimately, while Tobias had 'helped us a lot in the writing and the recording of this record and to me was a vital part of not only the band but also my life' he just wasn't interested in touring, which was why they eventually turned to Fortus to fulfil that role. 'We're fortunate to have found Richard. [He] has this vibe kind of like Izzy but with amazing feel. The first thing I heard Richard play was the beginning of "Stray Cat Blues" by the Stones and he did it with the right feel.' He also pointed out that Fortus was 'a proven professional. Basically, Richard's the guy that we always were looking for.' He went on: 'This is my shot and you can root for me to fail all you want, but there is simply way too much put into this to cater to someone else's selfish needs and destroy people's dreams I truly care about, including my own.'

He complained that he had given in to a lot of pressure while working on the *Illusion* albums 'both internally in Guns and externally in the press' and that both albums had 'suffered as a consequence [and] it's not something I'm too excited to have to live with again. There are a lot of new songs that were just done in the last year that we feel that "okay, well that bumps a lot of stuff off the previous list" but it's time to stop that now and wrap up the baby. It feels right, the timing, and a lot of things. We've sorted it down to what songs are on the record. What the sequence of the songs is. The album cover art is ready. Blah, blah, blah.'

He did sound one note of warning, however: 'If you're waiting . . . don't. Live your life. That's your responsibility, not mine. If it were not to happen you won't have missed a thing. If in fact it does you might get something that works for you, in the end you could win on this either way. But if you're really into waiting try holding your breath for Jesus, 'cos I hear the pay-off may be that much greater.'

A week later, as good as his word, Axl flew into London, ready for the band's show in Leeds on 23 August. As darkness descended on Temple Newsam, the sweeping rural idyll that plays host to the Leeds Carling Festival, the air of anticipation was palpable. It may have been nine years since the last GN'R appearance in Britain – even if it was a totally different band standing with the singer onstage – but some things, it seemed, would never change as far as Axl Rose was concerned. Backstage, it was almost 11.00 p.m. – over an hour past the advertised start – by the time Axl stepped from his private dressing-room and jumped into the chauffeur-driven stretch limo hired to carry him the scant fifty yards to the stage, weaving its way through a bemused assemblage of Prodigys, Offsprings and Slip-knots, the PA blasting out 'Gimme Danger' by Iggy Pop and the Stooges.

As he stood at the top of the side-stage steps, gazing out at the 60,000-plus crowd, Axl waited silently while the stage lights dimmed and the video screens erupted in an eye-scorching lava of screaming skulls and swirling psychedelia. The crowd, already teased to its limit, went predictably nuts as the familiar riff to 'Welcome To The Jungle' began bouncing around their heads.

Then Axl strode out, his long mane of intricately braided red plaits tumbling haphazardly from his trademark bandanna, his stocky form clad in a loose-fitting baseball jersey, his gaze predatory, almost feral. He may have been older, but he was back.

While Buckethead (the word 'Funeral' incongruously felt-penned across the brim of his upturned KFC bucket hat) and Finck (consigned to the role of straight-man now that Tobias was gone) proved that musically they were easily able to replicate Slash and Izzy's licks, the stage still seemed to some populated by ghosts. And while bassist Stinson and drummer Mantia were a perfectly effective rhythm section (technically maybe superior to the men they had replaced), it was hard not to reflect that Stinson would never be blond or punk-drunk enough to be Duff, and Mantia was simply too good to be ramshackle Steven and too slight to be muscle-bound Matt.

Indeed, other than Axl – who also, paradoxically, looked like a stand-in, heavier and furrow-browed from ten years spent creating a new band – the main visual foil were the video screens, with their relentless jump-cut images of the Columbine High School massacre (of three years before), the Gulf War (of eleven years before) and Mike Tyson (of even longer before, back when he was still known as a world champion boxer rather than the past-his-prime convicted rapist and ear-biter of the present). All of which only reinforced the view of some that Axl's points of reference – culturally, musically, *spiritually* – were solidly based in a past growing, ironically, ever more distant even as he strived to ensure Guns N' Roses remained relevant to the future.

If all you had come for was to hear the hits from a bygone age, you could close your eyes and imagine you really were there in 1987 when they first hit England like the actual hurricane that flattened it for real just weeks later. But if, like most people there, you had come to experience the band once dubbed the most dangerous in the world, you might have been sorely disappointed by the absence of the original players. 'Where's Slash?' cried one audience member during 'Patience'. 'He's up my ass, that's where he is. Go home!' fired back Axl.

There would be some new songs from the unreleased *Chinese Democracy* album previewed on this tour, as there had been in Las Vegas and Rio before, but none of the stature required to sit comfortably next to cornerstone classics like 'Sweet Child' or 'Paradise City', nor even the more knockabout numbers like 'You Could Be Mine'. The only one unveiled in Leeds, the portentous 'Madagascar', was accompanied by a video of burned-out cars, New York subway trains and the Martin Luther King speech it so conspicuously sampled. It also featured Buckethead's first solo: a lank, over-telegraphed affair pepped up by clichéd excursions into the theme tune from *Star Wars*, by way of a quick demonstration of his nunchaku skills and some off-kilter, '80s-style robot-dancing. It was for some excruciatingly awful, and as unlike anything previously seen at a Guns N' Roses show as could be imagined.

Indeed, the only moment in the whole show that was truly redolent of the original band was when Axl, seated at the grand piano for 'November Rain', announced: 'Well, it appears that we're gonna have an interesting evening. You see, the city council and the promoters say we have to, like, end the show.'

He looked out at the crowd, enjoying the frisson this visibly caused. Then he continued: '. . . they could say maybe I'm inciting a riot. Now I'm not, 'cos I don't want anyone to get arrested or anyone to get in trouble or anything like that. But I think we got a good seven or eight fuckin' songs left at least. And I didn't fuckin' come all the way over to fuckin' England to be told to go back fuckin' home, by some fuckin' asshole!' Most of the crowd were back on his side instantly, hooting and cheering lustily, though a small faction began to boo. Axl, only registering the cheers, continued regardless. 'All I've got for the last eight years is shit after shit after shit in the fuckin' press and Axl's this, Axl's that. I'm here to play a fuckin' show and we wanna play! So, if you wanna stay, I wanna stay and we'll see what happens. Everybody . . . Nobody try to get in trouble or anything. Try to have a good time.'

By then it was past midnight – official stage curfew time – but, as usual, Axl was not one to be unduly concerned with the trifles of petty bureaucracy. He glanced over to where several officials were standing nervously by the side of the stage. Having already witnessed a crowd of around 500 drunken fans gang together to fight police earlier in the day, knocking down and setting fire to seventy-one toilet blocks and a Portacabin, the officials took the hint and by the time the number was over had sensibly revised their decision and given the signal that they would allow the show to run over. A triumphantly grinning Axl then told the audience: 'We've got more time. And to whoever is responsible for that I'd like to say thank you.' When he and the band exited not long afterwards, amid a hail of wildly ejaculating tickertape and pyro, most of the crowd were pleased they'd been there to see them, whoever they really were. It was just before 1.00 a.m.

The following night in Belgium, headlining the Pukkelpop festival, the show was a virtual duplication of the preceding night's events; arriving onstage over an hour late to play an almost identical two-hour set. The only difference was the addition of two more new songs – 'Rhiad And The Bedouins' and 'Chinese Democracy' – though it was almost impossible to take their true measure amid the cacophony of noise the festival crowd made as they swilled beer and waited impatiently for the set to return to more familiar pastures.

Two days later, at London's Docklands Arena, it was possible to gather a more general impression of the new material as the crowd – who stood throughout – used the opportunity to pause and reseat themselves briefly. This time the three new numbers featured were 'Madagascar', 'The Blues', which sounded like it captured some of the old band's melodic swagger, and the puzzlingly titled 'Rhiad And The Bedouins'.

Axl told the Docklands audience that most of the new songs featured on the tour so far were no longer even scheduled to appear on *Chinese Democracy*. Instead, he said, the band had now completed work on the album's follow-up, concluding: 'By the time the record company release the second group of songs, and we do this all over again, who knows? Maybe I'll have finished the third album.'

Reviews were not encouraging. The *London Evening Standard* said of the Docklands show: 'A new album, *Chinese Democracy*, has been in the pipeline for an eternity, but Rose demonstrated that it wasn't a myth by playing several new songs, including the dirty riffs of the title track. However, there was little to indicate that they will eventually surpass their former glories – the new band had better keep practising the old songs.' While *Classic Rock* magazine described the new band as, 'the greatest Guns N' Roses tribute band in the world.'

Three days after the London show the band was in New York getting ready for their surprise appearance at that year's MTV Video Music Awards event. No one outside the immediate circle of MTV producers was even aware of the plan. But throughout the show publicists buzzed through the audience whispering about a surprise 'not to be missed' finale. Sure enough, just minutes before the end, a screen slid back to reveal Axl and his new band, hacking out the familiar opening to 'Welcome To The Jungle'. The crowd of ticket-holders and VIPs instantly went wild. Inevitably, the cameras mainly focused on Axl, looking stocky in a long, baggy baseball jersey, black leather pork-pie hat, his new red dreadlocks hanging down to his waist. By the time the band launched without introduction into 'Madagascar', it was clear that Axl was struggling, his voice lacking its familiar serrated edge and power.

The band ended with 'Paradise City'. Staring out from the stage like a wild animal caught in a trap, Axl brought his stilted performance to a theatrical close in typically messianic stance, arms aloft, eyes closed, mouthing the words: 'Round one.' Unfortunately, the planned round two – the band's autumn tour of the US – would end with the singer flat on his back in the middle of the ring . . .

First though, there was a two-month break during which Axl returned to Malibu, while Tommy Stinson took Richard Fortus into the studio to re-record those guitar parts which Paul Tobias had already laid down and Axl now decided to wipe from the album. With the band's first US tour for nine years due to start in November, even the understandably reticent executives at Interscope were quietly confident that *Chinese Democracy* would, finally, be released at some point in the next few months.

However, when the tour finally got underway in November, there was such a catalogue of disasters within the first two weeks – riots, no-shows, delayed appearances, cancellations, tantrums, 'health problems' – that all the old concerns came flooding back and Interscope braced themselves for the inevitable news that the album would not be ready for release in time for the tour after all.

Despite announcing via the official GN'R website beforehand that the US tour was 'our tour – that I have personally authorized', and vowing that 'for better or worse, we'll be there', the problems started on the very first night at the 10,000-seater General Motors Place arena in Vancouver, when understandably jittery promoters cancelled the show after Axl still hadn't shown up more than two hours after the band was due onstage. With shades of St Louis eleven years before, the ensuing riot by the angry mob of disgruntled fans caused damage estimated at several hundred thousand dollars, as the crowd wielded steel barricades to smash windows and police were forced to use attack-dogs and pepper-spray to disperse them.

Yet what could the promoters do? Axl wasn't even in the same city, let alone at the venue for the allotted stage time. Having left it to the day of the show to set off, an unexpected delay in his flight from Los Angeles meant he was still in the air when the decision to cancel the show was made. In an official statement to the press the next day, venue organizers said they were left with no option but to cancel 'when it was recognized that the band could not take the stage at a reasonable time'.

Sensing his mistake, Axl was keen to give his version of events when he agreed to speak, live on air, the next day to Seattle radio station KISW. 'We were going to play, and the plug got pulled on us,' he said, clearly feeling he was the injured party. 'Basically, the building manager just decided – in all of our opinions, prematurely – that the show was just cancelled. He didn't discuss it with anyone. [The road crew] found out over the public address system. We have a legal team looking into it.' Axl then brought the ten-minute interview to a close by explaining sarcastically that he had to 'get down to soundcheck before they cancel the [next] show.'

In the days that followed, other radio stations were also approached to allow Axl to give his side of events, though the offer now came with a series of conditions. Namely, that the interviews would have to be pre-recorded in order for Axl to approve them first, and they would have to adhere to a strictly agreed list of questions in advance. The Vancouver riot was no longer to be discussed, unless Axl brought the subject up himself. Instead, potential interviewers were instructed to enquire about the current tour and/or the 'forthcoming' *Chinese Democracy* album – specifically what it was like to have spent time in Hong Kong and written songs there. Finally, the stations would not be allowed to preview or promote the possibility of an Axl interview until the singer had personally given the go-ahead.

Despite these draconian measures several stations submitted to them. Shrewdly, perhaps, as once he had a microphone in front of him Axl couldn't help but stray into several of those topics of conversation he may not have wanted to talk about. Like the ever-thorny subject of Slash. 'I wasn't gonna get in a one-on-one war with the old guys, because I thought all that would do was bring attention to their albums,' he told Michigan radio station WRIF. 'I didn't want that at all. The reality was that I was going to do most of Slash's songs, in particular, but every time we got halfway near something that [could] be successful it was backed away from. There was a lot of stress.'

'Izzy and those guys,' he continued, 'none of them wanted to do the big shows. From day one, Izzy wanted to be the size of the Ramones, doing like 2,000-seaters, so there was always a little battle there, and the other guys had to be on so many substances to be able to deal with that.' Though he did concede that 'Slash could play great guitar on a lot of drugs.'

He was also still happy to take potshots at his old band during the shows themselves. Halfway through a show in Albany, upstate New York on 27 November, he stopped to tell the audience: 'Truth is they didn't want to be here for you at this level. And they don't want to take it farther. I mean, that's their business, right? But not at my expense – or yours.' The rant became more incoherent as he slipped occasionally into what sounded like Eddie Murphy doing his 'banana in the tail pipe' routine from *Beverley Hills Cop*. 'You've been played,' he told the partly cheering, partly baffled audience. 'You've been lied to, you've been used, you've been manipulated. So that, you know, they can ride around in limos and jam with Snoop Dog or whoever the fuck, I don't care . . .' He stopped to take a drink, then began lumbering around the stage again, as if talking to himself. 'I'm sorry, you know, I'm a little bit more blunt. I mean, Slash may sound like the De La Hoya, but he's the fucking Vargas. That's just how it is. And just because you got a bunch of guys agreeing, doesn't mean shit. But the truth is, is that they're a bunch of bad cops, and I'm the fucking Serpico.' Then the pay-off: 'And they can suck my dick!'

Of course, the audience responded with more whoops and cheers, but it was unclear whether it was for the appearance of the word 'dick' or what Axl was actually saying. Encouraged, he continued, complaining about fans that said things like 'without Axl and Slash we wouldn't have "November Rain" and "Estranged". Well,' he said, 'you don't know what the fuck I went through to get that guy to play those songs. You don't know about the argument we had at [the] studios because Duff and Slash came to me going, "We're not gonna do that song, Axl. We're not gonna do this song. No, no, we're just not gonna do it." But I wanna do it. We'll do it right now . . .'

The band, unsure how to proceed, began tinkling out the intro to 'November Rain', and Axl thankfully responded by getting ready to sing again. Another sticky moment passed, for now . . .

The tour continued through out of the way places like Boise, Idaho and Fargo, North Dakota, before arriving on 5 December at its first high-profile stop: Madison Square Garden in New York. With all the tickets having sold out the day they went on sale, this was to be the first major highlight of the band's return to the American road, and a big party was planned afterwards, to which everybody connected with the tour, including several record company higher-ups, were invited.

As preparations for the party reached completion all seemed to be going well. From the Garden stage that night a plainly relieved Axl told the crowd: 'I managed to get enough of myself together to do this.' His good mood even continued after the show when he told everyone he met how much he had enjoyed it, saying it was 'as good as the band could get' and that it was 'time to cut our losses' and get on with things again – specifically, the rest of the US tour and the imminent release of the new album.

Later at the party, however, things took on a more familiar aspect. One of the MTV reps reportedly overheard Axl bawling out one of his backstage staff, as well as Doug Goldstein. Buckethead also seemed upset about something. One onlooker said of him and his girlfriend, 'I wouldn't say they were having a fight, I think she was trying to coax him into taking off that mask.' But to no avail.

The atmosphere continued to deteriorate when Axl and entourage left the party in the early hours and headed off for a new fashionable Manhattan nightclub called Spa, where Axl was refused entry apparently on the grounds that he was wearing fur, which the club did not allow. A blazing argument was said to have ensued with Axl flying into a rage when it became clear that no exception would be made for him, while at the same time absolutely refusing to comply with the club's rules and take off the offending coat. A stand-off was reached and a furious Axl eventually stormed off. He was so incensed, in fact, that he was still raging about it the next day.

The next stop should have been the First Union Center arena in Philadelphia, on 6 December. However, armed police were again called in to quell what threatened to turn into another riot among the 14,000-capacity crowd when it was announced at the last minute that the show would have to be cancelled due to the non-appearance of the entire band. The crowd started ripping up seats and hurling broken beer bottles almost as soon as the announcement was made. Though police made no reported arrests, the next day a spokesman for First Union Center explained the decision by saying they had received a phone call 'shortly after 11.00 p.m.' informing them that an unspecified band member had been 'taken ill' and that the group would therefore not be able to perform that night.

However, a long-time Guns N' Roses fan from Virginia named Bob, who'd been following the tour, later emailed the renowned *Metal Sludge* rock website to voice his own disappointment – and shed an interesting light on what in his opinion had really happened that night. According to Bob, he'd been waiting to get autographs all day outside the band's hotel in New York, and had personally witnessed everybody in the band – with the exception of Axl – leave the hotel at 2.30 p.m. and board the tour bus for the two-hour trip to Philadelphia. Hoping to get Axl's autograph, Bob hung around the hotel for the rest of the afternoon, waiting for his hero to leave. But Axl never showed and Bob finally gave up waiting at about 7.30 p.m.

Nevertheless, Bob and his companions drove down to Philly in the belief that 'Axl would hit the stage by 10.30 or 11.00 p.m., which is usual. Anyway, when we got there [at 10.00 p.m.] it was a war zone. People were leaving and the [venue] was about half full. People were booing, chanting "Axl sucks!"' When the cancellation announcement was made around 11.00 p.m., people on the floor started destroying chairs. That's kinda late to cancel a show. Security were getting bombarded by [beer] cups and trash.' There were nearly more serious consequences when several female ushers later claimed to have been threatened with rape by 'half-crazed' fans, as all around them thousands chanted: 'Axhole! Axhole!' Fortunately, most of the Union Center's female employees were well used to boisterous crowds of young men at rock concerts and so stood firm in the ensuing mêlée, while the rest were rushed to a designated 'safe area', protected by male colleagues. In all, fifteen people were reported injured that night, while the band's mixing desk was totally wrecked, the interior of one of the private boxes was badly vandalized and graffiti sprayed across the venue's walls.

Two days later, the *Philadelphia Inquirer* backed up the report made by Bob on *Metal Sludge*, revealing that Axl hadn't even checked into the city's Ritz Carlton Hotel. The article went on to claim that Axl had preferred to remain in his New York hotel suite watching a basketball game rather than leave with the others for the show. There was no way of knowing if this were true but, appalled by this, local Philadelphia radio station 93.3 WMMR announced they would be boycotting all Guns N' Roses music for the next three weeks, as well as pledging not to play any of the new material from *Chinese Democracy* – if and when it was released – until Axl called the station personally and apologized to fans on air.

From here on in the tour seemed doomed. Within days of the Philadelphia debacle, shows in Washington DC, Albuquerque, Phoenix, Sacramento and San José were also unceremoniously cancelled. While no further excuses or explanations were offered by the band, promoters Clear Channel publicly warned ticket-holders to expect more cancellations. It seemed only a matter of time before the announcement was made that the whole tour would be pulled – which it eventually was on 11 December.

Axl's first major tour with his new band had ended on a low note. A Clear Channel spokesman issued the following terse press statement: 'The remainder of the Guns N' Roses concert dates promoted by Clear Channel Entertainment have been cancelled. Refunds will be available at point of purchase. Clear Channel Entertainment takes pride in bringing live entertainment to the public. We apologize for any inconvenience to all the fans who purchased tickets.'

What had caused the tour to end in such a fashion? Predictably, in the absence of an explanation from Axl rumours flew. Behind the scenes even his new band now threatened mutiny, with insiders going so far as to suggest this latest calamity effectively marked the end of the current line-up. Stinson and Finck were rumoured to have already tendered their resignations, while Buckethead was also said to be seriously considering his options.

What the truth was, no one really knew. According to an unnamed official source quoted in the *New York Post*, prior to the tour the band were 'getting along better than ever because something was finally happening'. But once it seemed clear the whole thing was about to fall apart again, the band looked likely to split. Even long-term friends and family were said to be wringing their hands over this latest downturn in events.

Needless to say, *Chinese Democracy* was once again 'put on the backburner'. Some of the more outlandish rumours even suggested that Interscope might insist on Axl being given some enforced 'help' by bringing in a professional songwriting team, as contemporaries like Bon Jovi and Aerosmith routinely did.

Whatever the truth of that rumour, it is likely there was more than one person at Interscope who would have been glad to wash their hands of the whole mess, but the fact was that after investing eight years and more than $10 million, they simply couldn't afford not to have the album come out at some point.

With the new band said to be fracturing around him, there was even talk of a possible reunion with the original Guns N' Roses line-up. With Slash, Duff and Matt coincidentally back together in LA at that very moment, and said to be keen to work with each other again, could it be that just as the old band were beginning a search for a singer, Axl was about to become a singer in search of a band? If so, who better to approach than the very people with whom he'd first made it happen? It was even suggested in some quarters that the same therapist who had helped heal the apparently insurmountable rift between Jon Bon Jovi and his guitarist Richie Sambora (and before that Steven Tyler and Joe Perry) could be brought in to do the same thing for Axl and Slash.

For the time being, however, all the talk remained just that – talk. The reality was that, whatever his future plans, Axl's immediate problem was to stave off a messy lawsuit from his promoters, Clear Channel. Gary Bongiovanni, editor of the US concert industry publication *Pollstar*, said he believed that even if Axl won the battle in the short term, it was almost certainly too late to salvage his reputation in the business.

'Rose has damaged his career,' Bongiovanni told *Entertainment Weekly*. 'This makes the band a riskier situation for promoters in the future.' To illustrate his point he went on to say that, in terms of ticket sales, the tour hadn't performed as well as everyone expected. According to *Pollstar*, the initial ten shows sold an average of just 7,344 tickets a night, often in venues that held more than twice that number of people. Bongiovanni gloomily concluded that 'the 2002 Guns N' Roses is [no longer] an arena act.'

Meanwhile, back in Malibu, the rumour mill went into overdrive again. 'Sources say that Rose is very close to checking himself into a psychiatric clinic to deal with "exhaustion",' reported the *Chicago Sun-Times* in January 2003. Quoting another unnamed source, the paper went on: 'Famous for his outrageousness, the aging rocker lately has been "even more whacked than usual". The singer himself has openly admitted he's battling inner demons.'

Certainly, the next twelve months would prove a torrid time for Axl Rose. Not long after the tour ended, Doug Goldstein bailed out. Axl had talked about putting 'the final touches' to *Chinese Democracy* for four years; the last tour had ended in cancellations. And every time it was Doug who stood up and took the rap – from the fans, from the critics, from the record company bigwigs, even from those members of the band who were close enough to see what was going on and should have known better. Now he'd had enough.

Privately and very discreetly, he let it be known he wanted out. By the summer of 2003 he got his wish by selling his management contract to the British-based Sanctuary Group for a rumoured $8 million and immediately retiring from the business to play golf in Hawaii. After all those years at the band's beck and call, who could blame him?

The rest of 2003 was similarly shaky for the singer. In April, photographer Robert John sued him for allegedly refusing to honour an earlier contract in which he agreed to pay $80,000 for hundreds of photos of the band that John had taken since 1985. As an old friend of Axl's, dating back to the Hell House days, the embattled singer took this latest setback particularly hard: another betrayal by a formerly loyal 'soldier'. They settled out of court.

Then, on 19 June, came a possibly even bigger blow – when Slash, Duff and Matt played their first official show together in LA, at the El Rey Theater, with their new singer – former Stone Temple Pilots frontman Scott Weiland. The new band even had a name: Velvet Revolver. Following favourable reviews in *Rolling Stone* and *Spin*, they also had a whopping multi-million dollar record deal with RCA to go with it.

Meanwhile, his own band appeared to have scattered to the four winds. In July, Tommy Stinson began a short solo tour with a spate of well-received shows in New York. That same month, the first recording by Velvet Revolver – a prime slab of twenty-first-century rock called 'Set Me Free' – entered the Mainstream Rock Tracks chart in *Billboard* at number thirty. A fortnight later it entered the top ten. It may have been no coincidence that Axl also chose July as the month to 'preview' tracks from *Chinese Democracy* during a late-night visit to the Crazy Horse Too strip club in West Hollywood, handing the DJ the CD to play while he sat himself down at a table in the VIP area, sipping champagne and signing autographs for some of the dancers.

What Axl hadn't bargained for was some of the tracks being played in August, on the New York classic rock station 104.3, where its regular Friday-night DJ, Eddie Trunk, broadcast to great fanfare the song 'I.R.S.'. According to news reports Trunk claimed he was given it to play by Oakland Athletics baseball star Mike Piazza, a friend of Axl's who said the singer had given him a CD of the track as a gift. Piazza then gave the CD to Trunk, who played it in the early hours of the morning. The new management office put a call through to Trunk 'requesting' that he 'refrain' from airing the track again – on pain of a lawsuit.

Interscope, meanwhile, were still awaiting news on when the finished album would be delivered. They decided to take action. Desperate to claw back at least some of its eight-figure investment, in August 2003 label executives announced their intention to release a Guns N' Roses greatest hits collection. Axl instructed Sanctuary to block the release. Having spent so long putting the new band together, the last thing Axl wanted was a greatest hits album taking the shine off any release of *Chinese Democracy*

Sanctuary persuaded the company to hold back on the greatest hits package. But by January 2004 the greatest hits package was once again back on the schedule. With the label's patience now at an end, they wrote to Axl. The *New York Times* reported that the letter, dated 2 February 2004, informed him via his new management offices at Sanctuary that, 'having exceeded all budgeted and approved recording costs by millions of dollars', it was now 'Mr Rose's obligation to fund and complete the album, not Geffen's'.

Over the next few weeks the open tab at the recording studio was closed and the band's gear packed away. Then, on 15 March the *Guns N' Roses Greatest Hits* album was released. Despite the complete lack of promotion from any of the original band members, a month later the album racked up worldwide sales of over three million, eventually going to number one in Britain and nine other European countries. Released a week later in the US, it quickly sold 1.8 million copies, entering the *Billboard* Hot 100 album chart at number three.

As chance would have it, exactly a week later the current band announced the cancellation of an appearance scheduled for May at the fourth Rock In Rio festival, relocated this time to the Portuguese city of Lisbon. According to the official press release, the show was cancelled because Buckethead had left the band. True to form, Axl added his own familiar brand of intrigue to the announcement with a further press release headed: A Message from W. Axl Rose.

It began: 'The band has been put in an untenable position by guitarist Buckethead and his untimely departure. During his tenure with the band Buckethead has been inconsistent and erratic in both his behaviour and commitment – despite being under contract – creating uncertainty and confusion and making it virtually impossible to move forward with recording, rehearsals and live plans with confidence.' There was more: 'There is not a member of this camp that is not hurt, upset and ultimately disappointed by this event. Regardless of anyone's opinions of me and what I may or may not deserve, clearly the fans, individuals in this band, management, crew and our support group do not deserve this type of treatment. On behalf of Guns N' Roses and myself, I apologize to the fans who planned to see us at Rock in Rio.'

He ended with one last dig at Buckethead: 'It appears his plans were to secure a recording contract, quit GN'R and use his involvement in the upcoming Guns release to immediately promote his individual efforts.' However, there was light at the end of the tunnel: 'This unfortunate set of circumstances may have given us the opportunity to take our recording that one extra step further. Regardless we hope to announce a release date within the next few months. Sincerely, W. Axl Rose.'

By now the whole Guns N' Roses story was becoming so stretched few paid this latest development much notice. Certainly the press in Britain and America gave it scant attention. Instead, they were much more interested in the story that emerged the following month concerning the lawsuit against Axl that Slash and Duff filed at the Los Angeles Superior Court, claiming he'd failed to consult them before turning down several lucrative offers from movie companies wanting to use the old band's music in their films. They claimed that, contractually, Axl was obliged to consult them.

Allegedly disgruntled that they were deliberately kept in the dark about offers from the makers of movies such as *We Were Soldiers*, *Death To Smoochy*, *Old School* and *Just Married*, the suit went on to claim that Axl also killed off negotiations with producers of the 2001 blockbuster *Black Hawk Down*, who approached him about using 'Welcome To The Jungle' on the soundtrack. Axl denied all the charges and set his own lawyers on the case.

But further ignominy from his former band mates was to come when the debut Velvet Revolver album, *Contraband*, was released in June – and promptly sold more than 250,000 copies in the US in its first week, making it the fastest selling debut album in American rock history, and sending it straight to number one! For the first time since they'd fought over the material on the two *Use Your Illusion* albums, it suddenly appeared as though Slash and Duff had the upper hand.

As the summer progressed the band set out on their own mammoth world tour, selling out arenas and making headlines everywhere they went. Publicly, Axl said nothing. Privately, did their success fill him with fear and envy? Axl may have been rash but he wasn't stupid. Surely he knew the success of Velvet Revolver threw his own attempts to reactivate Guns N' Roses into even more stark relief. Slash, Duff and Matt were now the architects of their own potential year-zero, giving the fans exactly what they really wanted: classic Guns N' Roses.

On 5 July, when VH1 – the adult offshoot of MTV – broadcast a programme in its popular series, *Behind The Music*, all about the band Axl had spent so many years trying to revive and keep cutting edge, he was nowhere to be seen – aside from the same old video clips the station had been running for years. All the new material and the best quotes and interviews came from Slash, Steven, Gilby and Matt and all the other people who were no longer part of the Guns N' Roses story.

There was one special mention reserved for Axl's new Guns N' Roses line-up, though. It came right at the end of the programme when it was announced that their first album together, *Chinese Democracy*, would be released in November that year.

Chapter Eleven

COLD BLACK CLOUD COMIN' DOWN

In September 2005, an internet rumour began circulating that Axl Rose had taken time to speak to the gaggle of fans who still kept a twenty-four-hour vigil outside the electric gates of his Malibu mansion. Nothing too unusual there: although he tended to sweep past them on the rare occasions he actually left the house, very occasionally he would roll down the window of his silver Ferrari and instruct Earl, his bodyguard, to allow the fans to approach for a few moments. Often all they wanted was for him to autograph their old copies of *Appetite For Destruction* or *Use Your Illusion II*. This was different, though. This time, Axl was the one who instigated the conversation, going outside and pointedly giving them the news they'd waited so long to hear: that *Chinese Democracy* – the album now over a decade in the making at a reported cost of over $13 million – would finally be released a few months later, at the start of 2006. Not only that, but a track from it would be featured on the soundtrack of the forthcoming movie version of the best-selling book *The Da Vinci Code*.

Although the rumour was never officially verified, Guns N' Roses manager at Sanctuary, Merck Mercuriadis, refused to deny it and by December whispers were emanating within the music business that steps were finally being taken behind the scenes to release the album in the New Year. Of course, as we now know, that wasn't to be. Just like dozens of other murmurs of the album's imminent release this one turned out to be no more than wishful thinking.

Unlike all previous rumours, however, this one persisted throughout 2006, starting with Axl's surprise appearance in the early hours of the morning at the launch party in January for

American post-grunge band Korn's latest tour, where he told a reporter from *Rolling Stone*: 'We're working on thirty-two songs, and twenty-six are nearly done.' Of the completed tracks, he added, thirteen would be included on *Chinese Democracy* and the rest on two subsequent 'sequels'. He even named his favourite tracks: 'Better', 'There Was A Time' and 'The Blues'.

Dressed in a Toronto Maple Leafs' jersey, and a large ornate cross hanging from his neck, he puffed on a cigar and insisted: 'People will hear music this year. It's a very complex record. I'm trying to do something different. Some of the arrangements are kind of like Queen. Some people are going to say, "It doesn't sound like Axl Rose, it doesn't sound like Guns N' Roses." But you'll like at least a few songs on there.'

Even Slash, of all people, said in an interview that same month with Virgin Radio in London that he'd heard the album, 'sounds great' and that it was finally 'coming out in March'. While the album wasn't released in March, at least four tracks – 'T.W.A.T.', 'The Blues', 'I.R.S.' and 'Better' – were played on the internet over the weekend of 4 and 5 March. A rumoured fourteen-track running order for the album was also put online: 'Chinese Democracy', 'This I Love', 'I.R.S.', 'Thyme', 'Substitute', 'The General', 'Seven', 'Madagascar', 'Ides Of March', 'Catcher In The Rye', 'Leave Me Alone', 'The Blues', 'Closing In On You' and 'T.W.A.T.' As a result, 'I.R.S.' was added, briefly, to the rotation of several US radio stations, with enough of them playing it to propel the song to number forty-nine on the trade magazine *Radio & Records*' Active Rock National Airplay chart for a week, before Axl's management team intervened.

The same month Axl's lawyer, Howard Weitzman, released a statement to the media in which he said that Slash had 'made an unannounced 5.30 a.m. visit' to Axl's home back in October 2005. He went on: 'Not appearing to be under the influence, Slash came to inform Axl that: "Duff was spineless," "Scott Weiland was a fraud," he "hates Matt Sorum" and that in this ongoing war, contest or whatever anyone wants to call it that Slash has waged against Axl for the better part of twenty years, that Axl has proven himself "the stronger". Based on his conduct in showing up at

Rose's home, Axl was hopeful that Slash would live up to his pronouncements that he wanted to end the war and move on with life. Unfortunately that did not prove to be the case.'

Singer Scott Weiland issued a vehement reply via the official Velvet Revolver website just four days later. To wit: 'Get in the ring . . . How many albums have you put out, man, and how long did it take the current configuration of this so-called "band" to make this album? How long? And without the only guys that validated the name [Guns N' Roses]. How dare you! Shame on you! How dare you call our bass player "spineless". We toured [the Velvet Revolver] album over a year and a half. How many shows have you played over the last ten years? Oh, that's right – you bailed out on your long awaited comeback tour, leaving your remaining fans feeling shall we say a trifle miffed?! I won't even list what I've accomplished because I don't need to.'

Even singer Mike Patton – whose band, Faith No More, toured with Guns N' Roses in 1992 – had a public dig when he smirked that Axl's hair looked 'like a bad reggae wig'. Slash later made a less hot-headed denial of the Howard Weitzman story in an interview in May with the Camp Freddy radio show on US station Indie 1031 FM. 'I'm not gonna go into the whole long thing [but] a lot of this stuff was built to promote the next Guns record and the tour and all that kind of stuff . . . this blatantly fabricated thing in there that I'd gone to his house and that he and I had a conversation in which I said all this stuff about my band-mates. And it's just blatantly untrue. For one, I have not talked to the guy in any way, shape or form since 1996, so it's going on eleven years. So that's basically it. There's just no truth to it . . .'

So who is right? Only the participants in this drama can know the full story. In the background of this public spat was the fact that Slash and Duff had, earlier in 2005, instigated another potentially even more damaging legal action than the one in which they sought damages for Axl's refusal to consult them over the use – or not – of the GN'R back catalogue in several different movies.

When it was announced in January 2005 that Axl had signed a new multi-million dollar publishing deal with the Sanctuary Group – the umbrella company of his management team – including sizeable advances for rights to the band's back catalogue, Duff's lawyer Glen Miskel admitted he was shocked to hear about the deal, saying, 'Neither Sanctuary nor Axl Rose have provided the remaining partners with a copy of that agreement' and accusing Axl of attempting to claim copyright over songs which were 'not owned by Mr Rose'.

The result, some months later, was a joint federal lawsuit from Slash and Duff accusing Axl of changing the publisher of their jointly owned copyrighted songs without their consent. As a result, they sought damages for 'fraud, copyright infringement and breach of fiduciary duty'. The suit also claimed that neither Slash nor Duff was even aware of the situation until royalty payments they were expecting had failed to arrive. Miskel told MTV News: 'When the ASCAP cheque didn't come, we called and they looked into it. We didn't know all the facts at first.' The lawsuit went on to claim that 'Rose's actions were malicious, fraudulent and oppressive, and undertaken in conscious disregard of property rights.'

Howard Weitzman launched his defence against Slash and Duff's joint lawsuit by filing a counterclaim, on Axl's behalf, asking the Federal Court to officially confirm the singer's ownership of 'his own creative works'. In a press release, as reported by the *Los Angeles Business Wire* on 6 March 2006, Weitzman claimed: 'Mr Rose believes that once apprised of the true facts the Judge or Jury deciding these lawsuits will rule in Axl's favour on every issue before them.' And that 'the Federal lawsuit Hudson and McKagan filed was based on a faulty premise from the start. What Hudson and McKagan attempted to portray as egregious misconduct by Axl was in fact – as Slash and Duff have learned – nothing more than a clerical error committed by ASCAP. Had Slash and Duff or their representatives bothered to pick up the phone the clerical error could have been easily sorted out without the need for filing an utterly baseless lawsuit which one can only assume had been filed for the purposes of self-publicity at Axl's expense.'

Weitzman went on to claim that 'Axl has at all times worked diligently to maintain the artistic integrity of the band' and '[taken] the high road in the face of Slash and Duff's attacks.'

Weitzman concluded: 'Axl regrets having to spend time and energy on these distractions but he has a responsibility to protect the Guns N' Roses legacy and expose the truth. Axl believes he has been left with no alternative but to respond to these lawsuits. It would have been Axl's preference to resolve disputes with Slash and Duff in private. The courthouse is not his choice of forum. However, Axl could no longer sit quietly and allow the continuing dissemination of falsehoods and half-truths by his former band-mates.'

While the lawyers continued to do battle in LA, Axl moved his operation to New York where he took over an entire floor, including suites for his entourage, at the mega-expensive Trump Tower Hotel. Often seen hanging out at late-late clubs like Stereo in the Chelsea district, which only gets going at 4.00 a.m. – the same time most New York nightclubs usually close – he treated patrons to a sneak unofficial preview of *Chinese Democracy* when he turned up out of the blue at 5.30 one morning, a few days before his forty-fourth birthday in February.

According to club owners Barry Mullineaux and Mike Satsky, Axl was enjoying himself so much he sent a minion back to the Trump to pick up two private CD copies of the album, each containing ten tracks. 'He was talking with everybody freely about how he's been off for ten years, and how even though Slash and the rest of the guys [had started] Velvet Revolver, he's been holding back,' recalled Mullineaux. 'He was freely answering questions about his work, the band, what happened with the split [with the original line-up], the direction he's headed in – and the music sounded great.' Mullineaux went on to claim that many of the tracks sounded like classic Guns N' Roses. He said that Axl 'kept telling me to put back track number three – I guess that was his favourite song. He wanted to play that one over and over, like six times. He was really getting into it and rockin' out. Everybody was surprised at how good it sounded. And that third track, that was the song where his voice sounded the best, the smoothest.'

It was also during his extended stay in New York that Axl bumped into Matt Sorum for the first time in years, at a private party they both happened to attend. 'I hadn't seen him in at least six years,' Matt later wrote on his website. 'I walked over and said "Hello". We shook hands and it was pleasant. Later that evening, I ended up in a loft somewhere in the East Village where Axl was again. We spoke for quite some time, and it was nice to clear some things up. I told him how great of a frontman he was while I was in the band and no hard feelings from me at all. It was an all-round good vibe, I think.'

As a result, it came as no big surprise locally when it was announced in May that Guns N' Roses would be playing four warm-up shows at the modest, 2,000-capacity Hammerstein Ballroom on West 34th Street in preparation for a full European tour in the summer, including a headline appearance in Britain at the annual Download festival in June – preceded a few days before by a further warm-up show at London's Hammersmith Apollo, and followed by more dates in July, including two shows, in Nuremberg and Leipzig, opening for the Rolling Stones (later cancelled after the well-publicized head injury Keith Richards suffered while on holiday). What was less expected was that Axl would show up on New York DJ Eddie Trunk's syndicated Saturday night radio show to publicize the gigs – and then proclaim that *Chinese Democracy* would finally be released 'sometime this fall or late fall. It will be out this year.'

The first radio interview Axl had given since the debacle of the curtailed 2002 US tour, it began when guest host, former Skid Row singer Sebastian Bach, called Axl on his cellphone and broadcast the subsequent conversation live on air. With the sound of the band rehearsing in the background, Seb took the bold step of inviting Axl to swing by the studio. To everyone's surprise, an hour later he did. While he was there Trunk asked why the original 2002 comeback tour had ended so badly. Axl refused to elaborate but insisted, however, that it hadn't caused him any regrets as the dates the band did play helped the new line-up to bond. The real comeback, he insisted, would begin with the forthcoming shows at the Hammerstein.

'Can you tell people why the tour ended at that point?' asked Trunk.

'Umm, no, not exactly,' Axl replied, refusing to add anything further.

Behind this relaxed facade, however, new tensions were mounting. With the recalcitrant Buckethead resisting all attempts to lure him back, Axl had initially been content to continue the band with just Robin Finck and Richard Fortus, but the closer they came to the four Hammerstein shows, the twitchier Axl grew about going out without a recognized guitar 'shredder'.

Eventually, it was decided Axl would get his own way and add a third guitarist to the band. Tour manager Rick Fagin was also apparently the recipient of a new addition to his team: a new 'assistant' in the shape of Axl's old friend Del James, a survivor of the Hell House days.

Although the new guitarist's name was only officially revealed onstage by Axl halfway through the first Hammerstein show on 12 May, it came as no surprise to insiders that the gig should go to New Yorker Ron 'Bumblefoot' Thal – a virtuoso guitarist and composer, known for his 'fusion' playing (once described as a heavy metal Frank Zappa). Thal had already admitted some weeks before that he'd auditioned for the band but got his wrist slapped for doing so by their management, at which point it seemed he'd blown his chances. Then, just a few days before the Hammerstein shows, he announced on his website the cancellation of several live solo dates that would have conflicted with the Hammerstein shows, and put up a message asking fans not to 'speculate' as they would 'find out why soon'.

Come the day of the first show, rumours about a new guitarist reached such a dizzying peak there was talk of Izzy Stradlin having rejoined the band, the result of Axl hinting broadly on the Trunk show that Izzy might be putting in an appearance at some point during the Hammerstein run. Rumour turned to fantasy among the crowd outside the Hammerstein ballroom that first night, with many fans talking excitedly about the possibility of both Slash and Duff having secretly signed on.

In fact, with the exception of the Bumblefoot/Buckethead

swap, the band that took to the stage to deafening cheers at just after 11.00 p.m. – an hour and fifteen minutes later than advertised – was almost identical to the line-up that had ground to such an ignominious halt three-and-a-half years before: Axl on vocals and occasional keyboards, guitarists Finck, Bumblefoot and Fortus, bassist Tommy Stinson, keyboardists Dizzy Reed and Chris Pittman and drummer 'Brain' Mantia. Huddled in the roped-off VIP area were stars headed by Sebastian Bach, Limp Bizkit frontman Fred Durst, Lenny Kravitz and actor Ethan Hawke.

Looking at images of the cramped stage you got the feeling that Axl was determined to cram the whole arena-sized show into it. Red arc lights shot out from both sides of the stage as dry ice flooded the room; long vertical, cream-coloured GN'R banners with a new Chinese font draped the backdrop and various flash-bombs and storms of confetti exploded throughout.

The first song, predictably, was 'Welcome To The Jungle' and as soon as the ringing guitar lines began echoing round the hall people started going crazy. 'I wanna hear you scream!' Axl roared unnecessarily. Old favourites 'It's So Easy' and 'Mr Brownstone' followed. The songs sounded more or less how everyone remembered them but of course the whole thing looked so different now. Finck had a full beard, while Fortus looked like any other guy in a band. Only Buckethead's replacement, Bumblefoot, made any real impact. Armed with an equally silly name as his predecessor, he also displayed an array of equally silly gimmicks, replacing the Kentucky Fried Chicken bucket with a bumblebee-coloured, foot-shaped guitar. While Axl looked exactly like what he was now: an older guy singing a younger man's songs. Not quite as grizzled as, say, Mick Jagger or Robert Plant but definitely carrying more weight than when he first performed this material twenty years before. Dressed in designer shades and battered blue jeans, a black leather shirt unbuttoned to the waist to reveal a large silver crucifix, his lush gold-coloured dreadlocks tied back in a ponytail.

At forty-four, and giving his first live performance for nearly four years, it was perhaps unfair to expect him to be at his best. Sure enough, over the course of the four shows he started to pace himself and find his voice more consistently.

According to *Variety*, the new numbers in the set 'ran the gamut from gripping to baffling'. 'Better' fell into the latter category. Though Axl and the band attacked the new numbers enthusiastically enough, when they then kicked into 'Sweet Child O' Mine', however, there was no coaxing necessary; the place exploded. 'Knockin' On Heaven's Door' – 'This is about a place I've been one too many times,' Axl announced melodramatically – followed to similarly predictable acclaim. *Night After Night* magazine also noted that audience reaction noticeably cooled again during the second new number of the night, 'Madagascar', at the end of which Axl introduced the band by name – the first chance the audience had to discover who the new third guitarist was.

The moment was quickly forgotten, as Brain's galloping drums signalled the intro to 'You Could Be Mine'. Once again, the mood was dissipated when they segued into a solo spot from Dizzy, which eventually led into another new number, 'The Blues'. The remainder of the set followed the same pattern, not surprisingly given the crowd's familiarity with the old material compared to the new. 'Out Ta Get Me' was received like a long lost friend; Bumblefoot's guitar solo, which followed, was treated to polite applause. Despite the video backdrops featuring the usual quasi-religious symbols, Martin Luther King speeches and so on, to some most of the new stuff sounded self-important. The *New York Times* described it as 'dystopian, tense . . . electronic rhythms, big keyboard sounds and droning repetition.'

It was after midnight by the time Axl seated himself at the piano for a typically overwrought stab at 'November Rain'. The audience-reaction needle went into red again when Sebastian Bach joined him onstage for 'My Michelle'. One moment of levity occurred between the last of the new songs – 'Chinese Democracy' and 'There Was A Time' – when Axl cried: 'I see you people singing the new songs. You downloaded them, fuckers!' He added, comically: 'You can hold your breath a lot longer than David Blaine. I want to thank you for that . . .'

The finale of the show was, again, a question of contrasts: a wonderfully evocative 'Patience' followed by the intense and gripping 'I.R.S.', which led into a second extended guitar break from Bumblefoot, culminating in a steaming version of 'Nightrain'. The predictable 'Paradise City' encore found Axl diving into the audience before being quickly fished out again by the massed ranks of security men patrolling the lip of the stage. And that was it – show over. Nobody really knew what to make of the new material since it was the first time most of them had heard it, despite the jokes about illegal downloads.

Would the other three shows be the same? Yes, almost identical in fact, except for the second show they added 'Rocket Queen' to the set, with Sebastian Bach once again invited to duet with Axl. Ticket demand was also less heated: *Rolling Stone* reported that touts were now offering 'last-minute' prices of $30-a-ticket.

'Happy Mother's Day, motherfuckers!' crowed Axl from the stage that night. He also dedicated the show to his own late mother, Sharon, as well as Sebastian Bach, who he said he hadn't spoken to for thirteen years before the other night.

Of the four shows, one of the highlights came during the last on 17 May, when Izzy did finally show up, joining Axl onstage where the two men embraced before the band ripped into 'Think About You', followed by 'Patience' during which Izzy wiped tears from his eyes, followed by 'Nightrain' featuring a preening Kid Rock. Axl tried to preface Izzy's arrival with a little speech but his words were drowned out by the screams from the audience as his old school pal sauntered onto the stage.

Izzy would be a recurring fixture of the subsequent tour. His solo career had hardly kept him over-busy and mutual friends claimed he was simply happy to play.

The following night the band (minus Brain, whose drums weren't needed, and the still clean-living Izzy, who had gone to bed) put in a surprise appearance at the newly opened Plumm club on West 14th Street, in the heart of New York's fashionable Meatpacking District. The occasion was the twenty-seventh birthday party for TV actress Rosario Dawson, star of *Rent* and *Alexander*. The unexpected surprise: a 'secret' acoustic set by Guns N' Roses.

A small venue holding less than a thousand people, its two

floors were packed with guests. It may have been a secret but word among the cognoscenti was obviously out. Spotted lurking in the crowd were Dawson's boyfriend and *Sex And The City* star Jason Lewis, Lenny Kravitz, Kid Rock, Mickey Rourke, Mischa Barton, Peter Beard, Molly Simms, Damon Dash, Ann Dexter Jones, Wentworth Miller, Lydia Hearst and several other famous New York faces – many of whom had also attended the launch of the Plumm's new weekly 'Incubator' night earlier that evening – co-hosted by Yellow Fever designer Jamison Ernest and Warner Music Group executive Todd Moscowitz.

There was the predictable commotion when Axl arrived, surrounded by the usual throng of bodyguards, assistants and hangers-on. Making his way slowly to his own private booth, an even bigger commotion suddenly broke out when fashion designer Tommy Hilfiger appeared to start a fight with him. The trouble began, according to Axl, after he moved a drink belonging to Hilfiger's girlfriend, Dee Ocleppo, so that it wouldn't get spilled. At which point Hilfiger went ballistic and started 'smacking' him. Speaking to LA radio station KROQ the next day, Axl said, 'He just kept smacking me . . . It was the most surreal thing, I think, that's ever happened to me in my life.'

Axl also said he thought the Plumm show was the smartest thing he'd done in ten years, comparing it to when Guns N' Roses had played at the famous new wave club, CBGB in 1987. He was also asked about the New York shows and whether it was true *Chinese Democracy* would finally be coming out later that year? 'Yes,' Axl said. 'Absolutely.'

Talking the next day to the *New York Daily News*, Hilfiger said: 'I'm not a fighter. I was just protecting myself. [Axl] was being rude and obnoxious, and I just told him to cool it. I went after him before he could get me . . .' Hilfiger's brother Michael H. tried to calm things down by claiming the pair hadn't recognized each other. However, earlier reports claimed Hilfiger disliked Axl because he'd been dating his brother's ex-wife, the model Diana O'Connor, during his stay in New York. Not so, said Michael, who claimed that he and Tommy were in fact good friends with Axl and Diana, and that he was 'happy for them to be in a relationship'. He added: 'I don't think Axl knew it was Tommy and I don't think Tommy knew it was Axl. But by the time they realized it, the fuse was already lit – and you can't put out the fuse on dynamite.' Claims backed up by the fact that Richard Fortus also played occasionally in Michael H.'s part-time band, the Bashers. 'I've seen Axl and my ex-wife practically every night for the past two weeks,' Michael said, 'and we're all cool. I'm sure that he and Tommy will make up over a drink or dinner someday.'

After the fight, Axl was overheard saying, 'I didn't even know who he was, but he was a complete psycho bitch!' He also took the time to fill out a police report. Lenny Kravitz left after the fight, possibly because he was a friend of Hilfiger's, while Kid Rock stood around looking nonplussed smoking a huge cigar and knocking back shots. He seemed more concerned that he hadn't been onstage again at the final Hammerstein show.

An hour later, things had just started to calm down when all hell broke loose again as Axl led the band onto the stage, which was so small and cramped that when the audience surged forward several tables were overturned, the floor suddenly awash with spilt beer and champagne. Then an unusually relaxed and smiling Axl looked around at the giant-sized TV monitor at the back of the stage with all the lyrics flashed up on it and jokingly described what they were about to do as the 'karaoke version' of Guns N' Roses.

Beginning at around 1.15 a.m. the set was arguably better and certainly less tense than any of the Hammerstein shows. They began with some older tunes from *GN'R Lies* that they hadn't done since the days of the original line-up, which Axl said they'd learned in just twenty minutes before going onstage. They also threw in a couple of new numbers. When it came to 'I.R.S.' Axl turned to the band and asked if they felt like giving it a go even though they hadn't rehearsed it, to which Tommy Stinson cried out, 'I'm fucking fearless, I'll try anything!'

Axl dedicated 'You're Crazy' to 'my good friend Tommy Hilfiger'. They also did a surprisingly moving version of 'November Rain', for which Robin did an electric solo. They eventually played for over an hour, zipping through 'Used To Love Her', 'Mr Brownstone', 'Welcome To The Jungle', 'Patience', 'Knockin' On Heaven's Door', 'The Blues', 'I.R.S.', 'Sweet Child O' Mine' and 'Paradise City', the crowd lapping up every minute.

When it was over, Axl jumped up to say, 'I forgot to do something because I'm a fuckin' idiot.' He then introduced Rosario Dawson onto the stage before leading everyone in the room to sing 'Happy Birthday' to her. Afterwards, Dawson grabbed the mike and shouted: 'They've never played all acoustic, this is history in the making! How much does this man fucking rock!'

Shortly afterwards, Axl and his entourage – including Kid Rock, Mickey Rourke, Lindsay Lohan and photographer Peter Beard – moved on to Stereo where they grooved to an after-hours set by cult underground turntable-spinner A.M., featuring a brief spot from Kid Rock, who got up and rapped over a special remix of The Who's 'Eminence Front'. Axl finally left the club at around eight o'clock the following morning. Some even claimed he was smiling as he stepped into his stretch limo for the short hop back to his suite at the Trump.

Although the incident with Hilfiger was gleefully reported around the world, reviews of the New York shows were mixed. Typical of the comments made was the notice in the *New York Times* which asked, 'What does [Axl] represent, at this stage of the game? Survival? Re-invention? Creative control? The tortured artist? The persistence of the yowl?' – before concluding: 'If the spirit of his age resides in him, his long postponement of an infamous album has diluted that spirit somewhat.' While *VH1.com* described Axl scampering 'around the stage like a schizophrenic with a hard-to-reach back itch, defying the extra poundage he's visibly added. However, his voice isn't what it once was.'

If Axl thought his US critics were overly harsh, the reception their British and European counterparts held in store for him was even more heated. As was the reaction of a great many of the audiences, particularly in Britain, starting at the Hammersmith Apollo on 7 June, where controversy raged after the band failed to come onstage until nearly 11.00 p.m. As reported in the

Observer, the booing began in earnest at 10 p.m. and got louder by 10.30 p.m. Younger crowd members were forced to leave early by irate parents not wanting to miss the last train or bus home. However, once the band hit the stage, the review continued, 'The ensuing two hours cancel out the pain of the last two. Much of the continuing pleasure of tonight's triumphant show, heavy on hits and explosions, derives from seeing Axl Rose in such fine fettle.'

The subsequent review in *The Times* was typical of the generally more sardonic media response. 'Rose appears very much at home as the grand rock showman,' it began, 'except for his red and yellow dreadlocks and ginger facial hair; they merely make him look like a cross between Mick Hucknall and Metallica's James Hetfield.'

The review in the *Telegraph* also noted how 'even after three songs, Rose seemed to be out of puff.' It also noted 'the irony' in the fact that the show closed, just before 1.00 a.m., with 'Nightrain', as 'the last rail service from these parts had departed ages ago.'

While Axl was in London he also experienced again the indiscreet charms of the British tabloids. No longer concerned with his so-called bad boy image, they now focused on his relationships with famous women. In this case, the suggestion of a one-night stand with model turned reality TV star – and reformed cocaine addict – Sophie Anderton. The pair reportedly met at Anderton's twenty-ninth birthday party at London's Boujis Club, with Sunday newspaper the *People* quoting a source as saying: 'Sophie and Axl are like chalk and cheese, but they couldn't resist each other. Everyone was a bit surprised to see them get it on – but they just clicked right away.' Who knows if this was true.

A few days after the London show came the band's headline appearance at the Download Festival, on the same site that once housed the Donington Monsters of Rock Festival where two fans died during the band's show eighteen years before. As if to confound his critics, instead of arriving late onstage, Axl and crew actually managed to appear thirty minutes earlier than advertised for Download. Although one reason Axl went onstage so early may be because he'd arrived at the festival site much earlier than planned after management arranged for him to visit the Formula One race taking place at Silverstone that same day. Maybe, as one insider speculated, 'It was a shrewd move because it meant that for once Axl wasn't on his own time for a gig. Silverstone is halfway between London and Donington anyway so after the race they just carried on up the motorway. Once he was actually there, Axl decided he may as well just go onstage – which is exactly what his management were banking on.'

Unfortunately, Axl coming on early was about the only thing that did go well that day. Clips on YouTube show that after the band took to the stage sections of the 59,000-strong crowd began hurling plastic bottles towards the stage. According to the *Leicester Mercury*, a water bottle filled with urine smacked Tommy Stinson on the head. Instead of hurling back some abuse of his own, as would have been expected at almost any other show, Axl seemed taken aback at the prospect of facing such a hostile crowd. Mumbling something about 'technical difficulties', he twice left the stage halfway through a song – the second time after slipping over during 'Sweet Child O' Mine', leaving the band to try and fill the gap by playing an impromptu instrumental version of 'Don't Cry'. At one point Tommy Stinson tried to intervene, threatening to leave if the crowd didn't stop throwing bottles. To which sections began shouting 'Fuck off then!' and 'Pussy!'

When Axl threatened to vacate the stage for a third and final time after new number 'Better', the bottle-throwing section of the crowd just continued to boo and jeer. Even the arrival onstage of Izzy – for 'Patience', 'Nightrain' and 'Used To Love Her' – and Sebastian Bach for 'My Michelle' didn't help, and again witnesses reported seeing people leaving the show early. The subsequent 0/5 review in *Kerrang!* reflected the disastrous nature of the gig.

After the show, Axl was beside himself with rage. Nobody could console him, everybody felt his wrath before he angrily jumped into the limo and ordered it to take him to the nearby airfield where a private plane was waiting to fly him back to London.

Returning to his Knightsbridge hotel, the Mandarin Oriental, in the early hours of the morning, he went straight to the bar and began drinking. Joining him was his old friend Lars Ulrich of Metallica and his latest girlfriend, Danish actress Connie Nielsen. Jon Bon Jovi, who was in town for shows of his own, also joined them for a drink.

After that, the tour left for Europe where the pattern of late arrivals onstage continued. At the Paris show on 20 June Axl came on almost two-and-a-half hours late, at which point the crowd was in an agitated state. The next show in Zurich was cancelled, according to an official press statement because drummer Brain had to return to America where his pregnant wife was having their baby earlier than expected.

A replacement, Frank Ferrer – an old friend of guitarist Richard Fortus' from his previous band, Love Spit Love – was flown out to take Brain's place in time for the Graspop Festival in Belgium on 24 June, while the cancelled Zurich show was hastily rescheduled for 1 July.

Then, on 27 June, came the most bizarre moment of the tour when Axl was arrested in Stockholm after an early-morning fracas at the band's hotel following their show at the 13,000-capacity Globe Arena the night before. Earlier, the band had attended a party at the Café Opera nightclub. When Axl made his entrance at 2.20 a.m., he was immediately surrounded by a bevy of leather-clad blonde females and figures from the local Stockholm music scene, including members of Ace Of Base, Backyard Babies and the Poodles.

According to Swedish newspaper *Espressen*, Axl had been involved in a dispute with the media prior to the concert, refusing to allow pictures to be taken during the show unless the photographers signed away their copyright to the band's management. Given this ultimatum, most Swedish photographers decided to boycott the concert. The Swedish reviewers were similarly unimpressed, *Espressen* calling it 'an OK joke. No more, no less.' Axl, needless to say, had a different viewpoint. 'It was a fantastic show. The Swedish fans were wonderful,' he told a reporter from daily paper *Aftonbladet*, as he tucked into one of the things he'd demanded at the party – Jack Daniel's. Axl had apparently also specifically asked to meet blonde Swedish girls: a request publicized in the local media. 'Yeah, I like it,' he said, as he sat down between two blondes and lit up a cigarette, in defiance of the smoking ban in bars and restaurants in Sweden. According to another guest, female Swedish TV presenter Gry Forssell, 'Axl was in a great mood. He was dancing, drinking and he was surrounded by girls. He gave me a shot and seemed to be having a very pleasant night.'

The trouble began when the party moved on to a large private house. By now there were only a handful of blondes left in a roomful of several dozen men. Axl ordered his entourage back to the Berns Hotel, where he was booked into their largest most plush suite. But still he was restless, and decided 'We're leaving! Get the taskforce!' The taskforce being the aircrew that flew the private jet Axl was ferried around in. But it was now almost dawn and everyone was sleeping. Instead, Axl went down to the lobby. According to Axl he was talking to Beta when security started giving them a hard time. Press reports described him as arguing, at which point the hotel security guard, an off-duty cop, felt impelled to intervene, wrestling Axl into a headlock. In response, Axl bit the guard on the leg so badly he later had to be taken to a nearby hospital where he was given a tetanus injection.

The hotel reception staff pushed the panic button and called in the police who arrived just before 7.30 a.m. as Axl was throwing a vase at the large wall mirror, shattering it.

The police wrestled him to the ground, then arrested him, put him in cuffs and marched him with his arms pinned behind his back out of the hotel and into their waiting squad car.

Tove Hägg, one of the arresting officers, told journalists Axl was being charged with damaging property, assaulting a security guard and threatening police in the squad car on the way to the station. Or as his fellow arresting officer, Fredrik Nylén, put it: 'He was aggressive and acting out.' Nylén added that in Sweden, 'threatening a police officer is punishable by jail time'.

While they waited for Axl's manager Merck to locate a suitable local lawyer the police decided to take a blood sample. When Axl initially resisted he was told he could either submit voluntarily or that it would be taken forcibly.

A furious Axl was then placed in a cell. Still he wouldn't calm down so they locked the door and left him to sleep it off. A lawyer was hired a few hours later. The situation must have been hitting home to the now sober singer. Found guilty of 'violent conduct', Axl could have faced up to four years in prison. Even the lesser 'misdemeanour' charge carried a maximum penalty of six months in prison. In the event, after admitting the charges, he was fined 40,000 kronor (approximately £3,000) and released some twelve hours later. He was also ordered to pay 10,000 kronor (approximately £750) in damages to the security guard.

But the nightmare didn't end there. With the hotel refusing to take him back and no other five-star hotel in Stockholm apparently willing to allow him through its doors either, Axl was boarded his private plane and flew direct that night to the tour's next destination: Oslo. On arrival there, however, he decided he'd had enough of hotels and decided that a suitable apartment should be found for him.

There must have been a temptation to cancel the show and move on, but in the event it went ahead as planned. As ever, the band came on late and the show didn't finish until almost 1.00 a.m. The day after the Oslo show Merck put out a press release claiming Axl only admitted to the 'violent conduct' charge in Stockholm in order to avoid cancelling the rest of the tour. The Swedish authorities, he said, 'continually threatened us over a twelve-hour period with between five days and three weeks incarceration without bail if Axl did not "co-operate". They were fully aware that there were millions of dollars at stake, not to mention the hopes of tens of thousands of fans who had paid for tickets to see Guns N' Roses.' He described the experience as 'tantamount to being held for ransom. If the context were any different, Axl would probably have preferred to spend the time in jail in order to ensure that all the facts were a matter of public record.'

In his own separate press release, Axl claimed: 'We had a great gig in Stockholm and I am not going to let this incident spoil that. My assistant Beta and I were talking in the lobby of the hotel when the security started to give us a hard time. My only concern was to make sure she was okay.'

There was clearly now a feeling building up around every Guns N' Roses show that things were not always quite what they seemed. After the show in Spain, the influential newspaper *El Diario Vasco* talked of '*una bullanguera formación de mercenarios al servicio del ego del vocalista*', which roughly translates as: 'a noisy bunch of mercenaries in the service of the vocalist's ego'. The Spanish press also talked about the endless Nigel Tufnelesque '*solos absurdos*' each of the band members go through every night.

The Spanish press also started a rumour about one of the strangest, yet largely unreported, aspects of the new show – Axl's frequent disappearances offstage, which they claimed were because he entered an oxygen chamber backstage from which he would emerge '*más fresco que una lechuga*' – fresher than a head of lettuce. Axl would run off stage several times during the course of every show. Sometimes he would re-emerge in a new stage outfit; often he would not. He did this every time one of his three guitarists performed their interminable solos. He also ran backstage at times when it appeared to make no sense at all, when his absence from the stage was most noticeable. It was a strange story which may have no truth in it, but whatever he was doing it did nothing for either the audience's enjoyment or the reviews of the tour, which suffered even more critical brickbats on its return to the UK for a spate of dates at the end of July.

At Newcastle's Metro Arena on 19 July, trouble was sparked when he delayed the show leaving the audience waiting restlessly in the sweltering heat. The *Newcastle Evening Chronicle* quoted fan Saskia Green saying, 'The crowd was booing because he was taking for ever. People were throwing stuff about and getting quite upset.'

The final show of the tour, the second of two at Wembley Arena, on 30 July, also ended early when Axl 'collapsed' backstage before the encores, handing the mike to Sebastian Bach to finish the show for him. Axl was suffering from 'low blood pressure and low blood sugar'. According to the official press release, Axl became 'ill after performing two concerts' the night before: the first at Wembley and the second an unannounced semi-acoustic at London's Cuckoo Club, which began at 4.00 a.m.

Apparently 'Rose became ill a couple of hours after the seventy-five-minute performance ended, with a doctor being called to his hotel room. The physician advised that Rose should be hospitalized and not perform Sunday evening.'

Without financial support from his record company since they finally lost patience and cut the purse-strings two years before, Axl had to pay out of his own pocket for the upkeep of both his band and the never-ending tinkering in the studio on *Chinese Democracy*. Hence, the restructured publishing deal with Sanctuary in 2005, and now the tour a year later. Far from receiving a cash injection from his summer tour, after three months playing to over half-a-million people at more than thirty shows in eighteen countries, by the time Axl and his entourage were ready to return to LA in August, the tour was said to be not the greatest financial success.

At this time Axl faced another legal battle following the purchase of a $2.3 million Andy Warhol painting of John Lennon. According to press reports, having paid a $1.15 million down payment, he was then accused of being unable to come up with the balance, forcing the Los Angeles art dealer who made the deal to sue him for damages. The Acquire d'Arte gallery in LA told a Superior Court hearing that after agreeing to buy the painting Axl's manager then advised them his client no longer liked the price and had insufficient funds to pay for it. Axl's lawyer Howard Weitzman told the *New York Daily News*, 'Axl owes nothing. [He] may be the victim of a fraud or misrepresentation.'

It was the same when the tour resumed in the US in September. By now it was obvious to everyone that the band could not make the money it used to. Where once they had easily filled 70,000-capacity sports stadiums, they now found it difficult to sell out at 10,000-seat arenas. Instead, the tour began in Las Vegas with a brace of shows at the modestly sized The Joint, and continued in San Francisco with two dates at the same Warfield Theater the band had used as a secret warm-up venue fifteen years earlier.

Still coming onstage hours behind schedule, Axl's new saying was 'This isn't McDonald's or Burger King. It isn't "Have it your way." ' It certainly wasn't. A clip posted on YouTube showed how during the Warfield gig on 21 September, he stopped the show midway through 'Sweet Child' to remonstrate with a fan down the front who had been audibly chiding him all night. 'Come up here on the stage and I'll knock you the fuck out, motherfucker,' Axl yelled through the mike. You could almost feel the audience sag as Axl leaned over to continue his rant. 'You think you're a bigger asshole than me? You got something to learn . . . King Dick!' There were a few cheers on the singer's behalf. He continued, 'What, your mummy bought you the ticket, that's why you don't care about how much you spent? I don't wanna throw my money in the toilet. I know Universal's hoping *they* didn't,' he added for the benefit, presumably, of his manager standing side-stage. At which point the venue security intervened and the fan was forcibly removed. 'Where do you wanna pick up guys?' Axl asked the band. Now used to such interruptions they went crashing straight back into the song exactly where they left off.

Forty-eight hours later, at the first official Guns N' Roses performance in LA for thirteen years, at radio station KROQ's Inland Invasion Festival in San Bernadino, even though they weren't scheduled to be onstage until almost midnight, Axl still managed to keep the audience waiting over an hour, not hitting the Hyundai Pavilion stage until just after 1.00 a.m. By then, many fans had already drifted off after watching the likes of Muse and actor Jared Leto's band 30 Seconds To Mars. Even more reportedly left after the band started playing new *Chinese Democracy* material instead of the expected hits. Sebastian Bach was still putting in his nightly appearances on 'My Michelle' and Izzy promised to show up for a handful of unspecified dates, but Guns N' Roses was no longer considered a 'dangerous' rock band by most American fans; they were now more of a curiosity, with even their staunchest fans speculating over the internet about how many hours they would arrive late onstage, how many numbers into the set would Axl stop the show or simply walk off and even how many shows on the tour would eventually be cancelled.

Undaunted, straight after the Invasion show Axl threw a party in the poolroom at his Malibu mansion where he treated guests to the album in full. According to Sebastian Bach, 'It was mind-blowing.' Bach, who had previously failed an audition for the job Scott Weiland later took in Velvet Revolver, was now the singer's most vociferous cheerleader. 'It's a very cool album,' he told *Rolling Stone*. 'It's badass with killer screams, killer guitar riffs, but it's got a totally modern sound. The word for it is "grand". It's fucking epic. He's reinvented himself yet again.' The same article also said that 'a source' now claimed the album would be released on 21 November. To which Merck Mercuriadis commented coyly: 'I don't know that we will announce a release date. You just might walk into your record shop one Tuesday and find it there.' A statement, made glibly, that would soon come back to haunt him.

There were a further six shows in California originally in the diary after San Bernadino but they were all cancelled and rescheduled (then cancelled again) in order for Axl to put the finishing touches to *Chinese Democracy*. Instead, the tour resumed in Florida at the end of October, by which time a new confidence emanated from tour staff as news was announced that the forthcoming show at Madison Square Garden on 10 November had sold out. The tour proper was also the chance for US critics to catch up with the band. To Axl's chagrin, there were many that were negative. Reviewing the appearance at the DCU Center in Worcester, Massachusetts on 8 November, the *Boston Herald* wrote: 'Rarely is a show so good and so disappointing. In the first moments . . . it looked like [Axl] was going to pull it off.' But 'cracks started to show' almost immediately. 'Rose's thin yet still unique voice barely made the list of problems. When you've got a band with no charisma and no personality, mediocre vocals aren't what hold you back. With only Rose left from the original GN'R line-up, the band is a bloated octet of soulless virtuosos . . . And after booking a venue he could only three-quarters fill, he started his show so late that fans began filing out long before its 2.00 a.m. finish.'

While the *Tribune* music critic, Greg Kot, described the tour as: '2002 all over again. The Gunners line-up had once again been shuffled around singer Axl Rose, and *Chinese Democracy* had still not been released.' Before concluding: 'Since his 1987–92 heyday, Rose has managed to alienate all his sidekicks and many of his fans. Now he stands alone atop GN'R, but there's the inescapable notion that it is now more of a brand than a band.' Where once Axl had been the charismatic frontman of the most dangerous band in the world, now he was merely the middle-aged mouthpiece for a bunch of 'pros doing what pros do when on six-figure retainers'.

The day this review appeared that night's show at Milwaukee's Bradley Center was cancelled because Axl had 'contracted an ear and throat infection'. Three days later, however, at the next show in Cleveland at the Quicken Loans Arena there was fresh controversy when Axl reportedly took exception to his own support band, the Eagles Of Death Metal, asking the audience: 'So how'd you like The Pigeons Of Shit Metal? Don't worry, that's the last show they're playing with us.'

In response, Eagles Of Death Metal leader Jesse Hughes told the press: 'Axl Rose is fucking out of his mind. He wasn't even there when we played. He got there about thirty minutes after we got done playing. He waltzed onto the stage and went nuts.' Speaking to *Nme.com*, Hughes added: 'By the end of the night [Axl] had caused a giant uproar. It was like a total mutiny on the part of his band and everyone. I could hear screaming in the dressing-room, "Those are our friends and you've insulted our friends!"

The band were so incensed they later placed a video interview about their clash with Axl on the internet, in which they declared that 'Being disapproved of by Axl Rose is like winning a fucking award.'

To add insult to injury, reviewing the Cleveland show for the influential US website *cinemablend.com*, J.P. Gorman wrote: 'An artist, who once struck such an iconic pose for so many hard rock fans, has blown up the self-parody scale and ventured down an unfortunate road normally reserved for former child stars named Corey. His current band is a mess – a reconstructed, revolving door that basically serves as the most legitimate GN'R cover band in America today.' Before concluding: 'If you are an old-school GN'R fan looking forward to seeing your old hero in action, here's what you should do: take the hundred dollars you would spend on a ticket, crumple it into a tiny little ball, and throw it down a sewer. Next, punch yourself as hard as you can in the stomach. Once you've recovered your wind but before the sickening pain subsides, go home, take out your old jean jacket and tight pants from twenty years ago and put them on. Tie your bandana tight around your head, restricting as much blood flow to your brain as possible. Put on *Appetite For Destruction*. Listen to "Paradise City". Remember the good old days long since passed. Cry yourself to sleep.'

From there the US tour descended into even further parody. Axl and his latest manager, Merck Mercuriadis, separated in the first week of December. Axl released his own statement via the internet. Under the heading, 'An open letter to our fans from Axl', dated Thursday, 14 December 2006, he began by announcing the cancellation of the band's January 2007 touring schedule, in order to save 'valuable time needed by the band and record company for the proper setup and release of . . . *Chinese Democracy*.'

He went on: 'To say the making of this album has been an unbearably long and incomprehensible journey would be an understatement. Overcoming the endless and seemingly insane amount of obstacles faced by all involved, notwithstanding the emotional challenges endured by everyone – the fans, the band, our road crew and business team – has at many times seemed like a bad dream in which one wakes up only to find that they are still in the nightmare. Unfortunately, this time it has been played out for over a decade in real life.'

Blaming 'ongoing, behind-the-scenes triumphs and casualties' and 'various legal issues' Axl said it was 'easy for people to point out how others [would] have handled similar situations' but that 'without full knowledge of the various dynamics and circumstances involved, these types of comments or commentary are just uninformed, disassociated, generally useless – and often hindering – speculation.'

But there was more. Despite his best efforts to have the album released 'by December 26 at the latest' Axl now regretted to say 'that the album will not be released by the end of the year'. Problems which had been 'compounded by an overall sense of a lack of respect by management' had also now resulted 'in the end of both Guns' and my managerial involvement with Merck Mercuriadis'.

He did, however, do something he had never done before and name a release date for the album: 6 March 2007. That is, pending 'certain minor – and I do mean minor – additions, as well as contract negotiations'. He concluded: 'We thank you for your patience . . . We do hope you can hold on just a bit longer, and if not, please take a break and we'll be more than glad – if you so choose – to see you again later.' It was like a letter to an old girlfriend. It ended: 'All the best to each and every one of you over this holiday season, thank you and God bless. Sincerely, Axl Rose.'

Merck then posted his own 'open letter' on the internet, dated 15 December, in which he gave his side of the story. He began by claiming he had 'written the blueprint' for Axl's letter 'two days ago'. He then explained that 'The reality is all of this year's touring was planned and agreed between Axl and myself, with a view to the album being in the stores before the 31st of December '06.' He said they had 'planned the tour in February, just after Axl's [44th] birthday and we were supposed to finish the album in May, before it started.' But that the engineers waited in New York 'for over a month for the muse to come but she never arrived'. He said they then 'scheduled sessions in London in August' after the Wembley shows but that 'August came and went and once again the muse did not show.' At which point, 'We postponed our proposed radio date of Labour Day for the first single and we came back to LA and tried to finish before the San Francisco, Las Vegas and Los Angeles shows but yet again [the muse] eluded us. Axl then asked me to postpone the North American tour which was due to start on 24th of September by a month and, finally, early in that period after the euphoria of Inland Invasion, Axl made a breakthrough and got two or three very productive days under his belt.'

He went on: 'At this point we were very excited as Axl's feeling was that we had two or three days of work left to tidy things up and we still had three weeks before the tour started, so we were in good shape. Unfortunately the muse disappeared just as fast as she came and the tour started with no single at radio to support it and the album still needing two or three days of work.' At which point, Merck said he had 'seriously considered postponing the start of the tour, again, as the album was of paramount importance but the reality was that our historic track record left us with very little good will with you, the fans [or US promoters], and we needed the money to be able to complete the album and keep the band alive.'

However, Merck continued, once again Axl failed to show up for planned sessions in New York and 'The record company refused to conclude the renegotiation until we were ready to hand over the finished album and refused to prepare a marketing campaign or commission video treatments until they had it in their hands. This is still their position as of this week.'

He concluded that, while he found 'some' of Axl's letter 'disappointing' no one could 'begin to comprehend the pressure he is under' and that 'I believe *Chinese Democracy* is one of the best albums ever made, Axl Rose is one of the greatest vocalists and front men and the new Guns N' Roses (which kicks the shit out of the old) is one of the greatest bands. What we accomplished in 2006 only hints at what is to come.'

Whether Axl or Merck's version is accurate only they know – both agreed however that so far as *Chinese Democracy* was concerned the fans would need to continue to show patience . . .

Epilogue

ESTRANGED

So what does the future really hold in store for W. Axl Rose? Sitting here, writing this at the start of 2007 my guess is that *Chinese Democracy* may not even be released this year. Even if it is, neither all of the critics nor many of the fans are behind him any more, and I believe the reception it's likely to receive from these quarters may well be hostile, regardless of the quality of the material.

None of which is fair but for many it is understandable. Work on *Chinese Democracy* has now been going on for so long it's not just Guns N' Roses that's changed beyond all recognition but the music industry itself. Having consolidated from the six major corporations that ran the business the last time Guns N' Roses released a new album down to just four, its concerns have drastically altered too. Fighting the twin threats of internet piracy and a much more niche-driven consumer market, major record company executives are more focused than ever on the bottom line and on musicians able to deliver the goods – on time and reasonably on budget – such as Robbie Williams, Madonna, Christina Aguilera and their ilk. Michael Jackson's last album, *Invincible*, in 2001 only took three years to make and a relatively paltry $2 million.

Even now, with the album apparently 'imminent' once again, the chief executives at Universal Music, which owns Interscope, have understandably adopted a 'we'll believe it when we see it' attitude. One London-based executive at the company (who asked to remain anonymous) told me recently he found it 'almost inconceivable' that any other artist could ever 'get away' with the kind of delays the company has experienced this past decade waiting for *Chinese Democracy*. When asked if he could envisage any artist being granted a $13 million budget to make a single album now, he said: 'No, I can't. But it all depends of course on how much you think you're going to recoup. Also, budgets don't exist these days the way they used to, because technology now allows artists to make albums in all sorts of different ways. Ultimately, though, whatever you spend, it still has to be paid back.' He estimated that *Chinese Democracy* would have to sell around ten million copies for the company to recoup their huge outlay and show a reasonably healthy profit.

The problem is that selling ten million copies of an album by a band whose sales peaked years ago is not guaranteed. The sheer longevity of the project may have already holed it beneath the waterline; the irony is that while Axl fretted over making the 'new' Guns N' Roses sound up-to-date, much of the core material he created with them may have slid steadily out of date – and worse, just as a new generation of rock fans have enthusiastically rediscovered and embraced the raucous visceral spirit of 'classic' Guns N' Roses. Consequently, for some there's a real danger that *Chinese Democracy* will already sound out of date before it even goes on sale.

It could be that the very thing that once made Axl so charismatic to his audience – his apparent indifference to the opinion of others – now seems out of place. That having achieved the state of psychological independence that is every adolescent's ideal – becoming the classic rock'n'roll anti-hero – Axl's defiant mien is now outdated.

Meanwhile, when he's not facing the inevitable iniquities of life on the road, he apparently still lives alone in his Malibu mansion, with Beta and her son Fernando for regular company. His only other companions in the house are the tanks full of spiders, snakes and lizards he began collecting after he split from Stephanie.

And yet . . . 'Sweet Child', 'Paradise City', 'November Rain', 'Patience' . . . Axl's best songs always come down to the same simple coda, the same brittle yearning for a place and time better than this one. Many fans wish he would make that dream a reality by picking up the phone and calling Slash, Duff, Izzy and the guys and inviting them back in. Alan Niven looks as though he would still come back into the fold. For as he wrote in an email to the *Metal Sludge* website in March 2006: 'I have no doubt [Axl] is still genuinely and profoundly gifted . . . I have held this opinion from those very first rehearsals, and consider him better employed by his former band, where he could take advantage of their composing abilities once more. Perhaps then we could all get down to the very serious, and big, business of reforming the greatest, and most relevant, rock band (dispensing with the court spats that suck the juice out of life itself) for the delight of millions of fans, a multitude of which, the second and third generation of admirers, have never had the chance to see floral artillery in living magnificence. The industry could certainly use a shot of genuinely talented firepower.'

As Slash himself told me: 'There's not a day that goes by without someone asking me something about that band.' Though he did add, somewhat sadly: 'Everybody keeps going on about a reunion, but the truth is, [Axl] doesn't want to see me any more than I want to see him.' But that's what he says now. What if Axl were to pick up the phone and make that call? Maybe Izzy too could be persuaded.

Of course this dream seems unlikely to come true before *Chinese Democracy* appears. Speaking on the subject of a possible reunion back in 2002, Axl still sounded defiant: 'I do not believe in any true effort or potential regarding most of my past relationships from the other party or parties, creatively or emotionally. Without that the money from a reunion doesn't mean much and though I'm sure the alumni is up for it, for me it would be as or more lacking than it was during our attempts to work together previously. As a friend and former friend of Slash said to me in regards to working with Slash, "You can only do so many pull-ups." '

But what price a Guns N' Roses reunion, at some point? Maybe after *Chinese Democracy* finally comes out? According to one insider very high up in the GN'R organization, speaking privately recently, 'It's bound to happen sooner or later. There's too much money involved for it not to.'

Notes and sources

The foundations of this book, in terms of quotes and the facts of the story – of both Axl Rose and Guns N' Roses – so far as I have gleaned them, are based on my own original investigations, beginning with interviews and conversations with Slash, Duff McKagen, Izzy Stradlin, Steven Adler and, of course, W. Axl Rose. I have also spent a great deal of time over the years compiling as much background material as possible from as much published material as there is available, including books, magazine and newspaper articles, websites, television and radio shows, DVDs, demo-tapes, bootleg CDs and any other form of media that contained useful information, the most important of which I have listed here.

A handful of articles proved especially helpful, in terms of adding to my own insights and investigations. First and foremost were the series of excellently written articles by Kim Neely published in *Rolling Stone* in the early 1990s. Her interviews with Axl were particularly insightful, and full credit should be paid to her here for the impact these breakthrough pieces have had on the writing of this book.

Credit also goes to Del James for his superb series of Axl interviews in *RIP* magazine between 1989 and 1992. A close personal friend of the singer's, James was in a position to ask the sorts of questions none of his music journalist peers of the time, including myself, would have been able to. They were enthralling reading when they were first published, and I found them no less so when writing this book.

There were also occasional one-off pieces, which were so exceptional that they forced me to rethink several parts of the overall story, such as the Duff McKagan interview published in *Hard Force* magazine in June 1999 and the stupendous oral history published in *Spin* in July 1999 under the heading 'Just A Little Patience'.

I would also like to draw attention to the sterling efforts of the most dedicated Guns N' Roses fan websites – such as www.heretodaygoneto hell.com and the official www.gnronline.com – whose Herculean efforts in keeping a detailed record of the ups and downs of Axl's incident-filled career go way beyond the realms of dedication. Only true love is likely to do that – God bless them for it.

BOOKS

Adler, Steven, *No Bed Of Roses* book synopsis

Aerosmith, with Stephen Davis, *Walk This Way: The Autobiography of Aerosmith*, Virgin Books, 1998

Azerrad, Michael, *Come As You Are: The Story Of Nirvana*, Virgin Books, 1993

Hoskyns, Barney, *Waiting For The Sun: Strange Days, Weird Scenes and the Sound of Los Angeles*, Viking, 1996

Humphrey, Clark, *Loser: The Real Seattle Music Story*, Harry N. Abrams, 1999

James, Del, *The Language of Fear*, Dell, 1995

King, Tom, *David Geffen: A Biography of New Hollywood*, Random House, 2000

Mötley Crüe with Neil Strauss, *The Dirt: Confessions of the World's Most Notorious Rock Band*, HarperCollins, 2001

Stenning, Paul, *The Band that Time Forgot*, Chrome Dreams, 2004

Sugarman, Danny, *Appetite for Destruction: The Days of Guns and Roses*, St Martin's Press, 1991

Thompson, Dave, *Red Hot Chili Peppers: True Men Don't Kill Coyotes*, Virgin, 1993

MAGAZINES & NEWSPAPERS

'To Live and Die in LA', *Spin*, 1986

'Colt Heroes' and 'Guns N' Roses Marquee, London' (review of first night), *Kerrang!*, 11–24 June 1987

'Thorn to be Wild' (*Appetite For Destruction* review) and 'Guns N' Roses Marquee, London' (review of second and third nights), *Kerrang!* 23 July-5 August 1987

'The world according to W. Axl Rose' by Del James, *RIP*, April 1989

'The Rolling Stone Interview with Axl Rose', *Rolling Stone*, August 1989

'Guns N' Roses Working Up a Sweat', *Metal Muscle*, May 1991

'Guns N' Roses the Illusion of Greatness', Lonn M. Friend, *RIP*, June 1991

'Tears Before Bedtime?', *Q*, July 1991

'Danger Lurks Beyond the Doors', *Observer*, 25 August 1991

'Guns N' Roses', *Sky*, August 1991

'Fans Riot at Guns Show', *Rolling Stone*, 22 August 1991

'Guns N' Roses Here Today Gone to Hell (And Lovin' It)', Del James, *RIP*, September 1991

'Guns N' Neuroses', Dean Kuipers, *Spin*, September 1991

'There's a Riot Going On!', *Musician*, September 1991

'Guns N' Roses – Outta Control', *Rolling Stone*, 5 September 1991

'Guns N' Roses: Wimps 'R' Us', *Village Voice*, 1 October 1991

'Slash Speaks', *Music Life*, 17 November 1991

'Axl Gets in the Ring', *Metallix*, 1992

'Guns N' Roses from the Inside: An Exclusive Report', Lonn M. Friend, *RIP*, March 1992

'Axl interview', *Interview Magazine*, March 1992

'Axl Rose: The Rolling Stone Interview', *Rolling Stone*, 2 April 1992

'No Axl to Grind: Rock Star Pleads Innocent', *New York Post*, July 1992

'Axl Rose: The Mussolini of Mass Culture', *The Modern Review*, Summer 1992

'I, Axl Part I', *RIP*, September 1992

'I, Axl Part II', *RIP*, October 1992

'I, Axl Part III', *RIP*, November 1992

'Trial by fire', *Guitar World*, November 1992

'On the road with Guns N' Roses', *Life Magazine*, December 1992

'Guns N' Roses interview', *Hit Parader*, July 1993

'Duff McKagan talks', *Kerrang!*, 1993

'Guns N' Roses', *Okej*, November 1993

'Guns N' Roses Blazing Hot', *Moving Pictures!*, 1994

'War of the Roses!', *Kerrang!*, 24 May 1994

'Four Bust-ups and a Single!', *RAW*, November 1994

'Welcome to Slash's Snakepit', *Toronto Sun*, 24 January 1995

' "I Spent a Week Jammin' with Guns N' Roses". Zakk Wylde to join GN'R?!', *Kerrang!*, 28 January 1995

'Coiled and Ready', *Rolling Stone*, April 1995

'In Bed with . . . Slash', *Kerrang!*, July 1995

'Excerpts from a Slash interview', *Folha De Sao Paulo Journal*, 21 July 1995

'Guns N' Roses: Is It All Over? Does Anyone Care?', *Metal Hammer*, November 1995

'Q&A with Slash', *Kerrang!*, 1996

'It's all in the Wrist Action . . .', *Metal Hammer*, February 1996

'Review of the Marshall 2555SL Slash Signature Amp', *Guitar World*, April 1996

'At home with Matt Sorum', *Metal Hammer*, July 1996

'Outsiders responsible for Guns N' Roses reuniting?', *Toronto Sun*, 4 September 1996

'Neurotic Outsiders: Duff and Matt talk records', *Kerrang!*, September 1996

'My Record Collection (Duff McKagan)', *Kerrang!* February 1997

'More than blanks', *Entertainment Weekly*, 31 July 1998

'At home with Slash', *Metal Hammer*, August 1998

'Welcome to the Videos', press release, Geffen, October 1998

'At home with Duff McKagan', *Metal Hammer*, January 1999

'Duff McKagan: Laying Down his Guns', *Hit Parader*, May 1999

'Snake, Rattle 'N' Roll', *Guitar World*, May 1999

'Duff McKagan Interview', *Hard Force Magazine*, June 1999

'Just A Little Patience', *Spin*, July 1999

'Guns N' Roses' 2-part article, *Kerrang!*, August, 1999

'Oh, My God' press release, Geffen, September 1999

'Dirty Deeds Done Dirty', *NME*, 25 December 1999

'Axl Speaks', *Rolling Stone*, January 2000

'Slash is still breathing', *FHM*, March–April 2000

'What Happened to Axl Rose: The inside story of rock's most famous recluse', *Rolling Stone*, 11 May 2000

'Modern life is rubbish', *Kerrang!*, 10 June 2000

'Slash's Snakepit: For the love of art' *Hard Rock Magazine*, October 2000

'Slash's Heroes & Villains', *NME*, 7 October 2000

'Axl talks at the pool side', *O Globo*, January 2001

'Interview with Beta Lebeis', *O Globo*, January 2001

GN'R Article, *Clarin*, February 2001

'The History of Hard Rock: The Eighties (Appetite For Destruction)', *Guitar World*, March 2001

'Didn't You Used to be Axl Rose?', *Q*, May 2001

'Slash Interview', *Steppin' Out Magazine*, 16 May 2001

'Democracy in Action', *Q*, July 2001

'Inside the Lonely Mixed Up World of Axl Rose', *Classic Rock*, January 2002

'Gilby Clarke, Staying True to His Roots', *Guitar Player*, April 2002

'Ready to rock again, or is bloom off the Roses?', *Florida Times Union*, 14 August 2002

Review of London Docklands show, *London Evening Standard*, 27 August 2002

Duff McKagan Interview, *Classic Rock*, October 2002

'A new bloom from GNR veterans', *Los Angeles Times*, 3 November 2002

'We're catching our groove again now' (Richard Fortus interview), *Albany NY Times Union*, 21 November 2002

'Meltdown', *Guardian*, 3 January 2003

'Appetite For Self-destruction', *Classic Rock*, February 2003

'Welcome to the Jungle: A Timeline of Axl's return to the road', *Classic Rock*, February 2003

'GN'R:The Inside Story', *Total Guitar*, June 2003

'Appetite for Reconstruction' (Velvet Revolver), *Kerrang!* 2 July 2003

'Velvet Revolver Set to Fire', *Hit Parader*, October 2003

'Tommy Grows Up', *Harper Magazine*, October–November 2003

Geffen Guns N' Roses DVD press release, Geffen Records, 15 October 2003

'The Big Bang' (Velvet Revolver), *Guitar World*, November 2003

'Guns N' Roses: The Scum Also Rises', *Q*, November 2003

'Spotlight on . . . Camp Freddy', *Metal Hammer*, January 2004

'Velvet Revolver Beating The Odds', *Hit Parader*, February–March 2004

'Appetite For Self Destruction', *Record Collector*, February 2004

'Guns N' Roses. Greatest Hits. For the First Time', press release, Geffen, 19 February 2004

'Gilby Clarke Moonlightin' With Sinatra', *Guitar One*, March 2004

'Where are they now? The 411 on 46 Missing Guitar Heroes: Izzy Stradlin', *Guitar One*, March 2004

'The Scum also Rises', *Revolver*, March 2004

'Welcome Back To The Jungle: Duff McKagan Reloads With Velvet Revolver', *Bass Player*, March 2004

'Shooting from the hip' (Velvet Revolver), *Classsic Rock*, March 2004

'Welcome to the Jungle', *Kerrang!*, 17 March 2004

'Ten Reasons Why Guns N' Roses Still Rock', *NME*, 20 March 2004

'Guns N' Roses Not Able to Perform at Rock in Rio', press release, Sanctuary Records Group, 30 March 2004

'Matt Sorum Rocks with Velvet Revolver', *Drum!*, April–May 2004

'Duff McKagan: Guns N' Roses/Velvet Revolver', *Total Guitar Bass Special*, April 2004

'Velvet Revolver: It's all gonna go so wrong', *Metal Hammer*, April 2004

'Velvet Revolver', *Total Guitar*, April 2004

'Meet "The Most Dangerous Band in the World" . . .' *Kerrang!*, 10 April 2004

'Hanging with . . . Slash – Velvet Revolver, *Kerrang!*, 10 April 2004

'Paradise Lost', *Classic Rock*, May 2004

'Bulletproof: Duff interview' (Velvet Revolver), *Guitar World's Bass Guitar*, June–July 2004

'Slash Answers your Questions', *Guitar World*, June 2004

'Velvet Revolver the Ego has Landed', *Revolver*, June 2004

'Mexican Food With . . . Velvet Revolver', *FHM*, June 2004

'I'm With Stupid' (Velvet Revolver), *Q*, June 2004

'Gunning It' (Velvet Revolver), *The Times*, 5 June 2004

'Top Gun' (Slash interview), *Guitarist*, issue 251, July 2004

'Slash and Burn', *Sunday Mail*, Brisbane, Australia, 29 August 2004

'Velvet Revolver Cocked & Loaded', *Circus*, October 2004

'Magnum Force' (Duff interview / Velvet Revolver), *Guitar & Bass*, October 2004

'GN'R Set the Record Straight' press release, Sanctuary / Business Wire, 12 October 2004

'Velvet Revolver – Drugs! Booze! Kung Fu! GN'R!', *Classic Rock*, November 2004

'Guns at the Ready Indie legend Tommy Stinson shoots solo first', *Guitar World's Bass Guitar*, December 2004

'An Appetite for Reconstruction: The Inside Story of Velvet Revolver', *Metal Edge*, December 2004

'Breaking the Big Machine' (Velvet Revolver), *Metal Edge*, January 2005

'Tommy Gun', *Classic Rock*, January 2005

'Radio Axl', *Classic Rock*, January 2005

'Matt Sorum', *Mojo*, January 2005

'Brain – Cheesy Fun And Cubist Funk', *DRUM!*, March 2005

'Nowhere else to go but forward' (Tommy Stinson), *Los Angeles Times*, 3 March 2005

'Tom Zutaut interview', *New York Times*, March 2005

'Steven Adler interview', *Classic Rock*, April 2005

'The Complete Classic Axl Rose Interview', *Hit Parader*, April 2005

'The Story Behind the Song: "Sweet Child O' Mine"', *Q*, December 2005

'Axl Rose Responds To Lawsuit', press release, 6 March 2006

'Hammerstein preview', *New York Times*, 13 May 2006

'GN'R Get In The Ring!', press release, 19 May 2006

'Guns N' Roses storm New York', press release, 22 May 2006

Review of Hammerstein Ballroom show, *Hollywood Reporter*, 25 May 2006

Review of Hammerstein Ballroom show, *News Day*, May, 2006

Review of Hammerstein Ballroom show, *Illinois Entertainer*, May, 2006

Review of Hammerstein Ballroom show, *Reuters*, May, 2006

Review of Hammerstein Ballroom show, *Chicago Tribune*, May, 2006

Review of Hammerstein Ballroom show, *Variety*, May, 2006

Review of Hammerstein Ballroom show, *New York Times*, May, 2006

Review of Hammerstein Ballroom show, *New York Post*, May, 2006

'Tommy Hilfiger fight', *Associated Press*, May 2006

'Axl Vs. the World', *Classic Rock*, May 2006

Review of Hammerstein Ballroom show, *Blender*, June, 2006

Review of Lisbon show, *El Diario Vasco*, Spain, May 2006

Review of Madrid show, *MTV Spain*, 26 June 2006

Review of Hammersmith Apollo show, *London Evening Standard*, 9 June 2002

Review of Hammersmith Apollo show, *Daily Telegraph*, 9 June 2002

Review of Hammersmith Apollo show, Channel Four Teletext, June 2006

Review of Hammersmith Apollo show, *NME*, June 2006

'Guns N' Babies!', press release, 21 June 2006

'Axl Rose held for "biting guard"', *Associated Press*, 27 June 2006

'Guns N' Roses Knock Out Stockholm', press release, 28 June 2006

'Axl in fight with security guard', *Expressen*, Sweden, June 2006

'Axl in fight with security guard', *Aftonbladet*, Sweden, June 2006

'Guns N' Roses Continue Through Europe!', press release, 30 June 2006

'Guns N' Roses Heat Wave', press release, 22 July 2006

'Guns N' Roses Win Big in Europe', press release, 11 August 2006

'Axl Rose Could Be Kept in Jail Until Friday', *Classic Rock*, August 2006

'The Final Comeback Of Axl Rose', *American GQ*, September 2006

'Axl Rose article', *New York magazine*, September 2006

'Guns N' Roses announce "Chinese Democracy" North American tour and strategic relationship with Major League Baseball Advanced Media', press release, 29 September 2006

Uncut, October 2006 (grunge cover)

'A polished Guns N' Roses now more brand than band', *Tribune*, 28 November 2006

'Show in Portland, Maine Cancelled', press release, 6 November 2006

'Christine Aguilera feature', *Blender*, November 2006

'GN'R lineup a thorn in Axl's side', *Boston Herald*, 10 November 2006

'New story', Los Angeles Business Wire, December 2006

INTERNET

Special mention should also go here to the many well-intentioned people who emailed stories and information to my website, www.mick wall.com, many of which were exceptionally helpful in compiling my investigations for this book. Also, thanks to www.contactmusic. com who filtered hundreds of related news items to my desk and to the brilliant www.metalsludge.com for providing laughs as well as good information and often inspiration. And to the equally wonderful www.youtube.com for allowing me to view many related television and video clips, both professional and amateur, from the past twenty years.

Specifically, though, I obtained useful information and quotes from the following sources:

'Transcript of Slash online chat, Pepsi Live', www.ticketmasteronline, 16 October 1996

'Music West in 3-D: Duff, Dallas and Drugs', taken from the e-zine File, 1997

'For Slash, Life After Guns Is Grand', www.rollingstone.com, October 2000

'Slash Exclusive: Appetite For Reconstruction', www.KNAC.com,
    October 2000
'Brain interview', www.dwdrums.com, 2001
'Izzy Stradlin interview', www.bol.com, March 2001
GN'R press release with Axl interview, gnronline.com, 14 August
    2002
'Guns N' Roses blooms again', Life & Mind Desk, 19 September 2002
GN'R North American tour press release, www.gnronline.com, 25
    September 2002
'Beneath The Bucket, Behind The Mask: Kurt Loder Meets GN'R's
    Buckethead', www.mtv.com, 21 November 2002
'Use Your Delusion', www.rollingstone.com, 3 June 2003
'Scott & Slash Speak', www. rollingstone.com, 17 June 2003
'Lonn Friend article', www.lasvegasweekly.com, 15 April 2004
'This tastes like pretzels: the Tommy Stinson interview', Here Today
    . . . Gone To Hell!, 10 October 2004
'Sanctuary Music Publishing has signed Axl Rose to a publishing deal',
    Sanctuary website announcement, 26 January 2005
'Steven Adler Interview', Metal Sludge, January 2006
Online review, Hammerstein ballroom show, www.rollingstone.com,
    15 May 2006
Review of Hammerstein Ballroom show, MTV News, 18 May 2006
'Tommy Hilfiger fight', www.PageSix.com, 20 May 2006
'Sophie Anderston romance story', Digital Spy Showbiz, 29 May 2006
'Slash interview', www.mtv.com, June 2006
'Axl onstage on the 2002 US tour', www.youtube.com, 27 June
    2006
'Axl's appetite for destruction', Pop Bitch, 29 June 2006
'On the road by Del James', www.GunsN'Roses.com, 3 November
    2006
'Concert review', www.cinemablend.com/music, November 2006
'Concert review', www.ifilm.com/video, December 2006
Various clips – www.nme.com
www.photo.wenn.com
www.sp1at.com
www.blabbermouth.net
www.holymoly.co.uk
www.allexperts.com
www.adlersappetite.com
www.mattsorum.com

Plus mostly unofficial, some claiming to be semi-official GN'R fan sites, most still active, some no longer so, such as: Aco's Guns N' Roses Unofficial Site; Belgian Democracy; Appetite Guns N' Roses; Chinese Democracy; Encyclopedia GN'R site; Evitaph's Guns N' Roses site; Garden Of Illusions: Guns N' Roses; Get.to/GnR; GnrDaily.com; GN'R en Español; GN'R Exclusive; GN'RLIVE.COM; Guns N' Roses: The Lost Rose Guns N' Roses Bootleg Page; Guns N' Roses Fans; Guns N' Roses in the Jungle; Guns N' Roses Videos; Gunz N' Roses; Here Today, Gone To Hell; Hugo's Guns N' Roses Bootleg Site; Intentional Illusions; John's GN'R bootleg page; Marcy's Guns N' Roses Page [Hungarian]; Mark's big GNR Collection; Nightrain; Portal Guns N' Roses; Rat's Guns N' Roses site; Right Next Door to Hell; Ryan's Guns N' Roses Page; Surfers Delight; The Tableture Incident; The Unofficial Uzi Suicide Homepage; Use Your Illusion; We Ain't Dead Yet; *Welcome to the Jungle*; and of course, the official sites such as www.newgnr.com, and Guns N' Roses – GN'R Online.

DVDS, TELEVISION AND RADIO

Axl on MTV in 1988 talking about 'One In A Million'
Axl Rose, A conversation with Kurt Loder, MTV US, 8 November 1999
Axl interview, Radio Rock And Pop Chile, January 2001
Axl interview, Rock & Pop FM Argentina, January 2001
Post VMA interview, by Kurt Loder, MTV, 29 August 2002
Axl interview – KISW Seattle, 8 November 2002
Songs leaked on internet, MTV News, 23 February 2006
Axl interview, KROQ, Los Angeles, May 2006

Plus:
Welcome to the Videos, DVD
Use Your Illusion World Tour 1992 In Tokyo, DVD
Axl Rose: The Prettiest Star, DVD
Guns N' Roses: Sex, Drugs N' Rock'n'Roll, DVD